RACE IN MIND

RACE IN MIND

Critical Essays

PAUL SPICKARD

with Jeffrey Moniz and Ingrid Dineen-Wimberly

University of Notre Dame Press

Notre Dame, Indiana

Library of Congress Cataloging-in-Publication Data

Spickard, Paul R., 1950– Moniz, Jeffrey, Dineen-Wimberl, Ingrid
Race in mind : critical essays / Paul Spickard ;
with Jeffrey Moniz and Ingrid Dineen-Wimberly.
Notre Dame, Ind. : University of Notre Dame Press, [2015]
Includes bibliographical references and index.
ISBN 9780268041489 (pbk. : alk. paper)
ISBN 0268041482 (pbk. : alk. paper)
Race. Ethnicity. Race relations. Multiculturalism.
HT1521.S624   2015
305.8—dc23
2015032735

7361

In memory of

Win Jordan

Contents

MIXED RACE

Figures and Tables

FIGURES

TABLES

Acknowledgments

As this manuscript goes to press, I find I owe debts of gratitude beyond my capacity to repay to two people. Patrick Miller has been a fellow traveler on many, many adventures over the years. He has never failed to retain his good humor while doing his best to restrain some of my rhetorical excesses. Reginald Daniel's name appears often in the notes to the pages that follow, but he deserves special mention, for he has been a boon companion and is the single person to whom my thinking about race owes the greatest debt.

At the University of Notre Dame Press, Chuck Van Hof showed enthusiasm for the project from the start. He and his colleagues Stephen Little, Rebecca DeBoer, and Sheila Berg have done a more than professional job of editing. I am grateful for both. Among those he recruited to help me make this book better are Roger Daniels, the dean of American immigration historians, and Maria Diedrich, the foremost African Americanist in Europe. Each encouraged my work and helped me make key improvements to the manuscript.

I would not have come to many of the understandings that appear in these pages were it not for three institutions where I have done time. The people at Garfield High School in Seattle and the Central District around it nurtured me as a youth and taught me more about the way race works in America than any other single source. The people of Brigham Young University–Hawai'i and the towns of La'ie, Kahuku, and Kane'ohe helped

xiii

me understand that identities are not only constructed, but complex and variable. The University of California, Santa Barbara, gave me a place to work, space to pursue my ideas, and colleagues to encourage me. I am especially grateful to librarians at these institutions, among them Riley Moffett, Barbara Lansdon, Sherri Barnes, and Gary Colmenar.

DeAundra Jenkins-Holder of Fisk University went far out of her way to take a photo of the statue of W. E. B. Du Bois that stands on her campus. Special thanks are due to Francisco Beltran and Laura Hooton, whose generous, skillful, and persistent research on another project freed me to complete this one.

For the past couple of decades I have enjoyed the company of the Hui—an endless stream of brilliant students who have taught me much and who never failed to provide entertainment as they went about their own projects. My wife, Anna Lucky Louise Spickard, has been a constant solace and source of intellectual engagement. My other debts are marked in the notes. By the time you reach the end of the book, you will likely understand why it is dedicated to Winthrop Jordan.

Introduction

In 1903, W. E. B. Du Bois famously foretold that "the problem of the Twentieth Century is the problem of the color-line,—the relation of the darker to the lighter races of men in Asia and Africa, in America and the islands of the sea."[1] Surely he was correct. No problem more deeply troubled the American people,[2] throughout the century that he was then entering and we have just left, than race, for which Du Bois chose the metaphor, "the color-line." Never just a matter of Black and White, race in all its pain and complexity was a problem for America throughout the twentieth century—from Jim Crow segregation to the orgy of lynching that spasmed across the decades; from attempts to wipe out Native peoples by dismantling Indian reservations in the 1920s to the racialized immigration laws of that same decade; from World War II race riots to the incarceration of the entire Japanese American people; from the midcentury fight for civil rights for African Americans to similar movements for the rights of Latinos, Native Americans, and others; from racial divides in opportunity and access to life's good things (even physical safety) that persisted into the twenty-first century to the racialized anti-immigrant, anti-Mexican, and anti-Muslim movements of our own generation.[3]

Du Bois lived ninety-five years. He published dozens of books, scores of pamphlets, and hundreds of articles. He wrote on many topics, but race was always at the core of his concern. I want to focus in this prefatory essay on three themes that seem to me to have been especially central to Du Bois's theoretical thinking about race.[4]

Fig. I.1.
Statue of W. E. B. Du Bois on the campus of Fisk University. Photo by DeAundra Jenkins-Holder. Courtesy of Fisk University.

The first was a tension between seeing race as a biological essence and understanding it as a set of relationships that are constructed in the social negotiations that occur between people. When Du Bois wrote his famous words, race was widely assumed, by him and by others, to be a biological thing. In one of his first published writings, "The Conservation of Races," he stated as a certainty:

> We find upon the world's stage eight distinctly differentiated races. . . . They are, the Slavs of eastern Europe, the Teutons of middle Europe, the English of Great Britain and America, the Romance nations of Southern and Western Europe, the Negroes of

Africa and America, the Semitic people of Western Asia and Northern Africa, the Hindoos of Central Asia and the Mongolians of Eastern Asia.[5]

A sentence like this could have appeared in any turn-of-the-century anthropology textbook.[6] Looking back from his later years, he reflected, "I was born in the century when the walls of race were clear and straight; when the world consisted of mutually exclusive races; and . . . there was no question of exact definition and understanding of the meaning of the word."[7] Du Bois even, on occasion, used the language of eugenics, for it was the way that educated people spoke and wrote in his era.

Although he used the language of biology and treated races as permanent and discrete categories, Du Bois knew race in another way as well. He was always conscious that he was constructing his own race over the course of his life. In "The Conservation of Races," he continued:

> But while race differences have followed mainly physical race lines, yet no mere physical distinctions would really define or explain the deeper differences—the cohesiveness and continuity of these groups. The deeper differences are spiritual, psychical, differences—undoubtedly based on the physical, but infinitely transcending them. The forces that bind together the Teuton nations are, then, first, their race identity and common blood; secondly, and more important, a common history, common laws and religion, similar habits of thought and a conscious striving together for certain ideals of life.[8]

As I describe in chapter 8, Du Bois grew up among White, small-town New Englanders and performed New England White culture perfectly. Only when he ventured out to attend college at Fisk (because White Harvard would not have dusky Burghardt Du Bois) did he make a decisive choice to see himself as unambiguously Black. Even then, all the rest of his long life, alongside a rock-solid commitment to being a member of and an advocate for African Americans, he acknowledged and maintained an acute interest in his White forebears. He knew he was a man who had racial options, and he opted to be Black.[9]

A second theme in Du Bois's writing is the interlocking global nature of race and its relationship to colonialism. Although Du Bois's early work, as an activist, sociologist, and historian, centered on the United States and the racial situation of people of African descent here, as the color-line quote makes clear, he was also aware from the beginning that race was an international issue. During his later career he became an eloquent speaker for African liberation—indeed, for the freedom of all colonized peoples— and eventually he relocated to Ghana. From his new vantage point he saw the panorama of peoples across the globe, the intimate connection between colonialism and racial hierarchy, and the recurring racialized relationships that existed in many local contexts.[10]

The third theme that lurks in the crevices of Du Bois's writing is racial complexity. This possibility occurred to me first in the mid-1980s, on a visit to Fisk University. Walking in a garden on a break from the archives, I came upon a slightly smaller than life-size bronze statue of what I took to be an Italian guy with a goatee. Up close, the plaque identified the gentleman as Fisk's most famous son, William Edward Burghardt Du Bois. In the quote about the color line, Du Bois spoke as if racial groups were discrete boxes—one was either Black or White, Red or Yellow, never both or in between. Yet in other writings, Du Bois showed his deep awareness of his own multiplicity, as I discuss in chapter 10.

Race in Mind is a gathering of what Keynes called "essays in persuasion,"[11] in this case, essays about race, considered both theoretically and empirically. It brings together work that I have been doing over more than two decades. Some of the essays printed here were first published in scattered, sometimes obscure places. Others are fresh creations for this volume. I have reworked each of the previously published essays thoroughly to bring it up to date and to correct any errors I may have made in the initial published form. I have tried to maintain the original content and tone insofar as possible and to indicate the context that gave birth to each essay.

My work on race over these decades has revolved around the three themes in Du Bois's work to which I alluded above:

- race-as-biology versus race as something constructed by social and political relationships;

- race as a phenomenon that exists not just in the United States, but in every part of the world, and even in the relationships between nations; and
- the question of racial multiplicity.

I did not set out consciously to follow Du Bois's themes; at the outset I had not even studied his work carefully, beyond an undergraduate's reading of *The Souls of Black Folk*. But over the years, as I sought to understand the ways that race has worked in the United States and in the modern world, I inevitably ran across Du Bois's ideas again and again. Every time I thought that I had a brand-new idea that no one had thought before, sooner or later I would discover that Du Bois had been there first. I hope to add to his legacy, but I cannot eclipse it.

Whatever our similarities of theme, the provenance of my thinking about race is quite different from the context out of which Du Bois came to think about the subject. He came of age intellectually in the late nineteenth century, a time when racialist science was all the rage.[12] People styling themselves scientists marked populations off by color and continent; measured their skulls, their limbs, their eyefolds; and aspired to deduce from these and other physicalities their moral character, their aptitude for education, and their fitness for citizenship. Du Bois rejected such eugenic determinism, but like other intellectuals of his time he was caught to some degree in the web of its terms and concepts. As Du Bois's critique and that of contemporaries like Franz Boas took hold, his prose broke freer of racialist terminology.[13]

I grew to adulthood in the 1960s and 1970s, when social scientists dominated the writing about race. Eminent scholars like E. Franklin Frazier, Gunnar Myrdal, Thomas Pettigrew, Kenneth Clark, Winthrop Jordan, and Milton Gordon had turned away from biological determinism to social explanations of the different life chances experienced by different racial groups. Yet even those writers seldom questioned the racial categories themselves. They assumed the existence of discrete races as social entities, even though they did not give credence to the theory that biology dictated social and cultural difference.[14] As with Du Bois and the eugenicists, my early writing in the 1980s hews more closely to the language of the social scientists who were judged to be the smart people when I was coming up. It was only later, in the 1990s and beyond, that I was able to begin to break free of the determinist language of social science. Although my 1980s writing made room for racial complicatedness, it was only later that I was able to articulate more fully the mixed, constructed, and contingent qualities of race that I have since come to see.[15]

The places I have lived have led me to see race in one respect quite differently than did Du Bois. He was a product of rural New England, educated at Fisk, a Harvard PhD, a professor in Atlanta. For him, race was primarily a Black and White affair. Late in life he wrote in solidarity with other peoples of color, but Blackness was the central issue in race as he understood it. I am a product of the West Coast of the United States, born and raised in central Seattle, educated in graduate school at Berkeley, now a professor in Santa Barbara for more than fifteen years. In between I spent long periods in Hawai'i, China, and Japan, and in recent years I have lived in Germany.

All this means that I have never understood race as just—or even primarily—a matter of Black and White. Central Seattle was home to a large African American population but also to many Chinese, Japanese, Filipinos, Indians, and working-class Whites. Race where and when I grew up had those six categories. In fact, race has been multipolar pretty much everywhere west of the Rockies. *Racial Fault Lines*, Tomás Almaguer's history of the making of race in nineteenth-century California, depicts a multiple-sided system: Indian, Mexican, Chinese, Japanese, Black, and White. Each of these racial groups had its own characteristics and historical evolution, even as their interaction was framed by an overall system of White supremacy. David Torres-Rouff's study of the making of race in the making of place—the built environment—in Los Angeles history reveals a similarly complex system, with all the groups that Almaguer describes but also with some people moving in and out of racial categories. It turns out that there were several different kinds of Mexicans, for example, and that both the meanings and the boundaries of Mexicanness changed over time. Hawai'i has a very different bouquet of racial groups than most of the continental United States, including Hawaiians, Chinese, Haoles (Whites), Japanese, Okinawans, Filipinos, Koreans, Samoans, Tongans, Mexicans, Blacks, a great variety of mixed people, and others. Hawai'i is not without racial hierarchy and conflict, but the racial map there is complex, multiple-sided, and different from that in other parts of the United States.[16]

The scientific racialists who framed the racial thinking against which the young Du Bois struggled would surely have been surprised to hear what I have learned about race over the years I have been writing this set of essays. What I have found out might have surprised Du Bois himself. It would surely have surprised many of the social scientists of race whose work I read as a young scholar, and it would have been news to my younger self. But over these years I have come to see race, not as a simple set of fixed categories, but as a moving, morphing, complex, and shifting array of relationships.

THIS IS A BOOK of racial theory, but it is quite unlike some other books of theory. Some writers represent themselves as Theorists with a capital *T* and eschew any accompanying adjective. In positioning themselves thus, it strikes me that they are either silly, or confused, or lazy, for I do not believe there is such a thing as theory in the abstract.[17] Theories are about things, problems, peoples, relationships, and the like. One can articulate a theory about the relationships between physical objects (Newton did that, as did Aristotle before him), a theory about the mechanics of flight (Leonardo), a theory about monetary policy (Milton Friedman), a theory about history (Fernand Braudel).[18] *Race in Mind* is a book about *racial* theory.

Let me be clear, however, about what theory is good for. Theory is not a substitute for ideas, observations, evidence, or clear thinking. Theory is supposed to be a spur to those things. Above all, theory is not a magical template that one can place over a field of data and thereby achieve understanding. I hope that the reader will engage the theoretical ideas I present in these essays, consider the contexts from which they spring, and investigate the problems they may illuminate. I would be appalled if someone were to take my ideas and apply them mechanically, as if they were a magical guide to understanding. Theories are tools that may help along the way but achieving understanding is the reader's job.

The book is arranged in two big parts. The first considers race and ethnicity theoretically. Among the threads that developed in my thinking over the decades during which I was writing these essays is my understanding of the relationship between race and ethnicity; chapters 1 and 4 in particular attend to the ways that race and ethnicity may be thought of as the same thing and the ways that they are different. It also has struck me, as it struck Du Bois, that racialized relationships exist in every part of the globe. The different countries of the world do not have the same racial system—there is no master model for how race works everywhere and always—but the local systems are related to one another, often through links of colonial relationship. Ultimately, all racial systems are about power, and specifically about the power to define difference and enforce privilege. Chapter 2 compares the systems of racial category construction in the United States and Britain. Chapter 4 sets up a way of thinking about racialized relationships at many points around the globe. Chapter 5 explores the racialized systems that have developed in a selection of countries in Northeast Asia and the Central Pacific. The other two essays in the book's first part offer cautionary tales. Chapter 3 examines the late 1990s to mid-2000s fashion of Whiteness studies and finds it less than satisfying. Chapter 6 warns against taking too seriously the claims of a relatively new form of pseudoscience: DNA ancestry testing for race.

The book's second part is about racial multiplicity. This is where the issue of constructedness comes to the fore, as people who are manifestly multiple in their racial ancestry manage their identities, affiliations, and loyalties. Chapter 7 describes how Asian Americans have dealt with an increasing level of multiplicity in their midst. In chapter 8, I tell the stories of several mixed people like W. E. B. Du Bois who had racial options but chose to affiliate themselves with their African American side. Chapter 9 explores the grounds and patterns by which Pacific Islander Americans, nearly all of them heirs to complex ancestral streams, choose among and express their ethnic identities. In chapter 10, Jeffrey Moniz and I explore the perhaps unique racial history and present of Hawai'i and offer a new model for thinking about race from the vantage point of the middle ground. Some scholars have been quite critical of the multiracial idea; chapter 11 takes those criticisms seriously and evaluates their merits. In chapter 12, Ingrid Dineen-Wimberly and I take issue with the very notion of models as ways of illuminating human experience, as we detail a number of times when the one-drop rule did not work as it was supposed to. The final chapter, built around the figure of Barack Obama as a racial emblem, looks back at the past twenty-five years of scholarship and activism around the multiracial idea, evaluates what those scholars and that movement have achieved, and points to places we might go in the years ahead. It also attempts to assess what President Obama as a racial figure means about the state of race in the United States.

NOTES

1. W. E. B. Du Bois, *The Souls of Black Folk* (New York: Dover, 1994; orig. Chicago: McClurg, 1903), 9.

2. Throughout this book I use the word *American* in the way that citizens of the United States, Britain, and some other countries habitually do: to stand for the people of the United States of America. I recognize, and am sympathetic to, the irritation that this generates among Canadians, Mexicans, Peruvians, and a whole lot of other people who can lay equal claim to being Americans. I do this, not to slight their claims to the title, but simply because American English doesn't work very well if I employ studious circumlocutions. I hope they will forgive me for this choice.

3. I explore the history of race in America through all these episodes and many more in *Almost All Aliens: Immigration, Race, and Colonialism in American History and Identity* (New York: Routledge, 2007).

4. I distinguish here between his theoretical thinking about race and his practical writing on the subject. His practical writings were far more numerous, and revolved around a series of unsurprisingly more practical themes: the actual conditions under which African Americans lived; defense of African Americans against discrimination and second-class citizenship; proposals for ameliorating the condition of poor African Americans; expressions of solidarity with other peoples of color and colonized people generally; and so forth.

5. W. E. B. Du Bois, "The Conservation of Races," in *W. E. B. Du Bois: A Reader*, ed. David Levering Lewis (New York: Holt, 1995), 20–27; orig. in American Negro Academy, *Occasional Papers*, No. 2 (1897).

6. See, e.g., A. H. Keane, *Ethnology* (Cambridge: Cambridge University Press, 1901).

7. W. E. Burghardt Du Bois, *Dusk of Dawn: An Essay toward an Autobiography of a Race Concept* (New Brunswick, NJ: Transaction, 1984; orig. 1940), 116.

8. Du Bois, "Conservation of Races," 22.

9. See Du Bois, "The Concept of Race," in *Dusk of Dawn*, 97–133; W. E. B. Du Bois, *The Autobiography of W. E. B. Du Bois: A Soliloquy on Viewing My Life from the Last Decade of Its First Century* (New York: International Publishers, 1968), esp. 61–131.

10. Some of Du Bois's writings on race and colonialism as international issues, and his calls for solidarity among colored and colonized peoples around the globe, can be found in *Africa, Its Place in Modern History* (Girard, KS: Haldeman-Julius, 1930); *Color and Democracy: Colonies and Peace* (New York: Harcourt, Brace, 1945); *The World and Africa, an Inquiry into the Part Which Africa Has Played in World History* (New York: Viking, 1947); *Worlds of Color* (New York: Mainstream, 1961); Bill V. Mullen and Cathryn Watson, eds., *W. E. B. Du Bois on Asia: Crossing the World Color Line* (Jackson: University Press of Mississippi, 2005).

11. John Maynard Keynes, *Essays in Persuasion* (London: Macmillan, 1931).

12. Arthur de Gobineau, *The Inequality of Human Races* (New York: Fertig, 1999; English orig. 1915; French orig. 1853–55); William Z. Ripley, *The Races of Europe: A Sociological Study* (New York: Appleton, 1899); Keene, *Ethnology*; United States Congress, *Reports of the Immigration Commission,* 61st Cong., 3rd sess., vol. 5: *Dictionary of Races and Peoples* (Washington, DC, 1910–11); Stephen Jay Gould, *The Mismeasure of Man,* rev. ed. (New York: Norton, 1996).

13. Franz Boas, *Race, Language and Culture* (Chicago: University of Chicago Press, 1940), collected essays. For Du Bois's development, compare the language in "The Conservation of Races" with that in *Dusk of Dawn*, cited above in notes 8 and 9.

14. E. Franklin Frazier, *The Negro Family in the United States* (Notre Dame, IN: University of Notre Dame Press, 2001; orig. 1939; E. Franklin Frazier, *Negro Youth at the Crossways: Their Personality Development in the Middle States* (New York: Schocken, 1967; orig. 1940); E. Franklin Frazier, *Black Bourgeoisie* (Glencoe, IL: Free Press, 1957); Gunnar Myrdal, *An American Dilemma: The Negro Problem and Modern Democracy* (New York: Harper and Row, 1962; orig. 1944); Thomas F. Pettigrew, *A Profile of the Negro American* (Princeton, NJ: Princeton University Press, 1964); Thomas F. Pettigrew, *Racially Separate or Together?* (New York: McGraw-Hill, 1971); Kenneth B. Clark, *Dark Ghetto: Dilemmas of Social Power* (New York: Harper and Row, 1965); Kenneth B. Clark, *Prejudice and Your Child* (Boston: Beacon, 1965); Kenneth B. Clark and Talcott Parsons, eds., *The Negro American* (Boston: Houghton Mifflin, 1966); Winthrop D. Jordan, *White over Black: American Attitudes toward the Negro, 1550–1812* (Chapel Hill: University of North Carolina Press, 1968); Milton M. Gordon, *Assimilation in American Life: The Role of Race, Religion, and National Origins* (New York: Oxford University Press, 1964). In fairness, Jordan was more open than these other scholars to questioning the shape of racial categories.

On the rise of social science generally in the decades after World War II, see Paul Boyer, "Social Science into the Breach," in his *By the Bomb's Early Light: American Thought and Culture at the Dawn of the Atomic Age* (New York: Pantheon, 1985), 166–77; and Kenton W. Worcester, *Social Science Research Council, 1923–1998* (New York: Social Science Research Council, 2001). Markers in the temporary dominance of the social sciences in American intellectual life include C. Wright Mills, *The Sociological Imagination* (New York: Oxford University Press, 1959); Peter L. Berger and Thomas Luckmann, *The Social Construction of Reality: A Treatise in the Sociology of Knowledge* (Garden City, NY: Doubleday, 1966); Erving Goffman, *The Presentation of Self in Everyday Life* (Garden City, NY: Doubleday, 1959); and Peter Winch, *The Idea of a Social Science and Its Relationship to Philosophy* (New York: Routledge, 2007; orig. 1958).

15. Among other writers who have had a particular influence on the way I think are Clifford Geertz, *The Interpretation of Cultures* (New York: Basic Books, 1973); Clifford Geertz, *Agricultural Involution: The Process of Ecological Change in Indonesia* (Berkeley: University of California Press, 1963); Clifford Geertz, *Local Knowledge: Further Essays in Interpretive Anthropology* (New York: Basic Books, 1983); Clifford Geertz, *Works and Lives: The Anthropologist as Author* (Stanford, CA: Stanford University Press, 1988); Clifford Geertz, *Islam Observed: Religious Development in Morocco and Indonesia* (New Haven, CT: Yale University Press, 1968); Clifford Geertz, *The Religion of Java* (Glencoe, IL: Free Press, 1960); Clifford Geertz, "Deep Hanging Out," *New York Review of Books* 45.16 (October 22, 1998); Lawrence Levine, *Black Culture and Black Consciousness: African American Folk Thought from Slavery to Freedom* (New York: Oxford University Press, 1977); Lawrence Levine, *Highbrow/Lowbrow: The Emergence of Cultural Hierarchy in America* (Cambridge, MA: Harvard University Press, 1988); Lawrence Levine, *The Unpredictable Past: Explorations in American Cultural History* (New York: Oxford University Press, 1993); Lawrence Levine, *The Opening of the American Mind: Canons, Culture, and History* (Boston: Beacon Press, 1998); Malcolm X, *The Autobiography of Malcolm X* (New York: Grove Press, 1966); Frantz Fanon, *The Wretched of the Earth*, trans. Constance Farrington (New York: Grove Press, 1965); Frantz Fanon, *Black Skin, White Masks*, trans. Charles Lam Markmann (New York: Grove Press, 1967); Gloria Anzaldúa, *Borderlands/La Frontera: The New Mestiza* (San Francisco: Aunt Lute Books, 1987); Edward Said, *Orientalism* (New York: Pantheon, 1978); Edward Said, *Culture and Imperialism* (New York: Vintage, 1994).

16. Tomás Almaguer, *Racial Fault Lines: The Historical Origins of White Supremacy in California* (Berkeley: University of California Press, 1994); David Torres-Rouff, *Before L.A.: Race, Space, and Municipal Power in Los Angeles, 1781–1894* (New Haven, CT: Yale University Press, 2013); Jonathan Y. Okamura, *Ethnicity and Inequality in Hawai'i* (Philadelphia: Temple University Press, 2008);

Candace Fujikane and Jonathan Y. Okamura, eds., *Asian Settler Colonialism: From Local Governance to the Habits of Everyday Life in Hawai'i* (Honolulu: University of Hawai'i Press, 2008); see also Gary B. Nash, *Red, White, and Black: The Peoples of Early North America*, 6th ed. (Boston: Prentice Hall, 2010).

These understandings of the multipolar nature of the American racial system stand in sharp contrast to the (I think mistaken) presentation of a single Black–White continuum, with groups like Asians and Latinos placed in between, as in Eileen O'Brien, *The Racial Middle: Latinos and Asian Americans Living beyond the Racial Divide* (New York: New York University Press, 2008). Neil Foley and Eduardo Bonilla-Silva are a bit more sophisticated but still I think in error in Foley, *The White Scourge: Mexicans, Blacks, and Poor Whites in Texas Cotton Culture* (Berkeley: University of California Press, 1997); and Bonilla-Silva and David G. Embrick, "Black, Honorary White, White: The Future of Race in the United States," in *Mixed Messages: Multiracial Identities in the "Color-Blind" Era*, ed. David L. Brunsma (Boulder, CO: Lynne Rienner, 2006), 33–48.

17. That said, among the many works of more or less abstract theory that have influenced me are Pierre Bourdieu, *Outline for a Theory of Practice* (Cambridge: Cambridge University Press, 1977); Pierre Bourdieu, *Distinction: A Social Critique of the Judgment of Taste* (Cambridge, MA: Harvard University Press, 1984); Pierre Bourdieu, *The Logic of Practice*, trans. Richard Nice (Stanford, CA: Stanford University Press, 1990); Stuart Hall, ed., *Representation: Cultural Representations and Signifying Practices* (Thousand Oaks, CA: Sage, 1997); Stuart Hall and Paul du Gay, eds., *Questions of Cultural Identity* (Thousand Oaks, CA: Sage, 1996); Stuart Hall et al., eds., *Modernity: An Introduction to Modern Societies* (Cambridge: Polity Press, 1995); Gayatri Spivak, "Can the Subaltern Speak?," in *Can the Subaltern Speak? Reflections on the History of an Idea*, ed. Rosalind C. Morris (New York: Columbia University Press, 2010), 21–80; Antonio Gramsci, *The Antonio Gramsci Reader: Selected Writings, 1916–1935*, ed. David Forgacs (New York: New York University Press, 2000); and Michel Foucault, *The Archaeology of Knowledge* (New York: Pantheon, 1972). References to specifically racial theorists abound in the notes to the chapters that follow.

18. Isaac Newton, *The Principia: Mathematical Principles of Natural Philosophy*, trans. I. Bernard Cohen, Anne Whitman, and Julia Budenz (Berkeley: University of California Press, 1999; orig. 1726); Aristotle, *Physics*, trans. Robin Waterfield (New York: Oxford, 1999); Milton Friedman, *Monetarist Economics* (Cambridge, MA: Blackwell, 1991); Fernand Braudel, *On History*, trans. Sarah Matthews (Chicago: University of Chicago Press, 1980).

Race and Ethnicity

1

The Illogic of American
Racial Categories

I wrote this essay in 1991 at the request of Maria Root, as a theoretical introduction to her landmark edited book, Racially Mixed People in America *(1992).[1] She asked me to explain the constructed nature of race and ethnicity. The reader may perceive that I was feeling my way to an initial framing of these issues. I called on a scientist, James King, for authority on biological ideas about race and on Alice Brues for expertise from physical anthropology, although I gave their ideas a historical framing of my own. This essay attracted a ready audience; indeed, it has been reprinted several times without my permission, once by the PBS website.[2] I choose to view that appropriation (they did at least list me as the author) as praise for the clarity with which I communicated fundamental ideas about race. This was my first attempt to sort out the way that race works conceptually and to provide a constructivist interpretation that has room for the possibility of multiraciality. I have left the argument and nearly all the prose as they were in the original. I have changed a few sentences for clarity and updated some of the numbers and references.*

The Mulatto to His Critics

Ashamed of my race?
And of what race am I?
I am many in one.
Thru my veins there flows the blood
Of Red Man, Black Man, Briton, Celt and Scot
In warring clash and tumultuous riot.
I welcome all,
But love the blood of the kindly race
That swarthes my skin, crinkles my hair
And puts sweet music into my soul.

—Joseph Cotter, 1918

This poem by Joseph Cotter,[3] a promising African American poet who died young early in the last century, highlights several of the ways Americans think about race. What is a race? And, if we can figure that out, what is a person of mixed race? These are central questions of this essay and this book.

In most people's minds, as apparently in Cotter's, race is a fundamental organizing principle of human affairs. Everyone has a race, and only one. The races are biologically and characterologically separate one from another, and they are at least potentially in conflict with one another. Race has something to do with blood (today we might say genes or DNA), and something to do with skin color, and something to do with the geographic origins of one's ancestors. According to this way of thinking, people with more than one racial ancestry have a problem, one that can be resolved only by choosing a single racial identity.

It is my contention in this essay, however, that race, while it has some relationship to biology, is not mainly a biological matter. Race is primarily a sociopolitical construct. The sorting of people into this race or that in the modern era has generally been done by powerful groups for the purposes of maintaining and extending their own power. Not only is race something different from what many people have believed it to be, but people of mixed race are not what many people have assumed them to be.

As the other essays in this volume amply demonstrate, people with more than one racial ancestry do not necessarily have a problem. And, in contrast to Cotter's earlier opinion, these days people of mixed parentage are often choosing for themselves something other than a single racial identity.

RACE AS A BIOLOGICAL CATEGORY

In the thinking of most Europeans and Americans (and these ideas have spread around the world in the last century), humankind can be divided into four or five discrete races. This is an extension of the admittedly artificial system of classification of all living things first constructed by the Swedish botanist and taxonomist Carolus Linnaeus in the eighteenth century. According to the Linnaean system, human beings are all members of the kingdom Animalia, the phylum Chordata, the class Mammalia, the order Primates, the family Hominidae, the genus *Homo*, and the species *Homo sapiens.* Each level of this pyramid contains subdivisions of the level above. In the century after Linnaeus, pseudoscientific racists such as Johann Friedrich Blumenbach and Joseph Arthur, comte de Gobineau, tried to extend the system down one more level to human *races*, on the basis of geography and observed physical differences.[4] Details of the versions differed, but most systems of categorization divided humankind into at least Red, Yellow, Black, and White: Native Americans, Asians, Africans, and Europeans. Whether Australian Aborigines, Bushmen, and various brown-skinned peoples—Polynesians and Malays, for example— constituted separate races depended on who was doing the categorizing.

There has been considerable argument, in the nineteenth century and since, over the nature of these "races." The most common view has been to see races as distinct *types.* That is, there were supposed to have been at some time in the past four or five utterly distinct and pure races, with physical features, gene pools, and character qualities that diverged entirely one from another. Over millennia there had been some mixing at the margins, but the observer could still distinguish a Caucasian type (light of skin, blue-eyed, and possessing fine, sandy hair, a high-bridged nose, thin lips, etc.), a Negroid type (dark brown of skin, brown-eyed, with tightly curled black hair, a broad flat nose, thick lips, etc.), an Asian type, and so on. There was debate as to whether these varieties of human beings all proceeded from the same first humans or whether there was a separate genesis for each race. The latter view tended to regard the races as virtual separate species, as far apart as house cats and cougars; the former saw them as more like breeds of dogs—spaniels, collies, and so forth. The typological view of races developed by Europeans arranged the peoples of the world hierarchically, with Caucasians at the top, Asians next, then Native Americans, and Africans at the bottom—in terms of both physical abilities and moral qualities.[5]

Successors in this tradition further divided the races into subunits, each again supposed to carry its own distinctive physical, genotypical, and moral characteristics. Madison Grant divided the Caucasian race into five subunits: the Nordic race, the Alpine race, the Mediterranean race, the extinct races of the Upper Paleolithic period (such as Cro-Magnon humans), and the extinct races of the Middle Paleolithic period (including Neanderthal humans).[6] Each of the modern Caucasian subunits, according to Grant, contained at least five further subdivisions. Each of the major subunits bore a distinctive typical stature, skin color, eye color, hair color, hair texture, facial shape, nose type, and cephalic index.[7] Each was also supposed to carry distinctive *intellectual and moral qualities*, with the Nordic being the highest type. According to Henry Fairfield Osborn, even where there was achievement of distinction in non-Nordic peoples, it came from a previous infusion of Nordic genes. He contended in a *New York Times* article that Raphael, Cervantes, Leonardo, Galileo, Titian, Botticelli, Petrarch, Columbus, Richelieu, Lafayette, Joffre, Clemenceau, Racine, Napoleon, Garibaldi, and dozens of other Continentals were all actually of Nordic origin—hence their genius.[8] In similar fashion, pseudoscientific racists saw White bloodlines as the source of the evident capabilities of Booker T. Washington, Frederick Douglass, and George Washington Carver.[9]

Over the course of the twentieth century, an increasing number of scientists took exception to the notion of races as types. James C. King, a prominent American geneticist on racial matters, denounced the typological view as "make-believe."[10] By the second half of the twentieth century, biologists and physical anthropologists were more likely to see races as *subspecies*. That is, they recognized the essential commonality of all humans and saw races as geographically and biologically diverging populations. Thus the physical anthropologist Alice Brues saw a race as "a division of a species which differs from other divisions by the frequency with which certain hereditary traits appear among its members."[11] They saw all human populations, in all times and places, as mixed populations. There never were any "pure" races. Nonetheless, there are populations in geographic localities that can be distinguished from each other by statistically significant frequencies of various genetic or physical traits, from blood type to hair color to susceptibility to sickle-cell anemia. Most such thinkers agreed, however, that the idea of race is founded in biology. Nineteenth-century Europeans and Americans spoke of blood as the agent of the transmission of racial characteristics. Throughout most of the second half of the twentieth century, genes were accorded the same role once assigned to blood. Nowadays, we speak of DNA.

The most important thing about races was the boundaries between them. If races were pure (or had once been) and if one were a member of the race at the top, then it was essential to maintain the boundaries that defined one's superiority, to keep people from the lower categories from slipping surreptitiously upward. Hence US law took pains to define just who was in which racial category. Most of the boundary drawing came on the border between White and Black. The boundaries were drawn on the basis, not of biology—genotype and phenotype—but of descent. For purposes of the laws of nine southern and border states in the early part of the twentieth century, a "Negro" was defined as someone with a single Negro great-grandparent; in three other southern states, a Negro great-great-grandparent would suffice. That is, a person with fifteen White ancestors four generations back and a single Black ancestor at the same remove was reckoned a Negro in the eyes of the law.[12]

But what was a "Negro"? It turned out that, for the purposes of the court, a Negro ancestor was simply any person who was socially regarded as a Negro. That person might have been the descendant of several Caucasians along with only a single African. Thus, far less than one-sixteenth actual African ancestry was required in order for an individual to be regarded as an African American. In practice—both legal and customary—anyone with *any* known African ancestry was deemed an African American, while only those without any trace of known African ancestry were called Whites. This was known as the "one-drop rule": one drop of Black blood made one an African American. In fact, of course, it was not about blood—or biology—at all. People with no discernible African genotype or phenotype were regarded as Black on the basis of the fact that they had grandfathers or other remote relatives who were socially regarded as Black, and they had no choice in the matter. The boundaries were drawn in this manner to maintain an absolute wall surrounding White dominance.

This leads one to the conclusion that race is primarily about culture and social structure, not biology. As the geneticist King admitted:

> Both what constitutes a race and how one recognizes a racial difference are culturally determined. Whether two individuals regard themselves as of the same or of different races depends not on the degree of similarity of their genetic material but on whether history, tradition, and personal training and experiences have brought them to regard themselves as belonging to the same group or to different groups. . . . [T]here are no objective boundaries to set off one subspecies from another.[13]

The process of racial labeling starts with geography, culture, and family ties and runs through economics and politics to biology, not the other way around. That is, a group is defined by an observer according to its location, its cultural practices, or its social connectedness (and their subsequent economic, social, and political implications). Then, on looking at physical markers or genetic makeup, the observer may find that this group shares certain items with greater frequency than do other populations that are also socially defined. But even in such cases, there is tremendous overlap between racial categories with regard to biological features. As King wrote, "Genetic variability within populations is greater than the variability between them."[14]

Take the case of skin color. Suppose people can all be arranged according to the color of their skin along a continuum:

darkest   2   3   4   5   6   7   lightest

The people Americans call Black would nearly all fall on the darker end of the continuum, while the people we call White would nearly all fall on the lighter end:

darkest   2   3   4   5   6   7   lightest
Blacks |- - - - - - - - - - - - - - - - -|
Whites | - - - - - - - - - - - - - -|

On the *average*, the White and Black populations are distinct from each other in skin color. But a very large number of individuals who are classified as White have darker skin color than some people classified as Black, and vice versa. The so-called races are not biological categories at all; rather, they are primarily social divisions that rely only partly on physical markers such as skin color to identify group membership.

Sometimes, skin color and social definitions run counter to one another. Take the case of Walter White and Poppy Cannon.[15] In the 1930s and 1940s, White was one of the most prominent African American citizens in the United States. An author and activist, he served for twenty years as the executive secretary of the NAACP. Physically, White was short, slim, blond, and blue-eyed. On the street he would not have been taken for an African American by anyone who did not know his identity. But he had been raised in the South in a family of very light-skinned Blacks, and he was socially defined as Black, both by others and by himself. He dedicated his life and career to serving Black Americans. In 1949, White divorced his light-skinned African American wife of many years' standing and married Cannon, a White journalist and businesswoman. Although Cannon was a White woman socially and ancestrally, her hair, eyes, and skin were several shades darker than her new husband's. If a person were shown pictures of the couple and told that one partner was White and the other Black, without doubt that person would have selected Cannon as the Afro-American. Yet, immediately on White's divorce, there

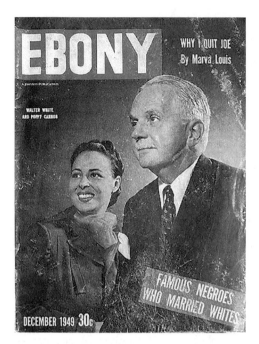

Fig. 1.1.
Walter White and Poppy
Cannon. Courtesy of *Ebony*
magazine.

was an eruption of protest in the Black press. White was accused of having sold out his race for a piece of White flesh and Cannon of having seduced one of Black America's most beloved leaders. White segregationists took the occasion to crow that this was what Black advocates of civil rights really wanted: access to White women. All the acrimony and confusion took place because Walter White was socially Black and Poppy Cannon was socially White; biology—at least physical appearance—had nothing to do with it.

All of this is not to argue that there is no biological aspect to race, only that biology is not fundamental. The origins of race are sociocultural and political, and the main ways that race is used are sociocultural and political. Race can be used for good as well as for ill. For example, one may use the socially defined category "Black" to target for study and treatment a population with a greater likelihood of suffering from sickle-cell anemia. That is an efficient and humane use of a racial category. Nonetheless, the origins of racial distinctions are to be found in culture and social structure, not in biology.

RACE AS A SOCIAL CATEGORY

Race, then, is primarily a social construct. It has been constructed in different ways in different times and places. In 1870, the US Bureau of the Census divided the American population into races: White, Colored (Blacks), Colored (Mulattoes), Chinese, and Indian.[16] In 1950, the census categories reflected a different social understanding: White, Black, and Other. By 1980, they reflected the ethnic blossoming of the previous two decades: White, Black, Hispanic, Japanese, Chinese, Filipino, Korean, Vietnamese, American Indian, Asian Indian, Hawaiian, Guamanian, Samoan, Eskimo, Aleut, and Other. In the 2000 census, the US government began to allow a person to report more than a single racial identity—a radical change brought about by the multiracial movement and the rising consciousness of racial multiplicity among the American public.[17] In 2010, the categories were "White; Black or African American; American Indian or Alaska Native—Print name of enrolled or principal tribe); Asian Indian; Chinese; Filipino; Japanese; Korean; Vietnamese; Other Asian—Print race, for example, Hmong, Laotian, Thai, Pakistani, Cambodian, and so on; Native Hawaiian; Guamanian or Chamorro; Samoan; Other Pacific Islander—Print race, for example, Fijian, Tongan, and so on; Some other race." This was complicated, of course, by the fact that people were allowed to check more than one box, so an elaborate system was devised to try to record both the numbers of people who placed themselves monoracially in each category and those who checked more than one box.[18]

In England in 1981, the categories were quite different: White, West Indian, African, Arab, Turkish, Chinese, Indian, Pakistani, Bangladeshi, Sri Lankan, and Other—because the sociopolitical landscape in England demanded different divisions.[19] Thirty years later, the British census categories were

- **White:** English/Welsh/Scottish/Northern Irish/British; Irish; Gypsy or Irish Traveller; Any other White background, please describe;
- **Mixed/Multiple ethnic groups:** White and Black Caribbean; White and Black African; White and Asian; Any other Mixed/Multiple ethnic background, please describe;

- **Asian/Asian British:** Indian; Pakistani; Bangladeshi; Chinese; Any other Asian background, please describe;
- **Black/African/Caribbean/Black British:** African; Caribbean; Any other Black/African/Caribbean background, please describe;
- **Other ethnic group:** Arab; Any other ethnic group, please describe.[20]

In South Africa, there were five racial categories: White, African, Coloured, Asian, and Other.[21] In Brazil, the gradations between Black and White were many: *preto, cabra, escuro, mulato escuro, mulato clara, pardo, sarará, moreno,* and *branco de terra.*[22] Each of these systems of racial classification reflects a different social, economic, and political reality. Such social situations change, and so do racial categories.

Social distinctions such as race and class come about when two or more groups of people come together in a situation of economic or status competition. Frequently such competition results in stratification—in the domination of some groups by others. In the era of the transatlantic slave trade, people in Africa did not experience their lives as Africans or as Blacks; they were Hausa or Ibo or Fon, or members of any of several other groups. But when they were brought to America they were defined as a single group by the Europeans who held power over their lives. They were lumped together as Africans or Negroes or Blacks, partly because they shared certain physical similarities, especially when contrasted with Europeans, and partly because they shared a common status as slaves.[23]

From the point of view of the dominant group, racial distinctions are a necessary tool of dominance. They serve to separate the subordinate people as Other. Putting simple, neat racial labels on dominated peoples—and creating negative myths about their moral qualities—makes it easier for the dominators to ignore the individual humanity of their victims. It eases the guilt of oppression. Calling various African peoples all one racial group, and associating that group with evil, sin, laziness, bestiality, sexuality, and irresponsibility, made it easier for White slave owners to rationalize holding their fellow humans in bondage, whipping them, selling them, separating their families, and working them to death.[24] The function of the one-drop rule was to solidify the barrier between Black and White, to make sure that no one who might possibly be identified as Black also became identified as White. For a mixed person, then, acceptance of the one-drop rule means internalizing the oppression of the dominant group, buying into the system of racial domination.

Race is by no means only negative, however. From the point of view of subordinate peoples, race can be a positive tool, a source of belonging, mutual help, and self-esteem. Racial categories (and ethnic categories, for they function in the same way)[25] identify a set of people with whom to share a sense of identity and common experience. To be a Chinese American is to share with other Chinese Americans at least the possibility of free communication and a degree of trust that may not be shared with non-Chinese. It is to share access to common institutions—Chinese churches, Chinatowns, and Chinese civic associations. It is to share a sense of common history—immigration, work on the railroads and in the mines of the West, discrimination, exclusion, and a decades-long fight for respectability and equal rights. It is to share a sense of peoplehood that helps locate individuals psychologically, and also provides the basis for common political action. Race, this socially constructed identity, can be a powerful tool, either for oppression or for group self-actualization.

AT THE MARGINS: RACE AS SELF-DEFINITION

Where does this leave the person of mixed parentage? Such people have long suffered from a negative public image. In 1912, the French psychologist Gustave LeBon contended that "mixed breeds are ungovernable." The American sociologist Edward Reuter wrote that "the mixed blood is [by definition] an unadjusted person." Writers and filmmakers from Thomas Nelson Page to D. W. Griffith to William Faulkner have presented mixed people as tormented souls.[26] Yet even if such a picture of pathology and marginal identity has ever been partially accurate, it certainly is no longer the case.

What is a person of mixed race? Biologically speaking, we are all mixed. That is, we all have genetic material from a variety of populations, and we all exhibit physical characteristics that testify to mixed ancestry. Biologically speaking, there never have been any pure races; all populations are mixed.

More to the point is the question of to which socially defined category people of mixed ancestry belong. The most illogical aspect of all this racial categorizing is not that we imagine it is about biology. After all, there *is* a biological component to race, or at least we identify biological referents— physical markers—as a kind of shorthand to stand for what are essentially socially defined groups. What is most illogical is that we imagine these racial categories to be exclusive. The US Census form said, until the 2000 census, "Check one box." If a person checked "Other," his or her identity and connection with any particular group was immediately erased. Yet what was a multiracial person to do?

Once, a person of mixed ancestry had little choice. Until fairly recently, for example, most Americans of part Japanese or part Chinese ancestry had to present themselves to the world as non-Asians, for the Asian ethnic communities to which they might have aspired to be connected would not have them.[27] For example, in the 1920s, seven-year-old Peter fended for himself on the streets of Los Angeles. He had been thrown out of the house shortly after his Mexican American mother died, when his Japanese American father married a Japanese woman, because the stepmother could not stand the thought of a half Mexican boy living under her roof. No Japanese American individual or community institution was willing to take him in because he was not pure Japanese.[28]

On the other hand, the one-drop rule meant that part Black people were forced to reckon themselves Black. Some might pass for White, but by far the majority of children of African American intermarriages chose or were forced to be Black. A student from a mixed family described his feelings in the 1970s: "At home I see my mom and dad and I'm part of both of them. But when I walk outside that door, it's like my mom doesn't exist. I'm just Black. Everybody treats me that way." When he filled out his census form, this student checked the box next to "Black."[29]

The salient point here is that once, before the last third of the twentieth century, multiracial individuals did not generally have the opportunity to choose identities for themselves.[30] In the 1970s and particularly the 1980s, however, individuals began to assert their right to choose their own identities—to claim belonging to more than one group, or to create new identities. By 1990, Mary Waters could write, "One of the most basic choices we have is whether to apply an ethnic label to ourselves." She was speaking of a choice of ethnic identities from among several White options, such as Italian, Irish, and Polish. Yet the concept of choice began to apply to mixed people of color as well.[31]

Some even dared to refuse to choose. In 1985, I observed a wise five-year-old. Dining with her family in Boston's Chinatown during Chinese New Year, she was asked insistently by an adult Chinese friend of the family, "Which are you really—Chinese or American?" It was clear the woman wanted her to say she was really Chinese. But the girl replied simply, "I don't have to choose. I'm both." And so she was.

This child probably could not have articulated it, but she was arguing that races are not types. One ought not be thrust into a category: simply Chinese or simply American, simply White or simply Black. Her answer calls on us to move our focus from the boundaries between groups— where we carefully assign this person to the White category and that person to the Black category—to the centers. That is, we ought to pay attention to the things that characterize groups and hold them together, to the content of group identity and activity, to patterns and means of inclusiveness and belonging. A mixed person should not be regarded as Black *or* White but as Black *and* White, with access to all parts of his or her identity. In the poem presented at the outset of this essay, Joseph Cotter's mulatto felt the pull of the various parts of his heritage but felt constrained to choose only one. Since the 1990s, that choice has still been available to mixed people, but it has no longer been *necessary.* In the twenty-first century, a person of mixed ancestry can choose to embrace multiple parts of his or her background. Many of the essays in this volume are about the issues attendant upon recognition of a multiracial identity. As the essays attest, the patterns of identity making and claiming are sometimes quite complex, but the one-drop rule no longer need automatically apply.

NOTES

1. Maria P. P. Root, *Racially Mixed People in America* (Newbury Park, CA: Sage, 1992), 12–20.

2. www.pbs.org/wgbh/pages/frontline/shows/jefferson/mixed/spickard.html (retrieved August 11, 2013).

3. Joseph Seamon Cotter, Jr., *Complete Poems*, ed. James Robert Payne (Athens: University of Georgia Press, 1990; orig. 1918), 27.

4. Carolus Linnaeus, *Systema Naturae* (1758), translated as *The System of Nature* (London: Lackington, Allen, 1806); Johann Friedrich Blumenbach, *On the Natural Varieties of Mankind* (New York: Bergman, 1969; orig. English 1865; orig. German 1775); Johann Friedrich Blumenbach, *The Anthropological Treatises of Johann Friedrich Blumenbach* (Boston: Milford House, 1973; orig. 1865); Arthur de Gobineau, *The Inequality of Human Races* (New York: Fertig, 1999; orig. English 1915; orig. French 1853–55); Michael D. Biddiss, *Father of Racist Ideology: The Social and Political Thought of Count Gobineau* (New York: Weybright and Talley, 1970); Michael D. Biddiss, ed., *Gobineau: Selected Political Writings* (New York: Harper and Row, 1970). For other leading early racial theorists, see Georges-Louis Leclerc, comte de Buffon, *A Natural History, General and Particular*, 2nd ed. (London: Strahan and Cadell, 1785); and Georges Léopold Cuvier, *Le règne animal* (1817), translated into English as *Animal Kingdom* (London: W. S. Orr, 1840).

This vector was carried into the twentieth century by, among others, William Z. Ripley, *The Races of Europe* (New York: Appleton, 1899); A. H. Keane, *Ethnology* (Cambridge: Cambridge University Press, 1901); Madison Grant, *The Passing of the Great Race or The Racial Basis of European History* (New York: Scribner's, 1916); Madison Grant and Charles Stewart Davison, eds., *The Alien in Our Midst, or "Selling our Birthright for a Mess of Pottage"* (New York: Galton, 1930); Lothrop Stoddard, *The Rising Tide of Color against White World Supremacy* (New York: Scribner's, 1920); Lothrop Stoddard, *The Revolt against Civilization: The Menace of the Under Man* (New York: Scribner's, 1923); Lothrop Stoddard, *Racial Realities in Europe* (New York: Scribner's, 1924); Lothrop Stoddard, *Clashing Tides of Colour* (New York: Scribner's, 1935); Earnest Albert Hooton, *Apes, Men and Morons* (New York: Putnam's, 1937); Earnest Albert Hooton, *Twilight of Man* (New York: Putnam's, 1939); Carleton Stevens Coon, *The Races of Europe* (New York: Macmillan, 1939); Carleton Stevens Coon, *The Story of Man* (New York: Knopf, 1954); Carleton Stevens Coon, *The Origins of Races* (New York: Knopf, 1962); Carleton Stevens Coon, *The Living Races of Man* (New York: Knopf, 1965); Carleton Stevens Coon, *Racial Adaptations* (Chicago: Nelson-Hall, 1982).

The tradition continues in current generations: Jerome H. Barkow, Leda Cosmides, and John Tooby, eds., *The Adapted Mind: Evolutionary Psychology and the Generation of Culture* (New York: Oxford University Press, 1992); Richard J. Herrnstein and Charles Murray, *The Bell Curve: Intelligence and Class Structure in American Life* (New York: Free Press, 1994); Samuel P. Huntington, *The Clash of Civilizations* (New York: Simon and Schuster, 1996); J. Philippe Rushton, *Race, Evolution, and Behavior*, 3rd ed. (Port Huron, MI: Charles Darwin Research Institute Press, 2000); Patrick J. Buchanan, *The Death of the West: How Dying Populations and Immigrant Invasions Imperil Our Country and Civilization* (New York: St. Martin's, 2002); Richard Lynn, *Race Differences in Intelligence: An Evolutionary*

Approach (Augusta, GA: Washington Summit Publishers, 2006); Nicholas Wade, *A Troublesome Inheritance: Genes, Race, and History* (New York: Penguin, 2014).

For analysis and critique, see Stephen Jay Gould, *The Mismeasure of Man*, rev. ed. (New York: Norton, 1996); Joseph L. Graves Jr., *The Emperor's New Clothes: Biological Theories of Race at the Millennium* (New Brunswick, NJ: Rutgers University Press, 2001); Jonathan Marks, *Human Biodiversity: Genes, Race, and History* (New York: Aldine de Gruyter, 1995); Ashley Montagu, *Man's Most Dangerous Myth: The Fallacy of Race* (New York: World, 1964); Thomas F. Gossett, *Race: The History of an Idea in America* (New York: Schocken, 1965); Audrey Smedley, *Race in North America*, 2nd ed. (Boulder, CO: Westview, 1999); William H. Tucker, *The Science and Politics of Racial Research* (Urbana: University of Illinois Press, 1994); C. Loring Brace, *"Race" Is a Four-Letter Word: The Genesis of the Concept* (New York: Oxford University Press, 2005).

5. There were two ways of conceiving this hierarchy, depending on which side of the Darwinian divide one inhabited. Pre-Darwinians thought of Adam and Eve as Caucasians, with Asians, Africans, and Native Americans representing degenerated descendants in separate lines. Those who came after Darwin and embraced the evolutionary view conceived of the human races as part of a continuum of ever-improving species and races, with great apes succeeded by chimpanzees, then by Africans, Asians, and Caucasians. The last were seen as the most complex and perfect of evolution's products. James C. King, *The Biology of Race*, 2nd ed. (Berkeley: University of California Press, 1981); Emmanuel Chukwudi Eze, ed., *Race and the Enlightenment* (Oxford: Blackwell, 1997); Ripley, *Races of Europe*.

6. Grant, *Passing of the Great Race*. The Nordics were people who could trace unmixed ancestry from Scandinavia, northern Germany, or the British Isles. Alpines were most minority peoples of Europe (Bretons, Basques, Walloons, etc.), French, southern Germans, northern Italians, Swiss, Russians, other Eastern Europeans, and so on. Mediterraneans included Iberians, southern Italians, northern Africans, Hindus, Persians, and many Middle Easterners.

7. The cephalic index was the ratio of the breadth of the head to its length, expressed as a percentage.

8. Henry Fairfield Osborn, writing in the *New York Times*, 1924; quoted in Jacques Barzun, *Race: A Study in Superstition* (New York: Harper and Row, 1965; orig. 1937), 224.

9. These ideas still had some currency as late as the 1980s. Consider a map in the 1982 *Bartholomew World Atlas* that divides up the world by skin color:

Light Skin Colour (*Leocodermi*)
    Indo-European: White skin, straight to wavy hair
    Indo-European: Light brown skin, wavy hair
    Hamitic-Semitic: Reddish brown skin, wavy hair
    Polynesian: Light brown skin, wavy hair

Yellow Skin Colour (*Xanthodermi*)
  Asiatic or Mongolian: Yellow skin, straight hair
  Indonesian: Yellow brown skin, straight hair
  American Indian: Reddish yellow skin, straight hair
Dark Skin Colour (*Melanodermi*)
  African Negro: Dark brown skin, kinky hair
  Pigmy Negro: Brown skin, kinky hair
  Melanesian: Dark brown skin, kinky hair
  Australo·Dravidian: Brown to black skin, wavy to kinky hair

There is also a map dividing the world by cephalic index:

Dolichocephalic (Long-headed)—primarily the peoples of Africa, Arabia, India, and Australia
Mesocephalic (Medium-headed)—Northwest Europe, North America, China, Japan, Persia
Brachycephalic (Broad-headed)—the rest of Europe, Latin America, the rest of Asia
Hyperbrachycephalic (Very broad-headed)—Russia

What the mapmakers imagined they were measuring and classifying is unclear, but it is clear that pseudoscientific racism was alive in the 1980s. John C. Bartholomew, *World Atlas*, 12th ed. (Edinburgh: Bartholomew, 1982).

10. King, *Biology of Race*, 112. One must be careful of even this appeal to argument by scientists. Much of the allure of the Blumenbach argument was that it was put forth on the supposed basis of science. Since some people regard science with a kind of ritual awe, they are unable to think critically about any idea, however preposterous, put forth in the name of science.

11. Alice Brues, *People and Races* (New York: Macmillan, 1977), 1.

12. Paul Spickard, *Mixed Blood: Intermarriage and Ethnic Identity in Twentieth-Century America* (Madison: University of Wisconsin Press, 1989), 274–75; Gilbert T. Stephenson, *Race Distinctions in American Law* (New York: Appleton, 1910), 12–20.

13. King, *Biology of Race*, 156–57.

14. Ibid., 158.

15. Poppy Cannon, *A Gentle Knight: My Husband, Walter White* (New York: Rinehart, 1956); Walter White, *A Man Called White* (Athens: University of Georgia Press, 1995; orig. 1948); Thomas Dyja, *Walter White: The Dilemma of Black Identity in America* (Chicago: Ivan Dee, 2008); Kenneth Robert Janken, *White: The Biography of Walter White, Mr. NAACP* (New York: New Press, 2003).

16. US Department of Interior, *Population of the United States: Ninth Census, 1870* (Washington, DC, 1872), 606–9.

17. Joel Perlmann and Mary C. Waters, eds., *The New Race Question: How the Census Counts Multiracial Individuals* (New York: Russell Sage Foundation, 2002); G. Reginald Daniel, *More than Black? Multiracial Identity and the New Racial Order* (Philadelphia: Temple University Press, 2002); Kim M. Williams, *Mark One or More: Civil Rights in Multiracial America* (Ann Arbor: University of Michigan Press, 2006); Jayne O. Ifekwunigwe, ed., *"Mixed Race" Studies: A Reader* (New York: Routledge, 2004), 205–60; Maria P. P. Root, ed., *The Multiracial Experience: Racial Borders as the New Frontier* (Thousand Oaks, CA: Sage, 1996), 15–48, 411–16.

18. www.census.gov/population/race/ (retrieved July 27, 2013). That some of these are also nationality labels should not obscure the fact that many in the United States and Great Britain treat them as domestic racial units, not simply statements of national origin.

19. Michael Banton, *Racial and Ethnic Competition* (Cambridge: Cambridge University Press, 1983), 56–57. Different constituent parts of the United Kingdom (England, Scotland, Wales, Northern Ireland) keep track of race and ethnicity in slightly different ways.

20. www.ons.gov.uk/ons/guide-method/measuring-equality/equality/ethnic -nat-identity-religion/ethnic-group/index.html#1 (retrieved July 27, 2013).

21. George M. Fredrickson, *White Supremacy: A Comparative Study in American and South African History* (New York: Oxford University Press, 1981).

22. Carl N. Degler, *Neither Black nor White: Slavery and Race Relations in Brazil and the United States* (New York: Macmillan, 1971), 103. See also G. Reginald Daniel, *Race and Multiraciality in Brazil and the United States: Converging Paths?* (University Park: Pennsylvania State University Press, 2006); Edward E. Telles, *Race in Another America: The Significance of Skin Color in Brazil* (Princeton, NJ: Princeton University Press, 2004).

23. Winthrop D. Jordan, *White over Black: American Attitudes toward the Negro, 1550–1812* (Chapel Hill: University of North Carolina Press, 1968); Michael A. Gomez, *Exchanging Our Country Marks: The Transformation of African Identities in the Colonial and Antebellum South* (Chapel Hill: University of North Carolina Press, 1998); Gwendolyn Midlo Hall, *Slavery and African Ethnicities in the Americas* (Chapel Hill: University of North Carolina Press, 2005).

24. Fredrickson, *White Supremacy*; Jordan, *White over Black*.

25. Since both are defined on the basis of social and not biological criteria, a race and an ethnic group are in essence the same type of group. They reckon (real or imagined) descent from a common set of ancestors. They have a sense of identity that tells them they are one people. They share culture, from clothing to music to food to language to childrearing practices. They build institutions such as churches and fraternal organizations. They perceive and pursue common political and economic interests. See Stephen Cornell, *The Return of the Native* (New York: Oxford University Press, 1985); Spickard, *Mixed Blood*, 9–17; Paul Spickard and

W. Jeffrey Burroughs, "We Are a People," in *We Are a People: Narrative and Multiplicity in Constructing Ethnic Identity* (Philadelphia: Temple University Press, 2000), 1–19.

26. Gustave LeBon, *La Revolution française et la psychologie des revolution* (1912), 53, 68, quoted in Barzun, *Race*, 227; Edward Byron Reuter, *Race Mixture* (New York: Negro Universities Press, 1969; orig. 1931), 216; Spickard, *Mixed Blood*, 329–39.

27. This was true for people of mixed Jewish and Gentile background as well. They were shunned by Jewish people and institutions and typically had to adopt Gentile identities.

28. Spickard, *Mixed Blood*, 110–17; see also Catherine Irwin, *Twice Orphaned: Voices from the Children's Village of Manzanar* (Fullerton: Center for Oral and Public History, California State University, Fullerton, 2008).

29. Spickard, *Mixed Blood*, 329–39, 360–61.

30. Sometimes the assignments were a bit arbitrary. The anthropologist Max Stanton tells of meeting three brothers in Dulac, Louisiana, in 1969. All were Houma Indians, had a French last name, and shared the same father and mother. All received their racial designations at the hands of the medical people who assisted at their births. The oldest brother, born before 1950 at home with the aid of a midwife, was classified as a Negro, because the state of Louisiana did not recognize the Houma as Indians before 1950. The second brother, born in a local hospital after 1950, was assigned to the Indian category. The third brother, born eighty miles away in a New Orleans hospital, was designated White on the basis of the French family name. I owe this information to a personal communication from Max Stanton in 1990; see also Max Stanton, "A Remnant Indian Community: The Houma of Southern Louisiana," in *The Not So Solid South: Anthropological Studies in a Regional Subculture* (Athens: University of Georgia Press, 1971), 82–92.

31. Mary Waters, *Ethnic Options: Choosing Identities in America* (Berkeley: University of California Press, 1990), 52.

2

Mapping Race

*Multiracial People and Racial Category Construction
in the United States and Britain*

*"Mapping Race" was a first foray into international compari-
sons of racial systems. Drawing on my work on multiraciality in
the United States, I examined the different ways that Britain was
dealing with an increasingly complicated domestic population,
racially speaking. The version here has been updated substantially from its 1996 incarnation. The essay made two main observations about race in Britain that some might have seen as
controversial at the time: (1) the coalition of pigment-rich
minority peoples then articulating themselves as politically
"Black"—whose ancestry was African, Caribbean, or South
Asian—was fragile and not likely to last; and (2) Britain seemed
ill poised to embrace the idea of racial multiplicity. In the nearly
two decades since I made those predictions, the former has come
true, and the latter has turned out to be quite in error.*

The social construction of what are often called "racial" categories has
proceeded differently in different places. The bases of ascription and
group identity, the placement of the boundaries between groups, and the

power dynamics between groups have changed dramatically over time and social and political circumstance in each place. This essay is a meditation and speculation on the ways that racial categories have been constructed and have changed in the United States and Britain over the course of the twentieth century.[1] It uses the identity situations of people of multiple ancestries—Black and White, Asian and African, and so on—as a tool to deconstruct the meanings assigned to racial categories and the power dynamics that underlie those categories.

The essay lays out some things that the situation of multiracial people—some of whose ancestors were Africans and some of whose ancestors came from somewhere else—tells us about the ways racial categories and meanings have evolved over the course of the twentieth century in the United States and in Britain. It finds, in sum, that White Americans have long had clearer ideas than White Britons about what they wanted to do with race; that over the past few decades those clear categories in the United States have been breaking down, in part because of the rise of a multiracial consciousness on the part of some people of mixed parentage; and that a British innovation of the 1970s and 1980s, a common Black identity for all non-White Britons, has not taken firm hold.

MIXED PEOPLE IN THE UNITED STATES

By early in the twentieth century, the United States had come to consensus that its race relations would be framed by the one-drop rule (what G. Reginald Daniel calls the "rule of hypodescent").[2] That is, America was deemed to be a two-category society racially. The White category was imagined to be biologically pure, and people with any known African ancestry ("one drop of Black blood") were assigned to the African or Black or Negro or Colored category. There were always other peoples in America (Native Americans, Asians, Latinos, others), but the dominant racial discourse was about Africans and Europeans, and the two categories were deemed to be sealed off from each other.

It was not that way always and everywhere. From very early on (the 1640s in Virginia) there was a pattern of equating African ancestry with slave status. Yet there always were some free people of African descent who constituted a small middle category. There also always were some mating and some marriage across the slave-free, Black-White line. Throughout most of the slave era, because of various factors such as masters manumitting their children and favoritism for very light slaves, a higher percentage of free people of color than slaves possessed mixed ancestry. The free population of color was a bit lighter than the slave. In fact, in a few places such as New Orleans and Charleston, "Mulattoes"—people of mixed ancestry—formed an intermediate caste between the two main races.[3]

After slavery was abolished, White Americans reinforced the line between themselves and their former slaves—and thus their dominance—in a number of ways. One was gradually to push the mixed population firmly and completely into the Black category. Joel Williamson records a number of subtle markers of the change, but even census categories reflected, crudely and somewhat belatedly, the evolving definitions of the races. From 1850 to 1920, the census usually recorded numbers of Negroes, Whites, and Mulattoes; thereafter, there were only Negroes and Whites, and by the 1920s, all mixed people were consigned to the Negro group.[4]

In such a two-category society, the place of mixed people was officially clear: they were supposed to be Black.[5] Mary Church Terrell, Booker Washington, and W. E. B. Du Bois were all emphatically Black leaders, although they were all of mixed parentage. Nonetheless, there were always issues for mixed people that the two-category system did not quite resolve. One was ambiguity. Walter White, executive secretary of the NAACP, and his father were functionally Black. Yet they were blond and blue-eyed, and no one on the street would have taken either for an African American. In 1931, Walter White's light brown uncle raced to the hospital in Atlanta where his brother-in-law, White's father, had been taken after being struck by a car. He could not find the elder man in the Colored ward and so went looking in the White wing of the hospital across the street. When the brown man found his brother-in-law, the horrified hospital staff dispatched their patient to the understaffed, underequipped wing for African Americans. There he died, perhaps in part for want of the treatment he could have received across the street.[6]

Another issue was choice. In the early decades of the twentieth century the writer Jean Toomer moved from a Mulatto consciousness to Blackness to Whiteness to an emphatic assertion that race was not an issue in his life. Toomer was on record in the public mind as Black by virtue of his pathbreaking Harlem Renaissance novel *Cane*, and he was pitied by some for his ambivalence. Other mixed people with lower profiles managed to make the break and pass as White. Contrast that with Herb Jeffries, a popular singer and star of all-Black movies from the 1930s to the 1950s. He eschewed the opportunity to pass as Spanish and claimed African ancestry, even, as he claimed, when it cost him mainstream movie roles. Later in life, Jeffries told interviewers that he in fact had no African ancestry at all but only Irish and Italian. He said he took on a Black identity because it allowed him entry into the Detroit jazz scene as a youth, and he stuck with that choice.[7]

Both Black and White publications from the 1920s through the 1950s titillated their readers with frequent tales of passing, which was usually viewed as a variety of psychopathology.[8] Some African Americans excoriated the practice; others celebrated it as putting one over on Whites. Whites, for their part, had a salacious interest in the subject of passing because of a lingering fear that the person beside one in bed might not be whom one supposed. What went unnoticed was that the majority of mixed people were denying their ancestry in a different way: they were passing for Black.

The mixing, of course, was not just between Black and White. The two-category racial system emphasized that dichotomy, but in fact more mixing took place between African Americans and Native Americans. Most African Americans recognize they have some Native American ancestors, and a much larger percentage of Native Americans than is generally recognized possess some African ancestry.[9] Then there were pockets of mixing of other sorts, such as between Blacks and Chinese in Mississippi and between Whites, Mexicans (themselves a mixed people), and Indians in the Southwest.[10] In short, the two-category system masked what was a multiethnic reality in American society all along.

Since World War II, and especially since the 1980s, at least three factors have begun to deconstruct the two-category system and rearrange the place of multiracial people. There has been an increase in interracial marriages of various sorts. The numbers are not completely clear, but it seems likely that the number of Black-White intermarriages about doubled each decade from the 1940s through the 2000s. However, the numbers were so small at the start of the period that the current figure is only about 17 percent.[11] Compare that to some other combinations, such as Asians and Whites or Native Americans and non-Indians, which approach an intermarriage rate of 50 percent.[12] More intermarriage begets more people with multiple ancestries, whose very existence and variety tend to disrupt the two-category system.

Perhaps more important, there has been a growing recognition that race in America is not just about Black and White. The racial categories in most of the reports of the 1940 census were White and Nonwhite (by which the census designers meant mainly African-derived people).[13] In 1950 and 1960, the categories were somewhat more elaborate: White, Negro, Indian, Chinese, Japanese, and Filipino, with a separate grid for people with Spanish surnames. After 1970, the categories began to multiply rapidly, so that by the 1990 census we had reached a total of forty-three different racial designations: White; Black or African American; American Indian, Eskimo, or Aleut; Asian or Pacific Islander, with eleven Asian subcategories (Chinese, Filipino, Japanese, Asian Indian, Korean, Vietnamese, Cambodian, Hmong, Laotian, Thai, and Other Asian) and four Pacific Islander subcategories (Hawaiian, Samoan, Guamanian, and Other Pacific Islander); Other Race; and across this a Hispanic Origin grid, with Mexican, Puerto Rican, Cuban, and Other Hispanic (Dominican, seven Central American subcategories, and seven South American subcategories). This proliferation of racial categories reflected the growing realization that America was not simply the "two nations, separate and unequal," of the 1968 Kerner Commission report but a vast mosaic of myriad hues.[14] In fact, it was always thus, but Americans at large were coming to realize it in the 1980s and 1990s.

The 1990s saw something of a challenge to the meaning of the category "Black or African American" by some people of mixed ancestry. With the multiplying of boxes came an increased awareness that many people possess more than one ancestry and may in fact regard themselves, be regarded by others, and function as multiracial people. Highly regarded books from the 1990s by Mary Waters, Karen Leonard, and Lise Funderburg bore the titles *Ethnic Options, Making Ethnic Choices*, and *Black, White, Other* respectively—reflecting notions that would have sounded absurd just a few years earlier.[15] It was widely remarked that the fastest-growing racial category in both the 1980 and the 1990 census was "Other."[16]

In the mid-1990s, such groups as the Association for Multi-Ethnic Americans, the Biracial Family Network, and Multiracial Americans of Southern California lobbied to change the category systems of the US Census Bureau and the Office of Management and Budget (hence school forms and many other pieces of bureaucratic paper) either to include a mixed category or to allow a person to check more than one box. Their efforts culminated in the 1997 OMB decision to allow individuals to check more than one racial box. The 2000 and 2010 censuses thus proved much more complex—not only having many monoracial categories but also with many people choosing to represent themselves as racially complex. It was a nightmare for the tabulators.[17]

The implications of this trend are several. On the one hand, one can view the trend toward recognition of multiplicity in mixed individuals as a healthy psychological development—getting in touch with all the parts of themselves, recognizing both parents, and so forth. Surely, if one has any compassion for the situation of individuals, this is a step forward from the days when people like Jean Toomer lacked a multiracial option.

On the other hand, there were some real dangers for African Americans as a group. One is blatantly political and has to do with access to power and funds. Many African American community leaders and pundits decried the advocates of multiracial identity as would-be escapees from Black America. They recognized that most people who were called African Americans also could legitimately acknowledge some other heritage. Yet they feared that opening the multiracial option would mean that some people would choose not to be African Americans at all, that the Black community would lose both their talents in service to the community and their numbers when apportionments of public services were being made—with, for example, fewer majority-Black congressional districts. As Joe Wood wrote, "Fair voting and fair employment and fair housing laws would need recalculation if a sizeable number of people abandoned Black. . . . [Since] the present generation of self-identified 'bi-racial' adolescents is mostly middle class, a light flight represents loss of middle-class people."[18] Finally, some suspected—mistakenly, I think— that choosing a multiracial identity implied a denigration of Blackness.[19]

These were real fears nonetheless, and they must be accounted for in the new shape the racial system has begun to take. Still, whether it is a good idea or not and whatever the costs to Black America, it seems clear that in recent decades the two-category system of American racial thinking and doing has gradually been dismantled, and a multicultural vision, including multiplicity within individuals, is taking its place.

MIXED PEOPLE IN BRITAIN

The shape of racial categorizing and the contents of those categories have been rather different in Britain than in the United States, mainly because of Britain's experience as the center of a polyglot, worldwide empire rather than a plantation economy. Whereas in the United States the main categories from very early on were Black and White, slave and free, in Britain the main distinction was between English and Other, and most of the Others were not in Britain. Much the same sense of national superiority and entitlement accompanied the British conquerors of Ireland as those who asserted hegemony over India, Hong Kong, and Kenya.[20] While British intellectuals took part in the pseudoscientific racial theorizing of the nineteenth century, while those ideas still hold the imagination of some silly people today, and while there is a resonant chord of hegemony in a lot of White British public discourse on racial questions, in fact British ideas about racial categories have never been clearly fixed.

There were not a lot of people of color in Britain before the mid-twentieth century, even though there were some racial incidents. A tiny African population existed in Britain from Roman times. Early in the twentieth century, a few thousand sailors whom native Britons called "Coloured"—men from places as varied as Aden, Somalia, Nigeria, India, and Jamaica—worked on British ships during World War I and then found themselves in ports like Cardiff and Liverpool at war's end. Some stayed, and some of those married White British women and started families (a few others chose mates from among the much smaller numbers of native Black British women). In 1919, White sailors and others rioted against these foreign workers in Cardiff, Liverpool, London, Glasgow, and elsewhere.[21] Six years later, the government joined the fray, passing the Coloured Alien Seamen Order, England's first overtly racist piece of legislation. This act forced some British subjects to register as aliens because they were not White; that made it hard for them to get work. The act also threatened legal resident aliens with deportation on account of their color. There was further pressure by White Britons, shipboard workers and others, throughout the 1930s.[22]

This seems quite a lot of attacking and restricting for a very small and inconsequential non-European population. The centerpiece of White public debate and the source of White fear was the fact that some of the non-European men had married British women and sired children. Quite a literature grew up about the "half-caste problem." Drawing on some of the same mythology as the Tragic Mulatto literature in the United States, there were extravagant suppositions that mixed people must be tortured and pathological souls.[23] There was even a philanthropic Liverpool Association for the Welfare of Half-Caste Children that operated in the 1920s and 1930s.[24]

What is arresting to note in all this is that people from all over the Empire and later much of the Commonwealth—East Africans, West Africans, East Indians, West Indians—were being treated together as "Coloured." That does not mean that they were in fact a single group or that they had or felt much in common, only that many native, White Britons could not or did not bother to tell them apart.[25]

The Nationality Act of 1948 granted British citizenship to citizens of the remaining colonies and the Commonwealth countries. In the next three decades there followed a rapid rise of labor immigration from the New Commonwealth Countries and from Pakistan, to the point that by 1978, 1.9 million residents of the British Isles (about 3.5 percent of the total population) were either immigrants from those countries or their children.[26] Immigration continued unabated through the 2000s, with increasing numbers from West, South, and East Asia, despite opposition from many White Britons.

Various government entities have attempted unsuccessfully to come to grips with race. From 1851 to 1961, the census included a question about nationality but none about race. The 1925 act, noted above, threw all pigmented peoples together as "Coloured" and chose them for discrimination together. Government people counters lately seem not to have been sure how to handle the multiracial reality in the United Kingdom. In 1970, the Department of Employment told its people to make a visual assessment of whether unemployed people belonged in the "Coloured" category; if these people were deemed "Coloured," then the department asked a question about origin. For the 1981 census a proposal was made to count people by the following categories: "White; West Indian; African; Indian; Pakistani; Bangladeshi; Arab; Turkish; Chinese; Other or Mixed (specify)." A 1979 Labour Force Survey took that list and further broke the Whites down into English, Welsh, Scottish, or Irish; Polish; Italian; and Other European.[27] The 1991 census arrived at this set of categories: "White; Black Caribbean; Black African or Black Other (please specify); Indian; Pakistani; Bangladeshi; Chinese; Any other ethnic group (please describe)." Significantly for my purposes here, after this list of categories in the 1991 census, there was this statement: "If the person is descended from more than one ethnic or racial group, please tick the group to which the person considers he/she belongs, or tick the 'Any other ethnic group' box and describe the person's ancestry in the space provided."[28] It is not clear what sorts of people in fact chose to exercise this last option, or what terms they then chose to describe their ancestry. In the 2011 census, the categories morphed again, as described in chapter 1. It is important to note here that the 2011 census tabulations made ample room for people to choose one of several mixed-race options.

These disparate peoples have not formed anything like a unified cultural or social group in the United Kingdom, and they only sporadically function in common politically. Nonetheless, from the late 1970s through the 1990s they were treated together as "Blacks" (sometimes NCWP— New Commonwealth and Pakistani), especially by political activists and scholars on the left.[29] Laura Tabili argued that her "use [of] the term 'Black' as it is used by [then] current scholars of Black British history and the contemporary Black movement in Britain, to refer to colonized people of Asia as well as of Africa and the Caribbean," is justified by "ample evidence of this usage in the 1920s and 1930s."[30] The term used in official documents in the 1920s and 1930s, of course, was not *Black* but *Coloured*, although *Black* had wide popular usage among the citizenry. Tabili showed that Britain's White government defined a widely diverse set of people as "Coloured" on the basis of common colonial subjection. That does not mean, however, that they perceived themselves as belonging to one group. Surely Tabili was right that the processes by which native White Britons dominated Africans, West Indians, and South Asians were parallel and related. Just as surely—her usage to the contrary—they were not the same people and did not think themselves so. Other scholars, like the anthropologist Susan Benson, regarded such linguistic agglomerations as "the New Commonwealth and Pakistani population" as "socially meaningless terms," but the proponents of bringing disparate groups together conceptually were undaunted.[31]

The British use of the term *Black* has evolved over the past several decades. It began as a charged political term borrowed from the US Civil Rights and Black Power movements of the 1960s. The boundaries, contents, and meanings of the category "Black" have always been ambiguous and contested. "Blackness" has involved three strains of meaning: (1) an externally imposed racist definition owing much to pseudoscience and the notion of races as subspecies, a definition that has much in common with similar definitions in the United States and South Africa; (2) the notion of Blacks as a people with common origins and a common culture, which in this case refers to African-derived peoples only; and (3) the idea of Blacks as all people who experience a common White racism and who together resist it, which meant, for a time at least in the 1980s and 1990s, people from the New Commonwealth countries and Pakistan—the definition that the activists preferred.[32] This is essentially a reflexive form of the first, White racist definition, one that empowers instead of oppresses. It is in some senses parallel to terms like *Asian American* and *Hispanic* in the United States—not natural groupings, but labels imposed by Whites, which nonetheless came to be used by the people to whom they were applied for purposes of self-empowerment.[33]

I do not propose to try to sort out the politics, much less the cultural complexities and personal dilemmas posed by this idea of Blackness. Let me just observe that while it may be politically important for oppressed peoples to band together as "Blacks" in order successfully to resist their oppression, it is highly unlikely that this is a category that organizes much of any person's life. I suspect there are very few Indian Britons who get up in the morning thinking, "I am Black." Their social networks and cultural expressions are almost certainly not Black but Indian, and probably one religious and language group of Indians.[34] At the level of personal relationships—and that is where most people live—there is almost no one, not even the most ardent Black activist, who would not view a marriage between a Pakistani man and a Jamaican woman as an intermarriage, and some might be faintly scandalized by it. Their child would be viewed by almost any observer as a mixed person with significant intercultural issues to confront.

So while an inclusive Black group may have been an important political category for organizing activism by peoples of color in the eyes of some 1980s and 1990s activists, it is not a useful analytical category. In addition, as Tariq Modood points out, when the category "Black" is widely applied, it is frequently done to subsume and then forget the non-African-derived peoples.[35] Modood suggests that South Asians, at least, are more appropriately thought of as a separate group or several.

> In the 1980s a political concept of blackness was hegemonic, but is increasingly having to be defended, even within the sociology of race. This is to be welcomed and seven reasons are given why the concept harms British Asians. The use of "black" encourages a "doublespeak". It falsely equates racial discrimination with colour-discrimination and thereby obscures the cultural antipathy to Asians and therefore the character of the discrimination they suffer. "Black" suggests also a false essentialism: that all non-white groups have something in common other than how others treat them. The fourth reason is that "black", being evocative of people of African origins, understates the size, needs and distinctive concerns of Asian communities. Fifthly, while the former can use the concept for purposes of ethnic pride, for Asians it can be no more than "a political colour",

leading to a too politicised identity. Indeed, it cannot but smother Asian ethnic pride—the pride which is a precondition of group mobilisation and assertiveness. Finally, advocates of "black" have tried to impose it on Asians rather than seek slower methods of persuasion, with the result that the majority of Asians continue to reject it. The new emphasis on multi-textured identities is therefore encouraging, as long as we are not simply exchanging a political for a cultural vanguardism.[36]

In the final event, most devotees of the inclusive Black identification cannot sustain their assertion of commonality. For example, Stephen Small, in a book on racialized barriers in the United Kingdom and the United States, quickly moved from a wide definition of Blackness to an African-derived definition "because inclusion of these [other] groups would have added considerably more complexity to an already complex topic."[37] Richard Skellington lumped the "Black and Asian population" together in a 1992 statistical study.[38] Several studies treated African-descended peoples together, whether their direct origins were in Africa, in the Caribbean, or elsewhere, and then treated Asian peoples separately but in parallel.[39] *The Oxford Companion to Black British History* treats all African-descended peoples as a monolith, no matter their origins or admixture, and ignores Asians utterly.[40]

All this testifies to several trends in British thinking about race. On the part of government statisticians, there was a groping after how to cope conceptually with the increasing diversity of British society, without a clear sense of what they were about. On the part of scholars and some community activists, there was an attempt for a time in the 1980s and 1990s to bring together colonized peoples conceptually if not practically. On the part of individual Asian Indians, Pakistanis, Arabs, Jamaicans, Trinidadians, and others whom some called "Black," there was an attempt simply to get on with life amid the racial disabilities White Britons would impose.

For a long time people of mixed ancestry did not fit anybody's boxes very well, despite the fact that there have been mixed people in Britain almost as long as there have been people of color. St. Clair Drake and Kenneth Little conducted studies in the 1940s of the communities in Cardiff, London, and Liverpool that reached back to the 1920s. One of the major themes of their work was interracial marriages and the mixed children who were produced by them. There have also been studies of the mixed children of British women and World War II–era African American soldiers. But only in the twenty-first century has people's racial mixture been widely recognized.[41]

The rates of intermarriage have been a bit more modest in the United Kingdom than in the United States, but intermarriages there have been, and the numbers are going up. In the 1970s, about 5 percent of Asian men, 2 percent of Asian women, 8 percent of West Indian men, and 1 percent of West Indian women married Whites, and presumably most of them had children.[42] Yet in that same period, about 9 percent of the population of color was mixed, and perhaps as many as 20 percent of the births involving NCWP parents were to mixed couples.[43] No one seems to have been keeping detailed records of interracial marriages in Britain in the new century, but something like 9 percent of British marriages and partnerships in 2008–10 were between native Britons and immigrants from other countries, according to the statistical arm of the European Union. And a 2009 study by the UK Equality and Human Rights Commission found that one in ten British children lived in a mixed-race household.[44]

The place mixed people have occupied in British society may have varied; at least there is not agreement on the subject. Most scholars and politicians for a long time assumed that mixed people were members of the Black group and placed them there in their writing and speeches.[45] More careful observation, such as that undertaken by Sheila Patterson in the 1960s, Susan Benson in the 1970s, and France Winddance Twine in the 2000s, suggests that most people of mixed Black West Indian and White British families possessed keen senses of themselves as mixed, not just as Black, and that in fact they had stronger cultural orientations toward and stronger connections with White British society than Black.[46]

The long history of White British racism, together with the intensity of the rhetoric of the Black British movement, once led me to conclude that widespread recognition of a multiracial identity was unlikely in the United Kingdom. However, in the past two decades a rich literature has grown up around racial mixedness in Britain. The census has kept statistics on mixed-race people since 2001. Multiracial organizations proliferate. There has been a sharp decline in public opposition to interracial marriage—from 50 percent in the 1980s to 15 percent in 2012. Mixed-race figures like the Olympic heptathlete Jessica Ennis have become emblems of British national identity. The United Kingdom is not without significant racial problems, but it has come to recognize multiraciality as part of its social fabric. In both these respects, the racial category system in the United Kingdom and the system in the United States have come to resemble each other.[47]

NOTES

This chapter first appeared in *Immigrants and Minorities* 15 (July 1996): 107–19. An earlier version was presented to the Collegium for African American Research in Tenerife, Canary Islands, on February 16, 1995. I am grateful for the comments of Sarah Meer, the late Robin Kilson, and Patrick Miller.

1. I will use "race" and "ethnic" more or less interchangeably in this essay. The relationships between these two terms are complex. My views on them are laid out elsewhere in this volume.

2. Winthrop D. Jordan, "Historical Origins of the One-Drop Racial Rule in the United States," ed. Paul Spickard, *Journal of Critical Mixed-Race Studies* 1 (2013): 98–132; Christine B. Hickman, "The Devil and the One-Drop Rule: Racial Categories, African Americans, and the U.S. Census," *Michigan Law Review* 95 (1997): 1175–76; G. Reginald Daniel, "Beyond Black and White: The New Multiracial Consciousness," in *Racially Mixed People in America*, ed. Maria P. P. Root (Newbury Park, CA: Sage, 1992), 333–41. The material for this section is more fully set forth in Paul Spickard, *Mixed Blood: Intermarriage and Ethnic Identity in Twentieth-Century America* (Madison: University of Wisconsin Press, 1989), 235–342; Maria P. P. Root, "Within, Between, and Beyond Race," in Root, *Racially Mixed People*, 3–11; G. Reginald Daniel, "Passers and Pluralists: Subverting the Racial Divide," in Root, *Racially Mixed People*, 91–107; F. James Davis, *Who Is Black? One Nation's Definition* (University Park: Pennsylvania State University Press, 1991); Virginia Dominguez, *White by Definition: Social Classification in Creole Louisiana* (New Brunswick, NJ: Rutgers University Press, 1986); Joel Williamson, *New People: Miscegenation and Mulattoes in the United States* (New York: Free Press, 1980); and Cynthia L. Nakashima, "An Invisible Monster: The Creation and Denial of Mixed-Race People in America," in Root, *Racially Mixed People*, 162–78.

3. Ira Berlin, *Slaves without Masters: The Free Negro in the Antebellum South* (New York: Random House, 1974); James Oliver Horton, *Free People of Color: Inside the African American Community* (Washington, DC: Smithsonian Institution Press, 1993); Joshua D. Rothman, *Notorious in the Neighborhood: Sex and Families in Virginia, 1878–1861* (Charlottesville: University of Virginia Press, 2007); Winthrop D. Jordan, *White over Black: American Attitudes toward the Negro, 1550–1813* (Chapel Hill: University of North Carolina Press, 1968); Emily Clark, *The Strange History of the Quadroon: Free Women of Color in the Revolutionary Atlantic World* (Chapel Hill: University of North Carolina Press, 2013); Sybil Klein, ed., *Creole: The History and Legacy of Louisiana's Free People of Color* (Baton Rouge: Louisiana State University Press, 2000); Arnold R. Hirsch and Joseph Logsdon, eds., *Creole New Orleans: Race and Americanization* (Baton Rouge: Louisiana State University Press, 1992).

From this intermediate caste and from the leadership positions that former free people of color held in the era of emancipation, as well as from continuing interactions with the dominant White caste, there emerged a color hierarchy that has plagued African Americans down to the present generation. See, e.g., Spickard, *Mixed Blood*, 317–24; E. Franklin Frazier, *Black Bourgeoisie* (Glencoe, IL: Free Press, 1957); Charles S. Johnson, *Growing Up in the Black Belt* (Washington, DC: American Council on Education, 1941); W. Lloyd Warner et al., *Color and Human Nature: Negro Personality Development in a Northern City* (Westport, CT: Negro Universities Press, 1970; orig. 1941); Kathy Russell et al., *The Color Complex: The Politics of Skin Color among African Americans* (New York: Doubleday, 1992); Gwendolyn Brooks, "If You're Light and Have Long Hair," in *Black-Eyed Susans*, ed. Mary Helen Washington (Garden City, NY: Doubleday, 1975), 37–42; Richard Udry et al., "Skin Color, Status, and Mate Selection," *American Journal of Sociology* 76 (1971): 722–33; Margaret L. Hunter, *Race, Gender, and the Politics of Skin Tone* (New York: Routledge, 2005); Cedric Herring et al., eds., *Skin/Deep: How Race and Complexion Matter in the "Color-Blind" Era* (Urbana: University of Illinois Press, 2004); Evelyn Nakano Glenn, ed., *Shades of Difference: Why Skin Color Matters* (Stanford, CA: Stanford University Press, 2009). For Asian Americans and colorism, see Joanne L. Rondilla and Paul Spickard, *Is Lighter Better? Skin-Tone Discrimination among Asian Americans* (Lanham, MD: Rowman and Littlefield, 2007).

4. Williamson, *New People*.

5. Silly myths about mulattoes with tortured psyches and split personalities, like those in D.W. Griffith's *Birth of a Nation* (Enoch Producing Corporation, 1915), need not detain us here; see Judith Berzon, *Neither Black nor White: The Mulatto Character in American Fiction* (New York: New York University Press, 1978).

6. Walter White, *A Man Called White* (Athens: University of Georgia Press, 1995; orig. 1948), 134–38.

7. Ingrid Dineen-Wimberly, "By the Least Bit of Blood: The Allure of Blackness among Mixed-Race Americans of African Descent, 1863–1916" (unpublished MS); BBC Radio, "From Our Own Correspondent: The Black Cowboy," March 21, 2013, www.bbc.co.uk/iplayer/episode/b01r9sks/From_Our_Own _Correspondent_The_Black_Cowboy/ (retrieved July 28, 2013). The social and psychic rewards and costs of passing are vividly portrayed in Nella Larsen's Harlem Renaissance novels, *Quicksand* (New York: Knopf, 1928) and *Passing* (New York: Knopf, 1928), and in Shirlee Taylor Haizlip's family memoir, *The Sweeter the Juice* (New York: Simon and Schuster, 1994). Reginald Daniel offers a provocative interpretation of the political-personal implications of passing in "Passers and Pluralists." Note that Toomer was not trying to pass as White. He was just trying to be all of himself (see chapter 8).

8. This fashion has come back to life in the twenty-first century in at least two unfortunate books: Brooke Kroeger, *Passing: When People Can't Be Who They Are* (New York: Public Affairs, 2003); Allyson Hobbs, *A Chosen Exile: A History of Racial Passing in American Life* (Cambridge, MA: Harvard University Press, 2014).

9. This is for at least two reasons. One of the largest southeastern tribes, the Seminole, were from the beginning a mixture of Creeks and runaway slaves. The Cherokee and Choctaw, on the other hand, were owners of large numbers of African American slaves, with whom they intermixed to a considerable extent, both in the Southeast and then in Indian Territory (now Oklahoma) after they were removed from their homeland by the US government in the 1830s. See Daniel F. Littlefield, *Africans and Seminoles: From Removal to Emancipation* (Jackson: University Press of Mississippi, 2001); Theda Perdue, *"Mixed Blood" Indians: Racial Construction in the Early South* (Athens: University of Georgia Press, 2003); Circe Sturm, *Blood Politics: Race, Culture, and Identity in the Cherokee Nation of Oklahoma* (Berkeley: University of California Press, 2002); James F. Brooks, ed., *Confounding the Color Line: The Indian-Black Experience in North America* (Lincoln: University of Nebraska Press, 2002); Claudio Saunt, *Black, White, and Indian* (New York: Oxford University Press, 2006); Tiya Miles, *Ties That Bind: The Story of an Afro-Cherokee Family in Slavery and Freedom* (Berkeley: University of California Press, 2005); Tiya Miles and Sharon P. Holland, eds., *Crossing Waters, Crossing Worlds: The African Diaspora in Indian Country* (Durham, NC: Duke University Press, 2006).

10. James W. Loewen, *The Mississippi Chinese: Between Black and White* (Cambridge, MA: Harvard University Press, 1971), 135–53.

11. Paul Taylor et al., *The Rise of Intermarriage: Rates, Characteristics Vary by Race and Gender* (Washington, DC: Pew Research Center, 2012); M. Kalmijn, "Trends in Black/White Intermarriage," *Social Forces* 72 (1991): 119–46.

12. Taylor et al., *Rise of Intermarriage*; Spickard, *Mixed Blood*.

13. For some parts of the 1940 census, there was a slightly further breakdown to White, Negro, Indian, and Other.

14. This is not to suggest that there was not what Stephen Small calls "racialised inequality"; *Racialised Barriers: The Black Experience in the United States and England in the 1980's* (London: Routledge, 1994). It is just to note that two categories were not enough.

15. Waters, *Ethnic Options*; Karen I. Leonard, *Making Ethnic Choices: California's Punjabi-Mexican Americans* (Philadelphia: Temple University Press, 1993); Lise Funderburg, *Black, White, Other: Biracial Americans Talk about Race and Identity* (New York: Morrow, 1994).

16. Paul Spickard, "Pacific Islander Americans and Multiethnicity: A Vision of America's Future?," *Social Forces* 73.4 (June 1995): 1365–83; US Bureau of the Census, *1980 Census of Population, 1B: General Population Characteristics: United States Summary* (PC80-1-B1) (Washington, DC: Government Printing Office, 1983), 22; US Bureau of the Census, *1990 Census of Population: General Population Characteristics: United States* (CP-1-1) (Washington, DC: Government Printing Office, 1992), 3.

17. Carlos A. Fernández, "Government Classification of Multiracial/Multiethnic People," in *The Multiracial Experience: Racial Borders as the New Frontier*, ed., Maria P. P. Root (Thousand Oaks, CA: Sage, 1996), 15–36; Susan R. Graham, "The Real World," in Root, *Multiracial Experience*, 37–62; Joel Perlmann and Mary C. Waters, eds., *The New Race Question: How the Census Counts Multiracial Individuals* (New York: Russell Sage Foundation, 2002); G. Reginald Daniel, *More than Black? Multiracial Identity and the New Racial Order* (Philadelphia: Temple University Press, 2002); Kim M. Williams, *Mark One or More: Civil Rights in Multiracial America* (Ann Arbor: University of Michigan Press, 2006); Jayne O. Ifekwunigwe, ed., *"Mixed Race" Studies: A Reader* (New York: Routledge, 2004), 205–60.

18. Joe Wood, "Fade to Black: Once upon a Time in Multiracial America," *Village Voice*, December 6, 1994, 25ff.

19. See, e.g., Jared Sexton, *Amalgamation Schemes: Antiblackness and the Critique of Multiracialism* (Minneapolis: University of Minnesota Press, 2008); Jon Michael Spencer, *The New Colored People: The Mixed-Race Movement in America* (New York: New York University Press, 2000); Rainier Spencer, *Spurious Issues: Race and Multiracial Identity Politics in the United States* (Boulder, CO: Westview, 1999); Michelle Elam, *The Souls of Mixed Folk: Race, Politics, and Aesthetics in the New Millennium* (Stanford, CA: Stanford University Press, 2011).

20. The most important distinction seems to have been between colonizer and colonized, although later a distinction arose between those who were citizens of Commonwealth countries that possessed patrial rights and those who were citizens of nonpatrial nations.

21. St. Claire Drake, "Value Systems, Social Structure and Race Relations in the British Isles" (PhD diss., University of Chicago, 1954); Paul B. Rich, *Race and Empire in British Politics* (Cambridge: Cambridge University Press, 1986).

22. See Rich, *Race and Empire*; Laura Tabili, *"We Ask for British Justice": Workers and Racial Difference in Late Imperial Britain* (Ithaca, NY: Cornell University Press, 1994); Laura Tabili, "The Construction of Racial Difference in Twentieth-Century Britain: The Special Restriction (Coloured Alien Seamen) Order, 1925," *Journal of British Studies* 33 (1994): 54–98. Tabili is at pains to insist that it was not White labor but the government that was behind this act; Rich thinks otherwise and is more believable. See also Laura Tabili, *Global Migrants, Local Culture: Natives and Newcomers in Provincial England, 1841–1939* (New York: Palgrave Macmillan, 2011); Panikos Panayi, ed., *Racial Violence in Britain in the Nineteenth and Twentieth Centuries*, rev. ed. (London: Leicester University Press, 1996).

23. Eve Allegra Raimon, *The "Tragic Mulatta" Revisited: Race and Nationalism in Nineteenth-Century Antislavery Fiction* (New Brunswick, NJ: Rutgers University Press, 2004); Teresa C. Zackodnik, *The Mulatta and the Politics of Race* (Jackson: University Press of Mississippi, 2004); Carolyn A. Streeter, *Tragic No More: Mixed-Race Women and the Nexus of Sex and Celebrity* (Amherst: University of Massachusetts Press, 2012).

24. St. Clair Drake, "The 'Colour Problem' in Britain: A Study in Social Definitions," *Sociological Review*, n.s., 3 (1955): 197–217; Rich, *Race and Empire*, 120–44.

25. St. Clair Drake, in interviews with sailors and their families in Cardiff in 1947–48, did find considerable friendly interaction among the various ethnic groups, especially such groups as Arabs and Somalis, who shared Islam. Yet each national origin group also maintained a separate identity in its own eyes. See Drake, "Value Systems, Social Structure and Race Relations," esp. 328–55.

26. New Commonwealth Countries are nations that joined the Commonwealth after World War II, nearly all pigment-rich peoples of the Global South. Usha Prashar et al., *Britain's Black Population* (London: Heinemann, 1980), 1–7. This increase occurred despite explicit attempts by Conservative governments to discourage non-White immigrants from coming to Britain. Kathleen Paul, *Whitewashing Britain: Race and Citizenship in the Postwar Era* (Ithaca, NY: Cornell University Press, 1997); Paul Gilroy, *"There Ain't No Black in the Union Jack": The Cultural Politics of Race and Nation* (Chicago: University of Chicago Press, 1987); Patrick Hennessy, "Blair Calls for Quotas on Immigrants from 'New Commonwealth,'" *Daily Telegraph*, June 6, 2004.

27. Heather Booth, "Identifying Ethnic Origin: The Past, Present, and Future of Official Data Production," in *Britain's Black Population*, ed. Ashok Bhat et al., 2nd ed. (Aldershot, UK: Gower, 1988), 23766.

28. Floya Anthias and Nira Yuval-Davis, *Racialized Boundaries: Race, Nation, Gender, Colour and Class and the Anti-Racist Struggle* (New York: Routledge, 1992), 148–55.

29. Prashar, *Britain's Black Population*; Centre for Contemporary Cultural Studies, *The Empire Strikes Back: Race and Racism in 70s Britain* (London: Hutchinson, 1982).

30. Laura Tabili, "'Keeping the Natives under Control': Race Segregation and the Domestic Dimensions of Empire, 1920–1939," *International Labor and Working-Class History* 44 (1993): 64–78.

31. Tabili, "Construction of Racial Difference"; Susan Benson, *Ambiguous Ethnicity: Interracial Families in London* (Cambridge: Cambridge University Press, 1981), 145–46.

32. Anthias and Yuval-Davis, *Racialized Boundaries*, 140–46.

33. Kwesi Owusu, ed., *Black British Culture and Society* (London: Routledge, 1999); Houston A. Baker Jr., *Black British Cultural Studies* (Chicago: University of Chicago Press, 1996); William Wei, *The Asian American Movement* (Philadelphia: Temple University Press, 1993); Yen Le Espiritu, *Asian American Panethnicity: Bridging Institutions and Identities* (Philadelphia: Temple University Press, 1992).

34. Tariq Modood, "Political Blackness and British Asians," *Sociology* 28 (1994): 859–76.

35. Tariq Modood, "'Black,' Racial Equality and Asian Identity," *New Commonwealth* 14.3 (1988): 397–404.

36. Modood, "Political Blackness"; Tariq Modood, Sharon Beishon, and Satnam Virdee, *Changing Ethnic Identities* (London: Policy Studies Institute, 1994); Tariq Modood, *Multiculturalism* (Cambridge: Polity Press, 2007), 101 passim. It is fair to point out that another prominent South Asian Briton, A. Sivanadan, took the opposite view, in *A Different Hunger: Writings on Black Resistance* (London: Pluto Press, 1991).

37. Small, *Racialized Barriers*, 35.

38. Richard Skellington, with Paulette Morris and Paul Gordon, *"Race" in Britain Today* (London: Sage/Open University, 1992).

39. E.g., Modood, Beishon, and Virdee, *Changing Ethnic Identities*; Dave Gunning, *Race and Antiracism in Black British and British Asian Literature* (Liverpool: Liverpool University Press, 2010).

40. David Dabydeen, John Gilmore, and Cecily Jones, eds., *The Oxford Companion to Black British Literature* (Oxford: Oxford University Press, 2007).

41. Drake, "Value Systems"; Kenneth Little, *Negroes in Britain* (London: Kegan Paul, Trench, Trubner, 1947); *No Mother, No Father, No Uncle Sam*, dir. Sebastian Robinson (Htv West, 1990).

42. Prashar, *Britain's Black Population*, 12.

43. Benson, *Ambiguous Ethnicity*, 145; Gary A. Cretser, "Intermarriage between 'White' Britons and Immigrants from the New Commonwealth and Pakistan," *Journal of Comparative Family Studies* 21.2 (1990): 227–38.

44. Giampaolo Lanzieri, "Merging Populations: A Look at Marriages with Foreign-Born Spouses in European Countries," *Eurostat: Statistics in Focus* (2012 report no. 29), http://ec.europa.eu/eurostat (retrieved July 29, 2013); Sholto Byrnes, "Mixed Blessings: Britain's Acceptance of Mixed-Race Relationships is a New and Precious Phenomenon," *The Guardian*, January 20, 2009.

45. Small, *Racialised Barriers*, 35; Michael Banton, *The Coloured Quarter: Negro Immigrants in an English City* (London: Jonathan Cape, 1955).

46. It is worth noting that many people of unmixed African heritage also identify themselves fiercely as Black Britons, though not all White Britons would acknowledge their claim. Sheila Patterson, *Dark Strangers: A Sociological Study of the Absorption of a Recent West Indian Migrant Group in Brixton, South London* (London: Tavistock, 1963); Benson, *Ambiguous Ethnicity*; France Winddance Twine, *A White Side of Black Britain: Interracial Intimacies and Racial Literacy* (Durham, NC: Duke University Press, 2010).

47. Louise Eccles, "Britain's Mixed Race Population Leaps over One Million as Research Reveals Prejudices Have Sharply Dropped," *Daily Mail*, December 9, 2012; Lanre Bakare, "Britain Is Now a Better Place to Grow Up Mixed Race; But Don't Celebrate Yet," *The Observer*, December 15, 2012; Peter Aspinall, "The Conceptualisation and Categorisation of Mixed Race/Ethnicity in Britain and North America: Identity Options and the Role of the State," *International Journal of Intercultural Relations*, 27 (2003): 289–92. Among the highlights of British mixed-race literature are Suki Ali, *Mixed-Race, Post-Race: Gender, New Ethnicities and Cultural Practices* (Oxford: Berg, 2003); Yasmin Alibhai-Brown, *Mixed Feelings: The Complex Lives of Mixed-Race Britons* (London: Women's Press, 2001); Peter J. Aspinall and Miri Song, *Mixed Race Identities* (London: Palgrave Macmillan, 2013); Jayne O. Ifekwunigwe, *Scattered Belongings: Cultural Paradoxes of Race, Nation and Gender* (London: Routledge, 1999); Jill Olumide, *Raiding the Gene Pool: The Social Construction of Mixed Race* (London: Pluto Press, 2002); David Parker and Miri Song, eds., *Rethinking "Mixed Race"* (London: Pluto Press, 2001); Miri Song, *Choosing Ethnic Identity* (Cambridge: Polity Press, 2003); Pnina Werbner and Tariq Modood, eds., *Debating Cultural Hybridity: Multi-Cultural Identities and the Politics of Anti-Racism* (London: Zed, 1997).

3

What's Critical about White Studies

I have left this essay substantially as it appeared in 2004, with updating mainly in the notes. The fashion in Whiteness studies has continued in the intervening decade in much the shape that it took then. Both the praise and the cautions I laid out originally still apply to this robust field of scholarship.

In the spring of 1966 many Black and some White and Asian students at Seattle's inner-city Garfield High School went on strike, asking the school board to devote more resources to educating minority children, hire more minority teachers, and install antiracist curriculum. One of the speakers at a rally and workshop at Mt. Zion Baptist Church was James Bevel, an organizer for the Southern Christian Leadership Conference and intimate of Dr. Martin Luther King. One of the White participants asked Bevel, "What is the place of White people in the Negro revolution?" (Remember, this was 1966, and the terminological turn to Black Power would not hit the streets of African American neighborhoods for another year.) He apparently regarded himself as a member of the liberal vanguard, was excited to be at this revolutionary gathering, and wanted specific direction as to how to be helpful. He may also have wanted to be told what a fine thing it was for a White person such as himself to do something on behalf of Blacks.

So it was with some dismay that he received Bevel's reply: "There is no place for White people in the Negro revolution. We are trying to organize ourselves to take control of our lives. White people are the problem. You need to go back to White people and teach them not to be racists." It was not what that White person wanted to hear, for he was looking for a way to be at the center of the action, where Black people were making a social revolution. Now he was being told not to sap the energy of the Black people around him, to go home and attend to a less glamorous chore, the subtle and difficult task of addressing White racism from within the White community. To his credit, he did just that, and spent much of the next decade talking to White people about their racism.

The sentiment in Bevel's injunction to go back to White people and teach them not to do bad stuff about race seems to be at the base of the enduring vogue in White studies. There has been an extraordinary outpouring of literature examining Whiteness. If one typed the word *Whiteness* into a library catalogue in 1995, one might pull up a half-dozen references. Typing the same word in 2002 yields hundreds. In the 2010s, typing it into Google yields thousands. This essay surveys the first decade of that literature, its premises, preoccupations, and themes. Further, it attempts to sort out what parts of the White studies literature are helpful in challenging the system of racial hierarchy that governs American social relations and what parts tend toward other effects—to determine, in short, what is critical about White studies.[1]

Jonathan Rutherford, a British critic, writes about his motivation to study Whiteness.

> I was prompted to start thinking about my own ethnic identity by the contemporary generation of black and Asian English intellectuals—Paul Gilroy, Stuart Hall, Kobena Mercer, Isaac Julien, Lola Young, Pratibha Parmar—who were thinking reflexively and historically about race, gender and ethnicity. My involvement in radical politics on the left had taught me to disavow the racial exclusivity of white ethnicity, but never to analyse or try and understand it. Being white was a vague, amorphous concept to get hold of; it wasn't a colour, it was invisible. And who wanted the risible, sometimes ugly, baggage of Englishness? Everything which signified Englishness—the embarrassing legacy of racial supremacy and empire, the union

jack waving crowds, the royalty, the rhetoric about Britain's standing in the world—suggested a conservative deference to nostalgia. The problem with intellectually disowning white English ethnicity was that the left never got around to working out what it was, and what our own emotional connections to it were.[2]

Noel Ignatiev and John Garvey pride themselves on being "race traitors." Like Rutherford, they are White but would disavow Whiteness. They begin with an insight with which this writer would not disagree: "the key to fundamental social change in the US is the challenge to the system of race privilege that embraces all whites." Their definition of Whiteness is perhaps a bit idiosyncratic: "The white race consists of those who partake of the privileges of white skin. . . . [P]eople were not favored socially because they were white; rather they were defined as 'white' because they were favored." Then, invoking the memory of John Brown, they issue a call to "focus on whiteness and the struggle to abolish the white race from within" by disavowing the privileges of White skin.[3]

This, they say, is the "key to solving the social problems of our age. . . . [T]he majority of so-called whites in this country are neither deeply nor consciously committed to white supremacy; like most human beings in most times and places, they would do the right thing if it were convenient. . . . By engaging these dissidents in a journey of discovery into whiteness and its discontents, we hope to take part . . . in the process of defining a new human community." They conclude, "The existence of the white race depends on the willingness of those assigned to it to place their racial interests above class, gender, or any other interests they hold. The defection of enough of its members to make it unreliable as a determinant of behavior will set off tremors that will lead to its collapse." What is not clear in this formulation is just how that "defection" from the White race is to be accomplished or how one can disavow one's Whiteness and make it stick.[4]

OLDER TRADITIONS IN WHITE STUDIES

Garvey, Ignatiev, and Rutherford would study Whiteness in order to dethrone it. This is a different business from most older studies of White people, although, as we shall see, there are some points of similarity.[5] The older Whiteness studies took several perspectives. First were the rantings of early-twentieth-century pseudoscientific racialists. Their name was legion, but among the most memorable of such writers were Madison Grant and Lothrop Stoddard. Grant's masterwork was *The Passing of the Great Race, or The Racial Basis of European History* (1916), in which he divided all of humankind into "races" on supposedly scientific principles and told why it was that vigor and virtue emerged out of competition among races as the distinctive qualities of Nordic peoples who drew their origins from Aryan ancestors. Grant argued that "conservation of [the White] race" was "the true spirit of Americanism." Hitler apparently read Grant and thought it the true spirit of the Third Reich as well. Stoddard followed soon after with *The Rising Tide of Color against White World-Supremacy* (1920), which made dire predictions of White people in Europe and North America being outbred and eventually overrun by fecund hordes of "inferior stocks"—Asians, Africans, and Latin Americans. Stoddard's writing and Grant's played a part in the racially inflected quotas and exclusions that distinguished the Immigration Act of 1924.[6]

Grant and Stoddard were crude, White supremacist race-baiters. Yet their racial assumptions have found marginally more genteel echoes in more recent times, covered by a thin veneer of pseudoscience and policy concern. Few were more prominent than Richard Herrnstein and Charles Murray's *The Bell Curve* (1994), an attack on affirmative action hidden in a welter of bad science and bogus statistics. Almost as widely read and no less pernicious was Peter Brimelow's *Alien Nation* (1996). Here, an Anglo-Saxon immigrant attempted to pull up the ladder behind him, charging that brown and yellow immigrants were "making America . . . a freak among the world's nations because of the unprecedented demographic mutation it is inflicting on itself." Patrick Buchanan strummed the same chords in *The Death of the West* (2002).

> Immigrant invasions imperil our county and citilization. . . . Uncontrolled immigration threatens to deconstruct the nation we grew up in and convert America into a conglomeration of peoples with almost nothing in common—not history, heroes, language, culture,

faith, or ancestors. Balkanization beckons. . . . Not only ethnically and racially, but culturally and morally, we are no longer one people or "one nation under God." . . . In half a lifetime, many Americans have seen their God dethroned, their heroes defiled, their culture polluted, their values assaulted, their country invaded, and themselves demonized as extremists and bigots.

Samuel Huntington adopted a more genteel, sometimes scholarly tone and talked about "culture" when he meant "race," but his message was essentially the same in *Who Are We?* (2005). These were relatively explicit celebrations of what the authors regarded as White superiority, a kind of literary Klanism.[7]

There has been a less overtly malevolent but still insidious literature: studies that focused on the experiences of White ethnic groups in such a way as to tend to ignore the fundamental differences between the experiences of White people and those of people of color in the United States. Books like Thomas Sowell's *Ethnic America* (1981), Nathan Glazer's *Ethnic Dilemmas* (1983), and Michael Novak's *The Rise of the Unmeltable Ethnics* (1973) wrote about African Americans and other peoples of color as if they were ethnic groups just like Greeks and Swedes. The tendency of such works was to focus on the hardships faced by some White immigrant groups, to bare their grievances, and to shade into justification of White privilege by denying its distinctive existence.[8]

Then there were quite a large number of studies of White immigrant groups that lacked the racist political agenda of the books described above. The list includes many excellent titles, for example, *The Transplanted*, by John Bodnar; *Voyagers to the West*, by Bernard Bailyn (1986); *Albion's Seed*, by David Hackett Fischer (1989); and *Ethnic Identity*, by Richard D. Alba (1990).[9] These authors and others like them focused on White people and tried to understand and represent their experiences without any particular racist edge to their interpretations.

Finally, there were studies of White attitudes about race. Again, the list includes many distinguished books: *The Nature of Prejudice*, by Gordon W. Allport (1954); *White over Black*, by Winthrop D. Jordan (1968); *The Black Image in the White Mind*, by George Fredrickson (1971);

American Slavery—American Freedom, by Edmund Morgan (1975); and *The White Man's Indian,* by Robert Berkhofer (1978).[10] These were varieties of Whiteness studies, too. They focused on the historical contexts in which and the social and psychological processes by which White people constructed the American racial system in slavery and colonialism and the outworkings of that system in White minds in later years.

This brief tour of older studies of Whiteness is not intended to assert direct lines of descent from, say, Madison Grant or Edmund Morgan to the Whiteness studies boom of the turn of the millennium. They were writers of different times, operating with different tools and insights and from different motives. I do intend to suggest, however, that the range of Whiteness studies in earlier eras—from studies of White racism to works on specific White groups to books that fail to recognize their racism and, finally, to those that openly express it—is echoed in the new. In the new Whiteness studies as in the old, there are substantial and important works that contribute vital insights to our understanding of race and racism; there are also other books, alas, that shade over into White-centeredness and finally into racist abuse. One of the tasks of this chapter is to sort out one from another.

NEW WHITENESS STUDIES

Among the older strands of Whiteness studies, the ones I have marked as racist (Stoddard, Herrnstein, Buchanan, et al.) had origins on the political right. The studies of White immigrant groups and White racial thinking before the 1990s hewed more to the middle of the road. The new Whiteness studies of the 1990s and the twenty-first century, by contrast, stem from the political left.

The founding parents of this latter movement were Alexander Saxton, David Roediger, and Toni Morrison. Saxton's book, *The Rise and Fall of the White Republic,* started the trend in 1990. It is an analysis of the role of racial thinking in the shifting class bases of political parties in the United States over the course of the nineteenth century. Saxton begins with the assumption that racial ideas began in North America as an attempt by Europeans to justify enslavement of Africans and expropriation and expulsion of Native Americans.[11] He then traces changes in racial thinking by various groups of Americans, as the vehicle by which he explains the changing alignments of White class groupings in the major political parties. In short, Saxton treats "the generation and regeneration of white racism 'as part of the process of class conflict and compromise.'"[12]

Saxton, then, is interested in the history of the creation and transformation of concepts about racial inequality. Underlying that, he is interested in the course of class conflict. He sees racial thinking primarily as a tool created and used by White people to pursue class-based political alliances among White people. This is not quite crude Marxism—race as mere false consciousness, a gloss on class. It nonetheless amounts to an admittedly sophisticated and informed attempt to reduce racial oppression to an expression of class conflict.[13] *The Rise and Fall of the White Republic* is a serious attempt to understand the ways that racial ideas and racial marking on the part of Whites shaped US politics in the nineteenth century.

David Roediger's much-acclaimed *Wages of Whiteness* (1991) is a book about class formation among Whites, too. Bearing the subtitle, *Race and the Making of the American Working Class*, it argues that White workers in the mid-nineteenth century gathered themselves into a self-conscious, activist working class, not only on the basis of class interests, but also on the basis of a racist intention to distance themselves from that other great part of the working class, Black workers. Roediger starts from an elaboration of W. E. B. Du Bois's notion of a psychic wage that accrued to Whites from their very Whiteness: "The pleasures of whiteness could function as a 'wage' for white workers. That is, status and privileges conferred by race could be used to make up for alienating and exploitative class relationships, North and South. White workers could, and did, define and accept their class positions by fashioning identities as 'not slaves' and as 'not Blacks.'" Thus, "working class formation and the systematic development of a sense of whiteness went hand in hand for the US white working class."[14]

The power of Roediger's book is enhanced by the subtlety of his argument and the variety of his methods and areas of inquiry. He examines political speech, crowd behavior, folklore, humor, and audience responses to minstrel shows, among other things. His argument is, in the end, equal parts psychological and class analysis: "Whiteness was a way in which workers responded to a fear of dependency on wage labor and to the necessities of capitalist work discipline. As the US working class matured, principally in the North, within a slaveholding republic, the heritage of the Revolution made independence a powerful masculine personal ideal. But slave labor and 'hireling' wage labor proliferated in the new nation. One way to make peace with the latter was to differentiate it sharply from the former. . . . [T]he white working class, disciplined and made anxious by fear of dependency, began during its formation to construct an image of the Black population as 'other'—as embodying the preindustrial, erotic, careless style of life the white worker hated and longed for."[15]

Roediger starts from the conviction, adopted from Coco Fusco, that "to ignore white ethnicity is to redouble its hegemony by naturalizing it."[16] This conviction stands at the ideological base of Whiteness studies. Yet if there is a criticism to be made of *The Wages of Whiteness*, it is that in it Roediger, like most of the Whiteness studies writers, expresses a rhetoric of normative Whiteness. "Workers" are assumed to be White unless they are racially marked as "Blacks," and the most important thing about Black workers is their Blackness, not their participation in the working class.[17] Roediger recognized the dangers in this posture and worked to undercut it in several later works. A volume of essays, *Towards the Abolition of Whiteness* (1994), took up several themes tangential to *The Wages of Whiteness*. More consistently than in the first book he treated Blacks and other people of color as actors in their own right, not merely as foils for White workers. In *Black on White: Black Writers on What It Means to Be White* (1998), Roediger reproduced the writings of four dozen African American writers, from Anna Julia Cooper to Lewis Gordon. Here was a book about Whiteness, but it was not fixed on the ideas of White people. Rather, it sought to dethrone White privilege by putting the analysis of Whiteness in the hands of Blacks. In *Working toward Whiteness: How America's Immigrants Became White* (2005), Roediger carried the story forward into the twentieth century and detailed how, he thought, immigrants at first were not White in America and how they worked hard to become Whites in the national imagination, against a tide of nativist sentiment and anti-immigrant legislation.[18]

Toni Morrison completed the foundation of the White studies movement in 1992 with *Playing in the Dark: Whiteness and the Literary Imagination*. Roediger and Saxton are interested in the White working class and its relationship to racial identity politics. Morrison's interest is American literature. Not only, Morrison said, has American literature been dominated by White male authors and White male critics, but the values of literary criticism, the decisions as to what is important and excellent and true, have been appropriated by White men in hegemonic ways that have denied that appropriation. Valuing the universal (read "White") over the particular (read "Black"), they have virtually erased Black characters, Black authors, Black themes, Black issues from the central part of American literature. But just as Saxton and Roediger find White workers defining their identities against Black workers, so, too, Morrison finds the White writers of the canon (Hemingway, Faulkner, and others) defining the major issues, indeed the national character, in relationship to Blackness. She argues that "the metaphorical and metaphysical uses of race occupy definitive places in American literature, in the 'national' character, and ought to be a major concern of the literary scholarship that tries to know it."[19]

The Wages of Whiteness, Playing in the Dark, and *The Rise and Fall of the White Republic*, then, are foundational examples of what is substantive and distinctive about Whiteness studies. Morrison, Roediger, and, less explicitly, Saxton analyze Whiteness in order, one might say, to decenter it, to make it less hegemonic, to reduce its power. Other useful examples of White studies abound.

Theodore Allen joined the discussion with *The Invention of the White Race* (1994, 1997). Instead of the nineteenth century as the critical time for White racial formation, Allen looks to America in the seventeenth and eighteenth centuries. He posits a time before the categories "White" and "Black" had social meaning, when national labels such as "English" and "Irish" were the modes of identity. He argues with polemical ferocity that the White race was invented no later than the middle of the eighteenth century by the planter elite of the Chesapeake colonies, as a deliberate measure of social control. The laboring classes were divided, White and free on one side, Black and slave on the other.[20]

Tomás Almaguer expanded the discussion beyond the Black/White dichotomy in *Racial Fault Lines* (1994). Roediger had made some mention of White workers defining themselves against Chinese workers in the West, but otherwise the authors discussed up to this point all saw race as a binary relationship between Black and White. Looking at the construction and uses of Whiteness in California in the second half of the nineteenth century, Almaguer paints a more complicated picture. Here there were not just White and Black people but Chinese, Japanese, Mexicans, and Native Americans as well.[21] Almaguer found White people coming to the West with preexisting convictions about White racial superiority and then creating a new racial hierarchy out of local materials.

For Almaguer, as for Saxton, Allen, and Roediger, race making is critically intertwined with class making. But unlike them, he argues for "the primacy of race. . . . Beginning in 1870 and intensifying dramatically in the 1880s, an economy based on wage labor eclipsed that based on the unfree labor system of the Mexican period. Once unleashed, this proletarianization absorbed both the indigenous Mexican population and the numerous white and nonwhite immigrant groups that settled in the area." "Racial status" played a "central role" in co-creating the new class structure.

> Far from being merely an ideological construct or an anachronistic status designation, race became the key organizing principle structuring white supremacist economic, as well as political, institutions that were introduced in California. White male immigrants became farmers, proprietors, professionals, and white-collar employees, while the Mexican, Japanese, Chinese, and Indian male populations were securely ensconced at the bottom end of the class structure as unskilled manual workers.[22]

The multiple sides of Almaguer's analysis may tempt some to conclude that *Racial Fault Lines* is something other than Whiteness studies. But though he is sensitive to the existence and issues of other groups, the actors in his story are White people, and the story is about the ways they drew lines between themselves and various peoples of color—the ways they defined and used Whiteness.

Neil Foley echoed Almaguer's description of a multiple-sided racial encounter in *The White Scourge* (1997). Set in the cotton country of Central Texas, mainly in the first decades of the twentieth century, *The White Scourge* examines the relationships between Blacks, Mexicans, and poor Whites. Where Almaguer focused on Whites making racial distinctions, Foley treats all three of the groups under study as actors and attends to the ways they negotiated their identities and class positions. For Foley, as for Almaguer, the critical item under negotiation was Whiteness. As cotton farming grew into agribusiness at the dawn of the century, former sharecroppers and tenant farmers became proletarian field workers. Foley finds that, for a time, poor Whites lost some of their racial privilege relative to Black and especially to Mexican agricultural workers. Conversely, for a brief period, Mexicans were able to negotiate a place for themselves partway between Black and White, taking on, Foley says, a measure of Whiteness.[23]

George Lipsitz turned a harsh lens on White privilege in an influential essay and book, both titled *The Possessive Investment in Whiteness* (1995, 1998).[24] Lipsitz offers a brilliant tour of American racial history, showing how, in each era from Jamestown up to the present, and in various sectors of the economy and polity, powerful Whites have chosen to establish structures that favored European-derived Americans over peoples of color and then masked those decisions behind the language of individualism. "From the start," says Lipsitz, "European settlers in North America established structures encouraging possessive investment in Whiteness. The colonial and early-national legal systems authorized attacks on Native Americans and encouraged the appropriation of their lands. They legitimated racialized chattel slavery, restricted naturalized citizenship to 'white' immigrants, and provided pretexts for exploiting labor, seizing property, and denying the franchise to Asian Americans, Mexican Americans, Native Americans, and African Americans."[25]

This drawing a line between Whites and people of color, and favoring the former over the latter, did not end with slavery, however. Lipsitz offers example after example of this practice, from the racist quality of the

American seizure of the Philippines to the 1978 *Bakke* decision against affirmative action to FHA housing policies that helped create all-White suburbs. Nonetheless, he concludes, almost hopefully, "The problem with white people is not our whiteness, but our possessive investment in it. Created by politics, culture, and consciousness, our possessive investment in whiteness can be altered by those same processes, but only if we face the hard facts openly.... How can we account for the ways in which white people refuse to acknowledge their possessive investment in whiteness even as they work to increase its value every day? We can't blame the color of our skin. It must be the content of our character."[26]

One of the most sophisticated examples of the merits of White studies is Matthew Frye Jacobson's *Whiteness of a Different Color: European Immigrants and the Alchemy of Race* (1998).[27] Jacobson attempts to chart the entire history of the European immigrant peoples of the United States and to examine the relationships among those peoples. He divides American racial history into three periods. The first was 1790–1840, when "free white persons" as designated in the first naturalization law was an amorphous category that had some element of hierarchy within it but that did not sharply delineate among varieties of European-descended peoples. For Jacobson, the crucial tool that made these peoples a common White race was republican ideology—an estimate of their fitness for self-government. In the second period, 1840–1924, Jacobson finds the White race broken up into some groups that are White and some that are less so—perhaps even some that are not White (he is not consistent on that point)—under the force of more varied immigration, the rise of industry, and pseudoscientific racial theorizing. That hierarchy among Whitenesses explains the Anglocentric quota system at the heart of the 1924 Immigration Act. In the third period, 1924–65, White people were mushed together again into an amorphous group called Caucasians.[28]

The strength of *Whiteness of a Different Color* is that it takes seriously the hierarchies that existed among White people and tries to account for them. There are some problems near the book's core, however. For one thing, although on nearly every page Jacobson speaks of the "racial" character of this or that distinction, at no place does he define what "racial" means for him.[29] So when he says that the differences among Anglo-Americans, Irish, and Jews were racial, we are not quite sure what he means. He seems to want to set up various European immigrant peoples as racially separate from the dominant group of Whites, especially in his middle period. Surely, there was hierarchy among Whites (and surely, by his own evidence but contrary to his schema, it existed in all three periods). But that does not mean that the disabilities suffered by Irish or Italians or Jews in the United States achieved the same scale as those suffered by peoples of color. Some people may have used "race" language in the middle period to describe what they called "ethnic" differences in another period, but that does not mean that the groups were more sharply divided in the middle period; it may only mean that the language fashion changed.

Jacobson very seldom even mentions African or Native or Mexican or Asian Americans, but on those few occasions when he does, it is clear that the disabilities suffered by subordinate White "races" pale by comparison. He writes:

> Reconstruction collapsed in the South, raising new questions about the relations among whites and blacks in an era of black Emancipation and the reintegration of the South into national political life. In the aftermath of Custer's demise . . . the Great Sioux Wars ended with the defeat of the Minneconjou Sioux; Sitting Bull escaped to Canada, and Crazy Horse surrendered to federal troops. A vocal and often violent anti-Chinese movement coalesced in the West, particularly in California, where white workers decried the labor competition of "Mongolians" and insisted upon a "white man's republic." The East and Midwest, meanwhile, were wracked by labor unrest which *raised questions* in some quarters about the white immigrant working class itself.[30]

"Raised questions" versus killed, enslaved, imprisoned on reservations, and excluded from the country. Yes, there were groups of Whites who were set off from the dominant group, and they had less privilege, but that does not mean that they were racially separate from dominant-group Whites or that their disadvantage came close to that experienced by peoples of color. They could vote, they were eligible for naturalization, and no one was killing them on account of their ethnicity. Theirs was, as the title suggests, not non-Whiteness but "Whiteness of a different color." Yet Jacobson's book is premised in part on their being more separate and disadvantaged than that, and the evidence just will not support such a claim.

Despite such shortcomings, *Whiteness of a Different Color*, like *The White Scourge*, *The Wages of Whiteness*, and other similar books, is a significant help to our understanding of the ways that race has been constructed and used. The best White studies are like these, historically grounded studies of how the White group was formed and how power has been employed to enhance and maintain it.[31]

There is a related movement—critical race theory—that is worth mentioning as an adjunct to Whiteness studies. Critical race theory is an intellectual movement primarily within legal scholarship circles.[32] Some progressive legal scholars saw the modest gains experienced by people of color during the Civil Rights movement disappearing in the 1970s. They grew impatient with the standard liberal approaches to racial justice. Turning to neo-Marxist and postmodern ideas, they fashioned a new approach to legal interpretation surrounding racial issues.[33] Critical race theory intersects with Whiteness studies through one of its offshoots: critical White studies. The branching began with an article by Cheryl Harris in the *Harvard Law Review*, "Whiteness as Property" (1993). There, she made from a legal point of view much the same argument that Lipsitz would later make in terms more broadly cultural and political. In *White by Law* (1996), Ian Haney López broadened Harris's analysis to show how Whites used the law to draw lines around their Whiteness and reinforce their privilege. Richard Delgado and Jean Stefancic (1997) widened the discussion of critical White studies in a massive compendium of writings by legal scholars and others on the ways that White people have created and maintained White privilege.[34]

WE ARE OTHER, TOO: THE PROBLEM WITH WHITENESS STUDIES

If these are the many strengths and important achievements of Whiteness studies, are there weaknesses, too? Alas, there are. The problems stem from what seem to be the motivations behind much of the White studies movement. One factor seems to be embarrassment on the part of some White people who regard themselves as sensitive to racial issues—embarrassment that they are White. Jonathan Rutherford, in the passage quoted early in this chapter, used that word to describe the root of his desire to study Whiteness.[35] No one wants to be part of the problem. People of sensitivity and goodwill want to be part of the solution. However, that desire may shade over into a longing to be at the center of action, racially speaking. Like the young man whose story opened this chapter, Whiteness studies people want to be on the side of progressive social change in racial matters.

Embarrassment and a desire to be at the center of action lead some people to want to flee their Whiteness. Rutherford writes of a longing to "disown . . . white English ethnicity," and Ignatiev and Garvey call on progressive Whites to "defect" from, in fact to "abolish," the White race.[36] That would neatly solve the embarrassment problem and perhaps put one at the center of the action, but how can one do that? The Black theologian James Cone put a positive spin on the dilemma in 1970, long before the White studies movement: "There will be no peace in America until whites begin to hate their whiteness, asking from the depths of their being: 'How can we become black?'"[37]

One way, perhaps, to lessen the tension is to suggest that one is not an oppressor because one is not quite so White as those bad Whites who are the main oppressors. This leads to the We Are Other, Too fallacy that is a significant subtheme in the Whiteness studies movement. Some White people, in desiring to flee or disavow their Whiteness, retreat into the comforting assertion that they (or some other Whites with whom they identify) are not, or were not always, quite so White as the main White oppressors.

They begin with the accurate observation that there has long been a hierarchy among White Americans along lines of ancestral nationality and that it has sometimes assumed a racial tone (i.e., the language people have used to describe it has sometimes referred to supposedly innate characteristics and phenotype). This hierarchy within Whiteness can be illustrated by the following exercise. More than two hundred audiences over thirty-five years—students, church groups, and people attending public lectures—have been asked to rank ten American ethnic groups "according to how closely they approximate the core of what it means to be an American." In every single case, the audience, on average, gave a ranking that looked about like this:[38]

1. English
2. Swedish
3. Irish
4. Polish
5. Jewish
6. Black
7. American Indian
8. Mexican
9. Japanese
10. Arab

Something very like this hierarchy was coded into the Immigration Act of 1924, which set strict quotas on Eastern and Southern European immigrants and banned Asians outright. Such a hierarchy was assumed by Florence Ewing, a kind White woman from Missouri, who early in the twentieth century wrote the names of all her high school friends next to their pictures in her scrapbook. The ethnicity of her Anglo-American, German, and Scandinavian Protestant and Irish Catholic friends went unmarked, but she felt compelled to write "Jewish" next to the names of those to whom that appellation might be applied. It did not mean that she was not equally their friend, only that their Jewish identity made them something less than other Whites.[39]

Starting from the observation of such a hierarchy among White people, some students of Whiteness take it a step further to the assertion that Jews or Irish or Italians or some other group of White people once were not White. Thus we see books and articles about How Whomever Became White. The unspoken assertion is, "We have race, too, the same as people of color. We are not part of the problem because we are Other, too."

The standard-bearer in this trend is Noel Ignatiev, in an influential book with the provocative title, *How the Irish Became White* (1995). Intrinsic to Ignatiev's argument is an idiosyncratic definition of Whiteness. He begins with the observations that race is not biological in origin but rather that people are assigned to races, and that there is an intimate "connection . . . between concepts of race and acts of oppression." One is not White in one's person, and a group of people are not a White group in their being. Rather, they are White insofar as they participate in oppressing others who are defined as the racial target for subordination. For Ignatiev, "The white race consists of those who partake of the privileges of white skin." This provides him with the conceptual foundation from which to argue that for Irish Americans in the nineteenth century, "to enter the white race was a strategy to secure an advantage in a competitive society."[40] That is, by the quirks of Ignatiev's definitions, the Irish were once not White, and then they worked to become White by drawing a distinction between themselves and people who were not White and actively oppressing those people.

Ignatiev argues there was a time in Ireland when Irish people were oppressed in something like racial terms. English people colonized Ireland, took away people's lands and livelihoods, and created an ideology of Irish innate, quasi-biological inferiority—not quite Black, but not like English people either. Irish people came to America and were slotted into low class positions—though not as low as slaves or free Blacks. Here, according to Ignatiev, instead of making class solidarity with African Americans, the Irish chose to be White—that is, to be oppressive—in order to distance themselves from Blacks and improve their social and economic possibilities. Through the Catholic Church, labor unions, and the Democratic Party they claimed a place in what was becoming the White Republic.

The important contributions of Ignatiev's polemic are his insistence on examining relations between White and Black members of the working class and his conclusion that adopting anti-Black attitudes and activities was essential to Irish Americans making a place for themselves above the bottom rung in the United States. His broader contention highlighted in the title, that the Irish were once not White and then chose to become White, is intelligible—but only if one recognizes and accepts his idiosyncratic definition of Whiteness not as biology or group identity but rather as choosing to act oppressively toward African Americans.

Yet the impact of the title and argument is quite different. Very few people comprehend Ignatiev's definition of Whiteness, and fewer still accept it as normative. This writer has heard dozens of times since Ignatiev's book was published, from White laypeople and scholars alike, some version of the following statement: "You know, the Irish weren't always White. Once they were not White, and then they became White." The implication is that the kind of mobility that Irish Americans are said to have experienced is readily available to people of color in the United States. It is an easy step from there to the racist conclusion that Blacks or Latinos or Indians or Asians have chosen not to become White out of their own perversity. Like the Irish, they could have become White and escaped the disabilities that are their lot.

Ignatiev would not own that interpretation. In *Race Traitor* and in *How the Irish Became White* he shows how vehemently he opposes White privilege and oppressiveness. That is why he wants to disown Whiteness. It is a noble urge but ultimately a misguided one. Ignatiev and other Whites (including this writer) cannot effectively disown our Whiteness, much as we might like to do so. We necessarily carry White privilege whether we want to do so or not. To illustrate: try as I may, I cannot change the fact that I can get a cab easily in midtown Manhattan, while a middle-aged Black man wearing similar clothing cannot. More consequentially, we will be seen differently when applying for a loan, seeking a job, or confronting a police officer. Whites as a group have better life chances than African Americans and other people of color. We can hate White privilege, we can denounce it, but until race is irrelevant in America—a distant day indeed—we cannot be not privileged. We can fight against racial hierarchy and oppression daily, but we cannot abolish the White race. We still enjoy the fruits of Whiteness, whether we want them or not.

The We Are Other, Too trend is carried further by Karen Brodkin in *How Jews Became White Folks and What That Says about Race in America.*[41] One hesitates to cast aspersions on a book as good as *How Jews Became White Folks.* Brodkin began the study as an attempt to understand how race, class, and gender interpenetrate one another in American society.

Gradually it turned, however, first into an exploration of changes in the nature of Jewishness and then into a kind of family history of racial identity. *How Jews Became White Folks* in fact does a superb job of illuminating how gender and class work together with race in the formation of identities and hierarchies in the American economic and political systems.

But in the more expansive theme that gives the book its title, Brodkin loses her way. Her central contention is that there was a time in American history when Jews were non-Whites. When she hews closer to her evidence, she describes Jews as being "not-quite white" or having "a whiteness of our own."[42] Here she refers to the fact that Jews have long held a lower position in the American ethnoracial hierarchy than White Gentiles (although that position has improved in recent generations and though it was never so low as any of the nation's peoples of color). But more frequently than such nuanced phrasings, Brodkin boldly asserts, again and again, and without any supporting evidence, that Jews were in fact not White.

This is an example of Whiteness studies run amok. If this trend continues, one can expect to see books before long on How the Italians Became White,[43] How the Swedes Became White, perhaps even How the English Became White. It is pretty silly, and disrespectful of the genuine disabilities faced by people of color in America's racial system.[44]

The ultimate absurdity on the theme We Are Other, Too is John Gennari's 1996 article, "Passing for Italian." On the cover of the once-trendy cultural studies journal *Transition* that title runs across a picture of Denny Mendez, Miss Italia 1996—an apparently Black woman. One might expect Gennari's article to be a meditation on the complexities of Italian identity in an age when immigrants (including the Dominican-born Mendez) are remaking the ethnic map of places that are frequently thought to be racially homogeneous. That would be a worthy subject. Instead, we are treated to a self-indulgent essay whose central contention is that there is "a distinct tradition of interethnic identification[,] . . . the black/Italian crossover fantasy," which Gennari calls "'goombah blackness'—an affective alliance between Italian and African Americans based on mutual desires and pleasures, and grounded particularly in a tradition of boisterous male assertiveness." Blacks and Italians, says Gennari, are natural pals.

Gennari's evidence? He has almost none, beyond assertions that Marvin Gaye admired Frank Sinatra, that Sinatra admired Billie Holiday, that Sinatra hung out with Sammy Davis Jr., and that Sinatra and some gangsta rappers had similar attitudes toward women. The suspicion lingers that Gennari is just a White guy attempting to appropriate Blackness in order to make himself look more hip. It does not work. Sinatra's attitudes may have been similar to those of some hip-hop artists, and there surely have been times and places where Blacks and Italians (and others) have interacted (see the description of Herb Jeffries's career in chapter 2). But I know of no Black neighborhood in the 1940s and 1950s where more than a tiny handful of people even listened to Frank Sinatra, much less thought him one of their own. There is no evidence at all of a special affinity between the Black and Italian American populations at large. "Passing for Italian" is pernicious silliness.[45]

Thus, many White studies authors assert, without adequate foundation, a parallel between racial divisions and the situations of White ethnic groups. And almost none ask the comparative questions that would be needed to prove their assumptions true. For example, precisely how *are* the disabilities suffered by Jews or Italians like—and how are they unlike—those suffered by Blacks and Indians? Do those disabilities stem from the same causes? Are they equally susceptible to remediation? These and questions like them are worth asking, but one will not find them asked in Whiteness studies.

There is another theme in some studies of Whiteness by White feminists, and it borders on an assertion that We Are Other, Too. It is the implication that femaleness Blackens, that because a White person or group is female that person or group does not partake of White privilege to the same degree as do White males. I take that to be a nearly spoken subtext in the interchange between Catharine MacKinnon and Martha Mahoney in the *Yale Journal of Law and Feminism* (1991, 1993).[46] I do not wish to contest or discount the very real disabilities faced by White women in a sexist society—quite the contrary. In fact, I offer this observation with the utmost tentativeness, as I am a White male and so am of the oppressing class on both counts. Nonetheless, there is something pernicious about adopting, even by subtle implication, the oppression of members of a group to which one does not belong. Salient refutations of such an assertion of common otherness are made by a number of feminists of color, among them bell hooks, Hazel Carby, Haunani-Kay Trask, and Donna Awatere.[47]

Finally, the We Are Other, Too vector in Whiteness studies extends to skinhead chic. The taking off point here is a smart, funny, subversive collection of essays called *White Trash* (1997), edited by Matt Wray and Annalee Newitz. The editors describe their project thus: "Poor or marginal whites occupy an uncharted space in recent identity studies, particularly because they do not easily fit the model of whiteness-as-power proposed by many multiculturalist or minority discourses. Associated in mainstream culture with 'trashy' kitsch or dangerous pathologies rather than with the material realities of economic life, poor whites are treated as degraded caricatures rather than as real people living in conditions of poverty and disempowerment."[48] Thandeka, in a *Tikkun* essay called "The Cost of Whiteness" (1999), echoed that analysis.

> I am not denying "white privilege." All whites . . . benefit from their wage of whiteness. Such talk of privilege, however, is incomplete unless we also speak of its penalty. For poorer wage earners without power, money or influence, their wage of whiteness functions as a kind of workers' . . . "consolation prize" to persons, who, although not wealthy, do not have to consider themselves losers because they are, at least, white. . . . These workers are, in effect, exploited twice: first as workers and then as "whites." . . . Whiteness functions as a distraction from the pervasive class problem.[49]

This is a convoluted way of saying that Thandeka wants the real problem to be class, not race. But it is also a serious attempt to address the disabilities faced by poor people who are White.

Where are the lines between (1) exploring Whiteness, (2) rescuing White working-class culture from abuse by outsiders, (3) celebrating Whiteness as a positive identity, and (4) embracing White supremacist racism? It is not always clear. A tour of who-bought-what-else from Amazon.com led from excellent Whiteness studies books by Roediger and

Jacobson to White trash books like Wray and Newitz's. Then the trail went on to Jim Goad's *Redneck Manifesto: How Hillbillies, Hicks, and White Trash Became America's Scapegoats* (1998). Finally, it landed in the heart of Aryan Nation: *They Were White and They Were Slaves* (1993) by Michael Hoffman and *The South Was Right!* (1994) by James Ronald Kennedy.[50] Where exactly was it that the antiracist intent of Whiteness studies shaded into advocacy of White racism? It is not clear, but that is the path it took.

Brodkin, Ignatiev, and nearly all the authors of the We Are Other, Too school express a desire to undermine White privilege. These authors, as much as Lipsitz, Roediger, and the other more successful writers on the theme, seem to be trying conscientiously to do what James Bevel instructed that White man to do in 1966: go back and teach White people about their bigotry. The best examples of Whiteness studies achieve that goal. Still, even the best authors in this field spend nearly all their time talking about White people. And there are so many authors, writing so much about Whiteness.[51] Each of them surely makes a contribution to the understanding of Whiteness. And White studies has opened up space for some very creative and insightful riffing on activities around race.[52] But they place White people at the center of investigation, saying by implication, "It is White people who are the important ones."[53]

The sheer volume of Whiteness studies overwhelms the senses. Even in the study of race, an exhorbitant amount of attention seems to be going to White people. Early in the 2000s, I was standing on a street corner talking with a Filipino American scholar about Whiteness studies. He asked, "Don't you White guys have enough already? You are the subject matter of almost all the departments on campus. Now you want ethnic studies, too?" His observation was not far off the mark. How sad that some of the makers of White studies should, in attempting to dethrone Whiteness, end up examining it obsessively and placing it at the center yet again.

NOTES

This chapter originally appeared in Paul Spickard and G. Reginald Daniel, eds., *Racial Thinking in the United States: Uncompleted Independence* (Notre Dame, IN:

University of Notre Dame Press, 2004), 248–74. It appeared again in *Affect and Power: Essays on Sex, Slavery, Race, and Religion in Appreciation of Winthrop D. Jordan*, ed. David J. Libby, Paul Spickard, and Susan Ditto (Jackson: University Press of Mississippi, 2005), 107–25. Patrick Miller, Lori Pierce, Nick Spreitzer, Puk Degnegaard, Stephen Cornell, Laurie Mengel, Reginald Daniel, David Torres-Rouff, Ingrid Page, Lynda Dumais, Ivana Lauro, and Jonathan Glickstein were all generous in contributing to my thinking about White studies; none should be held responsible for the final shape of this essay.

1. See also Eric Arnesen, "Whiteness and the Historians' Imagination," *International Labor and Working-Class History*, no. 60 (Fall 2001): 3–32; Eric Arnesen, "A Paler Shade of White," *New Republic* (June 24, 2002): 33–38. I am grateful for copies provided by Professor Arnesen. My take on the strengths and shortcomings of the Whiteness studies movement is different from Arnesen's, as my analysis proceeds from different principles and focuses on different issues. Arnesen takes David Roediger and other scholars of Whiteness to task for being less than careful about definitions and less than thorough in their research, in a jot-and-tittle analysis of their argument and evidence. I argue more broadly about themes, motives, and potential social impact. Despite our differences of approach, I find Arnesen's arguments and evidence generally convincing.

2. Jonathan Rutherford, *Forever England: Reflections on Masculinity and Empire* (London: Lawrence and Wishart, 1997), 5.

3. Noel Ignatiev and John Garvey, eds., *Race Traitor* (New York: Routledge, 1996), 1–2, 9–10.

4. Ibid., 10–14.

5. Of course, one might point out that most studies of US history and culture for many decades were studies of White people, for people of color were left out. In this essay I focus on works that explicitly addressed the White race and its standing in the world.

6. Madison Grant, *The Passing of the Great Race, or The Racial Basis of European History* (New York: Scribner's, 1916 [several later editions]), ix; Lothrop Stoddard, *The Rising Tide of Color against White World-Supremacy* (New York: Scribner's, 1920 [several later editions]). See also Homer Lea, *The Valor of Ignorance* (New York: Harper, 1909) and *The Day of the Saxon* (New York: Harper, 1912); F. G. Crookshank, *The Mongol in Our Midst* (New York: Dutton, 1924). For analysis, see Elazar Barkan, *The Retreat from Scientific Racism* (New York: Cambridge University Press, 1992); Ivan Hannaford, *Race: The History of an Idea in the West* (Baltimore: Johns Hopkins University Press, 1996).

7. Richard J. Herrnstein and Charles Murray, *The Bell Curve: Intelligence and Class Structure in American Life* (New York: Free Press, 1994); Peter Brimelow, *Alien Nation: Common Sense about America's Immigration Disaster* (New York: Harper, 1996), xxi; Patrick J. Buchanan, *The Death of the West: How Declining Populations and Immigrant Invasions Imperil Our Country and Civilization* (New

York: St. Martin's, 2002), 3–5; Samuel P. Huntington, *Who Are We? The Challenges to America's National Identity* (New York: Simon and Schuster, 2005). See also Patrick J. Buchanan, *State of Emergency: The Third World Invasion and Conquest of America* (New York: St. Martin's, 2007); Patrick J. Buchanan, *Suicide of a Superpower: Will America Survive to 2025?* (New York: Thomas Dunne Books, 2011); Samuel P. Huntington, *The Clash of Civilizations and the Remaking of World Order* (New York: Simon and Schuster, 1996); J. Philippe Rushton, *Race, Evolution, and Behavior* (New Brunswick, NJ: Transaction, 1997); Dinesh D'Souza, *The End of Racism: Principles for a Multiracial Society* (New York: Free Press, 1995); Jon Entine, *Taboo: Why Black Athletes Dominate Sports and Why We're Afraid to Talk about It* (New York: Public Affairs, 2000).

For correctives, see Steven Fraser, ed., *The Bell Curve Wars: Race, Intelligence, and the Future of America* (New York: Basic Books, 1995); Stephen Jay Gould, *The Mismeasure of Man*, rev. ed. (New York: Norton, 1996); William H. Tucker, *The Science and Politics of Racial Research* (Urbana: University of Illinois Press, 1994); Patrick B. Miller, "The Anatomy of Scientific Racism: Racialist Responses to Black Athletic Achievement," in *We Are a People: Narrative and Multiplicity in Constructing Ethnic Identity*, ed. Paul Spickard and W. Jeffrey Burroughs (Philadelphia: Temple University Press, 2000), 124–41; Jonathan Marks, *Human Biodiversity: Genes, Race, and History* (New York: Aldine de Gruyter, 1995); Joseph L. Graves Jr., *The Emperor's New Clothes: Biological Theories of Race at the Millennium* (New Brunswick, NJ: Rutgers University Press, 2001).

8. Thomas Sowell, *Ethnic America* (New York: Basic Books, 1981); Nathan Glazer, *Ethnic Dilemmas* (Cambridge, MA: Harvard University Press, 1983), esp. "Blacks and Ethnic Groups: The Difference and the Political Difference It Makes," 70–93; Michael Novak, *The Rise of the Unmeltable Ethnics* (New York: Macmillan, 1973).

9. Bernard Bailyn, *Voyagers to the West: A Passage in the Peopling of America on the Eve of the Revolution* (New York: Knopf, 1986); David Hackett Fischer, *Albion's Seed: Four British Folkways in America* (New York: Oxford University Press, 1989); Richard D. Alba, *Ethnic Identity: The Transformation of White America* (New Haven, CT: Yale University Press, 1990). One might even call a book like Langston Hughes's *The Ways of White Folks* (New York: Knopf, 1934) an example of Whiteness studies.

10. Gordon W. Allport, *The Nature of Prejudice* (Cambridge, MA: Addison-Wesley, 1954); Winthrop D. Jordan, *White over Black: American Attitudes toward the Negro, 1550–1812* (Chapel Hill: University of North Carolina Press, 1968); George M. Fredrickson, *The Black Image in the White Mind: The Debate on Afro-American Character and Destiny, 1817–1914* (New York: Harper & Row, 1971); Edmund S. Morgan, *American Slavery—American Freedom: The Ordeal of Colonial Virginia* (New York: Norton, 1975); Robert Berkhofer, *The White Man's Indian* (New York: Random House, 1978).

11. His ideas here are essentially those of Edmund Morgan in *American Slavery—American Freedom*. For a different view, see Jordan, *White over Black*.

12. Alexander Saxton, *The Rise and Fall of the White Republic: Class Politics and Mass Culture in Nineteenth-Century America* (London: Verso, 1990), 1–18, 387, passim.

13. Perhaps the preeminent attempt to free Marxist interpreters from the assumption that class trumps, in fact is formative of race, is Robert Miles, *Racism after "Race Relations"* (New York: Routledge, 1993). See also Michael Omi and Howard Winant, *Racial Formation in the United States from the 1960s to the 1990s*, 2nd ed. (New York: Routledge, 1994).

14. David Roediger, *The Wages of Whiteness: Race and the Making of the American Working Class* (London: Verso, 1991), 13, 8. Roediger acknowledges his debt to Du Bois. It is not clear whether he intends, as Du Bois did, to invoke the biblical contention that the wages of sin is death (Romans 6:23).

15. Ibid., 13–14.

16. Ibid., 6.

17. Ibid., 173 and passim. Roediger later apologized for what he regarded as a mistake in the subtitle: adopting the rhetorical position that Whites (and in his reading of his own book, males) were the only members of the working class. *The Wages of Whiteness*, 188–89.

18. David Roediger, *Towards the Abolition of Whiteness: Essays on Race, Politics, and Working Class History* (London: Verso, 1994); David R. Roediger, ed., *Black on White: Black Writers on What It Means to Be White* (New York: Schocken, 1998); David Roediger, *Working toward Whiteness: How America's Immigrants Became White: The Strange Journey from Ellis Island to the Suburbs* (New York: Basic Books, 2006). Roediger's collection of essays on the theme is *Colored White: Transcending the Racial Past* (Berkeley: University of California Press, 2002). See also James R. Barrett and David Roediger, "Inbetween Peoples: Race, Nationality and the 'New Immigrant' Working Class," *Journal of American Ethnic History* 16.3 (Spring 1997): 3–44.

19. Toni Morrison, *Playing in the Dark: Whiteness and the Literary Imagination* (Cambridge, MA: Harvard University Press, 1994), 63.

20. Theodore W. Allen, *The Invention of the White Race*, vol. 1, *Racial Oppression and Social Control* (London: Verso, 1994); vol. 2, *The Origin of Racial Oppression in Anglo-America* (London: Verso, 1997). Allen takes issue at length with the interpretations advanced by Jordan in *White over Black*. I find Jordan's arguments more persuasive, as they are based on a careful reading of the historical sources and advanced with little polemic aforethought. For a nuanced account of the other side of the coin—the making of African American identity—in a similar time period, see Michael A. Gomez, *Exchanging Our Country Marks: The Transformation of African Identities in the Colonial and Antebellum South* (Chapel Hill: University of North Carolina Press, 1998).

21. Truth be told, there were not just White and Black people in the places Saxton, Roediger, Allen, and Morrison examined, but they tended not to see Native Americans and others.

22. Tomás Almaguer, *Racial Fault Lines: The Historical Origins of White Supremacy in California* (Berkeley: University of California Press, 1994), 209, 104.

23. Neil Foley, *The White Scourge: Mexicans, Blacks, and Poor Whites in Texas Cotton Culture* (Berkeley: University of California Press, 1997).

24. George Lipsitz, "The Possessive Investment in Whiteness: Racialized Social Democracy and the 'White' Problem in American Studies," *American Quarterly* 47.3 (1995): 369–87; George Lipsitz, *The Possessive Investment in Whiteness: How White People Profit from Identity Politics* (Philadelphia: Temple University Press, 1998). See also the expanded edition, *The Possessive Investment in Whiteness*, rev. ed. (Philadelphia: Temple University Press, 2006); George Lipsitz, *How Racism Takes Place* (Philadelphia: Temple University Press, 2011).

25. Lipsitz, "Possessive Investment," 371.

26. Lipsitz, *Possessive Investment*, 233.

27. Matthew Frye Jacobson, *Whiteness of a Different Color: European Immigrants and the Alchemy of Race* (Cambridge, MA: Harvard University Press, 1998). The analysis and some of the language used here are drawn from my review of this book for *Social History* 26.1 (2001).

28. The periods were not that simple, of course; in fact, the processes were so complex that it takes Jacobson every bit of 135 pages just to describe them. Part of his problem is that his evidence does not fit his periodization very well; he is continually forced to explain why key developments happened outside the periods to which they belong thematically. The schema has a simple beauty at its most abstract level, but when Jacobson gets down to the details it does not hold together.

29. To be fair, neither does this chapter define race. For my take on the meaning of race, see Paul Spickard and W. Jeffrey Burroughs, "We Are a People," in *We Are a People: Narrative and Multiplicity in Constructing Ethnic Identity*, ed. Spickard and Burroughs (Philadelphia: Temple University Press, 2000), esp. 2–7; and chaps. 1, 2, and 4 of this book.

30. Jacobson, *Whiteness of a Different Color*, 140; emphasis added.

31. Other examples of excellence in Whiteness studies include Philip J. Deloria, *Playing Indian* (New Haven, CT: Yale University Press, 1998); Grace Elizabeth Hale, *Making Whiteness: The Culture of Segregation in the South, 1890–1940* (New York: Vintage, 1998); Robert G. Lee, *Orientals: Asian Americans in Popular Culture* (Philadelphia: Temple University Press, 1999); Nell Irvin Painter, *The History of White People* (New York: Norton, 2010); Melanie E. L. Bush, *Everyday Forms of Whiteness: Understanding Race in a "Post-Racial" World*, 2nd ed. (Lanham, MD: Rowman and Littlefield, 2011); Michelle Brattain, *The Politics of Whiteness: Race, Workers, and Culture in the Modern South* (Athens: University of Georgia Press,

2004); Sarah Gualtieri, *Between Arab and White: Race and Ethnicity in the Early Arab American Diaspora* (Berkeley: University of California Press, 2009).

There is a subgenre: practical manuals that encourage Whites to understand and work against their own racial privilege. Among these are Tim Wise, *White Like Me: Reflections on Race from a Privileged Son*, rev. ed. (Berkeley, CA: Soft Skull Press, 2011); Tim Wise, *Dear White America: Letter to a New Minority* (San Francisco: City Lights Books, 2012); Tim Wise, *Colorblind: The Rise of Post-Racial Politics and the Retreat from Racial Equity* (San Francisco: City Lights Books, 2010); Shelly Tochluk, *Witnessing Whiteness: The Need to Talk about Race and How to Do It*, 2nd ed. (Plymouth, UK: Rowman and Littlefield, 2010); Robert Jensen, *The Heart of Whiteness: Confronting Race, Racism, and White Privilege* (San Francisco: City Lights Books, 2005).

32. There is an unrelated movement bearing the name "critical race theory" in education studies, too, but it is less well articulated and has had less impact.

33. Kimberlé Crenshaw et al., eds., *Critical Race Theory* (New York: New Press, 1995); Richard Delgado, ed., *Critical Race Theory* (Philadelphia: Temple University Press, 1995).

34. Cheryl Harris, "Whiteness as Property," *Harvard Law Review* 106 (1993): 1707–91; Ian F. Haney López, *White by Law: The Legal Construction of Race* (New York: New York University Press, 1996); Richard Delgado and Jean Stefancic, eds., *Critical White Studies: Looking behind the Mirror* (Philadelphia: Temple University Press, 1997). Harris drew on a number of roots in earlier legal studies of race, including A. Leon Higginbotham, *In the Matter of Color: Race and the American Legal Process* (New York: Oxford University Press, 1978). The title of this chapter is a play on the name of this movement. Looking beyond merely legal studies, it seeks to determine just what is critical (and what may not be) about White studies.

35. Rutherford, *Forever England*, 5.

36. Ibid.; Ignatiev and Garvey, *Race Traitor*, 10.

37. James H. Cone, *A Black Theology of Liberation*, 2nd ed. (Maryknoll, NY: Orbis, 1986), vii.

38. I have reported on this exercise in more detail in "Who Is an American? Teaching about Racial and Ethnic Hierarchy," *Immigration and Ethnic History Society Newsletter* 31.1 (May 1999).

39. Scrapbook in the possession of the author.

40. Noel Ignatiev, *How the Irish Became White* (New York: Routledge, 1995), 1–2.

41. Karen Brodkin, *How Jews Became White Folks and What That Says about Race in America* (New Brunswick, NJ: Rutgers University Press, 1998). The analysis and some of the language used here are drawn from my review of this book for *Social History* 26.1 (2001). Far more thoughtful on the racial position of Jews in

America is Eric L. Goldstein, *The Price of Whiteness: Jews, Race, and American Identity* (Princeton, NJ: Princeton University Press, 2007).

42. Brodkin, *How Jews Became White Folks*, 22, 138.

43. In fact, Jennifer Guglielmo and Salvatore Salerno published an edited collection of essays, *Are Italians White? How Race Is Made in America* (New York: Routledge, 2003).

44. This is not to assert that White groups did not suffer terribly in other settings. The Irish in Ireland suffered bitter racialized oppression, as did Jews in Germany, Mennonites in Russia, and Armenians in Turkey. It is, however, to insist that there has been a qualitative difference between the disabilities suffered *in the United States* by lower-status Whites and those endured by people of color.

45. John Gennari, "Passing for Italian: Crooners and Gangsters in Crossover Culture," *Transition*, no. 72 (1996): 36–48.

46. Catharine A. MacKinnon, "From Practice to Theory, or What Is a White Woman Anyway?," *Yale Journal of Law and Feminism* 4 (1991): 13–33; Martha R. Mahoney, "Whiteness and Women, in Practice and Theory: A Reply to Catharine MacKinnon," *Yale Journal of Law and Feminism* 5 (1993): 217–51. For related themes, see also Abby L. Ferber, *White Man Falling: Race, Gender, and White Supremacy* (Lanham, MD: Rowman and Littlefield, 1998); Ruth Frankenberg, *White Women, Race Matters: The Social Construction of Whiteness* (Minneapolis: University of Minnesota Press, 1993); Hauraki Greenland, "Maori Ethnicity as Ideology," in *Nga Take: Ethnic Relations and Racism in Aotearoa/New Zealand*, ed. Paul Spoonley, David Pearson, and Cluny Macpherson (Palmerston North, NZ: Dunmore, 1991), 90–107; Jane Lazarre, *Beyond the Whiteness of Whiteness: Memoir of a White Mother of Black Sons* (Durham, NC: Duke University Press, 1996); Maureen T. Reddy, *Crossing the Color Line: Race, Parenting, and Culture* (New Brunswick, NJ: Rutgers University Press, 1994). Lewis Gordon makes a reflexive assertion that Blacks constitute a race gendered female, in "Sex, Race, and Matrices of Desire in an Antiblack World," in *Her Majesty's Other Children: Sketches of Racism from a Neocolonial Age* (Lanham, MD: Rowman and Littlefield, 1997), 73–88.

47. bell hooks, *Ain't I a Woman: Black Women and Feminism* (Boston: South End Press, 1981); bell hooks, *Talking Back: Thinking Feminist, Thinking Black* (Boston: South End Press, 1989); Hazel V. Carby, "White Woman Listen! Black Feminism and the Boundaries of Sisterhood," in *The Empire Strikes Back: Race and Racism in 70s Britain* (London: Hutchinson, 1982); Haunani-Kay Trask, "Pacific Island Women and White Feminism," in *From a Native Daughter: Colonialism and Sovereignty in Hawai'i* (Monroe, ME: Common Courage Press, 1993), 263–77; Donna Awatere, *Maori Sovereignty* (Auckland, NZ: Bradsheet, 1984), 42 and passim.

48. Matt Wray and Annalee Newitz, eds., *White Trash: Race and Class in America* (New York: Routledge, 1997), back cover. Wray carried this vector of argument to a triumphal conclusion in *Not Quite White: White Trash and the Boundaries of Whiteness* (Durham, NC: Duke University Press, 2006).

49. Thandeka, "The Cost of Whiteness," *Tikkun* 14.3 (May–June 1999): 33–38. See also Thandeka, *Learning to Be White: Money, Race, and God in America* (London: Continuum, 1999).

50. I made this investigation of www.amazon.com connections on July 29, 2000. Jim Goad, *The Redneck Manifesto: How Hillbillies, Hicks, and White Trash Became America's Scapegoats* (New York: Touchstone, 1998); Michael A. Hoffman, *They Were White and They Were Slaves: The Untold Story of the Enslavement of Whites in Early America*, 4th ed. (Dresden, NY: Independent History, 1993); James Ronald Kennedy, *The South Was Right!*, reprint ed. (Gretna, LA: Pelican, 1994). Cf. Jeffrey Kaplan, ed., *Encyclopedia of White Power: A Sourcebook on the Radical Racist Right* (Walnut Creek, CA: AltaMira, 2000).

51. See, e.g., Walter Benn Michaels, "Race into Culture: A Critical Genealogy of Cultural Identity," *Critical Inquiry* 18 (1992): 655–85; Avery Gordon and Christopher Newfield, "Critical Response: White Philosophy," *Critical Inquiry* 20 (1994): 737–57; Walter Benn Michaels, "Critical Response: The No-Drop Rule," *Critical Inquiry* 20 (1994): 758–69; Barbara J. Flagg, "'Was Blind, But Now I See': White Race Consciousness and the Requirement of Discriminatory Intent," *Michigan Law Review* 91 (1993): 953–1017; Micaela di Leonardo, "White Ethnicities, Identity Politics, and Baby Bear's Chair," *Social Text*, no. 41 (Winter 1994): 174–91; Shelly Fisher Fishkin, "Interrogating 'Whiteness,' Complicating 'Blackness': Remapping American Culture," *American Quarterly* 47.3 (1995): 428–66; Walter Benn Michaels, *Our America: Nativism, Modernism, and Pluralism* (Durham, NC: Duke University Press, 1995); Liam Kennedy, "Alien Nation: White Male Paranoia and Imperial Culture in the United States," *Journal of American Studies* 30 (1996): 87–100; Mike Hill, ed., *Whiteness: A Critical Reader* (New York: New York University Press, 1997); Michelle Fine et al., eds., *Off White: Readings on Race, Power, and Society* (New York: Routledge, 1997); Henry A. Giroux, "Rewriting the Discourse of Racial Identity: Towards a Pedagogy and Politics of Whiteness," *Harvard Educational Review* 67.2 (1997): 285–320; Howard Winant, "Behind Blue Eyes: Whiteness and Contemporary US Racial Politics," *New Left Review*, no. 225 (Sept.–Oct. 1997); Jonathan W. Warren and France Winddance Twine, "White Americans, the New Minority? Non-Blacks and the Ever-Expanding Boundaries of Whiteness," *Journal of Black Studies* 28.2 (1997): 200–218; Ruth Frankenberg, *Displacing Whiteness: Essays in Social and Cultural Criticism* (Durham, NC: Duke University Press, 1997); Richard Dyer, *White* (London: Routledge, 1997); Joe Kincheloe et al., eds., *White Reign: Deploying Whiteness in America* (New York: St. Martin's, 1998); Dana D. Nelson, *National Manhood:*

Capitalist Citizenship and the Imagined Fraternity of White Men (Durham, NC: Duke University Press, 1998); John Gabriel, *Whitewash: Racialized Politics and the Media* (New York: Routledge, 1998); Valerie Babb, *Whiteness Visible: The Meaning of Whiteness in American Literature and Culture* (New York: New York University Press, 1998); Thomas K. Nakayama and Judith N. Martin, eds., *Whiteness: The Communication of Social Identity* (Thousand Oaks, CA: Sage, 1999); Maurice Berger, *White Lies: Race and the Myths of Whiteness* (New York: Farrar, Straus and Giroux, 1999); Christine Clark and James O'Donnell, eds., *Becoming and Unbecoming White: Owning and Disowning a Racial Identity* (Westport, CT: Bergin and Garvey, 1999); Timothy B. Powell, ed., *Beyond the Binary: Reconstructing Cultural Identity in a Multicultural Context* (New Brunswick, NJ: Rutgers University Press, 1999); Chris Weedon, *Feminism, Theory, and the Politics of Difference* (Oxford: Blackwell, 1999); Sarah Barnet-Weiser, *The Most Beautiful Girl in the World: Beauty Pageants and National Identity* (Berkeley: University of California Press, 1999); Patricia McKee, *Producing American Races: Henry James, William Faulkner, Toni Morrison* (Durham, NC: Duke University Press, 1999); John Hartigan, *Racial Situations: Class Predicaments of Whiteness in Detroit* (Princeton, NJ: Princeton University Press, 1999); Chris J. Cuomo and Kim Q. Hall, eds., *Whiteness: Feminist Philosophical Reflections* (Lanham, MD: Rowman and Littlefield, 1999); Renee R. Curry, *White Women Writing White: H.D., Elizabeth Bishop, Sylvia Plath* (New York: Greenwood, 2000); Aime M. Carrillo Rowe, "Locating Feminism's Subject: The Paradox of White Feminity and the Struggle to Forge Feminist Alliances," *Communication Theory* 10.1 (2000): 64–80; Barbara A. Miller, "'Anchoring' White Community: White Women Activists and the Politics of Public Schools," *Identities* 6.4 (2000): 481–512; John Tehranian, "Performing Whiteness: Naturalization Litigation and the Construct of Racial Identity in America," *Yale Law Journal* 109.4 (2000): 817ff.; Kalpana Seshari Crooks, *Desiring Whiteness: A Lacanian Analysis of Race* (New York: Routledge, 2000); Nelson M. Rodriguez and Leila E. Villaverde, eds., *Dismantling White Privilege: Pedagogy, Politics, and Whiteness* (New York: Peter Lang, 2000); Walter Bronwen, *Outsiders Inside: Whiteness, Place and Irish Women* (New York: Routledge, 2001); Birgit Brander Rasmussen et al., eds., *The Making and Unmaking of Whiteness* (Durham, NC: Duke University Press, 2001); Diane Negra, *Off-White Hollywood: American Culture and Ethnic Female Stardom* (New York: Routledge, 2001); Melissa E. Steyn, *Whiteness Isn't What It Used to Be: White Identity in a Changing South Africa* (Albany: State University of New York Press, 2001); Mason Boyd Stokes, *The Color of Sex: Whiteness, Heterosexuality, and the Fictions of White Supremacy* (Durham, NC: Duke University Press, 2001); Bronwen Walter, *Outsiders Inside: Whiteness, Place, and Irish Women* (New York: Routledge, 2001); Vron Ware and Les Back, *Out of Whiteness: Color, Politics, and Culture* (Chicago: University of Chicago Press, 2002); John T. Warren, *Performing Purity: Whiteness, Peda-*

gogy, and the Reconstitution of Power (New York: Peter Lang, 2003); Bridget T. Heneghan, *Whitewashing America: Material Culture and Race in the Antebellum Imagination* (Jackson: University Press of Mississippi, 2003); Joe Feagin and Eileen O'Brien, *White Men on Race: Power, Privilege, and the Shaping of Cultural Consciousness* (Boston: Beacon, 2003); Warwick Anderson, *The Cultivation of Whiteness: Science, Health, and Racial Destiny in Australia* (New York: Basic Books, 2003); George Yancy, ed., *What White Looks Like: African American Philosophers on the Whiteness Question* (New York: Routledge, 2004); Todd Vogel, *ReWriting White: Race, Class, and Cultural Capital in Nineteenth-Century America* (New Brunswick, NJ: Rutgers University Press, 2004); Shelley Sallee, *The Whiteness of Child Labor Reform in the New South* (Athens: University of Georgia Press, 2004); Mike Hill, *After Whiteness: Unmaking an American Majority* (New York: New York University Press, 2004); Gary Taylor, *Buying Whiteness: Race, Culture, and Identity from Columbus to Hip-Hop* (New York: Palgrave Macmillan, 2005); Karyn D. McKinney, *Being White: Stories of Race and Racism* (New York: Routledge, 2005); Alfred J. Lopez, ed., *Postcolonial Whiteness: A Critical Reader on Race and Empire* (Albany: State University of New York Press, 2005); Linda Frost, *Never One Nation: Freaks, Savages, and Whiteness in US Popular Culture, 1850–1877* (Minneapolis: University of Minnesota Press, 2005); María DeGuzmán, *Spain's Long Shadow: The Black Legend, Off-Whiteness, and Anglo-American Empire* (Minneapolis: University of Minnesota Press, 2005); Martin A. Berger, *Sight Unseen: Whiteness and American Visual Culture* (Berkeley: University of California Press, 2005); Shannon Sullivan, *Revealing Whiteness: The Unconscious Habits of Racial Privilege* (Bloomington: Indiana University Press, 2006); Edwin R. Morris, *An Unexpected Minority: White Kids in an Urban School* (New Brunswick, NJ: Rutgers University Press, 2006); Bridget Byrne, *White Lives: The Interplay of "Race," Class, and Gender in Everyday Life* (New York: Routledge, 2006); Cynthia Skove Nevels, *Lynching to Belong: Claiming Whiteness through Racial Violence* (College Station: Texas A&M University Press, 2007); Cecily Jones, *Engendering Whiteness: White Women and Colonialism in Barbados and North Carolina, 1627–1865* (Manchester: Manchester University Press, 2007); Steve Garner, *Whiteness: An Introduction* (New York: Routledge, 2007); Julian B. Carter, *The Heart of Whiteness: Normal Sexuality and Race in America, 1880–1940* (Durham, NC: Duke University Press, 2007) ; Daniel Bernardi, ed., *The Persistence of Whiteness: Race and Contemporary Hollywood Cinema* (New York: Routledge, 2008); Elizabeth M. Smith-Pryor, *Property Rites: The Rhinelander Trial, Passing, and the Protection of Whiteness* (Chapel Hill: University of North Carolina Press, 2009) ; Zeus Leonardo, *Race, Whiteness, and Education* (New York: Routledge, 2009); Yiorgos Anagnosto, *Contours of White Ethnicity: Popular Ethnography and the Making of Usable Pasts in Greek America* (Athens: Ohio University Press, 2009); Gretchen Murphy, *Shadowing the White Man's Burden: US Imperialism and the Problem of the Color Line* (New York: New York University Press, 2010); David McDermott Hughes, *Whiteness in Zimbabwe: Race, Landscape, and the Problem of Belonging* (New York: Palgrave Macmillan, 2010); Simon Clarke and Steve Garner, *White Identities: A Critical Sociological Approach* (London: Pluto Press, 2010); Laurie Stras, ed., *She's So Fine: Reflections on Whiteness, Femininity, Adolescence, and Class in 1960s Music* (Burlington, VT: Ashgate, 2011); Francis Margot, *Creative Subversions: Whiteness, Indigeneity, and the National Imaginary* (Vancouver: University of British Columbia Press, 2011); Hamilton Carroll, *Affirmative Reaction: New Forms of White Masculinity* (Durham, NC: Duke University Press, 2011); Mary Buchholz, *White Kids: Language, Race, and Styles of Youth Identity* (Cambridge: Cambridge University Press, 2011); George Yancy, *Look, a White! Philosophical Essays on Whiteness* (Philadelphia: Temple University Press, 2012); Jennifer L. Pierce, *Racing for Innocence: Whiteness, Gender, and the Backlash against Affirmative Action* (Stanford, CA: Stanford University Press, 2012); Tracey Owens Patton and Sally M. Shedlock, *Gender, Whiteness, and Power in Rodeo: Breaking Away from the Ties of Sexism and Racism* (Lanham, MD: Lexington Books, 2012); Kristin Loftsdottir and Lars Jensen, eds., *Whiteness and Postcolonialism in the Nordic Region* (Burlington, VT: Ashgate, 2012); Matthew W. Hughey, *White Bound: Nationalists, Antiracists, and the Shared Meanings of Race* (Stanford, CA: Stanford University Press, 2012); Meghan A. Burke, *Racial Ambivalence in Diverse Communities: Whiteness and the Power of Color-Blind Ideologies* (Lanham, MD: Lexington Books, 2012); Harriet Pollack, ed., *Eudora Welty, Whiteness, and Race* (Athens: University of Georgia Press, 2013); Dianne Suzett Harris, *Little White Houses: How the Postwar Home Constructed Race in America* (Minneapolis: University of Minnesota Press, 2013).

52. See, e.g., *The White Issue*, no. 73 of *Transition* (1996).

53. Richard Delgado makes essentially the same point, expressing amazement at "how white people, even ones of good will, twist discussions concerning race so that the conversation becomes about themselves." Delgado, *Critical Race Theory*, xiii.

4

Race and Nation, Identity and Power

Thinking Comparatively about Ethnic Systems

This essay, in quite a different form, started out as a theoretical introduction to a book I edited, Race and Nation: Ethnic Systems in the Modern World.[1] *In that book seventeen scholars compared the ethnic systems in as many countries around the globe, from Brazil to the Punjab to Eritrea to France. We were seeking similarities, differences, and connections between systems around the world that people have called "racial" or "ethnic." Drawing on the work of my coauthors as well as other theorists, my essay describes the relationships between race and nation, race and ethnicity, race and religion, race and narrative, and race and colonialism. With respect to this last factor, it finds as much race-making going on in the Chinese empire or the Soviet empire as in the British empire or the American. It enunciates the concept of the* racial moment, *when people in a particular system come to perceive the differences between ethnic groups as not mutable but rather indelible features of other groups. It concludes that race is a story we believe about the relationships of power between peoples, and it is written on the body. It further concludes that there are many such different stories of race—many racial systems—in different parts of the world.*

85

The old man and I sat in the dust of the bazaar, our backs against a white-washed wall, hiding from the sun in what little shade we could find. Radio Beijing blared from a loudspeaker on a pole nearby, unheeded by the people around us. Like my companion and 95 percent of the people in Turpan, this little oasis town in the Takla Makan desert in China's far western borderlands, they were Uygurs.[2] Hawk-nosed, with slanted eyes and tawny complexions, they spoke a kind of Turkic and very little Chinese. When they talked about their Chinese colonial overlords they spat with contempt and used words like "hate" and "kill."

To pass the time, the old man and I tried to make conversation, using the few Chinese words we each could command.

"So you're Japanese," he declared.

"No, I'm American," I answered.

"What's that?" he asked. Aside from the radio playing overhead, there was no local means of learning about the outside world. No Uygur language radio, no television, no newspaper. Few outside visitors except for Chinese bureaucrats. No way of knowing about the United States or much else outside Turpan.

I tried to describe my country to the gentleman. He wasn't buying it. No place like that existed, so far as he was concerned.

He knew about three kinds of people. There were *people*—that is, Uygurs, of many tribes and lineages. There were Chinese, the hated colonizers. And there were Japanese. Every two weeks a minibus brought about a dozen Japanese tourists to Turpan. Outsiders, in this man's worldview, people who were neither Uygur nor Chinese, were ipso facto Japanese. So I, a White American, was Japanese.

I expect that things have changed a lot in Turpan since that hot spring day in 1989. Probably today I would not be labeled Japanese. But that day I was not *mistaken for* Japanese; I *was* Japanese, in the language of the Turpan racial system of that time.

VARIETY IN ETHNIC AND RACIAL SYSTEMS

My encounter in Turpan suggests a few themes that reemerge persistently throughout this book. First, there are many kinds of racial and ethnic systems in the world, many ways that groups of people with different ancestries come into contact with one another, interact, and assort themselves into socially significant groupings. Second, these groups may initially see one another as simply ethnic or cultural groups, but at some point—I will call this *the racial moment*—they begin to see themselves as fundamentally and irrevocably different from one another. And third, at such times power is at issue between the groups, and there is a tendency to associate physical markers with racial difference. In short, *race is about power, and it is written on the body*. I have more to say about each of these themes in the pages that follow.

In almost every place on earth where people live, there is more than just one kind of people. And in each such place, there is a system of ideas and a language describing the relationships between them. Most often, those peoples arrange themselves in hierarchies. Theoretically, a system of difference might be articulated without hierarchy, but historically I know of no situation where racial or ethnic difference has endured without some element of domination. Frequently we use the terms *racial* and *ethnic* to characterize those hierarchies. According to the estimates of scholars and government agencies:[3]

- Afghanistan is 42 percent Pashtun, 27 percent Tajik, 9 percent Hazara, 9 percent Uzbek, and 13 percent various other ethnicities.
- Angola is 37 percent Ovimbundu, 25 percent Kimbundu, 13 percent Bakongo, 2 percent Mestico (mixed European and African), 1 percent European, and 22 percent others.
- Belgium is 58 percent Fleming, 31 percent Walloon, and 11 percent mixed and others.
- Bosnia and Herzegovina is 48 percent Bosniak, 38 percent Serb, and 14 percent Croat.
- Brunei is 67 percent Malay, 15 percent Chinese, and 18 percent others.
- The Gambia is 42 percent Mandinka, 18 percent Fula, 16 percent Wolof, 10 percent Jola, 9 percent Serahuli, and 5 percent various others.
- Kazakhstan is 53 percent Kazak, 30 percent Russian, 4 percent Ukrainian, 3 percent Uzbek, 2 percent German, 1 percent Tatar, 1 percent Uygur, and 6 percent others.

- Malaysia is 50 percent Malay, 24 percent Chinese, 11 percent indigenous, 7 percent Indian, and 8 percent others.
- Samoa is 93 percent Samoan, 7 percent Afakasis (people of mixed Polynesian and European ancestry), and less than 1 percent Europeans.
- Serbia is 66 percent Serb, 17 percent Albanian, 4 percent Hungarian, and 13 percent others.
- Slovakia is 86 percent Slovak, 10 percent Hungarian, 2 percent Roma, and smaller numbers of Czechs, Ruthenians, Ukrainians, Germans, and Poles.
- Switzerland is 65 percent German speaking, 18 percent French, 10 percent Italian, 1 percent Romansch, and 6 percent others.
- Trinidad and Tobago is 40 percent East Indian, 38 percent African, 21 percent mixed, and 1 percent White, Chinese, and others.
- The United Arab Emirates is 19 percent Emiri, 23 percent other Arab and Iranian, 50 percent South Asian, and 8 percent other expatriates from the West and Asia.

In every one of these places, there are dynamics between peoples that observers would call "racial" or "ethnic."

As one can tell from this recital, what are the relevant racial and ethnic groups—and what one may mean by such terms as *race, ethnicity,* or even *people*—is quite different in different places. So, too, there is substantial variation in the ways that peoples relate to one another in such diverse places.

Such variety in ethnic or racial systems raises a number of questions: What is the nature of ethnic systems? Are they the same things around the globe, are they distinct but related things, or are they very different things in different places? We see enough similarity that we refer to them by common terms such as *racial* and *ethnic*, but are the similarities we perceive real? If so, what are the commonalities in ethnic and racial systems around the globe? And what are the sources and shapes of the differences that exist in different places?

It is fair to say, whatever the differences may be, that nearly all the parts of the world have systems of hierarchy that most observers call racial or ethnic. For example, Colombia lists its population as 58 percent Mestizo,

20 percent White, 14 percent Mulatto, 4 percent Black, 3 percent mixed Black and Indian, and 1 percent Indian. Peru reports its population as 45 percent Indian, 37 percent Mestizo, 15 percent White, and 3 percent Other.[4] What does it mean that in these places great care is made to note fractions of mixed ancestry? Some would say that it represents an attempt on the part of individuals to flee association with Blackness or Indianness by emphasizing that they have some European ancestry. Others would say that the ideal of a Mestizo nation is an attempt to erase the Indian element entirely; still others, that the distinctions are primarily ones of class, not of ancestry at all—that "Indians" are just poor, rural "Mestizos."[5]

To take another example, consider Israel, where 80 percent of the population is Jewish. We all are familiar with the Jewish domination of the 20 percent of the Israeli population who are ethnic Arabs. But we are probably less familiar with the complex dynamics among various groups we might call "ethnic" within the Jewish part of the population. Not only are there splits along lines of religious affiliation—secular Jews versus the ultra-Orthodox, to take the two extremes—but there are also differences among Jews with respect to their origin. To simplify, there are those born in Israel (21 percent of the total population), immigrants who were born in Europe and the Americas (32 percent), those born in Africa (15 percent), and so on. This is to say nothing of divisions along class and political lines. How all those groups and identities assort themselves in the Israeli nation (or is it the Israeli community?) is an incredibly complex affair.[6]

Myanmar is another polyglot place: 68 percent ethnic Burman, 9 percent Shan, 7 percent Karen, 4 percent Rakhine, 3 percent Chinese, 2 percent Mon, and 2 percent Indian. Outsiders are generally aware of the dictatorship that ruled Myanmar for a couple of decades and the struggles for democracy and human rights, but fewer of us know much about the ethnic character of some of that oppression. Karens, in particular, have a long history of suffering at the hands of ethnic Burmans.[7]

ETHNICITY, RACE, NATION, IDENTITY, POWER

Once upon a time, a book or an essay on race and ethnicity would attempt to come up with a set of more or less universal rules about how such systems work, everywhere and always—something like Robert Park's famous "race relations cycle."[8] I am not as convinced as the avatars of the social scientific paradigm once were that there is indeed a universal set of laws, stages, patterns, or processes that describes the ways all ethnic groups shape themselves or interact with one another in all times and places. But I do think there are tissues of similarity and webs of relatedness that may help us think productively about widely disparate ethnic systems alongside each other.

My concern is partly, but not primarily, about the nexus between race and nation. This essay is more broadly about systems of relationships in various places that are most often called "ethnic" (less often called "racial"). In such systems, race, power, identity, and nation are all factors that shape the relationships between peoples. For our purposes in this book, one might suggest that identity is the issue at stake, power is the means, race (or ethnicity) is the interpretation, and nation is the usual frame of analysis. It is more complex than that, of course, and the factors always morph and interweave, but that will give the reader an idea where we are headed. Many studies of race or ethnicity—especially but not only those by political scientists—operate in a teleological mode. Starting with the geographically and politically convenient unit of the state, they search for the grounds of identity (by which they usually mean citizenship) in the nation that they assume to be the ethnic core of the polity.

For scholars of nationalism such as Ernest Gellner, the most important question is the nature of the nation. For Gellner, a nation more or less equals an ethnic group. He sees a particular ethnic group—a specific people with a shared history, language, and ancestry—as the foundation of each nation. Multiethnic states, for Gellner, are conceptually incoherent and inherently unstable. His concern is the nation. He does not attend to the way that the ethnic group is constructed and maintained, what are its processes and permutations; he takes it as a given, and a near-synonym for the nation. Then he devotes most of his attention to the relationship between the nation and the state. The state is the governing apparatus. The nation is a collection of people who see themselves as one and who aspire to be governed together as one people. Gellner sees an intimate connection in European history between the formation of particular ethnic groups and particular nations.[9]

Other nationalism scholars, like Anthony D. Smith, are open to more detailed exploration of the nature of ethnic groups. But Smith's main concern, as much as Gellner's, is the nature of the nation. For him, as for Gellner, each nation is founded on an ethnic group. As Smith writes, "Modern nations—a fusion of premodern ethnic identities and modern 'civic' elements—require the symbols, myths and memories of ethnic cores if they are to generate a sense of solidarity and purpose. . . . [T]here is . . . [an] inner 'antiquity' of many modern nations."[10]

The term *nation*, then, implies aspirations to achieve political sovereignty, or statehood, whereas *ethnic group* is simply a people (more about that in a moment).[11] For example, people who call themselves and are called by others Jews share a common identity and fellow feeling; they are an ethnic group. By contrast, Zionists in the first half of the twentieth century expressed aspirations to achieve statehood; that is, they saw the Jewish people as a nation, the core of a potential state, something more than an ethnic group.

I am interested in turning the angle of investigation the other way around. I am interested in the nation but primarily as a frame for ethnic systems, or insofar as national dynamics may influence ethnic dynamics. My main concern is race and ethnicity, their relationships and interactions, and the various ways they have arranged themselves around the globe in the modern world. I am less interested in the ways that racial, ethnic, and national identities are put in the service of, or hinder, the projects of forming and maintaining states.

ETHNICITY AND THE RACIAL MOMENT

If ethnicity and race are the central concerns of this essay, what then are they? At the broadest level, I see at least two ways that people tend to think about these matters. One way comes to us from the eighteenth- and nineteenth-century pseudoscience of Blumenbach, Gobineau, Cuvier, and their intellectual descendants (right down to Charles Murray and Richard Herrnstein, J. Philippe Rushton, Jon Entine, and Nicholas Wade as the twentieth century turns to the twenty-first).[12] Their vision is the one that most laypeople assume to be the way things are.

According to the pseudoscientists, there are big races (perhaps four or five of them) and smaller, subsidiary ethnic groups. In this view, race is about biology, genes, phenotype, the body. It is physical, inherited, immutable. The races are discrete from each other. Each race has not only specific distinguishing bodily features—skin color, hair texture, nose shape, and so forth—but also specific character qualities that cannot be erased; they may be suppressed, but eventually they will out. In this same mode of thinking, ethnicity is based on smaller human subdivisions of race. The members of various ethnic groups within a race look very much, if not completely, alike. Their differences are based on cultural or national divisions, such as language, citizenship, religion, child-rearing practices, food habits, and clothing. Ethnic differences, in this view, are mutable. Ethnicity derives from an ancestral group, but it can be changed by changing behavior.

An alternative view emphasizes the plasticity and constructedness of groups, whether we call them races or ethnic groups.[13] It notes that groups that are often called races have cultures and that there are average physical differences that can be observed among the peoples who are called ethnic groups, so the race/ethnic group dichotomy tends to break down pretty quickly. It emphasizes that race is not a thing or a condition but a *process*. This alternative view notes further that the understanding of the pseudoscientists was created in a particular time and place (Europe and the United States in the late eighteenth to early twentieth century). It was created among a set of people who were trying to explain the varieties of peoples that Europeans and Euro-Americans were encountering as they made colonies around the globe. Some would say that they were trying to naturalize colonialism, to lay it on the genes of people.[14]

I have argued elsewhere in favor of using "ethnicity" over "race" as a generic term for kinds of groups that operate on more or less the same bases.[15] Both are social and political constructs based on real or fictive common ancestry, which were generated in particular contexts and which have gone through particular histories. If one is focusing on internal group processes, they are much the same kinds of groups, whether one calls them "races," "ethnic groups," "ethnoracial groups," or some other common term. To distinguish between "race" and "ethnicity" is, I have

contended, to give in to the pseudoscientific racists by adopting their terminology. It is to conjure up visions of large, physical, immutable races
and smaller, cultural subgroups that are ethnic groups.

In the United States, it is true, the markers of the largest social groups
do in fact more or less correspond to pseudoscientific racial categories:
red, yellow, black, brown, and white. Those are the meaningful racial formations in American society.[16] But elsewhere, it is other markers that
make the big divisions. In Britain, at least for a time in the 1970s and
1980s, people whom Americans would call Asians and Africans many
Britons joined together under the single term *Black*.[17] Taoufik Djebali
argues that in North Africa throughout much of its history it was religion
that constituted the big divider. There religion is, in power terms, a "racial" divider, in that people on either side of the religious divide see each
other as fundamentally, immutably different from themselves.[18] So, too,
Han Chinese and Tibetans, Japanese and Koreans have something like
"racial" differences between them.[19]

Despite such evident similarities between "racial" and "ethnic" groups,
there *is* nonetheless a critical juncture in relationships between peoples
when they come to see each other, and are seen by outsiders, as fundamentally, essentially, immutably different. At such a juncture, the differences
they perceive are often laid on the body and the essential character. That
is what I would call *the racial moment*. At such times, that racializing
move is accompanied by at least an attempt by one group to exert power
over the other, or to highlight its own disempowerment. It is worth noting
that *race* is a term that seems static and essential, while *racialize* emphasizes agency and process: ongoing action taken to make hierarchy, to
position oneself and to create an Other.

Not to make too fine a point of it, I would claim that, at its point of
origin and in its ongoing formations, race is about power, and it is written
on the body. That is, the dividing into peoples has usually been done for
reasons of asserting power vis-à-vis one another. Those with more power
have frequently dictated the shape of the division: who would be in each
group, what would be the criteria for group membership, what would be
the relationships between the groups, and what members of each group
would have to do henceforth. Subordinate groups may do some reflexive

policing of their own, but the impetus comes from the powerful. The purpose of writing racial division onto the body is to naturalize it, to make it inevitable and thus no one's fault.

In the United States, for instance, much of race relations has depended on the one-drop rule: race relations have been defined as being between Black and White, and any person with any known African ancestry has been regarded as Black.[20] That was in order to keep the part White sons and daughters of slave owners and slave women as slaves and to keep them from asserting any measure of Whiteness. Subordinate status was written onto the Black body itself. Whites (and others) assumed that the people who were defined as Black had particular character qualities and life chances and that people defined as White naturally, by virtue of their supposed biological inheritance, were blessed with more positive character qualities and better life chances.

Yet for other groups in the United States, the one-drop rule does not apply, at least not in the same way and with the same pervasiveness. People who are part Indian and part White are sometimes reckoned Native American and sometimes White, depending on the degree of their connectedness to Native peoples, cultures, and institutions. People who are part Indian and part Black are generally reckoned Black. People who are part Asian and part something else have much more complex sets of ethnic possibilities and constraints.[21]

RACE AND RELIGION

To what extent is the sense of difference between groups derived from one's sense of race, hence imputed to the genes and the body, and more broadly to ethnicity? Alternatively, to what extent is the sense of difference a derivative of the religious identity one may embrace? Douglas Monroy describes the dominance of Catholic Christianity in nineteenth-century California and the ways that converting to Catholicism allowed some Indians, if not to enter the dominant class, at least to elevate themselves from the ranks of the most despised class.[22] My own research on Fiji suggests that the dominant group—ethnic Fijians—defines itself nearly as much by its Protestant identity as by its racial difference from the Hindu and Muslim Indo-Fijian subject class.[23] In similar fashion, Howard Eissenstat speaks of the power of adherence to Islam to make one Turkish; Adrienne Edgar writes about how commitment to Marxism could make one Turkmen; and Djebali describes how in much of North Africa identification with Christianity rather than with Islam tended to make one French.[24] There was also a religious aspect to the difference my Uygur Muslim acquaintance perceived between himself and the Chinese (and probably me).

But even in such situations, where religion is the label dividing peoples, race lurks not far away. For example, when French Catholics imputed a fundamental, immutable viciousness to Algerians who failed to convert, or when Spanish Catholics expressed a similar assessment of Indians who were similarly reluctant, the conquerors were making something like a racial judgment. Further, one cannot ignore the ways a dominating power's religion may be used as a weapon, to destroy the cultural underpinnings of a dominated people, whether it be Spanish Catholics destroying Indian culture or Japanese conquerors imposing Buddhism and Shinto on Ainu in order to make of them Japanese subjects.[25]

COLONIALISM

The power dynamic that makes racial difference historically has been tied to colonialism. This is true not only in the case of European colonialism. Other peoples also make race. Over many centuries, people from the North China Plain expanded their power into surrounding territories and united them into the Chinese empire. Some they incorporated fairly fully, forcing the national language (or at least its writing system) on them and reckoning them Han, or members of the Chinese race. Others they kept at greater distance conceptually and socially, as conquered and colonized peoples: Uygurs in what became Xinjiang Province, Dai and Miao in the Southwest, Tibetans on the mountainous plateaus of Qinghai and Tibet. On these last they wrote a story of immutable biological separateness and cultural unassimilability. And the Han Chinese take on Tibetans is every bit as vicious as the most racist White Americans' take on Blacks. In fact, it has many of the same themes: Tibetans are supposed to be filthy, lazy, sneaky, dishonest, promiscuous, and intellectually incapable of higher orders of achievement. This discourse attributing primitivity to the less powerful is also found in the way that Khmer Cambodians talk about Vietnamese Cambodians and the way Nordic Germans talk about Turkish Germans.[26]

There are lots of varieties of colonialism, and they seem always to result in racialized hierarchies separating the conquering people and the conquered. Consider the colonial conquests achieved and ethnic hierarchies created by the British in South Africa and India, the French in North Africa, the Germans in Southwest Africa, the Euro-Americans in California and Hawai'i, the Soviet Russians in Central Asia, and the Italians in Eritrea. In each of those places the colonizers created a language of racial order with themselves at the top and the local peoples arrayed below.[27]

There seem to be some common elements in these colonial processes and some instances of conscious modeling. For example, the Japanese consciously modeled their treatment of the Ainu in Hokkaido after the US treatment of Native peoples in North America. They employed two strategies in alternating periods. At times they attempted to assimilate the Ainu, make farmers and citizens out of them, change their language and religion, and force them to take Japanese names—in essence, to wipe out difference and make the Ainu into ordinary Japanese. On other occasions they kept the Ainu separate, restricted them on reservations, kept their educational and economic level low, and settled ethnic Japanese onto their lands.[28] Similarly, White South Africans modeled their dominance of Black South Africans on US racial policies: the "homelands" policy was a frank imitation of the US Indian reservation policy; apartheid was a crude facsimile of Jim Crow segregation of Black Americans.[29] In this context the Euro-American domination of peoples of color in the United States stands indisputably as a colonial process.[30]

Colonialism brought many common impacts to the places that were colonized. One of these, in modern-era European colonialism in many places, was the rapid decline of indigenous populations. Colonialism caused massive destruction of human lives—of Hereros in Southwest Africa, of Hawaiians, of Maori in Aotearoa/New Zealand, of Native peoples in the Americas—many by violence, more by disease. In each place, the colonizers mounted a discourse touting the inevitable extinction of the native people. Within these cultural frames the local people were naturalized as part of the landscape, like beasts of the field and forest. The extinction of Hawaiians, of Indians, of Maori was seen as inevitable, like the sad disappearance of the buffalo from the Great Plains, a reminder of a bygone era that could be celebrated in iconic memory by the descendants of the people who had done the killing. Because it was inevitable, it was nobody's fault.[31]

Colonial connections brought new ideas to the colonized places. Among those that the French brought to North Africa were "race," "nation," "citizenship," and "anti-Semitism," in the European meanings of those terms. The French created new racialized distinctions between Arabs (whom they characterized as oppressors, bad people, and lazy) and Berbers (whom they pictured as good people and noble sufferers at Arab hands)—all this as a means of dividing and ruling the conquered peoples.[32]

Colonialism also brought new peoples, and not just the colonizers. European and American colonial enterprises brought Chinese workers to California; Indians to South Africa, East Africa, Fiji, and the Caribbean; and Chinese, Japanese, Filipinos, and Koreans to Hawai'i. In several instances, a key task for the colonizers was to turn these peoples, or local minorities who could be separated off from the bulk of the native populace, into middleman minorities. They formed a kind of local elite, working for the colonial governors and also in small business. This was the situation the French attempted to create with the Jews in Tunisia and the Berbers in Algeria and Morocco; that the British created with Indians in Fiji, Uganda, and Jamaica; and that the Americans created with Northeast Asian immigrants in Hawai'i.[33]

There was no guarantee that such middleman minorities would always side with the colonizers: for example, the Jews sided with the French in North Africa, but the Berbers did not. Nor is colonialism necessarily forever. In the fullness of time, Black South Africans overturned White hegemony and attempted to build a multiracial democracy. And in Aotearoa/ New Zealand, descendants of Europeans and descendants of Maori are remaking their postcolonial society as a bicultural nation, 150 years after the colonial imposition.[34]

NATIONALISM

Questions such as how the state is made up, what constitutes citizenship, and what is the common civic glue animate much of the literature that relates to ethnicity. This is especially true among political scientists, but one finds it among historians and sociologists as well. Whether ethnic groups are taken to be primordial entities or "invented traditions" and "imagined communities," they seem fundamental to modern notions of the state, at least in Europe.[35]

The idea of one people corresponding to one nation is a powerful one. But, as we have seen, most nations are in fact polyglot places. Moreover, ethnic processes are not bound by national borders. Pashtuns, Kurds, and Uzbeks live on both sides of several borders in western Asia, as do Mongols and Koreans in East Asia. And what is one to make of the fact that the primordial tie of ancestry does not seem to unite into one people Japanese whose families have never left the home islands and their cousins who later returned after three or four generations in Brazil, only to find that you can't go home again and still be regarded as Japanese?[36] There are perhaps several transnational dynamics at work here. So it is unclear to me that the nation-state is necessarily the appropriate frame for investigation of ethnic questions. And I am fairly certain that questions of construction of the polity are not the most important questions when dealing with racial and ethnic issues.

I am aware that some distinguished American scholars such as Nathan Glazer and the late Arthur Schlesinger Jr. would likely disagree with me on this point. Glazer and Schlesinger were former liberals who spent a good portion of their respective careers writing about White ethnic groups in the United States. While they showed interest in the lives, institutions, and cultures of various peoples within the United States, both always had, as their overarching concern, how to create a single, harmonious American polity. Their bottom-line concern was essentially a civic one. Thus, in the latter stages of their careers, they waxed cranky, criticizing people who advocated a multicultural view of the United States and insisting on a high degree of homogeneity (which I read as demanding conformity—dare one say "submission"?—to Anglo-American culture and identity).[37]

Monroy raises the question of the degree to which membership in the civic community will be based on *demos*, the idea of universal citizenship, deriving in the modern world from the age of democratic revolutions, versus *ethnos*, membership in a particular core cultural, ancestral, or racial group. Ethnos emphasizes a common language and *Leitkultur* and goes beyond these to metaphors of blood and the body. It speaks of the spirit and the essence of the people who are believed to be central to the nation's life. Demos places the people, the citizenry, at the center, and insists that all are equally members on the basis of their common accession to the social contract.[38]

France is perhaps the quintessential nation to operate on the demos idea. The French have long been proud of their commitment to the idea that, whatever one's ancestry, if one becomes a French citizen, then one becomes French. And for the French, citizenship laws operate on the principle of jus soli: if you are born on French soil you are French. Yet even the French have had some ethnic hesitations about how far to extend membership. One need only read a newspaper account of the resurgence of the National Party or the anti-Muslim and anti-Roma antics of French politicians to be reminded that even in France there is a counterdiscourse of blood and belonging.[39]

Like the French, the Americans have long prided themselves on their ideology of assimilation. The large lady who presides over New York Harbor invites, "Give me your tired, your poor/Your huddled masses yearning to breathe free/The wretched refuse of your teeming shore/Send these, the nameless, tempest-tost to me/I lift my lamp beside the golden door."[40] The idea is, if you will change your clothes, your food, your language, and perhaps your religion, you can become fully an American. Well, as long as you are White. Formally, the United States recognizes both jus soli and jus sanguinis, right of birth by ancestry. Anyone who was born in the United States or anyone who had American parents is a citizen. But for much of US history Americans denied citizenship to a large class of people—those of African descent—despite the fact that they were born in the United States. Not just slaves, but free people of color as well, were denied the right to vote, to bear arms, to testify in court throughout the antebellum South.[41] Native Americans, likewise, have only intermittently been regarded as US citizens. Native American citizenship rights have usually

been predicated upon accepting individual landownership and abandoning Native American culture, habits, clothing, and so forth—essentially,
upon performing Whiteness.[42] And for most of US history the American
majority chose, on a racial basis, to refuse to naturalize certain people:
Asian immigrants could not become citizens.[43] Perhaps more important,
people of color have never been accorded full membership in the body
social, whatever their formal citizenship may have been.[44] So the United
States is a mixed bag with regard to the question of the basis of membership in the nation.

Other nations do this differently. China is a classic empire, with
a vast congeries of peoples—with different histories, languages, and
physiognomies—all calling themselves Han and another array of peoples
treated as domestic dependents, not quite full citizens.[45] In Germany ethnos reigns. Modern Germany was born amidst images of shared blood
among people who spoke a variety of languages that are vaguely commonly denominated as "German." It became a nation accompanied by
a soaring hymn to the German *Volk* and dedicated to modern science,
which at the time highlighted pseudoscientific racism. Few Germans
today dispute the granting of citizenship to so-called Volga Germans:
people whose ancestors migrated into the Russian empire some centuries
ago and who themselves applied for German membership after 1989.[46]
Meanwhile, Turkish Germans and other children of immigrants, even
though they were born in Germany, have enjoyed less than the full blessings of citizenship (the government has belatedly indicated a limited willingness to naturalize foreigners).[47]

TERMS AND CONCEPTS

Words matter. In discussions of matters racial and ethnic, one finds several terms and concepts that are used in different contexts. Sometimes
they seem to be describing much the same sort of thing in each case; other
times, they may mean very different things.

Settler. One finds the term *settler* used to refer to British people who
came to Aotearoa to displace the local Maori, for Dutch people who came

to South Africa to displace the local Xhosa, for Europeans who came North America to displace the Native Americans, and for Jewish Israelis who went to the West Bank to displace the local Palestinians. This term implies that there was no one there before the "settlers" came, or that the people who were there were heathen barbarians—that it was a wild land in need of settling by civilized people like the British, Dutch, Europeans, and Israelis.

Tribe. One finds the word *tribe* used in different settings for very different types of people and social organization. *Tribe* does connote a group of people organized by lineage, but it also implies that the people to whom it refers are more primitive in cultural attainments and less civilized than the people who are describing them. It may imply that they are natural parts of the landscape, like rocks and trees and antelopes and cougars, and thus reasonable objects for removal or extinction. In European history, the Goths and Visigoths are often referred to as "tribes" in contradistinction to the more "civilized" Romans. In early California, "tribe" meant a very small group of people, at the level of the village, with perhaps only a few hundred people and a simple social organization that depended on personal leadership.

Compare that to a "tribe" in South Africa, which might have hundreds of thousands of members and a complex, hierarchically stratified social organization. Dunbar Moodie writes, "In Africa 'tribalism' trumps all other explanations." In South Africa, "race" is widely understood to be an idea imposed by Europeans, but "tribe" is supposed to be local and primordial. Yet Moodie and most other scholars who study the peoples of South Africa disagree with this assessment. For them, "tribalism" is a European import, too. Before Europeans arrived, the modes of social organization were homestead and lineage groupings. Europeans brought the idea of the ethnic group with them, but they called it "tribe" in Africa. Europeans perceived—indeed, reified— language groupings and divided the people according to them. They installed "chiefs" when they found no existing leaders at the level they deemed appropriate. Mangosuthu Buthelezi and the Inkatha Party turned this idea of "tribe" to their own purposes in claiming all the Zulu peoples for their own leadership. Moodie points out that White South Africans had their own "tribes" also: British and Afrikaners. He also demonstrates that supposedly primordial "tribal" identities have in fact been quite fluid in cities and mining districts. In short, Moodie sees the idea of "tribe" as an outside imposition, a tool of racist, colonialist oppression.[48]

It is arresting that the sizes and kinds of social organization that Moodie describes as "tribes" in South Africa, students of the Russian empire such as Adrienne Edgar call "nationalities" in Central Asia.[49] This is in accordance with Soviet ideology, which refused to regard what the Russians were doing in Central Asia as having anything to do with colonialism. So there the peoples they dominated in many of the same ways that British and Afrikaners dominated Black Africans went by the term *nationality* instead. But it was more or less the same thing. In Turkmenistan, as in South Africa and Fiji, the colonial power more or less created tribe and nationality out of many lineages and local chiefdoms. Unlike the British, the Soviets rejected racialist explanations, yet their actions led to racialized distinctions.

Mestizaje. *Mestizaje* is a term that wields considerable intellectual cachet. At its historical base, the term derives from the nation-building project of José Vasconcelos and other Latin American intellectuals of the 1920s. A Mexican politician and scientifico-mystic, Vasconcelos extolled his country people (and indeed all Latin Americans) as *la raza cosmica*, a people specially gifted to lead the world on account of their mixed European and Native American (especially Aztec) bloodlines. In more recent times, Gloria Anzaldúa brought the issue to the United States in one of the most frequently cited pieces of cultural criticism of the late twentieth century, *Borderlands/La Frontera: The New Mestiza*. Anzaldúa challenged all kinds of binary category constructions, from race to nationality to gender to sexuality to language. In the place of neat categories, she exalted mixedness, multiplicity, paradox, simultaneity, contrariness, and betweenness. Gary Nash followed with "The Hidden History of Mestizo America," his presidential address to the Organization of American Historians.[50] From the late 1990s through the opening decades of the new century, *mestizaje* and a cognate term, *hybridity*, came to be used promiscuously in literary and cultural studies, to the point that their meaning eroded in a flood of self-conscious fashion following.[51]

In nineteenth-century California, as in Mexico, the idea embraced the blending of Spanish and Indian but erased the African and Asian elements in the people's racial heritage. As Monroy writes, "How racial mixture and a concern for racial purity could exist congruously in the same society" was a powerful issue. The knowledge among the conquerors that they shared bloodlines with the people they dominated and feared lent force and vigor to their assertion of racial superiority. In El Salvador in the twentieth century, a hegemonic state discourse of mestizaje hushed public debate about discrimination against Afro-Latinos and Indians. Further, by defining ethnic politics as atavistic and even antinationalist, the mestizaje doctrine legitimized repressive state measures against ethnic and racial minorities.[52]

The flip side of mestizaje, of course, is the myth of racial purity. All populations are mixed, but for some groups in some places the fiction of purity played a critical role as social glue. Such was the case in pre–World War II Japan (but not during the earlier imperial period) and among Boers in South Africa.[53]

Blackness. There is an abiding fixation on the idea that race is something limited to, or generated from, the relationships between Black and White, and something found mainly in the United States. The scholarly literature on race in the United States is vastly richer than the literature on race or its analogues anywhere else in the world, and by far the majority of that literature is about Black and White.[54] There may be other racial groups in the United States and the world, but, in the words of one of African America's most accomplished scholars, "the Black-White relationship is the master narrative of racial studies."[55]

There are peoples called "Black" in several parts of the world. Their Blacknesses are related, but they are not always exactly the same thing. The Black Consciousness movement of South Africa in the 1960s had a specific content and meaning. It was a reaction against the White nationalist movement that had wedded Afrikaners and English descendants in creating the myth of White racial purity, the edifice of apartheid, and the oppressive fiction of Black "tribal" separate development in the Bantustans. That movement had only a tenuous place for many Coloureds, that is, people of mixed race.

There was also a Black Consciousness movement in Brazil, in the 1980s. It included echoes of its South African predecessor but operated in a very different context. In Brazil, the movement also sought to undermine White domination, but there that domination took place through the myth of a raceless society, not through walling people off in separate and supposedly pure social boxes. The social situation in Brazil in the 1980s in fact looked much more like the situation in Hawai'i in the 1990s and 2000s. Those farthest down seek to unite with those in the middle against the Whites at the top, except in the Brazilian case it is dark people and racially mixed people while in Hawai'i it is Hawaiians and Asians. In Hawai'i, Blackness plays no part in a thoroughly racialized social structure.[56]

All three of these racial situations are very far removed, though not totally uninfluenced by, Blackness in the United States. In the United States, Blackness was not a self-generated panethnic category created for self-defense but rather an oppressive imposition—the one-drop rule—though in the 1960s and after the Black Power movement it took on the form of positive self-assertion. In the United States, Blackness had no place for anyone who lacked African ancestors. Contrast that to political Blackness in Britain in the 1980s, which was an attempt to make common cause among many peoples descended from New Commonwealth countries, from Pakistan and the Middle East as well as the West Indies. Political Blackness in Britain for a time hid those differences and let West Indies–descended people dominate the Black agenda (see chapter 2).

There was a Black nationalist movement in Jamaica, too, identified with the person and ideas of Marcus Garvey. That movement influenced later US Black Consciousness movements, which in turn contributed to Jamaican Black nationalism. Another root of the Jamaican movement, however, was the idea of Ethiopia and the person of Haile Selassie, which made their influence felt through Rastafarianism and Reggae. All these racial movements were at least slightly affected by the Pan-African ideas of Garvey, W. E. B. Du Bois, Kwame Nkrumah, Sékou Touré, and others. That is even true in the Hawaiian case (if one counts the 1990s popularity of Jawaiian music, a strange blend of Reggae and slack-key guitar) and among Turkish-descended hip-hop youths in Germany.[57]

One place where outsiders regard the people as Black operated even more distinctly than these four: Eritrea. There people separate themselves from sub-Saharan Africans and see themselves more as part of the culture of the Middle East. Within the region Eritreans and Ethiopians have deep and abiding senses of identity and difference from each other, without recourse to an ideology of Blackness.[58]

There are many places where Blackness, far from being the master narrative, is a nonissue. In Japan, Hawai'i, Morocco, Tunisia, Algeria, Aotearoa, Cambodia, Turkmenistan, the Punjab, and China—in all these places and more, local people know that Black people exist, and they know some stereotypical things about Blacks. But no part of their highly racialized local scene is about people who are called Black. Blackness and African-descended people are hugely influential in modern racial issues, but they are far from the whole story, or even necessarily the main story.

Narrative. Among Pacific people, where I have spent a good bit of my adult life, before one speaks in public one must chant one's ancestry. The story begins back in the mists of time and accounts for all the main lines of one's genealogy. Only after I have told who my people are and what is the land that gave me birth can I speak of the matter of the day, for only when I have done so can you know who I am and judge my words. Stephen Cornell and others write eloquently of the power of narrative in ethnic identity. "We are the people who . . ." and, by implication, "you are not," are narratives that lie at the core of ethnic self-assertion and racial hierarchy making.[59]

I am impressed by the powerful role that is played by racial and ethnic narratives in creating social hierarchy and social glue. In Eritrea, it is the tale of descent from King Solomon and the Queen of Sheba. Among Afrikaners, it is the Great Trek and divine triumph over the Zulus at the Battle of Blood River. In Japan, the story of Emperor Jinmu was used as a tool in the forcible remaking of Okinawans and Ainu into ethnic Japanese as part of "the emperor's family-nation" since time immemorial. In Hawai'i, on the Hawaiian side, it is the story of the *mahele* and the overthrow of the Hawaiian monarchy by haole colonizers that gives vitality to Hawaiian ethnic self-assertion. On the White side, the aloha story of the multiracial Paradise of the Pacific attracts more Whites to the islands and quiets native resistance.[60]

These are examples of narrative's influence at the level of the group, as the most powerful sort of ethnic glue that holds a group together. But at the individual level, race is narrative, too. Race is the story of what we think we know about a person, a story we write on that person's features. For example, in California I may meet a person with light brown skin, brown eyes, black hair, and a slim build, and I may assume on the basis of what I read on his features that he is a Filipino. On interacting with him and learning his personal story, however, I may find out that he is Chicano, or Samoan, or Lebanese, or mixed Japanese and White. The same person might in another context be taken for Egyptian or Rom. Once, in 1989, far out of my usual context, I was even taken for Japanese.

CONCLUSION

Everywhere there are multiple peoples in one social space there develops a language of hierarchy that one may call "racial" or "ethnic." Such a hierarchy seems tied to colonialism and impositions of power by some groups over others, as well as defensive oppositions pursued by the less powerful. Racial thinking and signifying, then, are means to naturalize those oppressions and resistances. The formation of nations is often influenced by racial concerns, but nation making and the meaning of citizenship are not the primary objects of race making. Concepts such as "mestizaje" and "Black" that derive from particular racial contexts may be used in other contexts, but they do not necessarily mean the exact same thing in those other contexts. In fact, there is a host of different sorts of racial and ethnic systems in various places around the world. Each has its own configurations of peoples and issues; each generates its own language and hierarchy. Different systems may be related to one another, or they may not. There is no master narrative of racial and ethnic relationships.

NOTES

Steve Cornell is the person who first led me to think systematically about the territory this essay addresses. I am grateful for comments on the earlier manuscript by Reginald Daniel, Taoufik Djebali, Adrienne Edgar, Howard Eissenstat,

Rick Fogarty, Violet Showers Johnson, Cluny Macpherson, Patrick Miller, Doug Monroy, Dunbar Moodie, Lori Pierce, Elisabeth Schäfer-Wünsche, Christine Su, Virginia Tilley, Tekle Woldemikael, and Miyuki Yonezawa.

1. Paul Spickard, ed., *Race and Nation: Ethnic Systems in the Modern World* (New York: Routledge, 2005), 1–29.

2. I follow the Chinese Pinyin spelling here; some use the spelling *Uighur.*

3. Percentages in this section are taken from "Ethnicity and Race by Countries," www.infoplease.com/ipa/A0855617.html (retrieved December 2, 2011).

4. Ibid.

5. Marisol de la Cadena, *Indigenous Mestizos: The Politics of Race and Culture in Cuzco, Peru, 1919–1991* (Durham, NC: Duke University Press, 2000).

6. "Ethnicity and Race by Countries," www.infoplease.com/ipa/A0855617 .html (retrieved December 2, 2011).

7. Ibid.

8. Robert Ezra Park, *Race and Culture* (New York: Free Press, 1950). Other examples of this genre are Michael Banton, *Race Relations* (New York: Basic Books, 1967); Fredrik Barth, ed., *Ethnic Groups and Boundaries* (Boston: Little, Brown, 1969); H. M. Blalock Jr., *Toward a Theory of Minority-Group Relations* (New York: Wiley, 1967); Abner Cohen, ed., *Urban Ethnicity* (London: Tavistock, 1974); Oliver C. Cox, *Caste, Class and Race* (New York: Modern Reader, 1970; orig. 1948); Roger Daniels and Harry H. L. Kitano, *American Racism* (Englewood Cliffs, NJ: Prentice Hall, 1970); Arnold Dashevsky, ed., *Ethnic Identity in Society* (Chicago: Rand McNally, 1976); Harry H. L. Kitano, *Race Relations*, 4th ed. (Englewood Cliffs, NJ: Prentice Hall, 1991); Martin N. Marger, *Race and Ethnic Relations* (Belmont, CA: Wadsworth, 1985); R. A. Schermerhorn, *Comparative Ethnic Relations* (Chicago: University of Chicago Press, 1970); George Eaton Simpson and J. Milton Yinger, *Racial and Cultural Minorities*, 4th ed. (New York: Harper and Row, 1972).

9. Ernest Gellner, *Nations and Nationalism* (Ithaca, NY: Cornell University Press, 1983). See also E. J. Hobsbawn, *Nations and Nationalism since 1780*, 2nd ed. (Cambridge: Cambridge University Press, 1990).

10. Anthony D. Smith, *The Ethnic Origins of Nations* (Oxford: Blackwell, 1986), back cover. See also Anthony D. Smith, *Nationalism and Modernism* (London: Routledge, 1998).

11. See Paul Spickard and W. Jeffrey Burroughs, "We Are a People," in *We Are a People: Narrative and Multiplicity in Constructing Ethnic Identity*, ed. Paul Spickard and W. Jeffrey Burroughs (Philadelphia: Temple University Press, 2000), 1–19.

12. Johann Friedrich Blumenbach, *The Anthropological Treatises of Johann Friedrich Blumenbach* (Boston: Milford House, 1973; orig. 1865); Joseph Arthur, comte de Gobineau, *The Inequality of Races* (New York: H. Fertig, 1915; orig. 1856); J. Philippe Rushton, *Race, Evolution, and Behavior*, 3rd ed. (Charles Darwin Research Institute, 2000); Richard J. Herrnstein and Charles Murray, *The Bell*

Curve: Intelligence and Class Structure in American Life (New York: Free Press, 1994); John Entine, *Taboo: Why Black Athletes Dominate Sports and Why We're Afraid to Talk about It* (New York: Public Affairs, 2000); Nicholas Wade, *A Troublesome Inheritance: Genes, Race, and Human History* (New York: Penguin, 2014); Emmanuel Chukwudi Eze, ed., *Race and the Enlightenment* (Oxford: Blackwell, 1997); C. Loring Brace, *"Race" Is a Four-Letter Word* (New York: Oxford University Press, 2005).

Writers such as Dinesh D'Souza, Thomas Sowell, Samuel Huntington, and Thilo Sarrazin essentialize "culture" and use it to the same ends as the pseudoscientists use "race"; see D'Souza, *The End of Racism: Principles for a Multiracial Society* (New York: Free Press, 1995); Sowell, *Ethnic America* (New York: Basic Books, 1981); Huntington, *The Clash of Civilizations and the Remaking of World Order* (New York: Simon and Schuster, 1996); Huntington, *Who Are We? The Challenges to America's National Identity* (New York: Simon and Schuster, 2005); Sarrazin, *Deutschland schafft sich ab* (Germany Abolishes Itself) (Munich: Random House, 2010).

13. See, e.g., Miri Song, *Choosing Ethnic Identity* (Cambridge: Polity Press, 2003); Michael Omi and Howard Winant, *Racial Formation in the United States*, rev. ed. (New York: Routledge, 1994); Stephen Cornell and Douglas Hartmann, *Ethnicity and Race: Making Identities in a Changing World*, 2nd ed. (Thousand Oaks, CA: Pine Forge Press, 2007); Steve Martinot, *The Rule of Racialization* (Philadelphia: Temple University Press, 2003).

14. Reginald Horsman, *Race and Manifest Destiny: The Origins of American Racial Anglo-Saxonism* (Cambridge, MA: Harvard University Press, 1981); Matthew Frye Jacobson, *Special Sorrows: The Diasporic Imaginations of Irish, Polish, and Jewish Immigrants in the United States*, rev. ed. (Berkeley: University of California Press, 2002), 177–216; Catherine Hall, ed., *Cultures of Empire: Colonizers in Britain and the Empire in the Nineteenth and Twentieth Centuries* (New York: Routledge, 2000); Robert J. C. Young, *Colonial Desire: Hybridity in Theory, Culture and Race* (London: Routledge, 1995); Tomás Almaguer, *Racial Fault Lines: The Historical Origins of White Supremacy in California* (Berkeley: University of California Press, 1994); Stephen Jay Gould, *The Mismeasure of Man*, rev. ed. (New York: Norton, 1996); Bruce Dain, *A Hideous Monster of the Mind: American Race Theory in the Early Republic* (Cambridge, MA: Harvard University Press, 2002); Paul Spickard, *Almost All Aliens: Immigration, Race, and Colonialism in American History and Identity* (New York: Routledge, 2007); Paul A. Kramer, *The Blood of Government: Race, Empire, the United States, and the Philippines* (Chapel Hill: University of North Carolina Press, 2006); Matthew Frye Jacobson, *Barbarian Virtues: The United States Encounters Foreign Peoples at Home and Abroad, 1876–1917* (New York: Hill and Wang, 2001).

15. Spickard and Burroughs, "We Are a People," 2–7.

16. Of course, there are meaningful differences between peoples within each of the US races. Korean Americans and Vietnamese Americans are quite different from one another, much more so than are, say, Irish Americans and Italian Americans.

17. Stephen Small, *Racialised Barriers: The Black Experience in the United States and England in the 1980s* (London: Routledge, 1994); Floya Anthias and Nira Yuval-Davis, *Racialized Boundaries: Race, Nation, Gender, Colour, and Class and the Anti-Racist Struggle* (London: Routledge, 1992). See also chapter 2.

18. Taoufik Djebali, "Ethnicity and Power in North Africa: Tunisia, Algeria, and Morocco," in Spickard, *Race and Nation*, 135–54.

19. On the former, see Paul Spickard and Rowena Fong, "Ethnic Relations in the People's Republic of China," *Journal of Northeast Asian Studies* (Fall 1994): 26–48.

20. F. James Davis, *Who Is Black? One Nation's Definition* (University Park: Pennsylvania State University Press, 1991); G. Reginald Daniel, "Passers and Pluralists: Subverting the Racial Divide," in *Racially Mixed People in America*, ed. Maria P. P. Root (Newbury Park, CA: Sage, 1992), 91–107.

21. Circe Sturm, *Blood Politics: Race, Culture, and Identity in the Cherokee Nation of Oklahoma* (Berkeley: University of California Press, 2002); James F. Brooks, ed., *Confounding the Color Line: The Indian-Black Experience in North America* (Lincoln: University of Nebraska Press, 2002); Theda Perdue, *"Mixed Blood" Indians: Racial Construction in the Early South* (Athens: University of Georgia Press, 2005); Teresa Williams-León and Cynthia Nakashima, eds., *The Sum of Our Parts: Mixed Heritage Asian Americans* (Philadelphia: Temple University Press, 2001); Paul Spickard, "What Must I Be? Asian Americans and the Question of Multiethnic Identity," *Amerasia Journal* 23.1 (Spring 1997): 43–60.

22. Douglas Monroy, "Guilty Pleasures: The Satisfactions of Racial Thinking in Early-Nineteenth-Century California," in Spickard, *Race and Nation*, 33–52.

23. Michael C. Howard, *Fiji: Race and Politics in an Island State* (Vancouver: University of British Columbia Press, 1991); Brij V. Lal, *Broken Waves: A History of the Fiji Islands in the Twentieth Century* (Honolulu: University of Hawai'i Press, 1992); Stewart Firth and Daryl Tarte, eds., *20th Century Fiji* (Suva: USP Solutions, 2001); Deryck Scarr, *Fiji: A Short History* (Sydney: George Allen and Unwin, 1984); Victor Lal, *Fiji: Coups in Paradise: Race, Politics and Military Intervention* (London: Zed, 1990); Brij V. Lal, *Power and Prejudice: The Making of the Fiji Crisis* (Wellington: New Zealand Institute of International Affairs, Victoria University, 1988); Deryck Scarr, *Fiji: Politics of Illusion: The Military Coups in Fiji* (Kensington: New South Wales University Press, 1988); Jeremaia Waqanisau, "The Only Option: Fijian Coup d'État: A Product of Political Development" (MA thesis, Cartmel College, University of Lancaster, UK, 1989); Robert T. Robertson and Akosita Tamanisau, *Fiji: Shattered Coups* (Leichhardt, NSW: Pluto Press, 1988);

Robert T. Robertson, *Multiculturalism and Reconciliation in an Indulgent Republic: Fiji after the Coups, 1987–1998* (Suva: Fiji Institute of Applied Studies, 1998); Jon Fraenkel, Stewart Firth, and Brij V. Lal, eds., *The 2006 Military Takeover in Fiji: A Coup to End All Coups?* (Canberra: Australia National University Press, 2011); Jon Fraenkel and Stewart Firth, eds., *From Election to Coup in Fiji: The 2006 Campaign and Its Aftermath* (Canberra: Australia National University Press, 2011).

24. Howard Eissenstat, "Metaphors of Race and Discourse of Nation: Racial Theory and State Nationalism in the First Decades of the Turkish Republic," in Spickard, *Race and Nation*, 239–56; Adrienne Lynn Edgar, *Tribal Nation: The Making of Soviet Turkmenistan* (Princeton, NJ: Princeton University Press, 2004); Taoufik Djebali, "Ethnicity and Power in North Africa: Tunisia, Algeria, and Morocco," in Spickard, *Race and Nation*, 135–54.

25. Miyuki Yonezawa, "Memories of Japanese Identity and Racial Hierarchy," in Spickard, *Race and Nation*, 115–32.

26. Christine Su, "Becoming Cambodian: Ethnicity and the Vietnamese in Kampuchea," in Spickard, *Race and Nation*, 273–96; Paul Spickard, "Chinese Americans, Turkish Germans: Parallels in Two Racial Systems," in *Multiple Identities: Migrants, Ethnicity, and Membership*, ed. Paul Spickard (Bloomington: Indiana University Press, 2013), 290–302; Spickard and Fong, "Ethnic Relations in the People's Republic of China."

27. For insights into this general process, see Albert Memmi, *The Colonizer and the Colonized* (Boston: Beacon Press, 1967; orig. 1956). On South Africa, see T. Dunbar Moodie, *The Rise of Afrikanerdom: Power, Apartheid, and the Afrikaner Civil Religion* (Berkeley: University of California Press, 1975); Ivan Evans, *Bureaucracy and Race: Native Administration in South Africa* (Berkeley: University of California Press, 1997); Leroy Vail, ed., *The Creation of Tribalism in Southern Africa* (London: James Currey, 1989); T. Dunbar Moodie, *Going for Gold: Men, Mines, and Migration* (Berkeley: University of California Press, 1994).

On India, see Nicholas B. Dirks, *Castes of Mind: Colonialism and the Making of Modern India* (Princeton, NJ: Princeton University Press, 2001); Susan Bayly, *Caste, Society and Politics in India* (Cambridge: Cambridge University Press, 1999).

On French North Africa, see Djebali, "Ethnicity and Power in North Africa"; Ofra Bengio and Gabriel Ben-Dor, eds., *Minorities and the State in the Arab World* (Boulder, CO: Lynne Rienner, 1999); André Chouraqui, *Between East and West: A History of the Jews of North Africa*, trans. Michel M. Bernet (Philadelphia: Jewish Publication Society of America, 1968); Michael Laskier, *North African Jewry in the Twentieth Century* (New York: New York University Press, 1994).

On Germans in Southwest Africa, see Elisabeth Schäfer-Wünsche, "On Becoming German: Politics of Membership in Germany," in Spickard, *Race and Nation*, 195–211; Jeremy Sarkin, *Germany's Genocide of the Herero* (London:

James Currey, 2011); Jeremy Sarkin, *Colonial Genocide and Reparations Claims in the 21st Century: The Socio-Legal Context of Claims under International Law by the Herero against Germany for Genocide in Namibia, 1904–1908* (New York: Praeger, 2008).

On California, begin with Douglas Monroy, *Thrown among Strangers: The Making of Mexican Culture in Frontier California* (Berkeley: University of California Press, 1993); Almaguer, *Racial Fault Lines*; Albert Camarillo, *Chicanos in a Changing Society: From Mexican Pueblos to American Barrios in Santa Barbara and Southern California, 1848–1930* (Cambridge, MA: Harvard University Press, 1979); William Deverell, *Whitewashed Adobe: The Rise of Los Angeles and the Remaking of Its Mexican Past* (Berkeley: University of California Press, 2004); David Torres-Rouff, *Before LA: Race, Space, and Municipal Power in Los Angeles, 1781–1894* (New Haven, CT: Yale University Press, 2013).

On Hawai'i, places to start include Lilikala Kame'eleihiwa, *Native Land and Foreign Desires* (Honolulu: Bishop Museum Press, 1992); Jonathan Osorio, *Dismembering Lahui: A History of the Hawaiian Nation to 1887* (Honolulu: University of Hawai'i Press, 2002); Lori Pierce, "Creating a Racial Paradise: Citizenship and Sociology in Hawai'i," in Spickard, *Race and Nation*, 69–86; Pierce, "'The Whites Have Created Modern Honolulu': Ethnicity, Racial Stratification, and the Discourse of Aloha," in *Racial Thinking in America: Uncompleted Independence*, ed. Paul Spickard and G. Reginald Daniel (Notre Dame, IN: University of Notre Dame Press, 2004), 124–54; Haunani-Kay Trask, *From a Native Daughter: Colonialism and Sovereignty in Hawai'i* (Monroe, ME: Common Courage Press, 1993).

On Soviet Central Asia, see Edgar, *Tribal Nation*. On Eritrea, see Tekle M. Woldemikael, "Eritrea's Identity as a Cultural Crossroads," in Spickard, *Race and Nation*, 337–54.

28. Yonezawa, "Memories of Japanese Identity and Racial Hierarchy"; Michael Weiner, ed., *Japan's Minorities: The Illusion of Homogeneity* (London: Routledge, 1997); Brett L. Walker, *The Conquest of Ainu Lands: Ecology and Culture in Japanese Expansion, 1590–1800* (Berkeley: University of California Press, 2006); Isao Kikuchi, *Ainu minzoku to Nihonjin: Higashi Ajia no naka no Ezochi* (Tokyo: Asahi Shinbunsha, 1994). For the parallel developments in US Indian policy, see Francis Paul Prucha, *The Great Father: The United States Government and the American Indians*, abridged ed. (Lincoln: University of Nebraska Press, 1986); S. Lyman Tyler, *A History of Indian Policy* (Washington, DC: US Department of the Interior, Bureau of Indian Affairs, 1973).

29. Fredrickson, *White Supremacy*; Moodie, *Rise of Afrikanerdom*.

30. For an extended discussion of this issue, traced across four centuries of American history, see Spickard, *Almost All Aliens*.

31. Narratives of inevitable, therefore blameless, Native decline and disappearance are on display in Ralph S. Kuykendall, *The Hawaiian Kingdom*, 3 vols.

(Honolulu: University of Hawai'i Press, 1938–67), and in any United States history textbook written before 1970. Critiques of such narratives can be found in Brian W. Dippie, *The Vanishing American: White Attitudes and US Indian Policy* (Middletown, CT: Wesleyan University Press, 1982); Robert F. Berkhofer Jr., *The White Man's Indian: Images of the American Indian from Columbus to the Present* (New York: Random House, 1978); Trask, *From a Native Daughter*.

32. Djebali, "Ethnicity and Power in North Africa"; Richard S. Fogarty, "Between Subjects and Citizens: Algerians, Islam, and French National Identity during the Great War," in Spickard, *Race and Nation*, 171–94; Richard S. Fogarty, *Race and War in France: Colonial Subjects in the French Army, 1914–1918* (Baltimore: Johns Hopkins University Press, 2008).

33. Edna Bonacich, "A Theory of Middleman Minorities," *American Sociological Review* 38 (1970): 583–94; Jonathan H. Turner and Edna Bonacich, "Toward a Composite Theory of Middleman Minorities," *Ethnicity* 7 (1980): 144–58; Walter P. Zenner, "Middleman Minority Theories: A Critical Review," in *Sourcebook on the New Immigration*, ed. Roy Simon Bryce-Laporte (New Brunswick, NJ: Transaction, 1980), 413–25; Candace Fujikane and Jonathan Y. Okamura, eds., *Whose Vision? Asian Settle Colonialism in Hawai'i*, special issue, *Amerasia Journal* 26.2 (2000).

The literature on the Chinese diaspora is enormous. See, e.g., Maurice Freedman, "The Chinese in Southeast Asia," in *Race Relations in World Perspective*, ed. Andrew W. Lind (Honolulu: University of Hawai'i Press, 1955), 388–411; Adam McKeown, *Melancholy Order: Asian Migration and the Globalization of Borders* (New York: Columbia University Press, 2008); Adam McKeown, *Chinese Migrant Networks and Cultural Change: Peru, Chicago, and Hawai'i, 1900–1936* (Chicago: University of Chicago Press, 2001); Philip A. Kuhn, *Chinese among Others: Emigration in Modern Times* (Lanham, MD: Rowman and Littlefield, 2009); Lynn Pan, *Sons of the Yellow Emperor: A History of the Chinese Diaspora* (Tokyo: Kodansha, 1994); Laurence J. C. Ma and Carolyn L. Cartier, eds., *The Chinese Diaspora* (Lanham, MD: Rowman and Littlefield, 2003).

The literature on the South Asian diaspora is similarly immense. Some works with which to start are Jhumpa Lahiri, *Interpreter of Maladies* (Boston: Houghton Mifflin, 1999); John C. Hawley, ed., *India in Africa, Africa in India: Indian Ocean Cosmopolitanisms* (Bloomington: Indiana University Press, 2008); Sunil Bhatia, *American Karma: Race, Culture, and Identity in the Indian Diaspora* (New York: New York University Press, 2007); Vijay Prashad, *The Karma of Brown Folk* (Minneapolis: University of Minnesota Press, 2001); Sandhya Shukla, *India Abroad: Diasporic Cultures of Postwar America and England* (Princeton, NJ: Princeton University Press, 2003).

34. On Aotearoa/New Zealand, see Cluny Macpherson, "Reinventing the Nation: Building a Bicultural Future from a Monocultural Past in Aotearoa/New

Zealand," in Spickard, *Race and Nation*, 215–38; Donna Awatere, *Maori Sovereignty* (Auckland: Broadsheet Publications, 1984); Paul Spoonley, Cluny Macpherson, and David Pearson, eds., *Nga Patai: Racism and Ethnic Relations in Aotearoa New Zealand* (Palmerston North: Dunmore Press, 1996); Paul Spoonley and Cluny Macpherson, eds., *Nga Take: Ethnic Relations and Racism in Aotearoa/New Zealand* (Palmerston North: Dunmore Press, 1991).

35. The intersection between ethnic questions and national ones is discussed in Eric Hobsbawm and Terence Ranger, eds., *The Invention of Tradition* (Cambridge: Cambridge University Press, 1983); Benedict Anderson, *Imagined Communities: Reflections on the Origin and Spread of Nationalism*, rev. ed. (London: Verso, 1991); Gellner, *Nations and Nationalism*; Anthony D. Smith, *The Ethnic Origins of Nations* (Oxford: Blackwell, 1986); Smith, *Nationalism and Modernism*; Geoff Eley and Ronald Grigor Suny, eds., *Becoming National* (New York: Oxford University Press, 1996); Hobsbawm, *Nations and Nationalism since 1780*; John A. Armstrong, *Nations before Nationalism* (Chapel Hill: University of North Carolina Press, 1982).

36. Daniel Linger, *No One Home: Brazilian Selves Remade in Japan* (Stanford, CA: Stanford University Press, 2002); Joshua Hotaka Roth, *Brokered Homeland: Japanese Brazilian Migrants in Japan* (Ithaca, NY: Cornell University Press, 2002); Jeffrey Lesser, *Searching for a Homeland Abroad: Japanese Brazilians and Transnationalism* (Durham, NC: Duke University Press, 2003); Takeyuki Tsuda, *Strangers in the Ethnic Homeland: Japanese Brazilian Return Migration in Transnational Perspective* (New York: Columbia University Press, 2003).

37. Nathan Glazer, *Affirmative Discrimination: Ethnic Inequality and Public Policy* (Cambridge, MA: Harvard University Press, 1987); Nathan Glazer, *We Are All Multiculturalists Now* (Cambridge, MA: Harvard University Press, 1997); Arthur M. Schlesinger Jr., *The Disuniting of America: Reflections on a Multicultural Society*, rev. ed. (New York: Norton, 1998).

38. Monroy, "Guilty Pleasures"; see also Rogers Brubaker, *Citizenship and Nationhood in France and Germany* (Cambridge, MA: Harvard University Press, 1992).

39. "French Reform Targets Immigrants," *International Herald Tribune*, May 18, 2006; Elaine Sciolino, "Pan to Test Immigrants' DNA Divides France," *International Herald Tribune*, October 12, 2007; "Pseudoscientific Bigotry in France," *International Herald Tribune*, October 22, 2007; Elizabeth Bryant, "Immigration Stirs France: President Bids to Enforce Expulsion Rules as Lawmakers Debate Culture, Language Tests," *San Francisco Chronicle*, September 21, 2007; Devorah Lauter, "As the French Debate Their Identity, Some Recoil," *Los Angeles Times*, December 14, 2009; Devorah Lauter, "Muslims in France Feel Sting of Bias," *Los Angeles Times*, July 22, 2010; Elaine Sciolino, "Ban Religious Attire in School, French Panel Says," *New York Times*, December 12, 2003; Elaine Ganley,

"Muslims Protest French Plan to Ban Veils," *Oregonian*, January 18, 2004; Elaine Ganley, "French Lawmakers Pass Law to Ban Islamic Head Scarves," *Oregonian*, March 4, 2004; Elaine Sciolino, "France Vows to Enforce Scarf Ban Despite Threat," *New York Times*, August 30, 2004; Sebastian Rotella, "Most Muslim Girls Comply with France's New Head Scarf Ban," *Los Angeles Times,* September 3, 2004; "Banning the 'Burqa': France's Quest to Maintain Its Secular Identity," *Spiegel Online*, January 27, 2010; Devorah Lauter, "France Considers Burka Ban," *Los Angeles Times*, January 27, 2010; Stefan Simons, "France's Controversial Immigration Minister: The Man Who Launched the Burqa Debate," *Spiegel Online*, February 1, 2010; "Don't Ban the Burka," *Los Angeles Times*, February 3, 2010; Alexandra Sandels, "France Denies Citizenship over Burka," *Los Angeles Times*, February 5, 2010; "France's Veil Threat," *Los Angeles Times*, May 24, 2010; "The Burqa Debate: Are Women's Rights Really the Issue?," *Spiegel Online*, June 24, 2010; "France's Veil Threat: Basically, the Measure Is Simply Religious Discrimination against Muslims," editorial, *Los Angeles Times*, May 24, 2010; "Justice Minister Pushes Burka Ban," *Los Angeles Times*, July 7, 2010; Alison Culliford, "French National Assembly Approves Ban on Face Veils," *Los Angeles Times*, July 14, 2010; Gregory Rodriguez, "Behind France's Veil Ploy," *Los Angeles Times*, July 19, 2010; Pew Global Attitudes Project, "Widespread Support for Banning Full Islamic Veil in Western Europe," survey report (Pew Research Center, Washington, DC, July 8, 2010); Henry Samuel, "French Women Cause a Stir in Niqab and Hot Pants in Anti-Burka Ban Protest," *Daily Telegraph*, October 1, 2010.

For an interpretation of the headscarf issue that differs from my own, see Elaine R. Thomas, "Keeping Identity at a Distance: Explaining France's New Legal Restrictions on the Islamic Headscarf," *Ethnic and Racial Studies* 29.2 (2006): 237–59; Devorah Lauter, "France Cracks Down on Roma Migrants," *Los Angeles Times*, August 13, 2010; Stefan Simons, "Sarkozy Finds a Scapegoat," *Spiegel Online*, August 19, 2010; Devorah Lauter, "Deportations Fray Catholic Tie to Sarkozy," *Los Angeles Times*, August 25, 2010; Jan Puhl, "Unwanted in France, Unloved in Romania: A Desperate Homecoming for Deported Roma," *Spiegel Online*, August 31, 2010; "The Roma Are EU Citizens—Everywhere in the European Union," *Spiegel Online*, September 6, 2010; "'A Disgrace': EU Rebukes France over Roma Expulsions," *Spiegel Online*, September 14, 2010; Ullrich Fichtner, "Driving out the Unwanted: Sarkozy's War against the Roma," *Spiegel Online*, September 15, 2010; "France Has Acted Systematically against an Entire People," *Spiegel Online*, September 15, 2010; Hans-Jürgen Schlamp, "Paris vs. Brussels: Roma Row Dominates EU Summit," *Spiegel Online*, September 17, 2010; "Roma Ultimatum: Frances Pledges to Comply with EU Migration Rules," *Spiegel Online*, October 14, 2010.

The phrase is Michael Ignatiev's; see his *Blood and Belonging: Journeys into the New Nationalism* (Toronto: Penguin, 1993).

40. Alan M. Kraut, *The Huddled Masses: The Immigrant in American Society, 1880–1921,* 2nd ed. (Wheeling, IL: Harlan Davidson, 2001), 2.

41. James H. Kettner, *The Development of American Citizenship, 1608–1870* (Chapel Hill: University of North Carolina Press, 1978); Ira Berlin, *Slaves without Masters: The Free Negro in the Antebellum South* (New York: Random House, 1974); Eugene D. Genovese, *Roll, Jordan, Roll: The World the Slaves Made* (New York: Random House, 1974), 398–413; James Oliver Horton, *Free People of Color Inside the African American Community* (Washington, DC: Smithsonian Institution Press, 1993); Winthrop D. Jordan, *White over Black: American Attitudes toward the Negro, 1550–1812* (Chapel Hill: University of North Carolina Press, 1968), 122–28 and passim; John H. Russell, *The Free Negro in Virginia, 1619–1865* (New York: Dover, 1969; orig. 1913); Arthur Zilversmit, *The First Emancipation: The Abolition of Slavery in the North* (Chicago: University of Chicago Press, 1967).

42. Berkhofer, *The White Man's Indian*; Vine Deloria Jr. and Clifford Lytle, *The Nations Within: The Past and Future of Indian Sovereignty* (New York: Pantheon, 1984).

43. Sucheng Chan, *Asian Americans: An Interpretive History* (Boston: Twayne, 1991); Lisa Lowe, *Immigrant Acts: On Asian American Cultural Politics* (Durham, NC: Duke University Press, 1996); Erika Lee, *At America's Gates: Chinese Immigration during the Exclusion Era, 1882–1943* (Chapel Hill: University of North Carolina Press, 2003).

44. For the enduring hierarchy of ethnic and racial groups in American social life, see Paul Spickard, "Who Is an American? Teaching about Racial and Ethnic Hierarchy," *Immigration and Ethnic History Newsletter* 31.1 (May 1999).

45. Spickard and Fong, "Ethnic Relations in the People's Republic"; June Teufel Dreyer, *China's Forty Millions: Minority Nationalities and National Integration* (Cambridge, MA: Harvard University Press, 1976); Gladney, *Ethnic Identity in China*; Jonathan N. Lipman, *Familiar Strangers: A History of Muslims in Northwest China* (Seattle: University of Washington Press, 1997); Mette Halskov Hansen, *Lessons in Being Chinese: Minority Education and Ethnic Identity in Southwest China* (Seattle: University of Washington Press, 1999).

46. The historian Abraham Friesen contends that many of these people were not originally Germans at all but Dutch and possibly Danes. See Abraham Friesen, *In Defense of Privilege: Russian Mennonites and the State before and during World War I* (Winnipeg: Kindred Productions, 2006); Hans Werner, *Imagined Homes: Soviet Immigrants in Two Cities* (Winnipeg: University of Manitoba Press, 2007); Renate Bridenthal, "Germans from Russia: The Political Network of a Double Diaspora," in *The Heimat Abroad: The Boundaries of Germanness,* ed. Krista O'Donnell, Renate Bridenthal, and Nancy Reagin (Ann Arbor: University of Michigan Press, 2005), 187–218; Pieter Judson, "When Is a Diaspora Not a Diaspora? Rethinking Nation-Centered Narratives about Germans in Habsburg East

Central Europe," in O'Donnell, Bridenthal, and Reagin, *Heimat Abroad*, 219–47; Nancy R. Reagin, "German *Brigadoon?* Domesticity and Metropolitan Perceptions of *Auslandsdeutschen* in Southwest Africa and Eastern Europe," in O'Donnell, Bridenthal, and Reagin, *Heimat Abroad*, 248–66. News accounts report that Germany "grants all Jews from the former Soviet Union citizenship and automatic government benefits." Some Jewish organizations have questioned the Jewish bona fides of the immigrants, but "never again, officials said, would Germans sort out who is a Jew"; *Newsweek* (July 14, 2003): 34.

47. Deniz Göktürk, David Gramling, and Anton Kaes, eds., *Germany in Transit: Nation and Migration, 1955–2005* (Berkeley: University of California Press, 2007); Richard Alba, Peter Schmidt, and Martine Wasmer, eds., *Germans or Foreigners? Attitudes toward Ethnic Minorities in Post-Reunification Germany* (New York: Palgrave, 2003); Betigül Ercan Argun, *Turkey in Germany: The Transnational Sphere of Deutschkei* (New York: Routledge, 2003); Wesley D. Chapin, *Germany for the Germans? The Political Effects of International Migration* (Westport, CT: Greenwood, 1997); Thomas Faist, *Social Citizenship for Whom? Young Turks in Germany and Mexican Americans in the United States* (Aldershot: Avebury, 1995); Norbert Finzsch and Dietmar Schirmer, eds., *Identity and Intolerance: Nationalism, Racism, and Xenophobia in Germany and the United States* (Cambridge: Cambridge University Press, 1998); Simon Green, *The Politics of Exclusion: Institutions and Immigration Policy in Contemporary Germany* (Manchester: Manchester University Press, 2004); David Horrocks and Eva Kolinsky, eds., *Turkish Culture in Germany Today* (Providence, RI: Berghahn, 1996); Mark Terkessidis, *Migranten* (Hamburg: Rotbuch, 2000); Uli Bielefeld, *Das Eigene und das Fremde: Neuer Rassismus in der Alten Welt?* (Hamburg: Junius, 1991); Faruk Sen and Andreas Goldberg, *Türken in Deutschland: Leben zwischen zwei Kulturen* (Munich: Beck, 1994); Faruk Sen and Hayrettin Aydim, *Islam in Deutschland* (Munich: Beck, 2002).

48. Moodie, "Race and Ethnicity in South Africa." Nicholas Dirks sees caste in India in a related way, not as exactly created by the British, but as codified in the Indian-British encounter; see Dirks, *Castes of Mind*.

49. Adrienne Edgar, "The Fragmented Nation: Genealogy, Identity, and Social Hierarchy in Turkmenistan," in Spickard, *Race and Nation*, 257–72; Edgar, *Tribal Nation*.

50. José Vasconcelos, *The Cosmic Race/La raza cosmica*, trans. Didier T. Jaén (Baltimore: Johns Hopkins University Press, 1997; orig. Spanish 1925); Gloria Anzaldúa, *Borderlands/La Frontera: The New Mestiza* (San Francisco: Aunt Lute, 1987); Gary B. Nash, "The Hidden History of Mestizo America," *Journal of American History* 82.3 (1995): 941–64.

51. Examples of the trend include Juan E. DeCastro, *Mestizo Nations* (Tucson: University of Arizona Press, 2002); Ernst Rudin, "New Mestizos: Traces of a Quin-

centenary Miracle in Old World Spanish and New World English Texts," in *Cultural Difference and the Literary Text*, ed. Winfried Siemerling and Katrin Schwenk (Ames: University of Iowa Press, 1996), 112–29; Amy K. Kaminsky, "Essay, Gender, and *Mestizaje*: Victoria Ocampo and Gabriela Mistral," in *Politics of the Essay*, ed. Ruth Ellen B. Joeres and Elizabeth Mittman (Bloomington: Indiana University Press, 1993), 113–30; Nelson H. Vieria, "Hybridity vs. Pluralism: Culture, Race, and Aesthetics in Jorge Amado," in *Jorge Amado: New Critical Essays*, ed. Keith H. Brower, Earl E. Fitz, and Enrique E. Martinique-Vidal (New York: Routledge, 2001), 231–51; Julie Brown, "Bartok, the Gypsies, and Hybridity in Music," in *Western Music and Its Others*, ed. Georgina Born and David Hesmondhalgh (Berkeley: University of California Press, 2000), 119–42; Martha Cutter, "The Politics of Hybridity in Frances Harper's Iola Leroy," in *Unruly Tongue: Identity and Voice in American Women's Writing, 1850–1930* (Oxford: University Press of Mississippi, 1999), 141–60; Pnina Werbner and Tariq Modood, eds., *Debating Cultural Hybridity* (London: Zed, 1997); Avtar Brah and Annie E. Coombes, eds., *Hybridity and Its Discontents* (London: Routledge, 2000); Zipporah G. Glass, "The Language of Mestizaje in a Renewed Rhetoric of Black Theology," in Spickard and Daniel, *Racial Thinking in the United States*, 341–52; Javier Sanjines C., *Mestizaje Upside Down: Aesthetic Politics in Modern Bolivia* (Pittsburgh: University of Pittsburgh Press, 2004); Marilyn Grace Miller, *The Rise and Fall of the Cosmic Race: The Cult of Mestizaje in Latin America* (Austin: University of Texas Press, 2004); Alicia Arrizon, *Queering Mestizaje: Transculturation and Performance* (Ann Arbor: University of Michigan Press, 2006); Rafael Perez-Torres, *Mestizaje: Critical Uses of Race in Chicano Culture* (Minneapolis: University of Minnesota Press, 2006); Néstor Medina, *Mestizaje: Remapping Race, Culture, and Faith in Latina/o Catholicism* (Maryknoll, NY: Orbis, 2009); Theresa Delgadillo, *Spiritual Mestizaje: Religion, Gender, Race, and Nation in Contemporary Chicana Narrative* (Durham, NC: Duke University Press, 2011).

52. Monroy, "Guilty Pleasures"; Virginia Q. Tilley, "*Mestizaje* and the 'Ethnicization' of Race in Latin America," in Spickard, *Race and Nation*, 53–68; Virginia Q. Tilley, *Seeing Indians: A Study of Race, Nation, and Power in El Salvador* (Albuquerque: University of New Mexico Press, 2005).

53. Marks, *Human Biodiversity*; Yonezawa, "Memories of Japanese Identity"; Moodie, "Race and Ethnicity in South Africa."

54. I am well aware that there is a growing literature on other racial and ethnic groups in the United States. I have taught for many years in an Asian American studies department, and as I type these words I am looking at a wall full of books on Asian Americans; nearby are many shelves filled with books on Native Americans, Latinos, and multiracial people. Still, most scholars of race treat the encounter between Black and White in the United States as if it were the master narrative of race. It is not so.

55. Personal communication with the author.

56. G. Reginald Daniel, *Race and Multiraciality in Brazil and the United States: Converging Paths?* (University Park: Pennsylvania State University Press, 2007); Jonathan Y. Okamura, *Ethnicity and Inequality in Hawai'i* (Philadelphia: Temple University Press, 2008).

57. Violet Showers Johnson, "Racial Frontiers in Jamaica's Nonracial Nationhood," in Spickard, *Race and Nation*, 155–70; Ayhan Kaya, *Sicher in Kreuzberg: Constructing Diasporas: Turkish Hip-Hop Youth in Berlin* (Bielefeld: Transcript, 2001).

58. Woldemikael, "Eritrea's Identity."

59. Stephen Cornell, "That's the Story of Our Life," in Spickard and Burroughs, *We Are a People*, 41–53; Liisa Malkki, "Context and Consciousness: Local Conditions for the Production of Historical and National Thought among Hutu Refugees in Tanzania," in *Nationalist Ideologies and the Production of National Cultures*, ed. Richard G. Fox (Washington, DC: American Anthropological Association, 1990); Patricia Ewick and Susan S. Silbey, "Subversive Stories and Hegemonic Tales: Toward a Sociology of Narrative," *Law and Society Review* 29 (1995): 197–226; Phillip H. McArthur, "Narrating to the Center of Power in the Marshall Islands," in Spickard and Burroughs, *We Are a People*, 85–97; Coco Fusco, *English Is Broken Here* (New York: New Press, 1995); Amy Aisen Elouafi, "The Colour of Orientalism: Race and Narratives of Discovery in Tunisia," *Ethnic and Racial Studies* 33.2 (2010): 253–71; Ernesto Martinez, *On Making Sense: Queer Race Narratives of Intelligibility* (Stanford, CA: Stanford University Press, 2012); Marco Giudici, "Immigrant Narratives and Nation-Building in a Stateless Nation: The Case of Italians in Post-Devolution Wales," *Ethnic and Racial Studies* 37.8 (2014): 1409–26; Zana Vathi and Russell King, "'Have you got the *British*?': Narratives of Migration and Settlement among Albanian-Origin Immigrants in London," *Ethnic and Racial Studies* 36.1 (2013): 1829–48.

60. Woldemikael, "Eritrea's Identity"; Moodie, "Race and Ethnicity in South Africa"; Yonezawa, "Memories of Identity"; Pierce, "Creating a Racial Paradise."

5

From the Black Atlantic to the Racial Pacific

Rethinking Racial Hierarchy in Colonial and Postcolonial Contexts

This essay was written as the final chapter in a book edited by Heike Raphael-Hernandez and Shannon Steen that was planned as an exploration of the contours of race in Asia. As that book progressed from idea to paper, it became a volume of essays, not precisely on race in Asia, but rather on the specific connections between people of Asian descent and people of African descent, here and there—in North America, Asia, and the Caribbean, in fiction, film, music, and martial arts.[1] As the book took on a different shape, there seemed no point in including an analytical essay on race as an issue in Asia and the Pacific, and so the piece was withdrawn. It appears here for the first time.

Paul Gilroy, in *The Black Atlantic*, makes a wonderful interpretive move to extend the North American discussion of race across the Atlantic to northern Europe and also, somewhat differently, to Africa. He advocates attention to "a culture that is not specifically African, American, Caribbean, or British, but all of these at once, a black Atlantic culture whose themes and techniques transcend ethnicity and nationality."[2] That may be a salutary revision. But if it is, it probably does not go far enough. It is not just that there are racialized relationships involving African-descended peoples on both sides of the Atlantic (and that the sides are intertwined); there are other racialized relationships on both sides of the Atlantic, around the Mediterranean, among various peoples in Asia, and across the Pacific as well.[3] By "racialized relationships," I mean situations in which peoples confront each other with the result that some people dominate others; in that domination, a story of racial hierarchy—superiority and inferiority, dominance and submission—is written onto the bodies and into the genes of the peoples who are dominated.[4]

This essay explores the shapes of some of those other racialized relationships. It attempts to take quite a bit further the discussion that Gilroy began when he declared the African Atlantic: to examine the ways that systems of racialized relationships have been constructed halfway around the world, in Asia and in the Pacific.[5] It examines the ways that Japanese and Chinese people have imagined and treated Africans and African Americans. Then it moves on to analyze the ways some East Asians have racialized other peoples within their own geographic domains. Finally, it attends to the making of racial systems at two places in the Pacific, Fiji and Hawai'i.

RACE IN EUROPE

More and more, scholars and others are writing about race as a phenomenon in Europe, not just in the Americas.[6] Too frequently, the only "race" that seems to exist consists of people of African descent, hence Gilroy's limited and essentialist "Black" Atlantic. It seems to me that the racial reality of the Atlantic world is much more complex than that: Black there is, but there are several kinds of Black. Are Ethiopians and Eritreans Black in the same way (or is it ways?) that Igbo and Tutsis and Zulus are Black?[7] Are Algerians Black at all, even if they are treated as racially Other when they venture into European countries?[8] Just as there are many Blacks, there are several kinds of Whites, and others, too, in shades of yellow and brown. Racialized hierarchies and webs of social interrelationships are complex systems, not reducible to a simplistic binary.

It is true that, particularly in Britain, there is a group of scholars who have been writing for some time against the binary trend by doing racial analyses of, for example, the situations of Pakistanis or Chinese in the United Kingdom.[9] But the majority of race talk among scholars in Europe is about Blacks. Insofar as the discussion addresses other groups, in Britain and especially on the Continent, it seems to focus on the question of nationalism rather than race per se or on ways to manage a multiracial population.[10] Nonetheless, a small group of scholars has begun to talk about other groups on the Continent, such as Turks in Germany or Basques in Spain and France, in racial ways.[11]

As with European studies of race, so, too, in America, at least outside the West Coast. A major problem with the discussion of race in sociology and African American studies (as opposed to ethnic studies) has been that it has tended to see race as only a matter of Black and White. Or at least it has seen the Black-White encounter in the United States as the master racial project by which any others are to be understood. But race is a broader phenomenon, having to do with power relationships among peoples, which are then written onto the body and ascribed to the genes. Such relationships exist anywhere peoples encounter one another in confrontational and hierarchical ways.[12]

RACE IN ASIA

Asians and African-Descended People

Even before the Japanese began to have broad-scale interactions with the outside world in the 1850s, Japanese people had begun to adopt Europeans' prejudices regarding African-descended peoples. The first African-descended people they met were sailors on Dutch ships trading in Nagasaki Harbor. In 1787 a Japanese scholar wrote about those sailors:

These black ones on the Dutch boats are the natives of countries in the South. As their countries are close to the sun, they are sun-scorched and become black. By nature they are stupid. . . . Africa is directly under the equator and the heat there is extreme. Therefore, the natives are black colored. They are uncivilized and vicious in nature.[13]

Ukiyo-e, Japanese woodblock prints, from the Meiji era depict Africans as grotesque and bestial, with kinky hair sprouting at odd angles, exaggerated noses and lips, and very black skin.

More recently, Japanese popular culture—advertisements, movies, television, music videos, and the like—has had a particular fascination with people of part Japanese ancestry. They have exoticized half Europeans as inferior to full Japanese but sexy; half Africans, on the other hand, have often been depicted as inferior but beastlike and threatening. It is difficult for anyone who is not seen as pure Japanese to be accepted in Japan, but it is far more difficult for people of full or part African descent than for those of European descent.[14]

Chinese denigrations of Africans also predated the intrusion of Western ideas that came with colonialism in the nineteenth century. From the Tang dynasty on, reports filtered into China about Africa and its peoples, and indeed some African slaves arrived via the Silk Road in the employ of Arab and Persian merchants. Chinese observers described them as "simpleminded but courageous," "*yeren,* 'wild man', or *guinu,* 'devil slave'"; "frightening," "stupid." Later, when China was in thrall to Western science and ideas at the dawn of the twentieth century, Liang Qichao, one of the nation's foremost intellectuals and politicians, wrote, "All the black, red and brown races, by the microbes in their blood vessels and their cerebral angle, are inferior to the whites. Only the yellows are not very dissimilar to the whites. . . . [B]lacks and browns are lazy and stupid." On visiting the United States, he wrote, "The blacks' behaviour is despicable. They only die without regret if they have succeeded in touching a white woman's skin. They often lurk in the darkness of woods to rape them. Thereafter these women are murdered so that they will not talk. Nine out of ten cases of lynching are due to this crime." Kang Youwei, another prominent intellectual of the early twentieth century, wrote that darker races were unequal and should be eradicated by forcing them to intermarry, leave the nation, or be sterilized.[15]

Such attitudes have continued into the modern era. They permeated the treatment of African students at Chinese universities in the 1980s and 1990s. Several thousand students whose home countries lacked sufficient institutions of higher education accepted government scholarships and went to Chinese universities to study subjects like science and engineering. They were housed in segregated dormitories inhabited only by Africans. Officially, they were welcomed as foreign guests whose recourse to Chinese universities enhanced China's international stature, but socially they were ostracized and viewed with suspicion. At two universities in Tianjin in 1985, Chinese students rioted against African students whom they accused of approaching Chinese women students romantically and of stealing food. When the African students took refuge in a dining hall, the Chinese students threw rocks through the windows and attempted to break down the doors. Relations on those campuses were still tense four years later, in 1988–89, when similar riots occurred at Nanjing and several other universities across the country. Many African students were terrified, and most of those who were able to return home did so.[16]

In 1989, I made a survey of 169 Chinese students at Nankai University in Tianjin. I used the Bogardus Social Distance Scale to measure the social distance that they felt between themselves and various foreign nationalities. Chinese did not feel very close to any foreign people, but they put Americans, British, and Germans near the middle of their scale, with Russians, Mexicans, and Japanese rather distant; Africans tied for last place with Vietnamese. When I asked Chinese students to list adjectives that they felt usually applied to people in a particular group, they agreed on these for Africans: primitive, uncivilized, threatening, warlike, poor, simple, uneducated, ignorant, stupid, ugly.[17]

Indigenous Asian Racial Hierarchies

So both Chinese and Japanese people have had negative views of Africans and African Americans for a long time. Yet Asians' relationships with African-descended peoples are not the only racialized relationships in Asia, nor are they the most important ones. Most racialized relationships have been built in the context of colonialism; that is, they have been made by dominant peoples in the process of dominating other peoples. Examples include the British in India, the French and Germans in Africa, and the European-derived Whites in North America.[18] The Chinese were colonizers and race makers, too. Many non-Chinese have at least heard of Chinese domination (some would say genocide) of Tibetans.[19] Fewer Westerners are aware that the Han Chinese—those who regard themselves as the core Chinese people on the basis of descent from the peoples who lived within the empire during the Han dynasty (nearly 93 percent of the nation)—have created an elaborate system of racial hierarchy in which they rank internal minorities who inhabit the farther reaches of the Chinese empire, peoples like the Dai, Miao, Manchus, Liao, and Hui. My study of Han Chinese attitudes included questions about several such colonized domestic minorities. Han Chinese saw themselves, overseas Chinese, Uygurs, and ethnic Koreans living in China as smart, hardworking, brave, and kind. They perceived Manchus, Mongolians, Dai, and Yi as positive primitives: beautiful, friendly, adept at singing and dancing. Tibetans, the most brutally dominated of the peoples whom the Han have colonized, were characterized in much the same terms as Africans: primitive, threatening, warlike, stupid, dirty.[20]

The Japanese have long had the idea that they are an unusually pure race of people, separated by blood from all others and descended from the sun goddess Amaterasu Ōmikami. In fact, like all the world's peoples, the Japanese are a mixed multitude, the product of the merging of many peoples. In ancient times, at least two big waves of immigrants from the Korean peninsula came to the islands to join the native Ainu inhabitants and form the Yamato people. Their number and ethnic diversity were increased by several smaller waves of immigrants from the islands of the western Pacific. Early in the modern era, Japan was barely a single political entity. Each region had its own autonomous government, its own version of the Japanese language, its own identity.[21]

Such divisions were self-consciously erased in the second half of the nineteenth century by the makers of Meiji Japan. They propagated the ideology of racial unity and blood purity as a powerful glue to unite the nation. They set up the emperor as national patriarch, with State Shinto as the unifying religion. In the Meiji era and after, Japan engaged in colonial enterprises in Asia and the Pacific that added to the variety of peoples in

Japan, even as official policy denied that multiplicity. In 1905 the Japanese army invaded Korea, and in 1910 Japan incorporated the peninsula. From that time forward thousands of Korean workers were imported each year, and thousands of Korean women were impregnated by the colonizers. Several thousand ethnic Koreans were among those who died in the bombings of Hiroshima and Nagasaki. Japanese colonial ventures in the Pacific—in the Bonin Islands, the Ryūkyūs, and Micronesia—brought Japanese people to those places and their mixed offspring back to Japan. In addition to such colonial peoples, for centuries there have existed within Japan two groups that have been marked off as racially separate from other Japanese: the indigenous Ainu and a hereditary outcaste group known variously, and pejoratively, as *eta* and *hisabetsu burakumin*. Except for the Ainu, who have sometimes been treated in ways resembling the American treatment of native peoples, none of this variety was officially recognized. The government required people of non-Japanese ethnic origins to take Japanese names if they wanted to become citizens, and Korean- and Pacific-descended people were discriminated against sharply. Koreans and burakumin especially were targets of the language of racial dominance: they were characterized by other Japanese as unclean, violent, primitive, and sexually predatory.[22]

From the Meiji era through World War II, Japanese went abroad in large numbers to places as disparate as Brazil, Peru, Truk, Hawai'i, China, Manchuria, Mexico, Canada, and the United States. They maintained webs of connectedness with their fellow Japanese in widely separated locations for four generations. Yet when—in the 1980s, 1990s, and 2000s—some of those ethnic Japanese who had been born abroad in Brazil, Argentina, and other places migrated to the land of their ancestors, native Japanese did not view them as long lost relatives. Rather they enunciated a story of difference about Latin American Japanese immigrants. In those decades Japan's relatively robust economy and declining birthrate meant jobs were plentiful. Not only did ethnic Japanese come, but also Europeans and guest workers from places like the Philippines and Indonesia.[23]

Together, these groups of new immigrants and the descendants of burakumin, Koreans, Ainu, and others make Japan a much more self-consciously mixed place today than it was acknowledged to be in the past. The media are beginning to take notice of the mixed nature of the Japanese population. Models and TV stars show a greater variety of physiognomy. The government is relaxing its blood definition of citizenship—a naturalized Finn became a member of the Diet, the national legislature—although Japan's citizenship law remains one of the most ethnically restrictive on the planet. Some unmixed Japanese people have begun in recent decades to deliberately blur their features by altering the color of their hair, the shape and color of their eyes, the shape of their noses, even body dimensions. All these things point to a more relaxed, less racially determined definition of Japaneseness than was the case during the first century and a quarter of modern Japanese nationhood.

Khmer attitudes and actions toward Vietnamese in Cambodia point to another sort of racial system in another part of Asia. Most outsiders probably do not give much thought to the issue of race in Cambodia or to Cambodia at all. But there are profoundly racialized relationships between ethnic Khmers (the Cambodian majority group) and the sizable minority of Vietnamese origin. That is, the peoples regard themselves as not just culturally but also physically distinct, and each believes that the other has innate, negative characterological qualities. Christine Su, an ethnic Khmer scholar working in the United States, writes:

> In the midst of casual conversation, a close personal friend once told me that "it is *necessary* that we Cambodians hate the Vietnamese. . . . There is no why—it's just a fact." . . . Vietnamese are the "hereditary enemy," the perpetual "threat to Khmerness." They are thieves, gamblers, traitors, prostitutes. They are the antithesis of all that is Cambodian.[24]

I submit that throughout Asia such racialized relationships exist. The way Cambodians feel about their ethnic Vietnamese minority is not very different from the way Vietnamese talk about their ethnic Khmer minority, except that in the latter case the Vietnamese attribute the Khmer's supposed negative character qualities to their darker skin color. Similar racialized attitudes exist in the minds of Thais toward their ethnic Chinese fellow citizens, among Burmans toward their Karen fellow citizens, and so on.[25]

RACE IN THE PACIFIC

In the Pacific, I will talk about Fiji and Hawai'i, with reference to two axes of encounter: first, between European colonizers and indigenous peoples; and second, between indigenous peoples and Asian immigrants who were brought by colonialism but who have been established in the locale for several generations.

Fiji

Fiji has a long and troubled history of conflict between ethnic Fijians and Indo-Fijians that has been shaped decisively by the legacy of British colonialism. It was a loose, frequently warring collection of island peoples when England took it over as a colony in 1874.[26] The British government, in its possibly self-serving account of events, was initially reluctant to take on the colony, but did so at the request of some Europeans in the islands and also of a number of chiefs in eastern Viti Levu, the largest and most populous island. A year later Arthur Gordon arrived as colonial governor. He inherited a bankrupt administration and a native population ravaged by measles (forty thousand Fijians, more than a quarter of the population, died in the epidemic).

Gordon's limited resources dictated that he must rule indirectly, through those existing chiefs who had supported the British takeover. He encouraged Fijians to maintain their languages and cultural practices. He brought together the collaborating chiefs in a Great Council of Chiefs, which is a power in Fijian politics to this day. Finding that much of the best agricultural land had already been swept up by Europeans and that land law varied enormously throughout the islands, Gordon used the Great Council of Chiefs to standardize land tenure and sharply limit the ability of Fijians to alienate land to foreigners, enshrining the new system as "traditional."

In order to establish a tax base for his administration, Gordon completed negotiations with a large Australian firm, the Colonial Sugar Refining Company (CSR), to lease vast tracts of land for sugarcane production.

At first the workers were Fijians and contract laborers imported from the Solomon Islands and elsewhere in the Pacific. But the colonial government promised CSR that it would bring in tens of thousands of farmworkers from India to plant and harvest sugarcane. Between 1879 and 1916, 60,969 Indian laborers came to Fiji on five-year indentures. They lived and worked in miserable, slavelike conditions. At the end of their contracts they were free to go home, but they had been paid very little and no passage money was provided. The overwhelming majority stayed on in Fiji.

A population that was 90 percent ethnic Fijian in 1881 was nearly 30 percent Indo-Fijian in 1911, over 40 percent Indo-Fijian by 1936, and over 50 percent Indo-Fijian on the eve of independence in 1966. These were second-, third-, and fourth-generation residents of the islands, with no personal ties to any homeland other than Fiji. Yet British colonial policies and the CSR kept Indians and Fijians apart. Fijians held a monopoly on landownership but were a population by and large mired in poverty; Indo-Fijians owned and ran many businesses and were prominent in the professions. Most Fijians were fervent Christians; Indians were Muslims or Hindus. The two communities were strictly segregated. For example, the western end of the large island of Viti Levu—sugar country—is almost all Indian, the northern and eastern regions are almost all Fijian, and Suva, the capital, has de facto segregated neighborhoods.

The British government, on granting independence, insisted that all Fijian citizens—ethnic Fijian, Indo-Fijian, Chinese, Rotuman, European, other Polynesian, and so on—be allowed to vote and hold office. This was part of the Commonwealth's vision to create little British-inspired democracies around the globe, all tied together with the United Kingdom at the center. Up to that time, there had been a legislative council composed of representatives from three racial communities, with each community's representatives chosen by different rules: European men elected their representatives, Fijian members were chosen by the Great Council of Chiefs, and Indo-Fijian members were chosen by wealthy Indians.

Two budding political parties, the New Federation Party (NFP) and the Alliance Party, hammered out a constitution over several years. These parties were led, respectively, by an Indo-Fijian, A. D. Patel, and an ethnic Fijian chief, Ratu Kamisese Mara. Both parties were officially multiracial, but in fact nearly all Indo-Fijians voted for the NFP and nearly all ethnic Fijians voted for the Alliance. Ratu Mara's party won the first election in 1972, as well as the subsequent three elections. But in 1987 a coalition of the NFP and the new Labour Party won a narrow victory. An ethnic Fijian, Timoci Bavadra, headed the ticket, and the majority of his cabinet was Fijian, yet the new government was labeled "Indian dominated."

On May 14, 1987, a young ethnic Fijian lieutenant-colonel, Sitiveni Rabuka, and ten soldiers overthrew the multiracial government and put a Fijian at its head. Theirs was the first military coup against a democratically elected government in South Pacific history. In time Rabuka consolidated his hold on the country and promulgated a racial constitution that allowed only ethnic Fijians to vote and hold office. Indo-Fijians, who constituted a slim plurality of the nation's population, began leaving the islands by the thousands. Indo-Fijian department heads at the University of the South Pacific were replaced by ethnic Fijians.[27]

Over the course of nearly a decade and a half, Fijian politics opened up again. Commissions met and reported.[28] A new constitution was written. Indo-Fijians were allowed to vote and stand for office. Some began to agitate for the right to own land. In 2001, under the new constitution, the Chaudry government was elected and took power, briefly, and then it too was deposed. A failed businessman, George Speight, led a ragtag bunch of ethnic Fijians in taking over the parliament building and holding Chaudry and thirty people hostage for several weeks.[29]

The pattern was repeated. Indo-Fijians left in droves. Commissions met and recommended democratic reforms. A more ethnically open government began to assert itself. And in 2006 there was a third ethnic Fijian coup and restoration of dictatorial rule.[30]

The conflict continues. There is near-total segregation between ethnic Fijians and Indo-Fijians. Both sides, and especially the fundamentalists among the ethnic Fijians (a substantial group), lay the differences at the door of religion. But off the record they speak in racial terms about the body and essential racial character: a lot of Indians talk about Fijians as sexual, violent, irresponsible, and foul-smelling; many ethnic Fijians talk about Indo-Fijians as effeminate, money-grubbing, and heartless.

Hawai'i

Polynesian seafarers had inhabited the Hawaiian Islands for more than a millennium when James Cook, a British sea captain, made the first modern outside contact in 1776. Shortly thereafter, Kāmehameha, hereditary leader of one district on the Big Island, united the archipelago by force. He proclaimed himself king, and the kingdom he and his heirs ruled took on many of the features of European-style monarchy. American and European Protestant missionaries and businesspeople came, trading in sandalwood and souls. They also brought American and European diseases: a population that had numbered between 800,000 and 1.3 million at first European contact plummeted to 40,000 by the 1820s. People left their communal farms and fishponds in the countryside and went to newly established towns, where they worked for wages, interacted with the growing number of foreigners, and caught the foreigners' diseases. Hawai'i became a center for whaling and trade throughout the Pacific, and islanders traveled abroad, many never to return.[31]

By the 1840s, Haoles, or White foreigners, had married into the Hawaiian ruling class and taken over the government in all but name. Missionary influence outlawed the ancient sacred dance, the hula, and had a hand in the abolishment of the traditional system of *kapu*, the rules that had governed Hawaiian society for centuries. In place of the kapu came Western-style law codes and courts. In 1848, under intense pressure from Haole advisers, the king conducted the *mahele*, or land division. All lands had formerly belonged to the king but had been in the hands of the people organized in *ahupua'a*, or communal groups. Now 1.5 million acres were carved up and assigned as personal property to the noble class, one million acres became the personal property of the king, and 1.5 million acres were designated as crown lands to support the government. Some commoners were allowed to claim not ownership but *kuleana*, or stewardship, of small parcels of land if they had lived on them for more than a decade. Government land was not supposed to be alienated to non-Hawaiians, but by 1865 two-thirds of the government lands and much of the rest were in Haole hands.[32]

This gave rise to a financial oligarchy of foreign land barons. Haoles, mainly of American derivation, owned vast tracts of land in sugar and later pineapple cultivation. They brought in thousands of foreign workers, first from China, then from Japan, and later from the Philippines, Korea, and elsewhere. Soon the newcomers outnumbered Native Hawaiians. The various new peoples formed a mixed ethnic plantation working class that created a common mixed culture, including a language, Pidgin, and mixed local food customs. Power, however, remained in the hands of the Haole oligarchy. In the 1880s and 1890s, King David Kalākaua and his successor, Queen Liliʻuokalani, attempted to pull power back into Hawaiian hands but failed. Haole businessmen forced what has come to be called the Bayonet Constitution on Kalākaua in 1887, reducing his power still further. Then in 1893 they overthrew Liliʻuokalani, imprisoned her, and proclaimed a Hawaiian Republic with one of their own, the White missionary descendant Sanford Dole, as president. They applied for annexation by the United States, which was achieved in 1898; two years later Hawaiʻi formally became a US territory.[33]

The territorial period (1900–1959) saw the rise of a racialized system in Hawaiʻi that the historian Lori Pierce calls the Discourse of Aloha. This was accompanied by the rise of a tourist industry, civic boosterism, the 1930s and 1940s vogue of ersatz Hawaiian music and aloha shirts, the sexualization of island women, and the figurative emasculation of island men. The Discourse of Aloha cast the islands as a place of happy natives eager to sing and dance for visitors and make them welcome. At the same time, it pictured Native Hawaiians as a dying race, to be supplanted by "the golden men," in the novelist James Michener's phrase—a polyglot mixture of Whites and Asians (with perhaps a tiny element of Hawaiian ancestry) who were making the islands a peaceful "meeting place of East and West." A corollary to the Discourse of Aloha was the narrative of Native decline. Things Hawaiian were suppressed. Even at the Kāmehameha Schools—institutions for Native Hawaiian children, named after Hawaiʻi's first king—students were forbidden to speak Hawaiian or dance hula. The Hawaiian language nearly died out, and predictions were made that the people would disappear as well.[34]

Meanwhile the Haole oligarchy continued to dominate the islands. Five companies headed by missionary descendants—the so-called Big Five—ran not only the economy but also the Republican-controlled state legislature through the 1950s. Their hold was loosened a bit by the Democrat- and Japanese American–led campaign for statehood that culminated in 1959. Statehood brought demographic and economic booms to the islands. The colonial relationship to the United States was cemented. Native Hawaiians were honored culturally and ceremonially, even as they were impoverished and criminalized in fact.[35]

The years since statehood have seen a sharpening of race-based class divisions, with Haoles, Chinese, and Japanese (in that order) at the top of the social structure and Hawaiians, Samoans, and Filipinos (in that order) at the bottom. The first three groups are pictured in public discourse as productive, positively oriented toward family and education, civic-minded, and wholesome members of society. The darker three groups are often pictured as lazy, violent, sexual, and criminal.

The 1980s through 2000s saw a renaissance of Native Hawaiian cultural prestige and political activism. The Hawaiian language made a comeback. As a new century began, some Hawaiians began to contest the position of people they called "Asian settler colonialists," whom they portrayed as junior partners in Haole domination. Some Asian-descended Hawaiian residents supported this characterization of Asians as essentially illegitimate members of Hawaiian society; others resisted.[36]

CONCLUSION

There are profound racial dynamics in Asia and the Pacific. They include the experiences and images of African Americans in those places. Yet that is only a minor theme in Asian and Pacific racial relationships. In each part of Asia and the Pacific, there are profoundly important racial dynamics that are critical to the situation and future of the peoples in those places. They have little or nothing to do with African-descended people.

Frequently there is a colonial tie to this race making and maintaining in Asia and the Pacific. Sometimes the tie is to European or American colonialism: for example, race in Fiji was framed by British colonialism, and Chinese and Japanese ideas about Africans (but not other racialized peoples in their spheres) were more or less inherited from Americans and Europeans. Sometimes the colonialism is more regional, whether it be Chinese colonialism in Tibet and other territories ruled by China or Japanese colonialism in the western Pacific. The key issue in such racialized hierarchies is power: those who would rule write a narrative of inferiority onto the bodies and into the genes of those whom they would control.

Finally, I would ask, does the end of colonialism lead us in the direction of an end to racialized encounters and oppression? Sadly, my preliminary judgment is that it does not. If one looks at Fiji, one sees a former British colony that has been legally independent for decades, yet is still mired in racial hierarchy left over from the colonial period. In Hawai'i, some would say that the colonial era ended when the islands were incorporated into the United States as the fiftieth state; others would say that colonialism continues. Yet in either case it is clear that the racial regime that came with American colonialism persists.

NOTES

1. Heike Raphael-Hernandez and Shannon Steen, eds., *AfroAsian Encounters: Culture, History, Politics* (New York: New York University Press, 2006). See also Vijay Prashad, *Everybody Was Kung Fu Fighting: Afro-Asian Connections and the Myth of Cultural Purity* (Boston: Beacon, 2002), for another interesting take on the issues that Raphael-Hernandez and Steen ended up engaging.

2. Paul Gilroy, *The Black Atlantic* (London: Verso, 1993), back cover.

3. Paul Spickard, ed., *Race and Nation: Ethnic Systems in the Modern World* (New York: Routledge, 2005), 21–22 and passim.

4. Paul Spickard and W. Jeffrey Burroughs, "We Are a People," in *We Are a People: Narrative and Multiplicity in Constructing Ethnic Identity*, ed. Paul Spickard and W. Jeffrey Burroughs (Philadelphia: Temple University Press, 2000), 1–19; Lori Pierce, "The Continuing Significance of Race," in Spickard and Burroughs, *We Are a People*, 221–28; Michael Omi and Howard Winant, *Racial Formation in the United States*, 2nd ed. (New York: Routledge, 1994), 53–76; Paul Spickard and G. Reginald Daniel, "Independence Possible," in *Racial Thinking in the United States: Uncompleted Independence*, ed. Paul Spickard and G. Reginald Daniel

(Notre Dame, IN: University of Notre Dame Press, 2004), 1–17; G. Reginald Daniel, "Either Black or White: Race, Modernity, and the Law of the Excluded Middle," in Spickard and Daniel, *Racial Thinking in the United States*, 21–59; Emmanuel Chukwudi Eze, ed., *Race and the Enlightenment* (Oxford: Blackwell, 1997); Patrick B. Miller, "The Anatomy of Scientific Racism: Racialist Responses to Black Athletic Achievement," in Spickard and Burroughs, *We Are a People*, 124–41; Stephen Cornell, "That's the Story of Our Life," in Spickard and Burroughs, *We Are a People*, 41–53.

5. Many writers on international economics, politics, and business refer to "the Asia-Pacific." See, e.g., G. John Ikenberry and Michael Mastanduno, eds., *International Relations Theory and the Asia-Pacific* (New York: Columbia University Press, 2003); Michael Yahuda, *The International Politics of the Asia Pacific*, 3rd ed. (New York: Routledge, 2011); Simon Greenberg, Christopher Kee, and J. Romesh Weeramantry, *International Commercial Arbitration: An Asia-Pacific Perspective* (Cambridge: Cambridge University Press, 2011); Peter A. Petri, Michael G. Plummer, and Fan Zhai, *Trans-Pacific Partnership and Asia-Pacific Integration: A Quantitative Assessment* (Washington, DC: Peterson Institute for International Economics, 2012). The term *Asia-Pacific* makes no sense, and in fact it leads the reader astray. We can argue about whether or not "Asia" is a meaningful abstraction, but "Asia-Pacific" certainly is not. There is no Asia-Pacific region, culture zone, or field of intertwined economic activity. Tokyo, Beijing, Singapore, and Manila—even Mumbai—have a great deal in common with one another thematically, and they connect with each other economically, but none has much at all to do with Suva or Rarotonga; the former are Asian places, the latter Pacific places. Those who use the term *Asia-Pacific* in fact mean Asia (with the possible inclusion of Australia) and its trans-Pacific connections, and by this hegemonic usage they obscure the very distinct issues—even the existence—of Pacific peoples. See Epeli Hauʻofa, "Our Sea of Islands," in *A New Oceania: Rediscovering Our Sea of Islands*, ed. Epeli Hauʻofa, Eric Waddell, and Vijay Naidu (Suva: School of Social and Economic Development, University of the South Pacific, 1993), 2–16; Joanne L. Rondilla, "The Filipino Question in Asia and the Pacific: Rethinking Regional Origins in Diaspora," in *Pacific Diaspora*, ed. Paul Spickard, Joanne L. Rondilla, and Debbie Hippolite Wright (Honolulu: University of Hawaiʻi Press, 2002), 56–68; Arif Dirlik, *What Is in a Rim? Critical Perspectives on the Pacific Rim Idea*, 2nd ed. (Lanham, MD: Rowman and Littlefield, 1998).

6. E.g., Stephen Small, *Racialised Barriers* (London: Routledge, 1994); Paul Gilroy, *There Ain't No Black in the Union Jack* (London: Hutchinson, 1987); Floya Anthias and Nira Yuval-Davis, *Racialised Boundaries: Race, Nation, Gender, Colour and Class and the Anti-Racist Struggle* (London: Routledge, 1992); Robert Miles, *Racism after "Race Relations"* (London: Routledge, 1993); John Solomos, *Race and Racism in Britain* (London: Macmillan, 1993); Ika Hügel-Marshall,

Invisible Woman: Growing Up Black in Germany, trans. Elizabeth Gaffney (New York: Continuum, 2001); Hans J. Massaquoi, *Destined to Witness: Growing Up Black in Nazi Germany* (New York: Morrow, 1999); Yelena Khanga, with Susan Jacoby, *Soul to Soul: The Story of a Black Russian American Family, 1865–1992* (New York: Norton, 1992); Paul Mecheril and Thomas Teo, *Andere Deutsche: Zur Lebenssituation von Menschen Multiethnischer und Multikultureller Herkunft* (Berlin: Dietz Verlag, 1994); Darlene Clark Hine, Trica Danielle Keaton, and Stephen Small, eds., *Black Europe and the African Diaspora* (Urbana: University of Illinois Press, 2009); Trica Danielle Heaton, *Muslim Girls and the Other France: Race, Identity Politics, and Social Exclusion* (Bloomington: Indiana University Press, 2006); Jill Olumide, *Raiding the Gene Pool: The Social Construction of Mixed Race* (London: Pluto Press, 2002); Alessandro Portelli, "The Problem of the Color-Blind: Notes on the Discourse of Race in Italy," in Spickard, *Race and Nation*, 355–63.

7. Tekle Woldemikael, "Ethiopians and Eritreans," in *Case Studies in Diversity: Refugees in America in the 1990s*, ed. David W. Haines (Westport, CT: Praeger, 1997), 265–87; Tekle Woldemikael, "Eritrea's Identity as a Cultural Crossroads," in Spickard, *Race and Nation*, 337–52.

8. Craig S. Smith, "French-Born Arabs, Perpetually Foreign, Grow Bitter," *New York Times*, December 26, 2003; Craig S. Smith, "Third Bomb Attack Directed at France's First Muslim Prefect," *New York Times*, January 30, 2004; Taoufik Djebali, "Ethnicity and Power in North Africa (Tunisia, Algeria, and Morocco)," in Spickard, *Race and Nation*, 135–54; Paul Spickard, ed., *Multiple Identities: Migrants, Ethnicity, and Membership* (Bloomington: Indiana University Press, 2013); Alec G. Hargreaves, *Multi-Ethnic France: Immigration, Politics, Culture, and Society*, 2nd ed. (New York: Routledge, 2007); Deniz Göktürk, David Gramling, and Anton Kaes, eds., *Germany in Transit: Nation and Migration, 1955–2005* (Berkeley: University of California Press, 2007); Michèle Lamont, Ann Morning, and Margarita Mooney, "Particular Universalisms: North African Immigrants Respond to French Racism," *Ethnic and Racial Studies* 25.3 (2002): 390–414; Ruth Mandel, *Cosmopolitan Anxieties: Turkish Challenges to Citizenship and Belonging in Germany* (Durham, NC: Duke University Press, 2008); *Muslims in Europe: A Report on 11 EU Cities* (London: Open Society Institute, 2010).

9. E.g., David Parker, *Through Different Eyes: The Cultural Identities of Young Chinese People in Britain* (Aldershot: Avebury, 1995); Tariq Modood, "Political Blackness and British Asians," *Sociology* 28.4 (1994): 3–13; Tariq Modood et al., *Ethnic Minorities in Britain* (London: Policy Studies Institute, 1997); Paul Spickard, "Mapping Race: Multiracial People and Racial Category Construction in the United States and Britain," *Immigrants and Minorities* 15 (July 1996): 107–19; Miri Song, *Helping Out: Children's Labor in Ethnic Businesses* (Philadelphia: Temple University Press, 1999); Miri Song, *Choosing Ethnic Identity* (Cambridge: Polity

Press, 2003); Susan Benson, "Asians Have Culture, West Indians Have Problems," in *Culture, Identity, and Politics*, ed. T. O. Ranger, Y. Samad, and O. Stuart (Aldershot: Avebury, 1996).

10. E.g., Anthony D. Smith, *The Ethnic Origins of Nations* (Oxford: Blackwell, 1986); Anthony D. Smith, *Nationalism and Modernism* (London: Routledge, 1998); E. J. Hobsbawm, *Nations and Nationalism since 1780*, 2nd ed. (Cambridge: Cambridge University Press, 1990); Geoff Eley and Ronald Grigor Suny, eds., *Becoming National* (Oxford: Oxford University Press, 1996); John A. Armstrong, *Nations before Nationalism* (Chapel Hill: University of North Carolina Press, 1982).

11. See the references in note 8, plus Elisabeth Schäfer-Wünsche, "On Becoming German: The Politics of Membership in Germany," in Spickard *Race and Nation*, 195–211; David Horrocks and Eva Kolinsky, eds., *Turkish Culture in German Society Today* (Providence, RI: Berghahn Books, 1996); Gérard Noiriel, *The French Melting Pot: Immigration, Citizenship, and National Identity*, trans. Geoffroy de Laforcade (Minneapolis: University of Minnesota Press, 1996); Daniel R. Brower and Edward J. Lazzerini, eds., *Russia's Orient: Imperial Borderlands and Peoples, 1700–1917* (Bloomington: Indiana University Press, 1997).

12. See chapter 4.

13. Morishima Chūryō, *Kōmō Satsuwa* (Chitchats with the Dutch), ed. R. Ono (Tokyo, 1943), 54–55, 92; quoted in Hiroshi Wagatsuma, "The Social Perception of Skin Color in Japan," in *Color and Race*, ed. John Hope Franklin (Boston: Beacon, 1968), 135.

14. Discrimination against mixed-race Black Japanese seems to be lessening in the new century as Japan becomes a more cosmopolitan country. Nathan Oba Strong, "Patterns of Social Interaction and Psychological Adjustment among Japan's Konketsuji Population" (PhD diss., University of California, Berkeley, 1978); Miyuki Yonezawa, "Memories of Japanese Identity and Racial Hierarchy," in Spickard, *Race and Nation*, 115–32; Lily Anne Yumi Welty, "Advantage through Crisis: Multi-Racial American Japanese on Post–World War II Japan, Okinawa, and America, 1945–1972" (PhD diss., University of California, Santa Barbara, 2012). See also Frank Dikötter, ed., *The Construction of Racial Identities in China and Japan* (Honolulu: University of Hawai'i Press, 1997).

15. Frank Dikötter, *The Discourse of Race in Modern China* (Stanford, CA: Stanford University Press, 1992), 15–17, 38–39, 82, 89.

16. Field notes, Tianjin, 1988–89.

17. Rowena Fong and Paul R. Spickard, "Ethnic Relations in the People's Republic of China: Images and Social Distance between Han Chinese and Minority and Foreign Nationalities," *Journal of Northeast Asian Studies* 13.1 (1994): 26–48.

18. Spickard, *Race and Nation*, 14–16, 135–211; Reginald Horsman, *Race and Manifest Destiny: The Origins of American Racial Anglo-Saxonism* (Cambridge,

MA: Harvard University Press, 1981); Philip Mason, *Patterns of Dominance* (London: Oxford University Press, 1971); Nicholas B. Dirks, *Castes of Mind: Colonialism and the Making of Modern India* (Princeton, NJ: Princeton University Press, 2001); Anthony W. Marx, *Making Race and Nation* (Cambridge: Cambridge University Press, 1998), 29–46; Martin Daunton and Rick Halpern, eds., *Empire and Others: British Encounters with Indigenous Peoples, 1600–1850* (London: University College London Press, 1999); Albert Memmi, *The Colonizer and the Colonized*, rev. ed. (Boston: Beacon, 1991; orig. 1965); Michael Hechter, *Internal Colonialism* (Berkeley: University of California Press, 1975).

19. Melvin C. Goldstein, *The Snow Lion and the Dragon: China, Tibet, and the Dalai Lama* (Berkeley: University of California Press, 1999); Tsering Shakya, *The Dragon in the Land of Snows: A History of Modern Tibet since 1947* (New York: Penguin, 2000); John F. Avedon, *In Exile from the Land of Snows: The Definitive Account of the Dalai Lama and Tibet since the Chinese Conquest* (New York: HarperCollins, 1998); Warren W. Smith Jr., *China's Tibet? Autonomy or Assimilation* (Lanham, MD: Rowman and Littlefield, 2009); Blake Kerr, *Sky Burial: An Eyewitness Account of China's Brutal Crackdown in Tibet* (Ithaca, NY: Snow Lion Publications, 1997).

20. Fong and Spickard, "Ethnic Relations in the People's Republic of China." See also Emily Honig, *Creating Chinese Ethnicity: Subei People in Shanghai, 1850–1980* (New Haven, CT: Yale University Press, 1992); Stevan Harrell, *Ways of Being Ethnic in Southwest China* (Seattle: University of Washington Press, 2001); Stevan Harrell, ed., *Cultural Encounters on China's Ethnic Frontiers* (Seattle: University of Washington Press, 1995); Dru C. Gladney, *Ethnic Identity in China: The Making of a Muslim Minority Nationality* (Fort Worth, TX: Harcourt Brace, 1998); Dru C. Gladney, *Muslim Chinese: Ethnic Nationalism in the People's Republic* (Cambridge, MA: Harvard East Asian Monographs, 1991); Dru C. Gladney, ed., *Making Majorities: Constituting the Nation in Japan, Korea, China, Malaysia, Fiji, Turkey, and the United States* (Stanford, CA: Stanford University Press, 1998), 95–131; Dikötter, *Construction of Racial Identities in China and Japan*, 12–95; Dikötter, *Discourse of Race in Modern China*; Jonathan N. Lipman, *Familiar Strangers: A History of Muslims in Northwest China* (Seattle: University of Washington Press, 1997); Edward J. M. Rhoads, *Manchus and Han: Ethnic Relations and Political Power in Late Qing and Early Republican China, 1861–1928* (Seattle: University of Washington Press, 2000).

21. Yonezawa, "Memories of Japanese Identity and Racial Hierarchy"; Cullen Tadao Hayashida, "Identity, Race, and the Blood Ideology of Japan" (PhD diss., University of Washington, 1974); Kirsten L. Ziomek, "Subaltern Speak: Imperial Multiplicities in Japan's Empire and Post-War Colonialisms" (PhD diss., University of California, Santa Barbara, 2011). See in Dikötter, *Construction of Racial Identities in China and Japan*: Michael Weiner, "The Invention of Identity: Race

and Nation in Pre-War Japan," 96–117; Kazuki Sato, "'Same Language, Same Race': The Dilemma of *Kambun* in Japan," 118–35; Richard Siddle, "The Ainu and the Discourse of 'Race,'" 136–57; Louise Young, "Rethinking Race for Manchukuo: Self and Other in the Colonial Context," 158–76; Kosaku Yoshino, "The Discourse on Blood and Racial Identity in Contemporary Japan," 199–211. In Gladney, *Making Majorities*: Kosaku Yoshino, "Culturalism, Racialism, and Internationalism in the Discourse on Japanese Identity," 13–30; Emiko Ohnuki-Tierney, "A Conceptual Model for the Historical Relationship between the Self and the Internal and External Others: The Agrarian Japanese, the Ainu, and the Special-Status People," 31–51.

22. George DeVos and Hiroshi Wagatsuma, *Japan's Invisible Race: Caste in Culture and Personality*, rev. ed. (Berkeley: University of California Press, 1972); Richard Hanks Mitchell, *The Korean Minority in Japan* (Berkeley: University of California Press, 1967).

23. Lane Ryo Hirabashi, Akemi Kikumura-Yano, and James A. Hirabayashi, eds., *New Worlds, New Lives: Globalization and People of Japanese Descent in the Americas and from Latin America in Japan* (Stanford, CA: Stanford University Press, 2002); Jeffrey Lesser, *Negotiating National Identity: Immigrants, Minorities, and the Struggle for Ethnicity in Brazil* (Durham, NC: Duke University Press, 1999); Joshua Hotaka Roth, *Brokered Homeland: Japanese Brazilian Migrants in Japan* (Ithaca, NY: Cornell University Press, 2002); David T. Suzuki and Keibo Oiwa, *The Other Japan: Voices beyond the Mainstream* (Golden, CO: Fulcrum, 1999); Daniel Touro Linger, *No One Home: Brazilian Selves Remade in Japan* (Stanford, CA: Stanford University Press, 2001); James Brooke, "Sons and Daughters of Japan, Back from Brazil," *New York Times*, November 27, 2001.

24. Christine Su, "Becoming Cambodian: Ethnicity and the Vietnamese in Kampuchea," in Spickard, *Race and Nation*, 273–96.

25. Joanne L. Rondilla and Paul Spickard, *Is Lighter Better? Skin-Tone Discrimination among Asian Americans* (Lanham, MD: Rowman and Littlefield, 2007), 45–78; Khong Dien, *Population and Ethno-Demography in Vietnam* (Chiang Mai, Thailand: Silkworm Books, 2002); Nicole Constable, ed., *Guest People: Hakka Identity in China and Abroad* (Seattle: University of Washington Press, 1996); Craig J. Reynolds, ed., *National Identity and Its Defenders: Thailand Today*, rev. ed. (Chiang Mai, Thailand: Silkworm Books, 2002); Shamsul A. B., "Bureaucratic Management of Identity in a Modern State: 'Malayness' in Postwar Malaysia," in Gladney, *Making Majorities*, 135–50; Anthony Milner, "Ideological Work in Constructing the Malay Majority," in Gladney, *Making Majorities*, 151–69; Judith A. Nagata, "What Is a Malay? Situational Selectivity of Identity in a Plural Society," *American Ethnologist* 1 (1974): 331–50.

26. Sources for this section include Michael C. Howard, *Fiji: Race and Politics in an Island State* (Vancouver: University of British Columbia Press, 1991); Brij V.

Lal, *Broken Waves: A History of the Fiji Islands in the Twentieth Century* (Honolulu: University of Hawai'i Press, 1992); Stewart Firth and Daryl Tarte, eds., *20th Century Fiji* (Suva: USP Solutions, 2001); Deryck Scarr, *Fiji: A Short History* (Sydney: George Allen and Unwin, 1984); Padmini Gaunder, *Education and Race Relations in Fiji, 1835–1998* (Lautoka, Fiji: Universal Printing, 1999); Timothy J. Macnaught, *The Fijian Colonial Experience: A Study of the Neotraditional Order under British Colonial Rule Prior to World War II*, Pacific Research Monograph No. 7 (Canberra: Australian National University, 1982); K. L. Gillion, *Fiji's Indian Migrants: A History to the End of Indenture in 1920* (Melbourne: Oxford University Press, 1962); Alexander Mamak, *Colour, Culture, and Conflict: A Study of Pluralism in Fiji* (Rushcutters Bay, NSW: Pergamon Press, 1978); John D. Kelly, "Aspiring to Minority and Other Tactics against Violence," in Gladney, *Making Majorities*, 173–97; Martha Kaplan, "When 8,870 – 850 = 1: Discourses against Democracy in Fiji, Past and Present," in Gladney, *Making Majorities*, 174–214.

27. The 1987 coup is the subject of several books, including Victor Lal, *Fiji: Coups in Paradise: Race, Politics and Military Intervention* (London: Zed, 1990); Brij V. Lal, *Power and Prejudice: The Making of the Fiji Crisis* (Wellington: New Zealand Institute of International Affairs, Victoria University, 1988); Deryck Scarr, *Fiji: Politics of Illusion: The Military Coups in Fiji* (Kensington: New South Wales University Press, 1988); Jeremaia Waqanisau, "The Only Option: Fijian Coup d'État: A Product of Political Development" (MA thesis, Cartmel College, University of Lancaster, 1989); Robert T. Robertson and Akosita Tamanisau, *Fiji: Shattered Coups* (Leichhardt, NSW: Pluto Press, 1988).

28. Sir Paul Reeves, Tomasi Rayalu Vakatora, and Brij Vilash Lal, *The Fiji Islands towards a United Future: Report of the Fiji Constitution Review Commission, 1996*, Parliamentary Paper No. 34 (Suva: Parliament of Fiji, 1996); Brij V. Lal and Tomasi Rayalu Vakatora, eds., *Fiji Constitution Review Commission Research Papers*, 2 vols. (Suva: School of Social and Economic Development, University of the South Pacific, 1997).

29. One can follow the course of politics in the 1990s in the pages of such sources as Ralph R. Premdas, *Ethnic Conflict and Development: The Case of Fiji* (Aldershot: Avebury, 1995); Reeves, Vakatora, and Lal, *Fiji Islands towards a United Future*; Brij V. Lal and Peter Larmour, eds., *Electoral Systems in Divided Societies: The Fiji Constitution Review*, Pacific Policy Paper No. 21 (Canberra: National Centre for Development Studies, Research School of Pacific and Asian Studies, Australian National University, 1997); Robert T. Robertson, *Multiculturalism and Reconciliation in an Indulgent Republic: Fiji after the Coups, 1987–1998* (Suva: Fiji Institute of Applied Studies, 1998); Lal and Vakatora, *Fiji Constitution Review Commission Research Papers*; Stephanie Lawson, *Tradition versus Democracy in the South Pacific: Fiji, Tonga and Western Samoa* (Cambridge: Cambridge

University Press, 1996), 37–76; Kelly, "Aspiring to Minority and Other Tactics against Violence."

30. Jon Fraenkel, Stewart Firth, and Brij V. Lal, eds., *The 2006 Military Take-over in Fiji: A Coup to End All Coups?* (Canberra: Australian National University Press, 2009); Jonathan Fraenkel and Stewart Firth, eds., *From Election to Coup in Fiji: The 2006 Campaign and Its Aftermath* (Canberra: Australian National University Press, 2007).

31. Gavan Daws, *Shoal of Time: A History of the Hawaiian Islands* (Honolulu: University of Hawai'i Press, 1968); Ralph S. Kuykendall, *The Hawaiian Kingdom,* 3 vols. (Honolulu: University of Hawai'i Press, 1938–67); Michael Kioni Dudley and Keoni Kealoha Agard, *A Call for Hawaiian Sovereignty* (Honolulu: Nā Kāne O Ka Malo Press, 1990); O. A. Bushnell, *The Gifts of Civilization: Germs and Geno-cide in Hawai'i* (Honolulu: University of Hawai'i Press, 1993); David Stannard, *Before the Horror: The Population of Hawai'i on the Eve of Western Contact* (Honolulu: Social Science Research Institute, University of Hawai'i, 1989); J. Matthew Kester, *Remembering Iosepa: History, Place, and Religion in the American West* (New York: Oxford University Press, 2013); David A. Chang, "Borderlands in a World at Sea: Concow Indians, Native Hawaiians, and South Chinese in Indige-nous, Global, and National Spaces," *Journal of American History* 98.2 (2011): 384–403.

32. Lilikala Kame'ele'ihiwa, *Native Land and Foreign Desires* (Honolulu: Bishop Museum Press, 1992); George Cooper and Gavan Daws, *Land and Power in Hawai'i* (Honolulu: University of Hawai'i Press, 1985); Linda S. Parker, *Native American Estate: The Struggle over Indian and Hawaiian Lands* (Honolulu: University of Hawai'i Press, 1989); Sally Engle Merry, *Colonizing Hawai'i: The Cul-tural Power of Law* (Princeton, NJ: Princeton University Press, 2000).

33. Jonathan Osorio, *Dismembering Lāhui: A History of the Hawaiian Nation to 1887* (Honolulu: University of Hawai'i Press, 2002); Dudley and Agard, *Call for Hawaiian Sovereignty*; Lili'uokalani, *Hawai'i's Story by Hawai'i's Queen* (Rutland, VT: Charles E. Tuttle, 1964); Michael Dougherty, *To Steal a Kingdom: Probing Hawaiian History* (Waimanalo, Hawai'i: Island Style Press, 1992); Noenoe Silva, *Ku'e! The 1897 Petitions Protesting Annexation* (Honolulu: 'Ai Pohaku Press, 1998); Helena G. Allen, *The Betrayal of Lili'uokalani* (Honolulu: Mutual Publishing, 1982); Noenoe Silva, *Aloha Betrayed: Native Hawaiian Resistance to American Colonialism* (Durham, NC: Duke Universty Press, 2004); Tom Coffman, *Nation Within: The History of the American Occupation of Hawai'i*, rev. ed. (Kihei, Ha-wai'i: Koa Books, 2009).

34. Lori Pierce, "'The Whites Have Created Modern Honolulu': Ethnicity, Racial Stratification, and the Discourse of Aloha," in Spickard and Daniel, *Ra-cial Thinking in the United States*, 124–54; Pierce, "Creating a Racial Paradise: Citizenship and Sociology in Hawai'i," in Spickard, *Race and Nation*, 69–86. The

conquering and remaking of the Philippines by the United States in the same era was a similarly racialized encounter, though without the syrupy veneer. Stanley Karnow, *In Our Image: America's Empire in the Philippines* (New York: Random House, 1989); Angel Velasco Shaw and Luis H. Francia, eds., *Vestiges of War: The Philippine-American War and the Aftermath of an Imperial Dream* (New York: New York University Press, 2002); Paul A. Kramer, *The Blood of Government: Race, Empire, the United States, and the Philippines* (Chapel Hill: University of North Carolina Press, 2006).

35. Haunani-Kay Trask, *From a Native Daughter* (Monroe, ME: Common Courage Press, 1993).

36. Candace Fujikane and Jonathan Y. Okamura, eds., *Asian Settler Colonialism: From Local Governance to Habits of Everyday Life in Hawai'i* (Honolulu: University of Hawai'i Press, 2008); Jeffrey A. S. Moniz and Paul Spickard, "Carving Out a Middle Ground: Making Race in Hawai'i," in *Negotiating the Color Line: Multiracial Identities in the "Color-Blind Era,"* ed. David L. Brunsma (Boulder, CO: Lynne Rienner, 2006), 63–81.

6

The Return of Scientific Racism?

DNA Ancestry Testing, Race, and the New Eugenics Movement

Science has a lot of uses. It can uncover laws of nature, cure disease, inspire awe, make bombs, and help bridges to stand up. Indeed science is so good at what it does that there's a perpetual temptation to drag it into problems where it may add little or even distract from the real issues.

—H. Allen Orr, "Fooled by Science"

Ancestry.com, a popular website, extends an extravagant scientific promise to make a difference in how you understand your life: "Who Were Your People? For only $79, our test takes you back 30,000, 50,000 . . . even 100,000 years to discover your ancient ancestors—in addition to helping you connect with more recent genetic cousins." Spencer Wells, Ancestry .com's spokesperson and Harvard PhD, National Geographic book author, and PBS documentarian, writes in *Deep Ancestry: Inside the Genographic Project*:

Genetics has become a kind of genie of sorts, promising to grant our wishes with the magic spell of its hidden secrets. . . . By sending in a simple cheek swab sample, a participant can learn about his or her own place within the story of human migration while contributing to and participating in the overall Project.[1]

This sort of claim has a history. This chapter talks about that history and about the science, the pseudoscience, and the misconceptions that go with such promises from the DNA ancestry-testing industry. I enter this discussion as a student of race and society, rather than as a biologist, so I will engage the science of DNA ancestry testing mainly on conceptual rather than technical grounds. It will become apparent that the DNA ancestry-testing people—as distinct from serious DNA scientists—are selling bad science built on racist delusions of long standing.[2]

THE HERITAGE OF RACIALIST SCIENCE

The lineage of ideas about human ancestry, and specifically about race, that passed for science during much of the nineteenth century and the first decades of the twentieth is well known. People styling themselves as scientists made what they presented as racial distinctions and created hierarchies of those racial groups using supposedly scientific methods, categories, and ideas.[3]

The founding father of this movement was Carl Linneaus. In the 1750s Linnaeus did future generations the estimable service of creating a system for classifying all living things into a nested hierarchy of categories. Every organism belonged to one of two kingdoms, plant or animal. Then, proceeding downward through a multiplying hierarchy, organisms were divided into various phyla, the phyla into classes, the classes into orders, and thence to families, genera, and species. Supposedly, the species were fully distinct one from another. It was all very tidy, and it was quite an efficient device for organizing information about a multitude of organisms. For generations neither working scientists nor the thinking public had reason to question Linnaeus's system. Although species were not quite as sealed off from one another as the system represented and although it turned out that there were a lot of organisms, like bacteria, that were neither plant nor animal, still the system possessed a kind of elemental beauty. It was not a tested scientific theory so much as abstract philosophizing based on a lot of data about the structures of northern European plants and much less about other organisms. Yet it was useful for organizing a lot of information, and people thought of it as scientific.[4]

Subsequent generations of European scientists elaborated Linnaeus's system in several ways. On one hand, working biologists examined innumerable species, delimited them with care, discovered new ones, explored the relationships among them, and so on—all against the intellectual backdrop of Linnaeus's categories. That is, they developed the science of biology and what they called natural history. Taking off in another direction, philosophers inclined to think about human beings took Linnaeus's idea of species one step further, asserting that there were several distinct races of humankind, each with a separate physiognomy, intellect, and moral character. These were the pseudoscientific racialist speculators. Georges-Louis Leclerc, comte de Buffon, published his *Histoire Naturelle, Generale et Particuleire* in forty-four volumes between 1748 and 1804. He argued that all humans were one species but that they were divided into several races, each with its own location on the planet, its own physical type, character, and intellectual propensities. The source of the physical, intellectual, and moral differences, thought Buffon, came mainly from climate.[5]

Johann Friedrich Blumenbach, working in the 1770s, decided first that there were four and then that there were precisely five races—European, Mongolian, Ethiopian, American, and Malay—into which all human beings could be divided. He decided further that Europeans had been the original race and that the others had diverged and degenerated from European stock. Finally, he divided each race into what he called "nations," what people much later would come to call "ethnic groups."[6] He worked at around the same time as Georges Léopold Cuvier. Both Blumenbach and Cuvier decided that the Europeans, who by now were being called Caucasians, were the most beautiful of the races. They were called Caucasians in part because some people thought the Caucasus region was where

Europeans originated but mainly because in Cuvier's eyes, "various nations in the vicinity of Caucasus, the Georgians and Circassians, are . . . the handsomest on earth."[7] Cuvier was a scientist and the chancellor of the University of Paris, but this racial speculating sounds as if he had left science behind somewhere and wandered into poetry.

The villain of the piece, if there be one, was another French aristocrat, Joseph Arthur, comte de Gobineau. In a hugely influential treatise, *The Inequality of Human Races* (1853–55), still in print today in many languages, Gobineau arranged the races in a strict hierarchy of intellect, ability, and morality: Whites, Asians, Indians of the Americas, Malays, and Africans. Race, he said, explained everything in human affairs and human history. Some of his chapter titles give the flavor of his ideas: "Degeneration: The Mixture of Racial Elements," "Racial Inequality Is Not the Result of Institutions," "Some Anthropologists Regard Man as Having a Multiple Origin," "Racial Differences are Permanent," "The Human Races Are Intellectually Unequal," "The Different Languages Are Unequal, and Correspond Perfectly in Relative Merit to the Races That Use Them." And again, when he spoke of race and beauty: "Those who are most akin to us come nearest to beauty; such are the degenerate Aryan stocks of India and Persia, and the Semitic people who are least infected by contact with the black race. As these races recede from the white type, their features and limbs become incorrect in form; they acquire defects of proportion which, in the races that are completely foreign to us, end by producing an extreme ugliness." Richard Wagner welcomed Gobineau into his Bayreuth circle when the latter wore out his welcome in France, and Adolf Hitler admired his writing in a later generation.[8]

By the time these ideas reached Gobineau, what had hitherto been science—speculative science, to be sure, but arguably science nonetheless—was shading over into something quite different: popular intellectual underpinnings for a racialized public policy. Perhaps in part because of such public popularity, the racialist ideas of Blumenbach, Gobineau, and the others continued to shape scientific orthodoxy, especially among avatars of the growing discipline of physical anthropology. So one saw books like *The Races of Europe* (1899), by William Ripley, a professor of sociology at MIT and of anthropology at Columbia. Ripley's book had a lot of pictures of "racial types"—not just five big races, but subsidiary ethnic groups, and maps that showed the distribution of people according to their cephalic indexes. The cephalic index was an attempt to make racial and ethnic distinctions, the products of social interactions and mutual perceptions, arrived at in the context of colonial relationships, look more like science by quantifying them. One selected a "typical" member of an ethnic group, measured the breadth and length of that person's head, and calculated the relationship of those two numbers as a percentage. Each head shape was supposed to have its own characteristic temperament and intellectual capability.[9]

A. H. Keane, in a 1901 book, *Ethnology*, which became the standard textbook on its subject for generations, presented the family tree of humankind (which he called "hominidae," perhaps because that Latinate term sounded more scientific than "humankind"). He presented Anglo-Saxons as the central branch of the human species, with Anglo-Americans and other worldwide colonizers as their fullest expression. Slavs branched off earlier and were further removed from the Anglo-Saxon core group; Southern Europeans, Semites, and Ainu, before that; Polynesians, before that; and Asians, before that. Africans (with subgroups that included Australian Aborigines and Melanesians), Keane posited, had diverged so long ago as to be almost a separate species. Of course, Keane presented no data other than skin color on which to base his schema or the historical relationships he supposed to have existed between peoples (fig. 6.1).[10]

Vice president of the British Anthropological Institute and a professor of Hindustani at University College, London, Keane laid out his ideas about the current state of the races in a table I have reproduced as table 6.1. He placed religion and temperament alongside eye shape, nose shape, and skin color, as if they were all genetically determined. He used big words that sounded scientific (brachycephalous, orthognathus, mesodont, etc.). But he revealed his underlying social agenda—to excuse slavery and the colonial domination of Whites over darker peoples—in the final row: temperament. Dividing a welter of peoples into four ideal physical types and masking his enterprise in a cloud of pseudoscientific jargon, he expected his readers to follow him as he leaped to conclude that each type had a characteristic temperament that explained its social position. Hence, African-descended people were "sensuous, indolent, improvident; fitful,

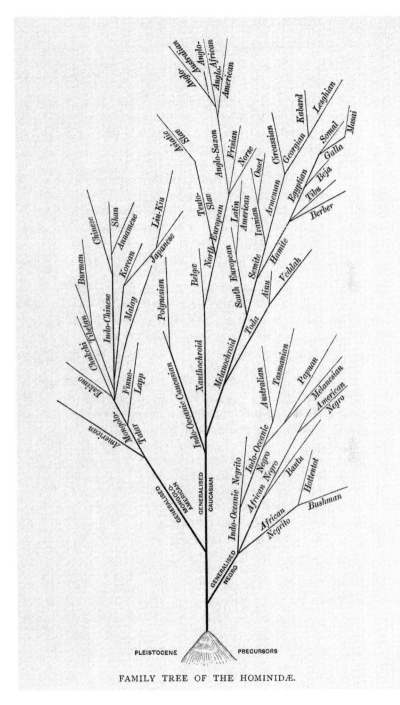

Fig. 6.1.
Family tree of humankind. From A. H. Keane, *Ethnology* (1901).

passionate, and cruel," with "easy acceptance of the yoke of slavery" and a lack of science and art. Europeans, by contrast, were "active, enterprising, imaginative," and either "serious, steadfast, solid and stolid" or "fiery, impulsive, fickle"—but in either case good at science and the arts. Africans were biologically destined to be slaves, said Keane and other pseudoscientists. Europeans were biologically destined to be scientists and poets. If it were in their genes, the implication was, it was no one's fault. This passed for science a century ago in the United States, Britain, and the rest of the colonizing countries of Europe and North America.

Such ideas, then, were accepted scientific orthodoxy, and they became unquestioned popular orthodoxy as well. A map that appeared in the 1904 *Annual Report* of the US Commissioner-General of Immigration made a "grand division of race" that presented the peoples who came to the United States as "Slavic," "Teutonic," "Iberic," "Keltic," "Mongolic," and "Hebrew," as if each of these "racial" distinctions had some scientific meaning. Similarly, one of the forty-one volumes of the 1910–11 report of the Dillingham Commission, a comprehensive report on US immigration, was titled *Dictionary of Races or Peoples*, which purported to lay out a definitive list of races and ethnic groups, their locations in the world and their characters and physiognomies, and other material.[11]

It was a short step from pseudoscientific ideas that had made their way into public life to using those ideas to advocate particular public policies. In fact, in the first decades of the twentieth century there appeared a slew of racist screeds against immigrants in general, Southern and Eastern European immigrants in particular, and Asian immigrants most especially. Social and marital mixing among divergent ethnicities was a topic of special scorn. None of the attacks was more pointed than Alfred Schultz's diatribe against race mixing and immigration, which he called "racial suicide." The book's full title tells its story: *Race or Mongrel? A brief history of the rise and fall of the ancient races of earth; a theory that the fall of nations is due to intermarriage with alien stocks; a demonstration that a nation's strength is due to racial purity; a prophecy that America will sink to early decay unless immigration is rigorously restricted.*[12]

One of the classic texts was Madison Grant's *The Passing of the Great Race*. Published first in 1916 and then in several editions, *Passing* had an

Table 6.1. Racial Types in Pseudoscience

	Ideal Negro Type	Ideal Mongol Type	Ideal American Type	Ideal Caucasic Type
Hair	a. Short, jet black, frizzly, flat in transverse section, little or no beard; b. Reddishbrown, woolly	Coarse, black, lustreless, lank, round in transverse section, beardless, but moustache common	Very long, coarse, black, lank, nearly round in section; beardless	a. Long, wavy, soft, flaxen; b. Long, straight, wiry, black; both oval in section; both full bearded
Colour	a. Blackish; b. Yellowish brown	Yellowish	Coppery, yellowish	a. Florid; b. Pale
Skull	a. Dolichocephalous: 72 b. Brachycephalous: 83	Brachycephalous: 84	Mesaticephalous: 79	a. Dolichocephalous: 74 b. Brachycephalous: 83
Jaws	Prognathous: 60	Mesognathous: 68	Mesognathous: 72	Orthognathous: 76
Cheek bone	Small, moderately retreating	Prominent laterally	Moderately prominent	Small; unmarked
Nose	Very broad, flat, platyrrhine: 56	Very small, mesorrhine: 52	Large, bridged or aquiline, mesorrhine: 50	Large, straight or arched, leptorrhine: 46
Eyes	Large, round, prominent, black; yellowish cornea	Small, black, oblique, outer angle slightly elevated, vertical field of skin over inner canthus	Small, round, straight, sunken, black	a. Blue; b. Black; both moderately large and always straight
Teeth	Large (macrodont)	Medium (mesodont)	Medium (mesodont)	Small (microdont)
Stature	a. Above the average: 5 ft. 10 in. b. Dwarfish: 4 ft.	Below the average: 5 ft. 4 in.	Above the average: 5 ft. 8 in.	a. Above average: 5 ft. 8 in. b. Average: 5 ft. 5 or 6 in.
Speech	Agglutinating of various prefix and postfix types	Agglutinating chiefly with post fixes; isolating with tones	Polysynthetic mainly	Chiefly inflecting; some agglutinating
Religion	Non-theistic, nature and ancestry worship; fetishism and witchcraft prevalent	Polytheistic; shamanism; Buddhism; Transmigration	Polytheistic; animism; nature worship	Monotheism: Judaism; Christianity; Mohammedanism
Temperament	Sensuous, indolent, improvident; fitful, passionate, and cruel, though often affectionate and faithful; little self-respect, hence easy acceptance of the yoke of slavery; science and art undeveloped	Sluggish, somewhat sullen, with little initiative but great endurance; generally frugal, thrifty and industrious, but moral standard low; science slightly, art and letters moderately developed	Moody, taciturn, wary; deep feelings masked by an impassive exterior; indifference to physical pain; science slightly, art moderately, letters scarcely at all developed	Active, enterprising, imaginative; a. serious, steadfast, solid and stolid; b. fiery, impulsive, fickle; science, art and letters highly developed in both.
	a = Negro; b = Negrito.			a = Xanthochroi; b = Melanochroi.

Source: A. H. Keane, Ethnology (Cambridge: Cambridge University Press, 1901), 228.

enormous influence on American public opinion, medical practice, and public policy. Grant argued that Europeans—in particular, a subset that he called at various stages Aryans, Nordics, and Teutons—were the central figures in all that was good, true, and beautiful in human history. He followed racial scientists in assigning scientific-sounding Latinate names to peoples—Dolicho-lepto, Lappanoid, etc.—and in assorting all European peoples into three groups: Nordics (*Homo sapiens europeau*), Alpines (*Homo sapiens alpinus*), and Mediterraneans (*Homo sapiens mediterraneus*). He arranged them according to what he believed to be their ancient linguistic roots, as well as their typical physical stature; eye, hair, and skin color; nose and face shape; and cephalic index. He claimed that each group, in addition to possessing a distinctive physical type, possessed a particular temperament and set of intellectual capabilities. Teutons, for instance, were a branch of the Nordic race of Europeans. They were tall of frame and had long heads and high, narrow faces. Their hair ran from flaxen to chestnut but never to black, their eyes from blue to gray to green. They were gifted in intellectual and artistic pursuits. The common feature of all Nordics was that their languages descended from ancient Aryan roots. This set them apart from other European races in his schema.

One can catch the flavor of Grant's polemic in the following excerpt, in which he dismisses the notion that non-Nordic immigrants could assimilate and become good Americans.

> With a pathetic and fatuous belief in the efficacy of American institutions and environment to reverse or obliterate immemorial hereditary tendencies, these newcomers were welcomed and given a share in our land and prosperity. The American taxed himself to sanitate and educate these poor helots, and as soon as they could speak English, encouraged them to enter into the political life, first of municipalities, and then of the nation.
>
> The result is showing plainly in the rapid decline of the birth rate of native Americans because the poorer classes of Colonial stock, where they still exist, will not bring children into the world to compete in the labor market with the Slovak, the Italian, the Syrian, and the Jew. The native American is too proud to mix socially with them,

and is gradually withdrawing from the scene, abandoning to these aliens the land which he conquered and developed. The man of the old stock is being crowded out of many country districts by these foreigners, just as he is to-day being literally driven off the streets of New York City by the swarms of Polish Jews. These immigrants adopt the language of the native American; they wear his clothes; they steal his name; and they are beginning to take his women, but they seldom adopt his religion or understand his ideals, and while he is being elbowed out of his own home the American looks calmly abroad and urges on others the suicidal ethics which are exterminating his own race.

There was a German edition, and it has been said that *The Passing of the Great Race* was Adolf Hitler's favorite book and one of the works that inspired Nazi racial policies in Germany.[13]

Not all pseudoscientific racism was directed toward blocking further immigration to the United States. Some of these ideas were used on unfortunate members of subordinate races and classes already here, in the form of a new pseudoscience: eugenics.[14] Eugenics grew to become a dominant influence from the 1920s through the 1950s in several scholarly circles: biology, anthropology, sociology, law, social work. The idea was that science could gauge the heredity of individuals, use that knowledge to judge their mental abilities and their degree of physical perfection, and then use *that* knowledge to perfect the human race by weeding out the unfit and selecting the fittest for special benefits, including increased access to procreation. Originally the brainchild of Francis Galton, a British aristocrat and adventurer who mapped parts of Africa and studied how weather worked, the idea of perfecting the race by selective breeding took hold in the United States, Britain, and Germany more than in other countries, though it had offshoots around the globe.

Eugenicists purported to bring together all the sciences in order to direct human evolution. It had both positive and negative dimensions. Positive eugenics would theoretically encourage people who were regarded as the best examples of the human species to breed and presumably create superior offspring. Some White Americans competed in the 1910s and

1920s, as Germans did in the 1930s and 1940s, to have babies who would be judged the finest physical and mental representatives of their race. There was not a national, government-sponsored program in the United States, as there was in Germany, to breed Aryan super-babies, but there were attempts to prevent breeding by people whom eugenicists deemed to be inferior. The anti-immigrant campaign of the 1910s and 1920s was argued partly in eugenic terms, and the US Surgeon General and leaders of the Public Health Service advocated screening immigrants to keep out "inferior stock." Eugenicists imposed a medical model of defective genetics on homosexuals. And, beginning in 1907, thirty states passed laws that empowered governments to force sterilization on women who were deemed to be "degenerates," "feeble-minded," "morally delinquent," or otherwise unfit. From Massachusetts to Hawai'i, girls and women were incarcerated, labeled "incorrigible" or "feeble-minded" because they appeared to enjoy sex or had borne babies out of wedlock, and sterilized—64,000 in all, most of them poor, and many of them women of color. The American eugenicist Henry Laughlin helped take the show on the road, as one of the authors of the Nazi regime's "race hygiene" law; two million Germans were sterilized as a result.

Eugenics was the force behind the vogue of intelligence testing that swept the nation in the wake of World War I and has been with us ever since.[15] The first intelligence test was created in France by two Galton devotees, Alfred Binet and Theodore Simon. Charged by the French government in 1904 to devise a method by which to detect "mentally deficient" children, Simon and Binet devised a standardized series of questions and problems that, they said, could determine the "mental age" of a particular child. The goal was then to devise particular curricula to fit the educational needs of children of different mental ages. Binet perceived there was a great deal of variability in mental age within any social group (and indeed within a given person over time), but this realization was overlooked when his test was brought to America in 1908 by H. H. Goddard, a former schoolteacher and University of Southern California football coach who was doing research at the Training School for Feeble-Minded Girls and Boys in Vineland, New Jersey.

Goddard distributed thousands of English-language copies of the test across the country and began a lifelong campaign to bring it into every arena of American life. He and other advocates convinced the US Army to use a similar test to determine the assignments of soldiers during World War I. As Lewis Terman, another devotee of intelligence testing, put it, "If the Army machine is to work smoothly and efficiently, it is as important to fit the job to the man as to fit the ammunition to the gun."[16] In 1912 Goddard convinced the authorities at Ellis Island to let him test immigrants, using two assistants. One assistant would scan the room for people who, to his eyes, looked stupid. They were pulled out of line and tested by the second assistant. If the test found them to be, in Goddard's terminology, an "idiot," an "imbecile," or a "moron," they were denied entry to the country. Goddard claimed that 40 percent of steerage passengers were "feeble-minded." As a result, at least for a time, the numbers of would-be entrants who were sent back to wherever they came from skyrocketed.[17] Carl Brigham, one of the army testers, contended that the tests indicated an ethnic difference in intelligence. Echoing the categories of Madison Grant, he concluded that the Alpine and Mediterranean "races"—that is, people of Central and Southern European origin—were "intellectually inferior to members of the Nordic race."[18]

New versions of the Binet-Simon test, including the famous Stanford-Binet test devised by Terman, made their way into business hiring practices and classrooms across the country. Goddard, Terman, Brigham, and others not only convinced the American public that intelligence was a measurable quantity. Without much scientific evidence, they also persuaded people that intelligence was an inherited, not an acquired, trait and that different groups of people—including races—tended to have different amounts of intelligence per capita. These ideas—founded in racial prejudice and nourished by dubious science—have not died. Goddard's and Terman's tests are the direct ancestors of today's SAT and GRE examinations for college and graduate school admission.[19]

Beginning in the 1920s, mainstream social science struck back, with a systematic refutation of pseudobiological ideas about race. Frank Hankins made a head-on assault in 1926 with *The Racial Basis of Civilization: A Critique of the Nordic Doctrine*. He inveighed against "Aryanism[,] . . .

Gobinism[,] . . . Teutonism[,] . . . Celticism[,] . . . Gallicism[,] . . . Anglo-Saxonism[,] and Nordicism" on philosophical, scientific, and pragmatic grounds. The legendary anthropologist Franz Boas and a generation of disciples made their careers (and the discipline of cultural anthropology) out of confronting and gradually undercutting racialist pseudoscience and substituting cultural analysis. In mainstream academic circles, pseudoscientific racialist ideas had been fairly conclusively refuted by the 1940s, although it took another two decades for the public to begin to catch on.[20]

Even so, throwbacks to pseudoscientific racism continued to pop up now and then. For more than four decades beginning in the late 1930s, the Harvard anthropologist Carleton Coon wrote a series of big books for an ever shrinking audience in which he pushed a pseudoscientific racial angle of analysis. The books lacked the vitriol and obvious policy agenda of Grant and Goddard, but Coon's analysis was not much different from theirs. Despite his pretense to objectivity, Coon had a barely hidden policy agenda. In 1959 he joined a number of colleagues in forming the International Society for the Advancement of Ethnology and Eugenics, with the expressed purpose of linking race and intelligence in order to win a reversal of the *Brown v. Board of Education* ruling that aimed to end school segregation.[21] Sociobiology in the 1980s and its stepchild of the 1990s and 2000s, evolutionary psychology, expanded on several of the tracks laid down by Keane, Grant, Stoddard, and Galton. But in scholarly circles, these have remained minority opinions.[22]

If the number of purportedly scientific treatments based on racialist ideas has declined, policy advocacy based partly on racialist science is still quite common. Stretching from Richard Herrnstein and Charles Murray's 1994 screed against affirmative action, *The Bell Curve*, through Peter Brimelow's *Alien Nation* (1995), Samuel Huntington's *The Clash of Civilizations* (1996) and *Who Are We?* (2004), and Jon Entine's *Taboo: Why Black Athletes Dominate Sports and Why We're Afraid to Talk about It* (2000) to Patrick Buchanan's *The Death of the West: How Dying Populations and Immigrant Invasions Imperil Our Country and Civilization* (2002) and *State of Invasion: The Third World Invasion and Conquest of America* (2006), popular racism based partly on long-discredited pseudoscience has been a regular feature on best-seller lists.[23]

DNA TESTING AND PROMISES ABOUT
YOUR ANCESTRY

Spencer Wells and the DNA testing people adopt a scientific posture, too, with the imprimatur of the National Geographic Society. They promise to find out the scientific truth about who your ancestors were, even if there are no historical records, and also to find out about your ancestry much further back in time than any historical records could go.[24] A similar organization, AlphaGenic Testing Services, says, "The ethnicity DNA test will provide you with an estimated percentage of Ethnicity from the four population groups: East Asians[,] . . . Native American[,] . . . Indo-European[,] . . . Africans"—Keane's four racial groups, which scientists say never existed as separate types, nonetheless brought back to life.[25] AlphaGenic promises help "if you are seeking to validate your eligibility for government entitlements such as Native American rights"—but they hedge, saying, "you will need to verify with the specific tribe or entity you are seeking benefits from, if they will accept this type of test."[26]

Other purveyors of DNA ancestry testing focus on more medical-sounding services. DNA Direct concentrates on projecting a medical image. Its website pictures doctors with stethoscopes, lab technicians, clean-cut health care plan managers, and smiling families. And it markets to those same four groups: "We deliver guidance and decision support for genomic medicine to patients, providers and payors—reducing health risks, preventing disease, and better targeting therapies." DNA Direct's website warns, for example, "Seven to ten percent of breast cancers are hereditary." Could you have diseased ancestors? You'd better find out. We'll sell you a test.[27]

DNA is real, and scientifically it is vitally important. Each human being, in the nucleus of every ordinary cell, has forty-six chromosomes. These are arranged in pairs—one inherited from each parent—two very long, narrow, complex, twined strips of deoxyribonucleic acid. Each of these chromosomes is made up of genes, tiny coded bits of material that instruct the cells how to grow. Genetic research and testing of individuals for medical purposes are, on balance, great things. There are several hundred tests that can be run for susceptibility to a host of different diseases and conditions. Some of them test for individual mutations, others for susceptibilities that may be inherited. For example, it is probable that predispositions toward some kinds of cancer are inherited. There is a limitation: increased susceptibility to many diseases seems to reside not on single genes but rather in the interaction of several, even myriads of genes.[28] Nonetheless, on the whole genetic research for medical purposes is probably good science. I have no problems with the scientific mechanics of DNA work, although there is a great deal of controversy over whether one can make meaningful racial aggregations of genetic data for medical purposes.[29]

I do have one small conceptual problem, however, not with the way DNA lab work is done but with the way it may be used. The scientists who do the DNA tests only check a couple or at most a very small number of genes out of the 20,000 to 40,000 that they think we have. That makes DNA testing less useful for identity confirmation and ancestry purposes than for medical uses. Since DNA testing only checks a tiny fraction of any person's DNA, it is only useful for proving a negative, a nonmatch. If one is checking an individual for a particular disease, one can be ruled in or out on the basis of a small number of markers.

But for establishing an individual's identity, one must analyze a lot more markers, and forensic DNA analysis does not do that. It can prove difference, for example, that a particular person's DNA was *not* on the bloodstained knife. But DNA testing, contrary to what you may have imagined from watching *CSI*, cannot prove sameness conclusively. It cannot prove that the blood on the knife *is* that of a particular person, only that it has a relatively small number of characteristics in common with the blood of that person. DNA testing for this kind of match assumes that the rest of the genes are irrelevant to the goal of making the match, because we did not test for them.[30]

There is also a much bigger problem, one that I believe invalidates the whole project of using DNA analysis for genealogical purposes—again, as distinct from medical ones. Historically speaking, using DNA analysis to prove genealogical links is nonsense. Wells writes, "I consider myself to be a historian."[31] If so, then he is a bad one. He makes a classic freshman mistake that no good historian would make: he assumes that there was a Time Before, when things were unchanging:

> By analyzing samples from people who have been living in the same place for a long period of time, so-called indigenous people, it is possible to infer details about the genetic patterns of their ancestors. . . . Once they enter the melting pot, their DNA loses the geographic context in which the genetic patterns create a clear trail. . . . In the Genographic Project, we . . . want to look at a representative sample of people from around the world. . . . [W]e need a database of the way things were before the mobility revolution began in the 19th century. . . . By assembling a database of genetic data from indigenous populations around the world we can reconstruct worldwide genetic patterns as they were before the mobility revolution began.[32]

Well, no. There was no Time Before. Wells assumes—contrary to all historical and archaeological evidence—that people before 1800 were stationary. It is just not true. Human history is nothing if not a record of many vast migrations. People have moved back and forth across great distances and mixed everywhere. The modern-day Turks are descended largely from people who came to Anatolia from Central Asia only recently—as late as the eleventh century—although since that time they have mixed with all the peoples of the Mediterranean basin and western Asia. Creeks and other Native peoples of the American Southeast migrated into what we think of as their home region in a similar time frame, and then they mixed with each other, with Europeans, and with Africans. Most of the ancestors of the Apaches once lived in central Canada, although the tribe came together out of several different peoples in the American Southwest. Polynesians spread throughout the wide Pacific in many waves of exploration, emigration, and mixing that occurred over more than two thousand years, probably including some visits to the western coasts of the American continents. Inuit from northeastern Canada have engaged in transpolar travel and marriage patterns with circumpolar relatives from northern Norway for many hundreds of years.[33]

It is possible that DNA analysis of very large populations might be useful to guess at very general movements of very large groups of people over very long periods of time. But we absolutely cannot pin down where X person's ancestors came from, much less what percentage of X's ancestors came from where. The lessons of recorded history, going as far back in time as we can go, and of archaeological evidence before that, are clear. Every group of people came to where they are from somewhere else. Every group of people has been mixing with other groups of people for many, many centuries. The dominant fact about any single person's ancestry is that it is mixed. It has always been so. The myth of primitive isolation and purity is just that: a myth.

Pick a genetic marker—almost any marker. There are people inside one's group who don't have it. There are other people outside the group who do have it. That means that the existence of a particular genetic marker says nothing at all about a particular individual's ancestry, for all analyses are based on percentages and frequencies.[34] Let us assume, for the sake of argument, that our judgment of African descent is based on possession of a certain chromosome configuration because we observe that 90 percent of the people whom we believe to be African-descended possess that marker. The problem is twofold: (1) the other 10 percent of the people we believe to be African descended don't have that marker, and (2) some people we believe to be White do have that marker. Does this mean that the socially White people who possess the marker are really Black? Some would say so, but that is false scientism, where technique trumps social reality. What about the 10 percent of the people who have lived Black lives but don't have the marker? Are they not Black? Then what of the lives they have lived, of the families to whom they are related and with whom they have lived?

Conceptually, all this amounts to the same thing as nineteenth-century racialist science. Instead of skin color, eye shape, nose shape, or cephalic index, the current generation of DNA racialist pseudoscientists substitutes a different kind of physicality—something deeper than the surface, in the chromosomes, and so perhaps we may assume it is more true somehow—and they pretend it trumps social experience. That is a dubious contention at best.

It is especially troubling when promoters use DNA to pretend to determine a particular individual's ancestry. There are some key logical leaps of faith that render the whole enterprise unworkable. Always the claims made by Wells and the online DNA testing marketers are carefully hedged so they cannot be held liable for false promises. They speak just enough about averages and percentage chances of relatedness between populations so that no one can win a lawsuit. They are pretending to sell something—concrete information about a person's ancestry—but actually they promise only percentage likelihoods, similar patterns in frequencies of appearances of particular genes in populations who currently live at various locations around the globe.

Yet that is not the way that consumers perceive the tests, and therein lies the problem. People who read the ads and hear the claims think that DNA testing is a magical device for divining one's ancestry. Erin Aubry Kaplan is a smart, well-educated journalist. In 2003 she wrote a Los Angeles newspaper column, "Black Like I Thought I Was." In it she told the story of Wayne Joseph, then a fifty-one-year-old Black man, descended from Louisiana Creoles, living in Los Angeles. He was a high school principal and an African American community activist. On a whim, he took a DNA ancestry test. Kaplan wrote:

> Here was the unexpected and rather unwelcome truth: Joseph was 57 percent Indo-European, 39 percent Native American, 4 percent East Asian—and zero percent African. After a lifetime of assuming blackness, he was now being told that he lacked even a single drop of black blood.

Well, no. Wayne Joseph was an African American man, and he had led the life of an African American man in California. Like most descendants of Louisiana Creoles, he likely had multiple ancestries, probably European as much as African, and Native American as well. The DNA ancestry test proved nothing, and it changed nothing about the life he had lived. Yet Kaplan appears to have believed it revealed a deeper, more essential truth about who he really was.[35]

Perhaps the most famous example of misconceiving the value of DNA ancestry testing appeared on PBS, in Henry Louis Gates Jr.'s TV series, *African American Lives*. Gates, like many thoughtful African Americans, was frustrated by the at best fragmentary knowledge of family history that is available to most African Americans. The era of slavery put an insurmountable roadblock in the path of many a would-be genealogist. Writes Gates:

> I was searching not just for the names of my ancestors but for stories about them, the secrets of the dark past of Negroes in America. . . . [S]earching for my ancestry was always a fraught process, always a mix of joy, frustration, and outrage. . . . I even allowed myself to dream about learning the name of the tribe we had come from in Africa. But . . . the people who created [slavery] so perversely designed it to destroy any possibility of maintaining the family ties necessary to tracing one's ancestry[,] . . . making us fragmented and not whole, isolated, discrete parts, not pieces of fabric stitched together in a grand pattern.[36]

So Gates set out to discover the histories of nineteen prominent African Americans, himself included. He sent a team of researchers to the archives and found out a lot of information that the celebrities did not know about their family histories. He also had the celebrities talk on camera about what they thought they knew about their ancestry. And he gave them a DNA ancestry test. Then he recorded their reactions when he revealed the DNA results.

Oprah Winfrey was shocked:

> She told me she's often been told she was a Zulu—a descendant of the great South African nation who fought so hard and so effectively against the British [*sic*] for so many years. She said, "When I'm in Africa, I always feel that I look Zulu. I feel connected to the Zulu tribe." . . . But Oprah's DNA told a different story.[37]

Anyone who has ever read the history of the Atlantic slave trade could have told Oprah that her chances of Zulu ancestry were infinitesimal: the vast majority of slaves were taken from West Africa; there are no records of slaves being abducted from Zulu territory in extreme southern Africa. The report that her DNA looked a lot like the DNA of West Africans apparently was a shock to her, but it should not have been a surprise.[38]

WHAT IS THE UPSHOT of all this? I have no objection to scientific data gathering—and that seems to be Spencer Wells's ulterior motive. He wants to help scientists find out as much about the whole human genome as possible. For that purpose, he recruits people to contribute DNA samples, and he gets them to pay for the privilege. Wells explains:

> We need more samples. A lot more. What we know about human migratory patterns is based on a few thousand people who have been studied for a handful of genetic markers. There might be as many as 10,000 people whose DNA has been studied if you add up all of the samples in every paper that has been published in the last few years. But this isn't a great sample of the world's 6.5 billion people. It's like attempting to describe the complexity of outer space with a pair of binoculars. We need to increase this number by at least an order of magnitude, to 100,000 or more, to have the power to answer some of the key questions about our past. That will give us the genetic telescope we need. . . . By sending in a simple cheek swab sample, a participant can learn about his or her own place within the story of human migration while contributing to and participating in the overall Project . . . by purchasing a kit.[39]

DNA analysis can be a good thing. It can tell a lot about *an individual's* potential susceptibility to certain diseases. DNA analysis may tell us some things about the frequencies of particular characteristics in groups we designate by social means. For example, it might be able to tell us that the people we perceive as Jews have a higher susceptibility to Tay-Sachs disease than the rest of the population; so if we want to test people for that disease, we should look first at the Jewish population. DNA analysis may tell us that the people we designate as Black have a higher frequency of occurrence of sickle cell anemia, so we can direct the majority of our sickle cell anemia prevention resources toward that population.

DNA analysis can also tell us some things about group characteristics. With regard to any of several major characteristics, DNA analysis can tell us that Blacks are like this *on average*, while Whites are like that *on average*. Of course, we already knew about Tay-Sachs and sickle cell anemia, but other characteristic group features may appear, and we should welcome knowledge from DNA research that allows us to target medical services to particular socially defined groups. What DNA analysis *cannot* tell us, however, is anything meaningful about the racial or ethnic group ancestry of a particular *individual*. For such a purpose, DNA analysis seems pretty clearly to be junk science.[40]

The British Society for Human Genetics and the British Association for Adoption and Fostering agree. Their "Statement on the Use of DNA Testing to Determine Racial Background" concludes, "The use of genetic testing to determine ethnic background is not recommended." The Human Genome Diversity Project at Stanford University concurs:

> Are ethnic groups genetically definable? As far as scientists know, no particular genes make a person Irish or Chinese or Zulu or Navajo. These are cultural labels, not genetic ones. People in those populations are more likely to have some alleles in common, but no allele will be found in all members of one population and in no members of any other. . . . There is no such thing as a genetically "pure" human population.[41]

So the DNA ancestry-testing sellers' scientific and historical claims are bogus. But even so, on the surface not much harm appears to have been done. It is not pleasant to see people being conned into giving money under false pretenses, either buying products of dubious value to make someone some money or thinking they are learning about their personal ancestry when what they are really doing is contributing data to Spencer Wells's big project. It's a bit like giving money to faith healers, and it's sad to see. But if they want to give their money to be entertained by test results of doubtful validity, then okay.

To be completely fair, DNA ancestry testing for race is bogus, annoying, and fraudulent, but it is not precisely eugenic. That is, although it is founded on the same intellectual principles as the earlier eugenics movement, it does not seek actively to alter the genetic character of particular populations, as the eugenics movement did. The same cannot be said for several other recent uses of scientific and medical technologies.

We must also ask, to what use will Wells and the DNA bankers put the data they collect through this fraud? Once they have collected the DNA, it is theirs to keep and use as they choose. Will they turn the the things they learn about the genome over to crime labs that one day might experiment with DNA profiling, picking people out as genetically predisposed to commit crimes? Terrie Moffitt, a Duke University researcher, asserts, "Today the most compelling modern theories of crime and violence weave social and biological themes together."[42] While other researchers emphasize that even predisposition is not destiny and that no DNA test can predict the conscienceless rapaciousness of a Bernie Madoff or the guys from Enron, afficionados of TV cop shows are likely not to appreciate the distinction. What is to keep us from going down the path predicted in the sci-fi film *Minority Report*, where people were sentenced for crimes they had yet to commit, on the basis of technologies predicting future behavior?[43] On the other hand, will future researchers use DNA technology and information for what some might see as more positive eugenic purposes? Will they, for example, enable rich parents to create designer babies? Some labs are already advertising in vitro fertilization services offering sex selection and screening for hereditary diseases.[44] Both criminal profiling and selecting the characteristics of babies fall well within the orbit of eugenic practices, and they seem to me ethically irresponsible.

There are other problems as well. This whole DNA business tends to reinforce some pernicious ideas. In the first place, the selling of DNA ancestry analysis tends to support the popular impression that science is a magical template—"a kind of genie of sorts," in Wells's words—that works with unerring, mechanical precision. Most practicing scientists know otherwise, but the public remains awed. Second, all this tends to reinforce the popular belief (really a new phenomenon since World War II and the Manhattan Project) that science is smarter than nonscience and therefore should be funded lavishly while other ways of exploring and understanding are impoverished.[45]

Worse still: although Wells contends that like Darwin he is searching for the underlying unity of humankind,[46] DNA analysis for ancestry purposes tends to reinforce the idea that there exist in fact indelible, measurable biological differences between groups. It focuses on tiny similarities within socially and historically defined groups. It ignores vast variations inside each of those groups. It ignores huge similarities across all people from all groups. That approach has worked out badly in the past (e.g., Nazi Germany). One is left, sadly, with the conclusion that DNA ancestry testing is very much like the eugenics movement, operating with much fancier technological tools.

NOTES

H. Allen Orr's "Fooled by Science" appeared in the *New York Review of Books* on August 18, 2011. I must thank Lily Welty, Mike Osborne, Edwina Barvosa, Anna Spickard, Jörg Hölscher, Jim Spickard, Patrick Miller, Ingrid Dineen-Wimberly, Reginald Daniel, Cathy Tashiro, Ryan Colon, and Terence Keel for listening to these ideas at various times over the past few years and giving me many suggestions for making them better. Miri Song hosted my presentation of a version of this paper at the University of Kent, and she shared ideas and materials. Michelle Gadpaille and Victor Kennedy did the same at the University of Maribor. I expect that none of them would want to take responsibility for all the things I write here, but I much appreciate their ideas, encouragement, and company on life's journey.

1. Spencer Wells, *Deep Ancestry: Inside the Human Genographic Project* (Washington, DC: National Geographic, 2007), 2, 8. See also Steve Olson, *Mapping Human History: Genes, Race, and Our Common Origins* (Boston: Houghton Mifflin, 2002); Chris Pomery, *Family History in the Genes: Trace Your DNA and Grow Your Family Tree* (Richmond, UK: National Archives, 2007); Megan Smolenyak and Ann Turner, *Tracing Your Roots with DNA: Using Genetic Tests to Explore Your Family Tree* (Emmaus, PA: Rodale, 2004); Bryan Sykes, *The Seven Daughters of Eve* (New York: Bantam, 2001). Other promoters include the International Society of Genetic Genealogy, www.isogg.org.

2. My argument here fleshes out in more historical and conceptual detail the findings published by several other authors in a key scientific article: Deborah A. Bolnick, Duana Fullwiley, Troy Duster, Richard S. Cooper, Joan H. Fujimura,

Jonathan Kahn, Jay S. Kaufman, Jonathan Marks, Ann Morning, Alondra Nelson, Pilar Ossorio, Jenny Reardon, Susan M. Reverby, and Kimberly TallBear, "The Science and Business of Genetic Testing," *Science* 318 (October 19, 2007): 399–400. They conclude, "Consumers often purchase these tests to learn about their race or ethnicity, but there is no clear-cut connection between an individual's DNA and his or her racial or ethnic affiliation. . . . [T]here is little evidence that four biologically discrete groups of humans ever existed." See also Kimberly TallBear, "DNA, Blood, and Racializing the Tribe," *Wicazo Sa Review* (Spring 2003): 81–107; Patricia McCann-Mortimer et al., "'Race' and the Human Genome Project: Constructions of Scientific Legitimacy," *Discourse and Society* 15 (2004): 409–32; Dorothy Roberts, *Fatal Invention: How Science, Politics, and Big Business Re-Create Race in the Twenty-First Century* (New York: New Press, 2011); Richard C. Lewontin, *Biology as Ideology: The Doctrine of DNA* (New York: Harper-Collins, 1991); Richard C. Lewontin, *It Ain't Necessarily So: The Dream of the Human Genome and Other Illusions*, 2nd ed. (New York: New York Review of Books, 2001); Sheldon Krimsky and Kathleen Sloan, eds., *Race and the Genetic Revolution: Science, Myth, and Culture* (New York: Columbia University Press, 2011); Keith Wailoo, Alondra Nelson, and Catherine Lee, eds., *Genetics and the Unsettled Past: The Collision of DNA, Race, and History* (New Brunswick, NJ: Rutgers University Press, 2012); Peter Wade, ed., *Race, Ethnicity, and Nation: Perspectives from Kinship and Genetics* (New York: Berghahn Books, 2007); Barbara A. Koenig, Sandra Soo-Jin Lee, and Sarah S. Richardson, eds., *Revisiting Race in a Genomic Age* (New Brunswick, NJ: Rutgers University Press, 2008).

3. It should be remembered that the scientific class did not enjoy in those days quite the high regard for intellectual dispassion and investigatory care that they were granted in later decades and, in any case, that there is not a great deal of similarity between the methods of scientists in those days and these. This section is adapted from my book *Almost All Aliens: Immigration, Race, and Colonialism in American History and Identity* (New York: Routledge, 2007), 262–73.

4. Linnaeus's masterwork is *Systema Naturae*, 10th ed. (1758), translated as *The System of Nature* (London: Lackington, Allen, 1806).

5. Georges-Louis Leclerc, comte de Buffon, *A Natural History, General and Particular*, 2nd ed. (London: Strahan and Cadell, 1785).

6. Johann Friedrich Blumenbach, *On the Natural Varieties of Mankind* (New York: Bergman, 1969; orig. English 1865; orig. German 1775); Johann Friedrich Blumenbach, *The Anthropological Treatises of Johann Friedrich Blumenbach* (Boston: Milford House, 1973; orig. 1865).

7. Georges Léopold Cuvier, *Le règne animal* (1817), translated into English as *Animal Kingdom* (London: W. S. Orr, 1840). Quotation is taken from Emmanual Chukwudi Eze, ed., *Race and the Enlightenment* (Cambridge, MA: Blackwell, 1997), 105. Terence Keel reminds me that though it was Cuvier who made this judgment, it was Blumenbach who coined the term *Caucasian*.

8. Arthur de Gobineau, *The Inequality of Human Races* (New York: Fertig, 1999; English orig. 1915; French orig. 1853–55), v–v1, 151; Michael D. Biddiss, *Father of Racist Ideology: The Social and Political Thought of Count Gobineau* (New York: Weybright and Talley, 1970); Michael D. Biddiss, ed., *Gobineau: Selected Political Writings* (New York: Harper and Row, 1970).

9. William Z. Ripley, *The Races of Europe* (New York: Appleton, 1899).

10. A. H. Keane, *Ethnology* (Cambridge: Cambridge University Press, 1901), 224.

11. United States Commissioner-General of Immigration, *Annual Report, 1904* (Washington, DC, 1904), endpaper; United States Congress, *Reports of the Immigration Commission*, 61st Cong., 3rd sess., vol. 5: *Dictionary of Races or Peoples* (Washington, DC, 1910–11).

12. Alfred P. Schultz, *Race or Mongrel?* (Boston: Page, 1908).

13. Madison Grant, *The Passing of the Great Race, or The Racial Basis of European History* (New York: Scribner's 1916); quote on 80–81. The German edition is *Der Untergang der grossen Rasse: Die Rassen als Grundlage der Geschichte Europas* (Munich: J. F. Lehmanns Verlag, 1925). See also Jonathan Spiro, *Defending the Master Race: Conservation, Eugenics, and the Legacy of Madison Grant* (Burlington: University of Vermont Press, 2008).

14. Sources on eugenics include Edwin Black, *War against the Weak: Eugenics and America's Campaign to Create a Master Race* (New York: Four Walls Eight Windows, 2003); Laura Briggs, *Reproducing Empire: Race, Sex, Science, and U.S. Imperialism in Puerto Rico* (Berkeley: University of California Press, 2002); Susan Currell and Christina Cogdell, eds., *Popular Eugenics* (Columbus: Ohio State University Press, 2006); Gregory Michael Dorr, *Segregation's Science: Eugenics and Society in Virginia* (Charlottesville: University of Virginia Press, 2008); John M. Efron, *Defenders of the Race: Jewish Doctors and Race Science in Fin-de-Siècle Europe* (New Haven, CT: Yale University Press, 2004); Amy L. Fairchild, *Science at the Borders: Immigrant Medical Inspection and the Shaping of the Modern Industrial Labor Force* (Baltimore: Johns Hopkins University Press, 2003); Mark H. Haller, *Eugenics* (New Brunswick, NJ: Rutgers University Press, 1963); John P. Jackson Jr., *Science for Segregation: Race, Law, and the Case against* Brown v. Board of Education (New York: New York University Press, 2005); Daniel J. Kevles, *In the Name of Eugenics* (Cambridge, MA: Harvard University Press, 1986); Nancy Ordover, *American Eugenics: Race, Queer Anatomy, and the Science of Nationalism* (Minneapolis: University of Minnesota Press, 2003); Gregory D. Smithers, *Science, Sexuality, and Race in the United States and Australia, 1780s–1890s* (New York: Routledge, 2009); Alexandra Minna Stern, *Eugenic Nation: Faults and Frontiers of Better Breeding in Modern America* (Berkeley: University of California Press, 2005); Tukufi Zuberi, *Thicker than Blood: How Racial Statistics Lie* (Minneapolis: University of Minnesota Press, 2001), esp. chaps. 3–5.

15. Sources on intelligence testing include Alfred Binet, *The Development of Intelligence in Children*, trans. Elizabeth S. Kite (Baltimore: Williams and Wilkins, 1916); N. J. Block and Gerald Dworkin, eds., *The IQ Controversy* (New York: Pantheon, 1976); Jeffrey M. Blum, *Pseudoscience and Mental Ability* (New York: Monthly Review, 1978); Paul L. Boynton, *Intelligence: Its Manifestations and Measurement* (New York: Appleton, 1933); Hans J. Eysenck, *Intelligence* (New Brunswick, NJ: Transaction, 1998); Jefferson M. Fish, ed., *Race and Intelligence* (Mahwah, NJ: Lawrence Erlbaum, 2002); Henry H. Goddard, *The Criminal Imbecile* (New York: Macmillan, 1915); Henry H. Goddard, *Feeble-Mindedness: Its Causes and Consequences* (New York: Macmillan, 1914); Henry H. Goddard, *The Kallikak Family: A Study in Heredity of Feeble-Mindedness* (New York: Macmillan, 1912); Henry H. Goddard, *School Training of Defective Children* (Yonkers-on-Hudson, NY: World Book, 1914); Stephen Jay Gould, *The Mismeasure of Man*, rev. ed. (New York: Norton, 1996); Seymour W. Itzkoff, *The Decline of Intelligence in America* (Westport, CT: Praeger, 1994); Nicholas Lemann, *The Big Test: The Secret History of the American Meritocracy* (New York: Farrar, Straus and Giroux, 2000); Henry L. Minton, *Lewis M. Terman: Pioneer in Psychological Testing* (New York: New York University Press, 1988); Ashley Montagu, ed., *Race and IQ* (New York: Oxford University Press, 1999); J. David Smith, *Minds Made Feeble: The Myth and Legacy of the Kallikaks* (Rockville, MD: Aspen Systems, 1985); Theta H. Wolf, *Alfred Binet* (Chicago: University of Chicago Press, 1973); Leila Zenderland, *Measuring Minds: Henry Herbert Goddard and the Origins of American Intelligence Testing* (Cambridge: Cambridge University Press, 1998).

16. Quoted in Kevles, *In the Name of Eugenics*, 81.

17. Henry H. Goddard, "Mental Tests and the Immigrant," *Journal of Delinquency* 2 (1917): 243–77; Gould, *Mismeasure*, 165. The historian Patrick Miller writes, "Goddard claimed that he could spot a moron amidst the mass of immigrants coming through Ellis Island—not just with the test but by eye—which may give new meaning to the word 'moron'" (pers. comm., April 14, 2004). Roger Daniels points out that immigrants and their advisers soon learned how to cope with the eyeballing and the testing, and the number of rejections dropped (pers. comm., March 23, 2013).

18. Carl Campbell Brigham, *A Study of American Intelligence* (Princeton, NJ: Princeton University Press, 1923), 197, quoted in Kevles, *In the Name of Eugenics*, 82–83. African Americans also were supposedly inferior to Whites. But differential access to education played a part. Midwestern Blacks scored higher on Brigham's measures of intelligence than did southern Whites.

Even scholars who held benign attitudes toward immigrants and peoples of color found their ideas all wrapped up with pseudoscientific racialist thinking. Caroline Bond Day, a Radcliffe-educated instructor at all-Black Atlanta University, was a protégé of the anthropometrist Earnest Hooton. Hooton described Day as "an approximate mulatto, having about half Negro and half White blood." The fractions seemed important to both Day and her mentor. Hooton sponsored the publication of Day's *Study of Some Negro-White Families in the United States* by Harvard's Peabody Museum. It is an inexpressibly detailed accounting of the body parts of several hundred people whom Day interviewed, measured, and photographed, all of whom she marked as having some racial mixture. She displayed hundreds of pictures of racially mixed people, tying them together in family trees and listing them by racial fractions ("Jewett Washington, 7/16 N 9/16 W"), across scores of quarto pages. The book offered nearly a hundred tables recording detailed measurements of body parts for various categories of people. There were four tables on lips alone ("Lips, Integumental Thickness," "Lips, Membranous Thickness," "Lips, Eversion," "Lip Seam"), eleven on noses, and, of course, cephalic indexes. Day's work is a monument to misbegotten precision and the piling up of data without thinking about what they are for. Caroline Bond Day, *A Study of Some Negro-White Families in the United States* (Cambridge, MA: Peabody Museum, 1932).

Julie Kelley made a similar study among Asians in Hawai'i, with similar photographs, measurements, and tables. Sidney Gulick, one of the great defenders of Asian immigrants against their critics, nonetheless felt compelled to preface his book on race in Hawai'i with thirty-two race-fractionated photographs and to include sections such as "Psycho-Physical Race Differences," "Psychological Race-Differences," "Intelligence Tests on Race-Mixtures," and "Comparative Racial Intelligence (IQ)." Julie P. Kelley, "A Study of Eyefold Inheritance in Inter-Racial Marriages" (MS thesis, University of Hawai'i, 1960); Sidney L. Gulick, *Mixing the Races in Hawaii* (Honolulu: Hawaiian Board, 1937). See also Louis Wirth's chapter, "The Jewish Type," in *The Ghetto* (Chicago: University of Chicago Press, 1926).

19. On the SAT, see Rebecca Zwick, *Fair Game? The Use of Standardized Admissions Tests in Higher Education* (New York: Routledge Falmer, 2002); Rebecca Zwick, *Rethinking the SAT: The Future of Standardized Testing in University Admissions* (New York: Routledge Falmer, 2004); Lemann, *The Big Test*.

20. Frank H. Hankins, *The Racial Basis of Civilization: A Critique of the Nordic Doctrine* (New York: Knopf, 1926); Franz Boas, *Race, Language, and Culture* (New York: Free Press, 1940); Edward H. Beardsley, "The American Scientist as Social Activist: Franz Boas, Burt G. Wilder, and the Cause of Racial Justice," *Isis* 64 (1973): 50–66; Elazar Barkan, *The Retreat of Scientific Racism* (Cambridge: Cambridge University Press, 1992).

21. Carleton Stevens Coon, *The Races of Europe* (New York: Macmillan, 1939); Carleton Stevens Coon, *The Story of Man* (New York: Knopf, 1954); Carleton Stevens Coon, *The Origin of Races* (New York: Knopf, 1962); Carleton Stevens Coon, *The Living Races of Man* (New York: Knopf, 1965); Carleton Stevens Coon, *Racial*

Adaptations (Chicago: Nelson-Hall, 1982); Wesley Critz George, *The Biology of the Race Problem* (Richmond, VA: Patrick Henry Press, 1962); Jackson, *Science for Segregation*; Carleton Putnam, *Race and Reason* (Washington, DC: Public Affairs, 1961); Carleton Putnam, *Race and Reality* (Washington, DC: Public Affairs, 1967).

22. Pierre L. van den Berghe, *The Ethnic Phenomenon* (New York: Elsevier, 1981); J. Barkow, Leda Cosmides, and John Tooby, *The Adapted Mind: Evolutionary Psychology and the Generation of Culture* (New York: Oxford University Press, 1992). While this vector in research is a less than reputable minority opinion, it is well funded. Among its prominent supports is the Pioneer Fund, which has also given large sums to support the research of the eugenicists Arthur Jensen, Hans Eysenck, and J. Philippe Rushton; see www.pioneerfund.org (retrieved September 2, 2009). Among their writings are Arthur R. Jensen, *Genetics and Education* (New York: Harper and Row, 1972); Arthur R. Jensen, *Educability and Group Differences* (New York: Harper and Row, 1973); Arthur R. Jensen, *Straight Talk about Mental Tests* (New York: Free Press, 1981); Arthur R. Jensen, *The G Factor: The Science of Mental Ability* (Westport, CT: Praeger, 1998); Frank Miele, *Intelligence, Race, and Genetics: Conversations with Arthur R. Jensen* (Boulder, CO: Westview, 2002); H. J. Eysenck, *The Scientific Study of Personality* (London: Routledge and Kegan Paul, 1952); H. J. Eysenck, *The Biological Basis of Personality* (Springfield, IL: Thomas, 1967); H. J. Eysenck, *The IQ Argument: Race, Intelligence, and Education* (New York: Library Press, 1971); H. J. Eysenck, *The Inequality of Man* (London: Temple Smith, 1973); H. J. Eysenck, *A Model for Intelligence* (Berlin: Springer, 1982); H. J. Eysenck, *Intelligence: A New Look* (New Brunswick, NJ: Transaction, 1998); J. Philippe Rushton, *Race, Evolution, and Behavior: A Life History Perspective*, 3rd ed. (Port Huron, MI: Charles Darwin Research Institute, 2000).

23. Richard J. Herrnstein and Charles Murray, *The Bell Curve: Intelligence and Class Structure in American Life* (New York: Free Press, 1994); Peter Brimelow, *Alien Nation: Common Sense about America's Immigration Disaster* (New York: Random House, 1995); Samuel P. Huntington, *The Clash of Civilizations* (New York: Simon and Schuster, 1996); Samuel P. Huntington, *Who Are We? The Challenges to America's National Identity* (New York: Simon and Schuster, 2004); Jon Entine, *Taboo: Why Black Athletes Dominate Sports and Why We're Afraid to Talk about It* (New York: Public Affairs, 2000); Patrick J. Buchanan, *The Death of the West: How Dying Populations and Immigrant Invasions Imperil Our County and Civilization* (New York: St. Martin's, 2002); Patrick J. Buchanan, *State of Emergency: The Third World Invasion and Conquest of America* (New York: St. Martin's, 2007); Nicholas Wade, *A Troublesome Inheritance: Genes, Race, and Human History* (New York: Penguin, 2014). Sometimes Huntington uses the word *culture* when he really is talking about racialized distinctions; the other authors are not so squeamish.

24. www.ancestry.com (retrieved February 13, 2009).

25. Bolnick et al., "The Science and Business of Genetic Testing."

26. www.alphagenic.com (retrieved February 13, 2009).

27. www.dnadirect.com (retrieved October 2, 2009).

28. Benedict Carey, "Gene's Link to Depression Now Questioned," *New York Times*, June 18, 2009. It is worth noting that it was once common medical wisdom that tuberculosis was inherited; Jean Dubos, *The White Plague: Tuberculosis, Man, and Society* (New Brunswick, NJ: Rutgers University Press, 1987).

29. Some places to begin on that controversy are Nadia Abu El-Haj, "The Genetic Reinscription of Race," *Annual Review of Anthropology* 36 (2007): 283–300; Nikolas Rose, "Race, Risk and Medicine in the Age of 'Your Own Personal Genome,'" *BioSocieties* 3 (2008): 423–39; Troy Duster, "Race and Reification in Science," *Science* 307 (February 18, 2005): 1050–51; Priscilla Wald, "Blood and Stories: How Genomics Is Rewriting Race, Medicine and Human History," *Patterns of Prejudice* 40.4–5 (2006): 303–33; Sander L. Gilman, "Alcohol and the Jews (Again), Race and Medicine (Again): On Race and Medicine in Historical Perspective," *Patterns of Prejudice* 40.4–5 (2006): 335–52; Katya Gibel Azoulay, "Reflections on Race and the Biologization of Difference," *Patterns of Prejudice* 40.4–5 (2006): 353–79; Judith S. Neulander, "Folk Taxonomy, Prejudice and the Human Genome: Using Disease as a Jewish Ethnic Marker," *Patterns of Prejudice* 40.4–5 (2006): 381–98; Sharon L. Snyder and David T. Mitchell, "Eugenics and the Racial Genome: Politics at the Molecular Level," *Patterns of Prejudice* 40.4–5 (2006): 399–412; Philip Alcabes, "The Risky Gene: Epidemiology and the Evolution of Race," *Patterns of Prejudice* 40.4–5 (2006): 413–25; Troy Duster, "The Molecular Reinscription of Race: Unanticipated Issues in Biotechnology and Forensic Science," *Patterns of Prejudice* 40.4–5 (2006): 427–41; Sandra Soo-Jin Lee, "Biobanks of a 'Racial Kind': Mining for Difference in the New Genetics," *Patterns of Prejudice* 40.4–5 (2006): 443–40; Kelly E. Happe, "The Rhetoric of Race and Breast Cancer Research," *Patterns of Prejudice* 40.4–5 (2006): 461–80; Joseph L. Graves Jr. and Michael R. Rose, "Against Racial Medicine," *Patterns of Prejudice* 40.4–5 (2006): 481–93; Jonathan Michael Kaplan, "When Sociological Determined Categories Make Biological Realities: Understanding Black/White Health Disparities in the US," *The Monist* 93.2 (2010): 281–97; Elizabeth M. Phillips et al., "Mixed Race: Understanding Difference in the Genome Era," *Social Forces* 86.2 (2007): 795–820; Richard S. Cooper, Jay S. Kaufman, and Ryk Ward, "Race and Genomics," *New England Journal of Medicine* (March 20, 2003): 1166–70; Jenny Beardon, "Decoding Race and Human Difference in the Genomic Age," *Differences: A Journal of Feminist Cultural Studies* 15.3 (2004): 38–65; Barbara A. Koenig, Sandra Soo-Jin Lee, and Sarah S. Richardson, eds., *Revisiting Race in a Genomic Age* (New Brunswick, NJ: Rutgers University Press, 2008); Rick Kittles and Charmaine Royal, "The Genetics of African Americans: Implications for Dis-

ease Gene Mapping and Identity," in *Genetic Nature/Culture*, ed. Alan Goodman, Deborah Heath, and M. Susan Lindee (Berkeley: University of California Press, 2003), 219–33; Joe Markman, "New Law Bars Bias Based on Genetics," *Los Angeles Times*, November 21, 2009; Nadia Abu El-Hau, *The Genealogical Science: The Search for Jewish Origins and the Politics of Epistemology* (Chicago: University of Chicago Press, 2012).

30. For a judicious appraisal of the usefulness and limits of DNA forensic analysis, including privacy concerns and a range of other issues, see Sheldon Krimsky and Tania Simoncelli, *Genetic Justice: NDA Data Banks, Criminal Investigations, and Civil Liberties* (New York: Columbia University Press, 2011), esp. chap. 8, "The Illusory Appeal of a Universal DNA Bank," and chap. 16, "Fallibility in DNA Identification." See also Richard Lewontin, "Let the DNA Fit the Crime," *New York Review of Books* (February 23, 2012): 28–29; Jason Felch and Maura Dolan, "FBI Resists Scrutiny of 'Matches': A Crime Lab's Findings Raise Doubts about the Reliability of Genetic Profiles," *Los Angeles Times*, July 20, 2008; Helen Briggs, "Dispute over Number of Human Genes," *BBC News Online*, July 7, 2001.

Human Genome Project people say humans have 20,000 to 25,000 genes, as we have an unusual number of genes that control other genes. Other scientists estimate 40,000 to 60,000 to 100,000. We don't test for a lot of these genes partly because we don't know what they do. It is a little like the assumption once made about the Mayans and writing. I was taught in school in the 1950s and 1960s that the Mayans, who left a lot of texts full of symbols, did not have writing because at that time no one knew how to read those texts. Now we can read them because we have learned to decipher their characters. See, e.g., Gerardo Aldana, *The Apotheosis of Janaab' Pakal: Science, History, and Religion in Classical Mayan Palenque* (Boulder: University Press of Colorado, 2007).

31. Wells, *Deep Ancestry*, 11.

32. Ibid., 4, 44–45, 48.

33. Carter Vaughn Findley, *The Turks in World History* (New York: Oxford University Press, 2004); Alice Beck Kehoe, *America before the European Invasions* (London: Longman, 2002), 8–12; Dean R. Snow, "The First Americans and the Differentiation of Hunter-Gatherer Cultures," in *Cambridge History of the Native Peoples of the Americas*, vol. 1, pt. 1, ed. Bruce G. Trigger and Wilcomb E. Washburn (Cambridge: Cambridge University Press, 1996), 61–124; E. James Dixon, *Quest for the Origins of the First Americans* (Albuquerque: University of New Mexico Press, 1993); Tom D. Dillehay, *The Settlement of the Americas: A New History* (New York: Basic Books, 2000); David E. Stannard, *American Holocaust: The Conquest of the New World* (New York: Oxford University Press, 1992), 261–68; Patrick Vinton Kirch, *The Lapita Peoples: Ancestors of the Oceanic World* (Cambridge, MA: Blackwell, 1997); David Lewis, *We, the Navigators: The Ancient Art of Landfinding in the Pacific* (Honolulu: University of Hawai'i Press, 1994).

34. Jonathan Marks, *What It Means to Be 98% Chimpanzee: Apes, People, and Their Genes* (Berkeley: University of California Press, 2002).

35. Erin Aubrey Kaplan, "Black Like I Thought I Was," *LA Weekly*, October 7, 2003. On Louisiana Creoles, see Andrew Jolivétte, *Louisiana Creoles: Cultural Recovery and Mixed-Race Native American Identity* (Lanham, MD: Lexington Books, 2007); Gwendolyn Midlo Hall, *Africans in Colonial Louisiana: The Development of Afro-Creole Culture in the Eighteenth Century* (Baton Rouge: Louisiana State University Press, 1995); Sybil Kein, ed., *Creole: The History and Legacy of Louisiana's Free People of Color* (Baton Rouge: Louisiana State University Press, 2000); Gary Mills, *Forgotten People: Cane River's Creoles of Color* (Baton Rouge: Louisiana State University Press, 1977); Arnold Hirsch and Joseph Logsdon, eds., *Creole New Orleans: Race and Americanization* (Baton Rouge: Louisiana State University Press, 1992).

36. Henry Louis Gates Jr., *In Search of Our Roots: How 19 Extraordinary African Americans Reclaimed Their Past* (New York: Crown, 2009), 5–6. Gates reprised the act on PBS in 2010 with a new series, *Faces of America with Henry Louis Gates Jr.*, as well as another book, *Faces of America: How 12 Extraordinary People Discovered Their Roots* (New York: New York University Press, 2010), commented on by Matea Gold, "In 'Faces,' Blood Will Tell," *Los Angeles Times*, February 10, 2010. He took a third shot at the same theme on PBS in 2013 with *Finding Your Roots*.

37. Gates, *In Search of Our Roots*, 222. Actually, the Zulu fought a war of resistance against the Boers, who were descendants of Dutch, not British, colonists.

38. On the demography of the slave trade, see David Eltis, *Routes to Slavery: Direction, Ethnicity, and Mortality in the Atlantic Slave Trade* (New York: Routledge, 1997); David Eltis, Stephen D. Behrendt, David Richardson, and Herbert S. Klein, *The Transatlantic Slave Trade* (Cambridge: Cambridge University Press, 2000).

39. Wells, *Deep Ancestry*, 6, 8.

40. For concurring opinions, see Bolnick et al., "Policy Forum: Genetics: The Science and Business of Genetic Ancestry Testing"; TallBear, "DNA, Blood, and Racializing the Tribe"; and Roberts, *Fatal Invention*.

41. British Association for Adoption and Fostering and British Society for Human Genetics, "Statement on the Use of DNA Testing to Determine Racial Background," www.baaf.org.uk/info/lpp/adoption/ethnictesting.pdf (retrieved October 18, 2009); Morrison Institute for Population and Resource Studies, Stanford University, Human Genome Diversity Project, "Frequently Asked Questions," www.Stanford.edu/group/morrinst/hgdp/faq.html (retrieved February 22, 2008).

42. Patricia Cohen, "Genetic Basis for Crime: A New Look," *New York Times*, June 19, 2011; Michael Haederle, "Brain Function Tied to Risk of Criminal Acts,"

Los Angeles Times, July 15, 2013. Troy Duster of New York University adamantly disagreed; see his book, *Backdoor to Eugenics* (New York: Routledge, 1990).

43. Stephen Spielberg, dir., *The Minority Report* (Dreamworks, 2002).

44. See the web page of the Fertility Institutes, www.fertility-docs.com (retrieved January 29, 2013). Linda L. McCabe and Edward R. B. McCabe critique the designer baby industry in "Are We Entering a 'Perfect Storm' for a Resurgence of Eugenics? Science, Medicine, and Their Social Context," in *A Century of Eugenics in America*, ed. Paul A. Lombardo (Bloomington: Indiana University Press, 2011), 193–218. Nikolas Rose takes a more sanguine view in *The Politics of Life Itself: Biomedicine, Power, and Subjectivity in the Twenty-First Century* (Princeton, NJ: Princeton University Press, 2006).

45. Paul Boyer, *By the Bomb's Early Light: American Thought and Culture at the Dawn of the Atomic Age* (New York: Pantheon, 1985).

46. Adrian Desmond and James Moore, *Darwin's Sacred Cause: How a Hatred of Slavery Shaped Darwin's Views on Human Evolution* (Boston: Houghton Mifflin, 2009).

Mixed Race

7

What Must I Be?

Asian Americans and the Question of Multiethnic Identity

This chapter began as a contribution to a conference at UCLA titled "Multiple Tongues: Centering Discourse by People of Color"—truly awful prose that hid a vital purpose. The idea of the conference was for people who were relatively new to the academy and disempowered there (mostly scholars of color) to speak back against the perspectives of the powerful people (mostly White) who then dominated academic writing. The panel of which I was a part was the only one at that conference that did not assume monoraciality. All the other scholars sought to undermine the "dominant discourse"—that is, the way most White people framed things—by proposing a monoracial Black, Asian, Latino, or Native American alternative. The members of our panel tried to suggest that race was more complicated than that and that racial complexity was also a position from which one could resist White domination. "What Must I Be?" criticized the "dominant discourse" presented by White American scholars, but it also resisted what I called the "subdominant discourse" presented by those Asian Americans and others who refused to recognize and credit the mixed identities of multiracial people who had part Asian ancestry.

That paper, revised, went on to have quite an afterlife, first as an article published in Amerasia Journal, *the flagship publication in Asian American studies, in a special issue on mixed-race Asians edited by Teresa Williams and Velina Hasu Houston. That article, in turn, was reprinted three times in widely used anthologies edited by Min Zhou, Jim Gatewood, Jean Wu, and Min Song.[1] Here it is revised and updated once more, although the argument of the original has been preserved.*

In 1968 Asian American studies was born out of the Third World Strike at San Francisco State. By the mid-1980s Asian American studies had spread to most large public West Coast universities. Then in the 1990s and 2000s Asian American studies exploded across the country to institutions public and private, large and small. Times and institutions change, as has the definition of who is an Asian American.

When I took the first Asian American studies class at the University of Washington in 1970, "Asian American" meant primarily Japanese and Chinese Americans, with a few Filipinos allowed a place on the margin. By the 1990s, when I chaired the department at the University of California, Santa Barbara, "Asian American" included Koreans, Vietnamese, Thais, Burmese, Laotians, Cambodians, Hmong, Asian Indians, and Asians of several other sorts. The multiplication of significant Asian American populations, and their relative inclusion or lack of inclusion in the pan-Asian group, is the subject of another essay.[2] The topic here is more elusive and perhaps more subtle: the inclusion or lack of inclusion of people of multiple ancestries who are, as some would say, "part Asian."

THE IDENTITY QUESTION

Opinions vary widely about whether it is possible to have more than one ethnic identity, and if it is possible, how such multiple identities ought to be conceived and managed. In *Hunger of Memory*, Richard Rodriguez asserted that members of ethnic minority groups must choose between private and public identities. By this he meant that, in order to make satisfactory places for themselves in American society, either they must retain the ethnic culture of their youth, family, and community, or they must eschew their ethnicity and adopt the culture, values, and viewpoints of the dominant Anglo-American group. The ethnic, or "private," identity Rodriguez regarded as inferior and limiting; the dominant group, or "public," identity he found superior and liberating, even as he eloquently recounted the emotional costs of choosing to flee his own ethnicity.[3] This is not the occasion to question Rodriguez's use of the terms *public* and *private* in this way, or to mourn his willing alienation from his family, his ancestral culture, even himself. The point here is that Rodriguez, and the pundit Patrick Buchanan, and Malcolm X—to name just three examples—declared that one must choose. They said that a person can have only one ethnic identity. One cannot live in more than one community simultaneously. One cannot be Black *and* White, Asian *and* American. A person can be only one thing.[4]

W. E. B. Du Bois had a different view. He contended that every African American, whether that person liked it or not, possessed and was possessed by a double consciousness, two identities in dialectical conversation. In a famous *Atlantic Monthly* essay in 1897, DuBois wrote:

> The Negro is a sort of seventh son, born with a veil, and gifted with second-sight in this American world,—a world which yields him no self-consciousness, but only lets him see himself through the revelation of the other world. It is a peculiar sensation, this double-consciousness, this sense of always looking at one's self through the eyes of others, of measuring one's soul by the tape of a world that looks on in amused contempt and pity. One ever feels his two-ness, an American, a Negro; two souls, two thoughts, two unreconciled strivings; two warring ideals in one dark body, whose dogged strength alone keeps it from being torn asunder. The history of the American Negro is the history of this strife,—this longing to attain self-conscious manhood, to merge his double self into a better

and truer self. In this merging he wishes neither of the older selves to be lost. He does not wish to Africanize America, for America has too much to teach the world and Africa; he does not wish to bleach his Negro blood in a flood of white Americanism, for he believes—foolishly, perhaps, but fervently—that Negro blood has yet a message for the world. He simply wishes to make it possible for a man to be both a Negro and an American without being cursed and spit upon by his fellows, without losing the opportunity of self-development.[5]

Questions of double identity—of ethnicity and nationality—are concerns for nearly all people of color in the United States. For no group of people is the dilemma of double identity more pointed than for people of multiple ancestry. They find themselves continually defined by people other than themselves. Regardless of how they construct their own identities, they must always be in dialogue with others who would define them from outside. Those others may be school or census authorities (White people, usually) who insist that an individual "check one box" for ethnicity on a survey form. Worse, when the individual disobeys and checks more than one box, those officials may invalidate the form or simply pick one of the checked ethnicities and allot the individual to that category, thus denying the person of mixed ethnicity the right to define him- or herself.

In "Guessing Game" the Amerasian Santa Cruz poet Douglas Easterly rebels against being defined by Whites:

> Five seconds and they've gotta have you figured
> or it gnaws at them all night in a tiny
> part of their brain till they come up and ask you
>   what *are* you?
> like you're from another planet
>
> You see, though they also listen to your voice
> and study your name
> it's primarily a visual thing

Someone will see the curly hair
and hear you do well in school
and ask
      are you Jewish?
Or maybe it'll be
the guy who cuts you off at the intersection
yelling
      wetback go home!
Or maybe it'll be
that high school football coach
asking if you got so big
because you're part Samoan
      look just like one of 'em I coached once . . .

Tell 'em that your mother's Japanese
then it's easy.
      Oh I see now the eyes and maybe the nose
      and look at his stocky Japanese build
      and look at how he works at school I bet
      he probably studies all day
      I knew he was a Japanese when I saw him
      but I just wasn't positive.

                 *   *   *

Leaving you
      a footnote
      in race relation theory
      a symbol
      for the intersection of two worlds,
          one foot in each of them
      so you can be dissected
      stuffed into labeled boxes—

         Are you more white or more Japanese?
         Race: check only one box below
           What's it like only being half Japanese?
         Half-breed!

And you're denied
    completeness
    wholeness
    and put on display

What *are* you?[6]

Cindy Cordes, a woman of White and Filipino ancestry raised in Hawai'i, has a different problem. Cordes says, "I have a *hapa* [multiple-identity] mentality. I look white but I don't identify with white culture. I grew up with a Filipino mother in an Asian household. We ate Asian food, had Filipino relationships, Filipino holidays, with Filipino values of family. In Hawaii, I always felt comfortable, so much of our culture is a conglomeration of cultures." But then she went to Columbia University and found that other Asian Americans "look at me as white." When she went to a meeting of an Asian American student group, she said, "They asked me, 'Why are you here?'"[7]

For multiracial Asians like Cordes and Easterly, one task is to defend themselves against the *dominant discourse* imposed by White America in order to establish control of their own identity. But there is a second task that at least Cordes sees as equally important: defending herself against the *subdominant discourse* imposed by monoracially identified Asian Americans. Throughout their history, like Whites, Asian Americans have chosen definitions for people of part Asian descent[8] without regard to their actual life situations or wishes. And they have been quite successful in making those identities stick. In thus specifying identities for mixed people of Asian ancestry, Asian Americans have been as guilty of stereotyping and oppressing, of mythologizing and dominating, as have Whites. Throughout their history, however, multiracial Asian Americans have also chosen identities for themselves. There are patterns in these identity-specifyings and identity-choosings, and there are portents for the future. Those patterns and portents are the subject of this article. It begins by describing the previous status of multiracial people of Asian descent—prior to the 1960s, when a major change began to take place—and the stereotypes that both Whites and Asians held of mixed racial people. It then moves to a contemplation of the changes that have taken place since the 1960s and the variations in recent dynamics of Amerasian multiraciality. The article ends by considering the implications of choosing a multiracial identity, both for Amerasian individuals and for Asian communities.

AMERASIANS AND IDENTITY: PATTERNS OF THE PAST

It is a commonplace observation that intermarriage is on the rise. Take the case of Japanese Americans. During the 1910s and 1920s, the rate of out-marriage by Issei, or first-generation Japanese immigrants, was 2 or 3 percent. The percentage of Nisei (second-generation Japanese Americans) who married non-Japanese before or during World War II was about the same. The number reached around 10 percent among the younger Nisei who married in the 1950s. Out-marriage exploded in the third (i.e., Sansei) generation. It reached roughly 25 percent in the mid-1960s and 45 percent by the mid-1970s. By the turn of the millennium, as the Yonsei (fourth generation) and Gosei (fourth generation) were reaching marriageable age, the number of Japanese Americans marrying outside the group approached 50 percent.[9]

The numbers for other Asian American peoples are similar, although a bit smaller, because none of the other groups is so fully removed from the immigrant generation as are Japanese Americans. Nationally in 1980, only 15 percent of Chinese Americans were married to non-Chinese. But among those born in the United States who married in New York City in 1982, a third married out. By the 2000s, about a quarter of the entire Chinese American population who were married had non-Chinese partners. More than a quarter of the Filipino American population in 1980 was married to non-Filipinos. By the 2000s, the number of out-marriages by Filipinas approached 50 percent.[10] The rising number of intermarriages—attributable both to the length of time Asian peoples have spent in the United States and to the general easing of White prejudices and discrimination against Asians since World War II—has meant an ever-increasing number of people who have more than one kind of ancestry.

For most of the history of mixing between Asians and non-Asians in the United States, people of part Asian ancestry have not had much choice about how to identify themselves. Either the Asian minority or the White majority told them what they must be.

Prior to the 1960s, most Asian American peoples were so opposed to intermarriage that they shunned not only the intermarried couples but also their mixed children. That is in marked contrast to the situation for multiracial people of African American descent, who found at least a grudging welcome among African Americans and who were in any case forced by White Americans to identify as Black.[11] Chinese-Hawaiians in the 1930s, by far the largest group of Amerasians in that era, were far more readily accepted in the Hawaiian community than in the Chinese community.[12] In that same period, Japanese Americans thrust out of their midst most mixed people. The Los Angeles Japanese community ordinarily took care of any of its members who were in need. One result was that only 101 orphans had to be cared for by the Japanese American Children's Village in 1942. But nineteen of them were people of mixed ancestry. That was far more than their percentage in the Japanese American child population at large. Most of them, probably, were children who had been abandoned and whom no Japanese family was willing to adopt.[13]

White Americans also opposed intermarriage with Asians, and they were not inclined to celebrate the presence in their midst of multiracial people of Asian descent. But the number of Amerasians was so small that Whites could ignore such individuals and let them slide by on the margins of White society.[14]

Whites had some strange ideas about multiracial people of Asian descent. Those ideas are important because they shaped people's life chances then, and they continue to do so. The fullest exploration of this topic is an essay by Cynthia Nakashima.[15] White ideas about mixed-race people proceed from a set of biological ideas propounded by pseudoscientific racists in the late nineteenth and early twentieth century. Reasoning from the physical properties of plants and animals to the physical and moral qualities of human beings, pseudoscientific racists put on the American intellectual agenda a set of vicious assumptions about multiracial people that still plague mixed people today. Nakashima summarizes them ably as follows:

that it is "unnatural" to "mix the races"; that multiracial people are physically, morally, and mentally weak; that multiracial people are tormented by their genetically divided selves; and that intermarriage "lowers" the biologically superior White race[;] . . . that people of mixed race are socially and culturally marginal, doomed to a life of conflicting cultures and unfulfilled desire to be "one or the other," neither fitting in nor gaining acceptance in any group, thus leading lives of confused loneliness and despair.[16]

The dominant discourse about Amerasians has been largely in terms of this set of myths of degeneracy, confusion, conflict, and despair. Edward Byron Reuter, the foremost academic authority on racial mixing in his day, had this to say in 1918:

Physically the Eurasians are slight and weak. Their personal appearance is subject to the greatest variations. In skin color, for example, they are often darker even than the Asiatic parent. They are naturally indolent and will enter into no employment requiring exertion or labor. This lack of energy is correlated with an incapacity for organization. They will not assume burdensome responsibilities, but they make passable clerks where only routine labor is required.[17]

About the same time, a White journalist in California wrote, "The offspring are neither Japanese nor American, but half-breed weaklings, who doctors declare have neither the intelligence nor healthfulness of either race, in conformity with the teaching of biology, that the mating of extreme types produces deficient offspring."[18] Even Whites who fancied themselves defenders of Asians found themselves debating in terms set by the pseudobiological argument. Sidney L. Gulick, a prominent White opponent of Japanese exclusion, felt compelled to give evidence that (1) unlike mules, Amerasians were not sterile; and (2) far from being weak and imbecilic, they were stout and smart.[19]

There is a particular image abroad in popular culture of Amerasians as sexual enthusiasts. This is related to a mechanism of dominance that attributes lack of sexual control to dominated peoples—women especially—as a way to excuse White male abuses of those women.[20] Domination is sexually exciting, but it is her fault. This dynamic, the "myth of the erotic exotic," is compounded for women of mixed race.[21] Speaking of Amerasians, Nakashima writes, "The mixed-race person is seen as the product of an immoral union between immoral people, and is thus expected to be immoral him- or herself. . . . [M]ultiracial females are especially likely targets for sexual objectification because of their real and perceived vulnerability as a group . . . in the sense that they are mentally, emotionally, morally, and socially weak, powerless, and tormented, and very often the product of sexual and racial domination."[22]

The marketers of blue movies and pulp novels are more lurid. They advertise: "Erotic Fantasies of an Eurasian Nymph. She's a new breed of woman. Part Oriental, part European. She'll jolt you right out of your seat!" And: "Daughter of Violence. She was the child of the savage coupling of her beautiful Chinese mother and her handsome, brutal American father. She had her first lessons in life and love in the most elegant and depraved brothel in the Far East—and learned of passion in the arms of a lawless and forbidden lover. She came to America to be sold into an ultimate hell of degradation—and began her climb toward wealth and power man by man, selling her irresistible flesh to feed her insatiable ambition. She was Li-Li, the stunning Eurasian girl torn between the disparate worlds of East and West."[23] This erotic image of Amerasians is related to the oft-articulated and seemingly more benign idea that Amerasians are especially beautiful people, who somehow invariably combine the most attractive physical qualities of East and West.[24]

Sometimes the dominant group's thinking about Amerasians took an especially vicious twist. Such was the case during World War II, when White Americans put Japanese Americans into concentration camps on account of their ancestry. A small but significant number of mixed-race people—perhaps 700 Amerasians out of 110,000 inmates in all—shared that experience. The US government's handling of them shows the ambivalence and confusion among White Americans about how to conceive of and deal with multiracial people of Asian descent. The army and the War Relocation Authority (WRA) ruled that all persons of full Japanese ancestry living on the West Coast had to be imprisoned. Some had non-Japanese spouses; the spouses could choose whether or not to go to the government's prison camps. Amerasians presented a special problem. Were they more Japanese, in which case they should be required to go to the prison camps? Or were they more American, in which case they might remain at liberty with their non-Japanese parent? First the government incarcerated all multiracial people of Japanese ancestry, then they tried to figure out what to do with them.

The government's policy was confused and vacillating, but it emerged that the WRA would make a judgment about each Amerasian's prewar environment. This judgment was made on the basis of the gender of the non-Japanese parent. Amerasian children who had White fathers and Japanese mothers could leave the camps and return to their presumably "Caucasian" (the army's term) prewar homes. Amerasian children who had Japanese fathers and non-Japanese mothers were presumed to have been dominated by their fathers, so while they could leave the prison camp, they were not allowed to return to the West Coast until it was reopened to all Japanese Americans late in the war. Adult Amerasians could leave the camps but only if they had "fifty per cent, or less, Japanese blood" and could demonstrate that their prewar environment had been "Caucasian."[25]

Whites, then, were confused about Amerasians and uncertain exactly where to place them. They had a number of stereotypes of multiracial people (Amerasians especially) that were perverse and demeaning. Asians were less confused than Whites: generally, they rejected multiracial people of Asian ancestry, and they told them they could not be Asians.[26]

This made life problematic for many multiracial people of Asian descent. Take the case of Kathleen Tamagawa. Born at the turn of the century, she did not like being an Amerasian. She opened her autobiography with the words, "The trouble with me is my ancestry. I really should not have been born." There follows a tale of tortured passage through her young life in America and Japan, undermined rather than supported by parents who had problems of their own. She was, by her own reckoning, a "citizen of nowhere," but by that she meant that she could find no place for herself in Japan. In time, in fact, she married a nondescript, middle-class White American man and faded into White suburban life.[27]

Peter, a half Japanese, half Mexican boy, had a tougher time of it in Los Angeles in the 1920s. His Mexican mother died when he was very young, and he never established ties to any Chicanos. His father remarried, this time to a Japanese woman who did not like Peter. She beat him, ridiculed him, refused to feed him, and finally threw him out of the house. School authorities found him running unsupervised in the streets at age seven. Peter's father told him, he said, that "he wished that I had never been born; and at times I have even wished that myself. I have often wished that I were [a White] American and not a Japanese or Mexican." Juvenile court authorities found that Peter was "an outcast" from both the Japanese and Chicano communities. They tried to find a foster home for Peter, but no one would take him because of his mixed ancestry. He finally was sent to the state reformatory.[28]

For every Kathleen or Peter who suffered for their mixed raciality, however, there were others much happier. Kiyoshi Karl Kawakami, a prominent writer and interpreter of Japan to America and America to Japan, married Mildred Clark of Illinois and had two children, Clarke and Yuri. The younger Kawakamis spoke positively of their Eurasianness when interviewed in 1968. They grew up from the 1910s to the 1930s, mainly in the Midwest, well educated and insulated from life's blows by their father's money and status. They had almost nothing to do with Japanese Americans except for their father and in fact looked down on monoracial Nisei as people suffering from an "inferiority complex."[29] The common thread is that prior to the 1960s nearly all mixed-race people of Asian descent had to make their way outside of Asian American communities, for Asian communities would not have them.

This was true even for the great Asian American journalist and short story writer Sui Sin Far. Born Edith Maude Eaton in 1865, daughter of an English father and a Chinese mother, she was raised and lived her adult life in several parts of Canada and the United States. She chose to identify with Chinese people to the extent of choosing Chinese themes and a Chinese pseudonym, and she wrote prose sympathetic to the sufferings, fears, and hopes of Chinese North Americans. But she was nonetheless always more on the White side than the Chinese: she lived and worked among White people, they were her friends, and it is from their point of view that she wrote. In Sui Sin Far's writing, she did not mark the race of White people (they were just people), but she always marked the race of Chinese people. In part this was because her literary aspirations demanded that her work be intelligible to a White audience, in part because Chinese people treated her as an outsider, albeit a friendly one. For example:

> Some little Chinese women whom I interview are very anxious to know whether I would marry a Chinaman. I do not answer No. They clap their hands delightedly, and assure me that the Chinese are much the finest and best of all men. They are, however, a little doubtful as to whether one could be persuaded to care for me, full-blooded Chinese people having a prejudice against the half-white.[30]

Like other part Asians before the 1960s, Sui Sin Far spent her life mainly on the White side.

WINDS OF CHANGE

Increased Acceptance

The situation for people of mixed Asian descent began to change in the 1960s, when substantial numbers of Asian Americans began to marry non-Asians. By the 1970s, the numbers of Chinese and Japanese who married outside their respective groups and then had children were large enough that those communities were forced to begin to come to terms with the existence of mixed people. The decades since have seen a steady increase in the acceptance that Asian communities have accorded both intermarrying couples and their mixed racial offspring.

There were some limitations on this acceptance, however. Many Asian Americans became involved in the Asian ethnic assertiveness movement that began in the late 1960s and 1970s. Early on, that movement seldom had a place for people of multiple ancestry or their distinct issues. Stephen Murphy-Shigematsu describes the dynamic: "It has been difficult to include biracial Asian Americans in Asian American communities. The subject of biracial Asian Americans relates directly to interracial couples—an issue that is often seen as threatening to Asian American communities and individuals. There is a feeling that openly discussing this topic amounts to sanctioning interracial marriage and endorsing the death of Asian American ethnic groups."[31] Cynthia Nakashima agrees: "People of color who marry Caucasians are often labeled 'sellouts' and 'traitors' by other non-Whites. Multiracial people who are part White are seen as inherently 'whitewashed'; they are harassed for their light skin or light hair, their loyalty is always in question, and they are not allowed to discuss their multiraciality if they want to be included as legitimate 'persons of color.'"[32]

While such sentiments were undoubtedly dominant in the 1970s and 1980s, by the 1990s and especially after 2000, most Asian American communties had come to see multiracial people as an inevitable, and not necessarily undesirable, part of their future.

A New Identity Choice: Multiethnicity

Multiracial people of Asian descent took a number of paths to ethnic identity. Very few were inclined or able to identify solely with one part of their inheritance. Many adopted what Amy Iwasaki Mass calls "situational ethnicity." They would act and feel mainly White or Black or Latino (according to their mix) when among White or Black or Latino relatives and friends, mainly Asian when among Asians.[33] Some went through periods growing up when they emphasized one side and then periods when they turned the other way.

Joy Nakamura (a pseudonym) grew up in Brooklyn, in most respects a normal, not very observant Jewish girl in a Jewish neighborhood, except that her father was Japanese. Her Nisei father seldom talked about his childhood in California, her Japanese American relatives were far away, and, although she felt somehow connected to Japan, she never had an opportunity to explore the connection until she entered a large eastern university. "I met more Asians my first year [in college] than I had ever known," she said. "When one Japanese-American called me on the phone to invite me to join a Japanese-American discussion group, I was very excited. I went to the group meetings a few times, but my 'white-half' began to feel uncomfortable when the others began putting down whites." So she stopped going. She took classes on Japanese language and culture and enrolled in a seminar on Asian Americans. "I was desperately trying to find myself as an Asian-American woman, but I was not succeeding." She had clashes with her White boyfriend over racial issues, and she tried to ignore her Jewishness. Pressure from an African American activist friend helped Nakamura clarify her feelings. He said, "'You must decide if you are yellow, or if you are white. Are you part of the Third World, or are you against it?' I laughed at his question. How could I possibly be one and not the other? I was born half-yellow and half-white. I could not be one and not the other any more than I could cut myself in half and still exist as a human being." At length she decided, "I do not feel guilty about not recognizing my Asianness. I have already done so. I have just readjusted my guilt feelings about ignoring my Jewish half. . . . My Jewishness is something that can be easily hidden. I do not want to hide that fact. I want to tell the world that I am [also] a Jew."[34]

When I told Joy Nakamura's story at a conference on Jewish history and identity, one member of the audience—a distinguished senior Jewish scholar—snorted loudly that Nakamura was obviously a sick person. On the contrary, she was healthy and whole. Her choice to embrace both halves of her identity in the mid-1970s was a point of mature self-understanding to which increasing numbers of multiracial people have come in the decades since. There is no question that to embrace both (or all) parts of their identity is a healthier situation than to cling to one and pretend that the other does not exist. The general thinking here is to overturn the idea of a tortured "half-breed," torn between two unreconcilable identities. One has, not a split consciousness, but an integrated identity fused from two. "I am a whole from two wholes," is the way one Japanese-White man put it.[35]

Since the 1990s a number of organizations of multiracial Asian Americans have sprung up around the country where people can go to explore their multiraciality. There has also grown up a veritable cottage industry of scholarly studies by and about multiracial people of Asian descent.[36]

Asian American Responses

For many years, most mainstream Asian American groups did not know quite what to do with multiracial Asian Americans. And until the 1990s there was no place for multiracial people in Asian American studies curricula; now multiracial courses are common. Cynthia Nakashima analyzes the problem.

> People asserting their multiracial heritage confuse and threaten the boundaries that so comfortably mark people off from each other. It is not only the dominant White group that treasures these boundaries, but all racial and ethnic groups. . . . The treasuring of clear boundaries is evident in the fact that multiracial African Americans are "allowed" to be full members of the African American community, but only as long as they do not assert multiracial identities; and multiracial Asian Americans, especially when they are part Black, are generally considered "outsiders" and have very limited entree into Asian American communities.[37]

What was happening was that Asian Americans were adopting the boundaries set by White America. In so doing, they internalized the oppression that circumscribed their lives. They then visited that oppressive system of boundaries on Amerasians. The 1990–91 controversy over the Broadway version of the hit musical *Miss Saigon* illustrates the point. The play's lead character is a Eurasian pimp. The play's producer and director chose a White person for the role. Asian American actors and community activists protested bitterly, saying the role should go to an Asian. Lost in the shuffle was the fact that if ethnicity were the casting criterion, the only appropriate actor would be neither a Caucasian nor an Asian but a person of mixed ancestry.[38] Multiracial Asian Americans exist (and in large numbers), and no amount of ignoring them will cause them to go away or to mutate into something else.

Increasing numbers of Amerasians are inclined to regard themselves as a variety of Asian Americans, and increasingly they find that Asians of unmixed ancestry will accept them as fellow ethnics. Across the country, it is hard to find a Japanese American or Chinese American church that does not have interracial couples, biracial children, and biracial adults. Sometimes, as Nakamura complained, Asian groups will accept Amerasians only if they renounce their non-Asian background.[39] But with increasing frequency Asian American institutions, from athletic leagues to community newspapers to social welfare organizations, seem inclined to admit Amerasians as something like full participants.[40]

Creating Amerasian Culture

Most Amerasians do not link up primarily with other Amerasians. But in some cultural respects they nonetheless constitute a distinct group. A generation who grew up in Japan in the 1970s and 1980s, for example, the children of American soldiers and Japanese women, created a social world of their own, different but not walled off from the Japanese or the Americans around them. They socialized more with each other than with non-Amerasians and formed a third culture that mixed the languages, values, and symbol systems of their two parental cultures.[41] Nakashima's research suggests that American-born multiracial people of Asian ancestry are also culturally distinct. Multiracial Japanese Americans to whom she administered an ethnic identity questionnaire scored higher on several measures of "Japaneseness" than did unmixed Japanese Americans, even immigrants. Conversely, with regard to their interactions with Whites, the Amerasians showed more skill and comfort than did unmixed Japanese Americans.[42]

Intra-Asian Ethnic Variations

In all this, one must remember that there are large differences between different sorts of Asians. Asian Americans are not a single group, and one ought not assume a monolith. No one has studied comparatively the different meanings and trajectories of multiraciality for people whose Asian ancestry is Chinese versus Filipino versus Vietnamese versus Japanese versus Korean versus Asian Indian.[43] Nor has anyone studied the meaning of multiethnicity for people who have more than one sort of Asian background—whose parents are, for instance, Chinese and Japanese Americans. Do such people tend to identify with the Chinese side or the Japanese? Or do they regard themselves (as some Asian activists might wish) as simply Asian Americans?

A few observations can be made, however. It seems clear, for example, that the community acceptance level for Filipino Amerasians has long been much higher than for other groups. This is largely because the Filipino immigrant population was so heavily male that until after World War II almost any Filipino man who married had to find a non-Filipina mate. The majority of the American-born generation was multiracial. In addition, there was a long history of mixing in the Philippines under the Spanish colonial regime, so Filipinos have long had a stronger sense of being a mixed people than have other Asian groups.[44]

To take another example, the situation for multiracial Japanese Americans is necessarily different from that for multiracial Chinese Americans. The difference has to do mainly with structural differences in the two communities. Japanese Americans were an almost entirely American-born ethnic group until the 1990s. The bulk of the adult population are members of the third or fourth generation. By contrast, over half the current Chinese American population is made up of immigrants. The unmixed Japanese Americans are, as a group, much more assimilated to American society and culture at large and somewhat more accepting of intermarriage and multiracial people.[45]

A third difference is between Korean and Vietnamese Amerasians, on the one hand, and Amerasians whose Asian ancestry is from the other countries mentioned above. Most Amerasians are American born and raised, the children of Asian Americans and other sorts of Americans. Many adult Korean and Vietnamese Amerasians, however, were born in Asia, the children of American GIs and Asian women. Many of the Korean Amerasians were given up for adoption and came to the United States at a very young age. They were raised by people with names like Lund and Anderson in the Midwest. Their life trajectories and their identity issues are quite different from those of other sorts of Amerasians. These frequently revolve around how to connect with their Korean background when they grew up in rural Minnesota knowing only Swedish American culture. Most Vietnamese Amerasians, like Koreans, were born in Asia. But the Vietnamese typically came to the United States at a later age, in their teens and twenties. They were multiracial people, but they also were adult immigrants who had to make their own way in an often hostile land without much external support. Generally, the Korean and Vietnamese communities have been less eager to include Amerasians than have other Asian groups, although the increasing out-marriage rates in both communities have reduced the opposition.[46]

Geographic Differences

If there are intra-Asian ethnic differences, there are also substantial differences depending on one's geographic location. Ethnic dynamics in Hawai'i, for example, are quite different from those in the continental United States. For one thing, there has been a great deal of intermarriage in Hawai'i, and therefore a large number of Hapas, or people of mixed ancestry, for about a century and a half. That means that in Hawai'i most people are more or less comfortable with the idea that some of the people around them will have mixed identities. Ethnicity is very important in Hawai'i. When one meets another person, one very carefully calibrates the proportions of various ethnicities that make up that person. But mixed identity is viewed as a normal part of human affairs.[47]

To some extent, in Hawai'i the continental patterns of ethnic acceptance are inverted. Island Chinese seem more accepting of multiracial Asians than do island Japanese communities. Hawai'i's Chinese community may once have shunned people of mixed parentage, but in the past several decades that community has learned to make room for part Chinese. One finds people in Chinese churches with Chinese names who look Hawaiian and went to the Kāmehameha Schools, which are reserved for people of Hawaiian ancestry. By comparison, island Japanese communities and institutions have less room for multiracial Japanese Americans. There are a substantial number of Japanese Amerasians in Hawai'i, but generally they are not tightly connected to Japanese community institutions. They find places in the social system but usually in a wider, mixed sector that includes Whites, various Asians, some Polynesians, and other mixed people. To be Hapa among Chinese in Hawai'i is more acceptable; to be Hapa among Japanese in Hawai'i is less acceptable. A Japanese-White woman reported from Hawai'i that a Japanese relative twirled her auburn hair in her finger and snorted, "What part of you is Japanese—your big toe?"[48]

The reverse is true in most West Coast cities. There intermarriage by Japanese Americans is more frequent than in Hawai'i, and mixed people are more likely to be included in Japanese American communities. By contrast, multiracial Chinese Americans in cities like San Francisco and Seattle are more likely to be treated with suspicion and are less likely to be included in Chinese community institutional life, although that too is changing as interracial marriage becomes more common.[49]

Perhaps the biggest difference, however, is between the Pacific states, where there are large Asian communities, and most of the rest of the country, where Asians are more of a novelty. Those large communities tend to retard the rate of Asian out-marriage.[50] But they also encourage non-Asians to regard Asian Americans as ordinary parts of the social fabric. That acceptance of Asians extends to Amerasians: Amerasians (like un-mixed Asians) are less likely to be harassed by Whites in Monterey Park, California, than they are in Columbus, Birmingham, or Boston.[51]

Physical Appearance

Another way in which the experiences of multiracial people of Asian descent vary has to do with their physical appearance. There is some indication that physical appearance may affect how one is perceived and how one identifies oneself. University of Washington professor Jim Morishima tells the story of Kimiko Johnson (a pseudonym), whom on the basis of her last name and appearance he took to be a Japanese American married to a Caucasian. She had a good deal to do with other Japanese Americans and for a time even worked for the Asian American studies department at the University of Washington. When Morishima asked her about her husband, she replied cryptically that she was not married and had never been married but would show him his mistake. Soon she reappeared with an African American youth whom she introduced as her brother. The brother spoke Black English and identified himself as Black. The two Johnsons had the same set of parents—an African American father and a Japanese American mother—yet they identified themselves differently, one as Japanese, one as Black, because that is the way they looked and therefore the way other people treated them.[52]

Physical appearance, however, does not completely determine one's identity. Christine Hall, Michael Thornton, and Teresa Williams, in studying children of Japanese American intermarriages, all found some people whose features appeared to favor the Japanese side but who nonetheless identified more strongly with their American heritage (White or Black). Conversely, they found others who appeared physically more American but who for reasons of their upbringing felt more attached to their Japanese identities. Williams found that "darker-skinned Afroasians did not automatically relate to African Americans, nor did lighter-skinned Afroasians necessarily identify with their Japanese parentage. Eurasians who appeared more Caucasian did not always blend in naturally with Euro-Americans; those who looked relatively more Asian did not always accept their Japanese background willingly and readily."[53] Jill Joiner (a pseudonym) was a Black-Japanese woman who never met her father and was raised in Okinawa by her mother's parents. She looked to both Japanese and Americans like an African American, and she tended to be treated by them as such. But her mannerisms, style of speech, attitudes, and aspirations were in every sense those of an unmixed Japanese woman. That was a problem for her, because Japanese people would not let her be Japanese, yet she really was not comfortable living anywhere but Japan. When I interviewed her, she broke down in tears, saying, "They [unmixed Japanese in Japan] never let me forget that I am different. I know I'm different. They know it. Why do they have to keep telling me? Why can't they just let me be?"[54]

Different Mixes

Some mixed people have more options than others. The editors of a prominent anthology by and about Asian American women were quite ready to include work by Barbara Posadas, the daughter of a Filipino man and a White woman, but they had no place for the work of the celebrated playwright Velina Hasu Houston, the daughter of a Black–Native American man and a Japanese woman. The reason for their decision is unclear, but it can have had little to do with the relative literary merits of their proposed contributions. Did their decision to exclude Houston derive in part from the fact that her non-Asian parent was Black? Or in part from the fact that the non-Asian parent was male? Or was it simply that Houston took a more aggressive stance in favor of a multiracial identity? An interview with one of the editors did not clear up the question of motivation.[55] But it is clear from a regular reading of almost any Asian community newspaper that people whose Asian ancestry is mixed with White are generally accorded a warmer reception than those whose non-Asian parent is Black.

In instances of conspicuous achievement, Asian communities are perhaps more willing to treat mixed people of African American parentage as insiders. This is related to what Nakashima calls the "claim-us-if-we're-famous syndrome."[56] It is not likely that many San Francisco Japanese Americans thought of the attorney Camille Hamilton as one of their own until she was named by *Ebony* magazine one of "Fifty Black Leaders of the Future" in 1990. After this *Hokubei Mainichi* was quick to feature her accomplishments. That a Japanese American community newspaper would claim a Black-Japanese American as one of their own was in itself a remarkable step forward; it could not have happened a decade earlier.[57]

IMPLICATIONS OF MULTIPLE IDENTITIES

The number of intermarriages, and thence the number of multiracial people of Asian ancestry, has soared over the past two generations, and there is every indication it will continue to do so. An increasing number of people who are of mixed ancestry have chosen to embrace multiple identities. That makes sense, for they are in fact possessors of multiple heritages. It also is a decision that engenders personal wholeness. Psychological studies by Amy Iwasaki Mass, George Kitahara Kich, and others suggest that a choice of a biracial identity is, for most mixed people, a healthier one than being forced to make an artificial choice that results in denial of a major part of their heritage.[58] In helping individuals make their way to identity choices, family support is crucial. To quote Mass:

> Parents are the key agent in making decisions and marshaling resources to aid children in the development of self-esteem. Con-

tributing to the development of a positive racial self-concept in their children includes trying to choose a home community where the sense of being different or unacceptable is minimized. Children need help to deal with issues related to growing up in a society where there is a hierarchical preference for certain races over others. Children need both parts of their racial heritage accepted and affirmed; maintaining positive connections with people from both cultures is a concrete way parents can provide such experiences for their interracial children.[59]

One must add here, however, that since the pull of the dominant Anglo-American culture is so strong in America, if a child is of mixed Asian and White descent, it is prudent to emphasize the Asian heritage.

In addressing multiracial people of Asian descent, the task for the dominant group in America is to rearrange its understandings to accommodate the reality of that multiracial identity. Like the dominant group, the subdominant group—Asian Americans—has begun the no less necessary task of rearranging its understandings. This means redefining in more inclusive terms what it means to be an Asian American. In the case of some Asian groups—certainly Japanese Americans and probably Chinese, Koreans, Vietnamese, and Filipinos before long—their very survival in an era of high intermarriage depends on coming to terms with and incorporating multiracial Asians.

Asian American studies programs, to take just one example, ought to do more to include Amerasians. Stephen Murphy-Shigematsu has been especially articulate on this issue. He laments:

> Some biracial Asian Americans are clearly intimidated about joining such Asian American contexts as Asian American studies. They speak of knowing that they are Asian and American, but not being sure if they are *Asian American*. They are not sure if others will think they are in the right place, afraid that others will reject them. Some biracial Asian Americans are unsure if they will see their lives and their family's lives represented in the curriculum. They are sometimes concerned that attention will be drawn to their face, their hair

color, their skin color, their name, or that their loyalty and authenticity will be challenged. This self-consciousness can be crippling.

But Murphy-Shigematsu offers hope:

> One way to combat this absence of voice is to include biracial issues in the Asian American studies curriculum. When biracial people see their concerns expressed as legitimate within the context of Asian American issues, there is a greater opportunity for continued interest and involvement and less chance of alienation. When they are free to acknowledge their non-Asian heritage as an integral part of who they are as a people, without fear of rejection, then their ability to study and work among other Asian Americans will grow.[60]

The good news is that a growing number of Asian American studies programs—and many other Asian institutions—are doing just that. They are including the issues and persons of multiracial people of Asian descent.

NOTES

This chapter first appeared in print in *Amerasia Journal* 22.4 (Spring 1997): 43–60. An earlier version was given at the conference, "Multiple Tongues: Centering Discourse by People of Color," at UCLA. I am grateful to the sponsors and other participants at that conference. My education on the subject of multiethnic Asian Americans has occurred over many years at the patient hands of many mentors. Perhaps I learned more, early on, from Sonnet Takahisa and Irene O'Connor than from anyone else and, later, from Naomi Spickard, Daniel Spickard, Laurie Mengel, and Dorri Nautu. Cynthia Nakashima was particularly helpful with some of the ideas and documents that appear here, and she, Teresa Williams-León, and Velina Houston have always been wonderfully supportive colleagues and friends. Since this was first published, a horde of friends and students have helped me to learn more. They are too numerous to name individually here—they include almost every student who has taken Asian American Studies 137 or History 168N over the past twenty years—but they know who they are. Most of my other debts will be apparent from the notes.

1. Min Song and Jean Wu, eds., *Asian American Studies* (New Brunswick, NJ: Rutgers University Press, 1999), 255–69; Min Zhou and James V. Gatewood, *Con-*

temporary Asian America (New York: New York University Press, 2000), 606–21; Min Zhou and J. V. Gatewood, *Contemporary Asian America*, 2nd ed. (New York: New York University Press, 2007), 718–48.

2. See Yen Le Espiritu, *Asian American Panethnicity* (Philadelphia: Temple University Press, 1992); William Wei, *The Asian American Movement* (Philadelphia: Temple University Press, 1993); Paul Spickard "Who Is an Asian? Who Is a Pacific Islander? Monoracialism, Multiracial People, and Asian American Communities," in *The Sum of Our Parts: Mixed Heritage Asian Americans*, ed. Teresa Williams-León and Cynthia Nakashima (Philadelphia: Temple University Press, 2001), 13–24; Helen Zia, *Asian American Dreams: The Emergence of an American People* (New York: Farrar, Straus and Giroux, 2001); Paul Spickard and Debbie Hippolite Wright, "Pacific Islander Americans and Asian American Identity," in *Contemporary Asian Pacific American Communities*, ed. Linda Trinh Vo and Enrique Bonus (Philadelphia: Temple University Press, 2002), 105–19; Paul Spickard, "Whither the Asian American Coalition?," *Pacific Historical Review* 76.4 (2007): 585–604; Daryl Joji Maeda, *Rethinking the Asian American Movement* (New York: Routledge, 2011); Dina G. Okamoto, *Redefining Race: Asian American Ethnicity and Shifting Ethnic Boundaries* (New York: Russell Sage, 2014).

3. Richard Rodriguez, *Hunger of Memory: The Education of Richard Rodriguez* (New York: Godine, 1982).

4. Buchanan's sentiments on the need to obliterate ethnic differences and the need to put strict limits on non-northwestern European immigrants because they are, in his view, harder to "assimilate," were much in the news during his 1992 run for the US presidency. See, e.g., DeWayne Wickham, "Buchanan Is Mounting a Racist Campaign," *Honolulu Star Bulletin*, December 16, 1991; and Buchanan's *The Death of the West: How Dying Populations and Immigrant Invasions Imperil Our Country and Civilization* (New York: St. Martin's, 2002). Malcolm X called on African Americans, most of whom shared his mixed ancestry, to denounce their White background and embrace the Black. In his autobiography he recounted, "I learned to hate every drop of that white rapist's blood that is in me." When he came to Black self-consciousness as a member of the Nation of Islam, he changed his name: "For me, my 'X' replaced the white slave-master name of 'Little' which some blue-eyed devil named Little had imposed upon my paternal forbears." *The Autobiography of Malcolm X* (New York: Grove, 1965), 2, 199.

5. W. E. Burghardt Du Bois, "Strivings of the Negro People," *Atlantic Monthly* 80 (August 1897): 194–95.

6. Douglas P. Easterly, "Guessing Game," in Asian/Pacific Islander Student Alliance, *Seaweed Soup*, vol. 2 (Santa Cruz: University of California, Santa Cruz, Pickled Plum Press, 1990), 26–27.

7. Susan Yim, "Growing Up 'Hapa,'" *Honolulu Star-Bulletin and Advertiser*, January 5, 1992, B3.

8. Terminology for mixed-descent people is problematic and cumbersome, and there is no standard. In this essay, I most frequently use the term *Amerasian* to refer to people who have Asian ancestry on one side and American (White, Black, Native American, etc.) on the other. *Eurasian* refers specifically to people whose non-Asian heritage is European. I also use a number of descriptions, such as "multiracial Asians," "mixed people of Asian ancestry," and "people of part Asian ancestry," more or less interchangeably. I do not wish here to enter into a discussion of the difference or lack of difference between "race" and "ethnicity." Here I use "multiethnic" and "multiracial" interchangeably. By describing a person as having "part Asian ancestry," I specifically do *not* mean to imply that she is less than a fully integrated personality or that she is less than fully entitled to membership in an Asian American community. If in any of this I offend a reader, I can only apologize, plead that the offense is unintentional, and ask that the reader attend to the argument and evidence presented here rather than to taxonomy.

9. Spickard, *Mixed Blood*, 47–60; C. N. Le, "By the Numbers: Dating, Marriage, and Race in Asian America," www.asian-nation.org (retrieved August 7, 2013).

10. Betty Lee Sung, *Chinese American Intermarriage* (New York: Center for Migration Studies, 1990), 18, 31; Le, "By the Numbers."

11. Spickard, *Mixed Blood*, 329–30.

12. Doris M. Lorden, "The Chinese-Hawaiian Family," *American Journal of Sociology* 40 (1935): 453–63; Everett V. Stonequist, *The Marginal Man* (New York: Russell and Russell, 1965; orig. New York: Scribner's, 1937), 41.

13. It is perhaps significant that most of the non-Japanese parents of these mixed orphans were not Caucasians. Of the fourteen whose ethnicity investigator Helen Whitney could identify, six had Mexican ancestry, three Native American, one Filipino, and only four White. Several possibilities present themselves: (1) there were fewer children of Japanese intermarriages with Whites than with darker-skinned and lower-status groups; (2) children of White-Japanese parentage were not as frequently abandoned to the care of an institution; (3) White-Japanese children were more readily adopted than other mixed children; (4) abandoned White-Japanese children were cared for by the White social service network, not the Japanese. Helen Elizabeth Whitney, "Care of Homeless Children of Japanese Ancestry during Evacuation and Relocation" (MSW thesis, University of California, Berkeley, 1948), 65–68. Catherine Irwin, *Twice Orphaned: Voices from the Children's Village of Manzanar* (Fullerton: California State University, Fullerton, Oral History Project, 2008), brings the story up to date.

14. By contrast, Whites found the much larger group of mixed African–European–Native American ancestry—essentially, the entire population we call African Americans—much more troublesome. Whites felt constrained to enforce a rule that assigned every multiracial person of African ancestry to the Black

category. Consider the antimiscegenation laws that were passed at one time or another by thirty-seven states. Thirteen of those expressly forbade intermarriage between Whites and Asians. All thirty-seven of the laws considered anyone with generally acknowledged African ancestry to be a member of the African American group; twelve specified the degree of racial inheritance required. But no state systematically placed Amerasians in the Asian category, and none specified a degree of inheritance that made a part Asian fully Asian for legal purposes. Spickard, *Mixed Blood*, 374–75; Gilbert T. Stephenson, *Race Distinction in American Law* (New York: Appleton, 1910), 12–20. In somewhat similar fashion, Asians were such a small group themselves that they were quite troubled by mixed people of part Asian descent and found it important to exclude them. One must be careful, however, about using the word *group*: Asian Americans in the 1930s and 1940s were not a single group. They are not today. In the decades before World War II, they were Chinese and Japanese and Filipinos and (a few) Koreans. They had little in common with each other besides the fact that most Whites could not tell them apart. In the 1950s and 1960s, there began to emerge among young Asian Americans a sense of similarity, even of partial commonality, based on growing up near one another in West Coast Asian ghettoes and being treated alike by non-Asians. Beginning in the very late 1960s and early 1970s, that impulse toward commonality grew into an as yet incompletely successful attempt by some community activists to merge the several Asian groups into one. See, e.g., Amy Tachiki et al., *Roots: An Asian American Reader* (Los Angeles: UCLA Asian American Studies Center, 1971); Emma Gee, ed., *Counterpoint* (Los Angeles: UCLA Asian American Studies Center, 1976); Espiritu, *Asian American Panethnicity*; Wei, *Asian American Movement*; Zia, *Asian American Dreams*; Maeda, *Rethinking the Asian American Movement*; Okamoto, *Redefining Race*.

15. Cynthia L. Nakashima, "An Invisible Monster: The Creation and Denial of Mixed-Race People in America," in *Racially Mixed People in America*, ed. Maria P. P. Root (Beverly Hills, CA: Sage, 1991), 162–78. Nakashima writes about the images of all sorts of mixed-race people, but her findings apply especially to the Amerasian case. See also Williams-León and Nakashima, *Sum of Our Parts*.

16. Nakashima, "Invisible Monster," 165.

17. Edward Byron Reuter, *The Mulatto in the United States* (New York: Negro Universities Press, 1969; orig. PhD diss., University of Chicago, 1918), 29. See also E. B. Reuter, "The Personality of Mixed Bloods," in *Race Mixture* (New York: Negro Universities Press, 1969; orig. New York: Whittlesey House, 1931), 205–16.

18. Quoted in Kiyoshi K. Kawakami, *Asia at the Door* (New York: Revell, 1914), 71.

19. Sidney L. Gulick, *The American Japanese Problem* (New York: Scribner's, 1914), 153–57.

20. For fuller treatment of this theme, see Spickard, *Mixed Blood*, 35–42, 252–59; Calvin Hernton, *Sex and Racism* (New York: Grove, 1965); Winthrop D. Jordan, *White over Black* (Chapel Hill: University of North Carolina Press, 1968), 154ff.

21. Elaine Louie speaks of Asian women in general, not specifically of Amerasians, in "The Myth of the Erotic Exotic," *Bridge* 2 (Apr. 1973): 19–20.

22. Nakashima, "Invisible Monster," 168–69.

23. Pornographic movie advertisement section, *San Francisco Chronicle*, November 20, 1975; Gillian Stone, *Land of Gold Mountains* (New York: New American Library, 1980), back cover. Hiroshi Wagatsuma points to a similar set of associations in Japan between mixed racial people and sexual licentiousness, in "Some Problems of Interracial Marriage for the Japanese," in *Interracial Marriage*, ed. Irving R. Stuart and Lawrence E. Abt (New York: Grossman, 1973), 247–64. See also Strong, "Patterns of Social Interaction," 115–29. The African American analogue to the Eurasian nymph theme is explicated and denied in Ella Wheeler Wilcox, "An Octoroon," *New York Evening Journal*, no. 7, 800 (n.d.); and Emily Clark, *The Strange History of the American Quadroon: Free Women of Color in the Revolutionary Atlantic World* (Chapel Hill: University of North Carolina Press, 2013). Some Whites (and some Japanese in Japan) find that a special thrill of sinful associations attaches to persons of mixed race whose non-Japanese parent is Black. There is apparently a compounding of mythic effects. With both African Americans and people of mixed ancestry regarded as sinful and exciting, the combination of the two is overwhelming. See Nathan Oba Strong, "Patterns of Social Interaction and Psychological Accommodations Among Japan's Konketsuji Population" (PhD diss., University of California, Berkeley, 1978); Christine C. Iijima Hall, "Please Choose One: Ethnic Identity Choices for Biracial Individuals," in Root, *Racially Mixed People*, 250–64.

24. This author has heard that sentiment expressed uncountable times, by Asians, by Whites, by Blacks, and sometimes by Amerasians. See also Nakashima, "Invisible Monster," 169–70.

25. Paul Spickard, "Injustice Compounded: Amerasians and Non-Japanese Americans in World War II Concentration Camps," *Journal of American Ethnic History* 5.2 (Spring 1986): 5–22.

26. Rejection of multiracial people of Asian descent was common in China and Japan as well as among Chinese and Japanese Americans. Filipino communities were an exception to this rule of rejection (see below).

27. Kathleen Tamagawa Eldridge, *Holy Prayers in a Horse's Ear* (New York: Long and Smith, 1932; repr. New Brunswick, NJ: Rutgers University Press, 2008), 1, 220, passim.

28. William C. Smith, "Life History of Peter," Major Document 251-A, Survey of Race Relations Papers (Hoover Institution Archives, Stanford University); Wil-

liam C. Smith, "Adjutant M. Kobayashi on the Second Generation," Major Document 236, Survey of Race Relations Papers.

29. Clarke Kawakami and Yuri Morris, interviewed by Joe Grant Masaoka and Lillian Takeshita, May 22, 1968 (Bancroft Library, Berkeley, CA, Phonotape 1050B:10). Other elite Eurasian children inhabited similarly comfortable positions, aware of the Asian aspect of their identities—even trading on it in their careers—but essentially White in outlook and connections. See, e.g., the autobiographical portions of Isamu Noguchi, *Isamu Noguchi: A Sculptor's World* (Tokyo: Thames and Hudson, 1967); Masayo Duus, *The Life of Isamu Noguchi: Journey without Borders*, trans. Peter Duus (Princeton, NJ: Princeton University Press, 2004); *The Life and Times of Sadakichi Hartmann* (Riverside, CA: Rubidoux, 1970); and (also on Hartmann) Gene Fowler, *Minutes of the Last Meeting* (New York: Viking, 1954). Others in less comfortable circumstances had to struggle—psychically, interpersonally, and financially—to make places for themselves. See, e.g., Sui Sin Far, "Leaves from the Mental Portfolio of an Eurasian," *The Independent* 66, no. 3136 (January 7, 1909): 125–32.

30. Sui Sin Far, *Mrs. Spring Fragrance and Other Writings*, ed. Amy Ling and Annette White-Parks (Urbana: University of Illinois Press, 1995), 223. The essay is titled, "Leaves from the Mental Portfolio of an Eurasian."

31. Stephen Murphy-Shigematsu, "Addressing Issues of Biracial/Bicultural Asian Americans," in *Reflections on Shattered Windows*, ed. Gary Y. Okihiro et al. (Pullman: Washington State University Press, 1988), 111.

32. Nakashima, "Invisible Monster," 174.

33. Amy Iwasaki Mass, "Interracial Japanese Americans: The Best of Both Worlds or the End of the Japanese American Community?," in Root, *Racially Mixed People*, 265–79. See also Maria P. P. Root, "Resolving 'Other' Status: Identity Development of Biracial Individuals," in *Complexity and Diversity in Feminist Theory and Therapy*, ed. L. Brown and M. P. P. Root (New York: Haworth, 1990), 185–205.

34. Joy Nakamura (pseud.), letter to the author, May 22, 1974.

35. Jean Y. S. Wu, "Breaking Silence and Finding Voice: The Emergence of Meaning in Asian American Inner Dialogue and a Critique of Some Current Psychological Literature" (EdD diss., Harvard University, 1984), 173–82.

36. See, e.g., Nakashima, "Invisible Monster"; Cynthia Nakashima, "Research Notes on Nikkei Hapa Identity," in Okihiro et al., *Reflections on Shattered Windows*, 206–13; Barbara Posadas, "Mestiza Girlhood: Interracial Families in Chicago's Filipino American Community since 1925," in *Making Waves: An Anthology of Writings by and about Asian American Women*, ed. Asian Women United of California (Boston: Beacon Press, 1989), 273–82; Murphy-Shigematsu, "Biracial/Bicultural Asian Americans"; Stephen Murphy-Shigematsu, "The Voices of Amerasians: Ethnicity, Identity, and Empowerment in Interracial Japanese Americans"

(EdD diss., Harvard University, 1986); Hall, "Please Choose One"; Christine C. I. Hall, "The Ethnic Identity of Racially Mixed People: A Study of Black-Japanese" (PhD diss., University of California, Los Angeles, 1980); Strong, "Japan's Konket-suji"; Teresa Kay Williams, "Prism Lives: Identity of Binational Amerasians," in Root, *Racially Mixed People*, 280–303; Mass, "Interracial Japanese Americans"; George Kitahara Kich, "The Developmental Process of Asserting a Biracial, Bicultural Identity," in Root, *Racially Mixed People*, 304–17; George Kitahara Kich, "Eurasians: Ethnic/Racial Identity Development of Biracial Japanese/White Adults" (PhD diss., Wright Institute, 1982); Michael C. Thornton, "A Social History of a Multiethnic Identity: The Case of Black Japanese Americans" (PhD diss., University of Michigan, 1983); Kieu-Linh Caroline Valverde and Chung Hoang Chuong, "From Dust to Gold: The Vietnamese Amerasian Experience," in Root, *Racially Mixed People*, 144–61; Ana Mari Cauce et al., "Between a Rock and a Hard Place: Social Adjustment of Biracial Youth," in Root, *Racially Mixed People*, 207–22; Ronald C. Johnson, "Offspring of Cross-Race and Cross-Ethnic Marriages in Hawaii," in Root, *Racially Mixed People*, 239–49; Cookie White Stephan and Walter G. Stephan, "After Intermarriage: Ethnic Identity among Mixed Heritage Japanese-Americans and Hispanics," *Journal of Marriage and the Family* 51 (1989): 507–19; Ronald C. Johnson and Craig T. Nagoshi, "The Adjustment of Offspring of Within-Group and Interracial/Intercultural Marriages: A Comparison of Personality Factor Scores," *Journal of Marriage and the Family* 48 (1986): 279–84; Lorraine K. Duffy, "The Interracial Individual: Self-Concept, Parental Interaction, and Ethnic Identity" (MA thesis, University of Hawai'i, 1978); Julia María Schiavone Camacho, *Chinese Mexicans: Transpacific Migration and the Search for a Homeland, 1910–1960* (Chapel Hill: University of North Carolina Press, 2012); Kip Fulbeck, *Part Asian/100% Hapa* (San Francisco: Chronicle Books, 2006); Rebecca Chiyoko King-O'Riain, *Pure Beauty: Judging Race in Japanese American Beauty Pageants* (Minneapolis: University of Minnesota Press, 2006); Rudy P. Guevarra Jr., *Becoming Mexipino: Multiethnic Identities and Communities in San Diego* (New Brunswick, NJ: Rutgers University Press, 2012); Karen I. Leonard, *Making Ethnic Choices: California's Punjabi-Mexican Americans* (Philadelphia: Temple University Press, 1994); Stephen Murphy-Shigematsu, *When Half Is Whole: Multiethnic Asian American Identities* (Stanford, CA: Stanford University Press, 2012); Kathleen Tyau, *A Little Too Much Is Enough* (New York: Norton, 1996); Williams-León and Nakashima, *Sum of Our Parts*.

37. Nakashima, "Invisible Monster," 175–76.

38. It has been asserted by some that the part was originally written for an Asian pimp and then transformed into a Eurasian so that a White person could play the part. If that be true, then the situation is similar to the controversy over the *Kung-Fu* television series of the early 1970s, for which an originally Chinese leading character was rewritten as a Eurasian so that a White actor could play the

part. If that is the situation here, then my analysis must be revised. However, to my knowledge this assertion has never been supported by any hard evidence.

39. See also Mass, "Interracial Japanese Americans."

40. For the convoluted limits on part Asians' participation in Asian American athletic leagues, see Rebecca Chiyoko King-O'Riain, "Eligible to be Japanese American: Counting on Multiraciality in Japanese American Basketball Leagues and Beauty Pageants," in *Contemporary Asian American Communities: Intersections and Divergences*, ed. Linda Trinh Vo and Rick Bonus (Philadelphia: Temple University Press, 2002); Kathleen S. Yep, *Outside the Paint: When Basketball Ruled at the Chinese Playground* (Philadelphia: Temple University Press, 2009).

41. Williams, "Prism Lives"; Strong, "Japan's Konketsuji."

42. Nakashima, "Research Notes on Nikkei Hapa Identity."

43. Obviously, there are other Asian groups, but these are the largest in number. People sometimes include Pacific Islanders as Asians. Asian community newspapers sometimes refer, for example, to "the Asian Pacific Islander community" ("New Director for Law Caucus," *Hokubei Mainichi*, December 10, 1991). That is silly. There are almost no points of historical similarity or connectedness of experience between Asians and Pacific Islanders. The cultural frame of reference—Confucianism—that does the most to make similar several otherwise disparate Asian groups (Chinese, Japanese, Koreans, Vietnamese) is completely lacking in the Pacific Islands. There has been some historical contact in a couple of locations: (1) between Chinese and Hawaiians in Hawai'i since the nineteenth century; (2) between Asian Indians and Fijians in Fiji in the same period; and (3) between Japanese conquerors and various island peoples, mainly in Micronesia, during World War II. But otherwise Asians and Pacific Islanders have been peoples apart. Among the distinctions is that almost all Pacific Island people see themselves as mixed—e.g., Marquesans from Tahiti, Indo-Fijians, Tongans, living in Samoa—while all the Asians except Filipinos make quite a point of their ethnic purity (see, e.g., Cullen T. Hayashida, "Identity, Race, and the Blood Ideology of Japan" [PhD diss., University of Washington, 1974]). For Pacific Islander American ethnic identity, see chapter 9.

44. Posadas, "Mestiza Girlhood."

45. Spickard, *Mixed Blood*, 61–70; Sung, *Chinese American Intermarriage*, 74–86.

46. Valverde and Chuong, "From Dust to Gold"; Nancy Cooper, "'Go Back to Your Country': Amerasians Head for Their Fathers' Homeland," *Newsweek* (March 18, 1988): 34–35; Kien Nguyen, *The Unwanted: A Memoir* (Boston: Back Bay Books, 2002); K. W. Lee, "Korean War Legacy," *Boston Herald Advertiser*, March 24, 1974; Eleana J. Kim, *Adopted Territory: Transnational Korean Adoptees and the Politics of Belonging* (Durham, NC: Duke University Press, 2010).

47. See chaps. 9 and 10.

48. Personal communication, 1996.

49. A unique transition occurred for one group of Amerasians during the period 1930–60. These were the children of mixed Chinese-Black families in the Delta region of Mississippi. During that period, according to the sociologist James W. Loewen, Chinese gradually rose in status, from being segregated along with African Americans in the bottom layer of Mississippi life to being granted a kind of acceptance at the lower margin of the White group. In the decades before that transition, quite a few Chinese immigrant men had married African American women. Those mixed couples and their offspring, according to Loewen, were left behind by the unmixed Chinese as they made their ascent. Loewen, *The Mississippi Chinese: Between Black and White* (Cambridge, MA: Harvard University Press, 1971), 135–53.

50. Spickard, *Mixed Blood*, 73–84.

51. There is also, of course, the enormous difference between the ways multiracial Asians are perceived and treated in the United States and the ways they are treated in various Asian countries. See, e.g., Strong, "Japan's Konketsuji"; Williams, "Prism Lives"; "Court Rejects Japan Nationality for Children of U.S. Fathers," *Japan Times Weekly*, April 4, 1981; Elizabeth Anne Hemphill, *The Least of These* (New York: Weatherhill, 1980); Valverde and Chuong, "From Dust to Gold." There is another difference in harassment that is very difficult to express clearly. Insofar as Asians or Whites may be bothered by the presence of multiracial people of Asian descent, Whites are more likely than Asians to be open about their opposition. Whites are more likely to use a racist epithet in public or to snub a person openly. In part that may be because Asians are more likely to be indirect, even passive-aggressive in the ways they express disapproval. But also the characteristic—the Asianness of the Amerasian—that sets off a White bigot is perceived by the latter as a disempowering thing. The White person's sense of advantage over the Amerasian may encourage the White bigot to express openly her or his hostility. By contrast, the distinct characteristic—the Americanness of the Amerasian—that sets off the Asian bigot is perceived by the Asian as an empowering thing. The Asian's sense of threat or disadvantage relative to the Amerasian may encourage the Asian bigot to keep quiet about her or his hostility.

52. James Morishima, "Interracial Issues among Asian Americans" (Panel discussion, Association for Asian/Pacific American Studies, Seattle, November 1, 1980).

53. Christine Hall finds that Whites and people of color emphasize different characteristics when they consider the physical aspects of racial identity: "It seems that Whites concentrate primarily on skin color, while people of color (who vary tremendously in skin color and ancestry) attend to other features, such as eyes, hair, nose, body build, and stature." Hall, "Please Choose One," 260. See also Williams, "Prism Lives"; Thornton, "Multiethnic Identity"; Mass, "Interracial Japanese Americans."

54. Jill Joiner (pseud.), interview by the author, St. Paul, MN, September 25, 1981.

55. The anthology in question is Asian Women United of California, *Making Waves*. See note 36 above.

56. Nakashima, "Invisible Monster."

57. *Hokubei Mainichi*, April 1990). Rex Walters, a Eurasian from San Jose, was also an object of the claim-us-if-we're-famous syndrome, on the basis of his basketball exploits for the University of Kansas and in the NBA; "Japanese American Athletes," *Hokubei Mainichi*, January 1, 1992. And then there is the Thai-Chinese golfer Tiger Woods.

58. Mass, "Interracial Japanese Americans"; Kich, "Eurasians"; Hall, "Ethnic Identity of Racially Mixed People."

59. Mass, "Interracial Japanese Americans."

60. Murphy-Shigematsu, "Biracial/Bicultural Asian Americans."

8

The Power of Blackness

Mixed-Race Leaders and the Monoracial Ideal

"The Power of Blackness" began as a speculative essay, published in a volume called Racial Thinking in the United States *along with essays by historians and sociologists charting the contours of American racial ideas. Upon its publication in 2004, the essay attracted considerable criticism for suggesting that multiracial people who adopted uncomplicated Black identities were passing for Black. Passing, the critics said, occurred when a "really" Black person (who had mixed parentage) passed for White. If the same person identified as Black, then he or she was just being who he or she was. Passing, in the critics' view, was racial fraud and betrayal of one's proper relationship to Black America.*

In the years since this essay first appeared, it has become less controversial. That Walter White, W. E. B. Du Bois, and others chose to pass as Black has come to be seen as unremarkable. That Jean Toomer's identity was complex and contingent is no longer viewed as psychosis or racial betrayal on his part. Time and experience with the multiracial idea have changed how we see these things.

Four of the most prominent African American political and cultural leaders of the last half of the nineteenth century and the first half of the twentieth—W. E. B. Du Bois, historian, sociologist, cofounder of the NAACP, editor of the *Crisis*, and pan-Africanist leader; Jean Toomer, herald of the Harlem Renaissance; Walter White, novelist and NAACP executive secretary; and Frederick Douglass, antislavery firebrand and African America's first national leader—had mixed racial ancestry, at least Black and White and perhaps also Native American. They, and others like them, were members of what one might call the *beigeoisie*—that coterie of light-skinned, multiracial people who formed an elite upper class within African American society in the generations after slavery.[1] All but Douglass might have passed for White had they chosen to do so. Instead, all—with the revealing exception of Jean Toomer—consistently chose to pass for Black. I use the phrase "pass for Black" advisedly. Reginald Daniel argues that passing was a strategy used by people of mixed ancestry to take advantage of their phenotypical ambiguity to acquire a measure of White privilege—to "pass" for White. That is the sense in which the term *passing* has ordinarily been used. But if the student of such matters is balanced conceptually, then he or she will admit that people of mixed ancestry who presented themselves in public as Black were passing, too.[2] This essay is a meditation on why some multiracial people made the choice to adopt a Black social and political identity—to pass for Black—and what implications their choice has for the construction of race (at least, of Black and White) in this period in American history.[3]

A few matters should be clarified at the outset. The first concerns the issue of choice. Often a choice is not entirely freely made. So we must ask, to what extent did these individuals choose a public racial identity, and to what extent was their choice constrained by circumstance? Passing for White may have been a choice, but it came with a cost. One had to be wealthy enough or desperate enough to move away from family and friends, or else one risked exposure and collapse of the life one was attempting to build. One had to be psychologically strong enough or scarred enough to abandon a former identity, the comforts of kin, and familiar surroundings. One had to have the education or the skill or the luck to be able to make a living in the world of White people. Passing for Black was the choice dictated by the dominant racial ideology. The power of racial ideologies lies in their very power to deny us absolutely free choices. Each of the persons discussed here made a choice to identify as Black. For some, this was an act with a substantial element of freedom; they could have made another choice. For others, the choice was more constrained. In each case, I have examined the writings of the individual and the work of biographers to try to ascertain the pattern in their choosing of public and private racial identities.

Second, there has been a long history of racial mixing in the United States. Several historians have observed that during the early colonial period there was more interracial mating than at any later time in American history. White slave masters took Black slave concubines, Black freemen married White women, and so forth. Such practices continued, often without widespread public acknowledgment, throughout the slavery period.[4] Some have asserted that early in US history the lines of race and class were not so rigid as they later became. For example, it has frequently been alleged that Alexander Hamilton was of mixed Black and White descent. Hamilton was born to a White mother, the product of an adulterous affair, on the West Indian island of Nevis in 1755. When Hamilton rose to the heights of American government in the early years of the republic, his political opponents sometimes alleged his mother's paramour had been Black or mulatto in an attempt to discredit Hamilton in a White-dominant society—a difficult charge to refute given the blurred racial lines in the islands in the era of his birth. If indeed Hamilton had African ancestry, then he was a racially mixed person who reached the highest levels of society as White.[5]

Whatever the merits of the stories about Hamilton's parentage and however much flexibility may have existed in the racial system of the eighteenth century, it is clear that by the end of the nineteenth century the options afforded a multiracial person were more limited. Many authors have observed that there were places in the South under slavery where elements of racial mixedness were recognized.[6] Yet, as Joel Williamson argues convincingly, in the period 1850–1915 American society at large came to embrace that peculiarity, the one-drop rule. To ensure the racial hierarchy as slavery came under attack and was eclipsed, White people began to reckon as Black any person who had known African ancestry, no matter how remote, and free people of mixed race were pushed into an externally undifferentiated Black class. Williamson asserts:

> The period between 1850 and 1915 marked a grand changeover in race relations in America. . . . A long-running intolerance of miscegenation and mulattoes among whites in the upper South joined with the rising and crystallizing intolerance among whites in the lower South to exert tremendous pressures upon both whites and mulattoes. Whites who mixed found themselves abused and ostracized. Under heavy fire from a seemingly universal racism, the previous ambivalence of mulattoes toward both whites and blacks turned during the Civil War toward a steadily growing affinity with blacks. . . . [T]he engagement of mulattoes and blacks was firmly cemented, though obvious vestiges of a preference for lightness lingered for two or three generations. By the 1920s the great mass of mulattoes saw their destiny as properly united only with that of their darker brothers and sisters. They saw themselves as fusing with blacks and together forming a whole people in embryo. . . . Negroes accepted the blackness of the seemingly pure white . . . and of others strikingly light—they too accepted the one-drop rule.[7]

Over those decades, this binary Black-White construction hardened as a keystone of the ideology of White supremacy. The creation of the one-drop rule required a substantial assault on what might have been known about people's genealogies. The US population, whatever its monoracial labels, was in fact a mixed multitude, with a substantial amount of mixing between White and Black and between both of those and Native peoples. But multiracial ancestry was a fact that White supremacists wanted to forget and one whose memory they strove to eradicate. The notion became entrenched, across the color line, that place in society was bound to race and that racial difference was timeless and immutable. Not only the European Americans who asserted dominance but also the people of African ancestry who were dominated by the system came to view it, not as a political construction, but as an unquestioned biological fact: White people, it was agreed by all, were unmixed; mixed people were deemed to be Black. This taking on of the dominant group's racial ideology by the subordinate people is an example of what Antonio Gramsci termed "hegemony"—that domination so thorough that one knows not that one is dominated but thinks it the natural order of things.[8]

Nearly all of the people who informed W. E. B. Du Bois's notion of the Talented Tenth and who populate Willard Gatewood's study of aristocrats of color fell into this category: Black-identified people of mixed European and African (and perhaps Native American) ancestry, many of whom could have passed for White had their Black ancestry not been known and had they chosen to do so.[9] This essay makes a start at understanding how the *multiracial fact* (their ancestry) encountered the *monoracial fact* (their identity) in the lives and the minds of some such people, who were prominent Black intellectuals and political leaders. I am emphatically not arguing that it was their admixture of European ancestry that brought such people to prominence. In slavery, being the master's child may have brought some privilege, education, even manumission. In freedom, White descent may have brought some social advantage. But there is no evidence, contrary to the opinions of both Du Bois and Edward Byron Reuter, that White ancestry brought greater ability.[10] Here, then, are their stories and some observations.

W. E. B. DU BOIS

William Edward Burghardt Du Bois was one of the most famous African Americans of the early decades of the twentieth century and is the figure most admired by the last two generations of intellectuals. Du Bois was racially mixed, although the mixing had taken place some generations back in his ancestral past. Du Bois's forebears were Africans, French Huguenots, and Hudson Valley Dutch. His father, Alfred, born in Haiti, was so light and smooth-haired as to be able to live as White.

In *Dusk of Dawn*, one of several autobiographies, Du Bois wrote fondly of his childhood in Great Barrington, Massachusetts, where his playmates were White, he attended a White church, and he was culturally "quite thoroughly New England," unconscious of race. His mother's family had resided in western Massachusetts for more than a century. "Living with my mother's people I absorbed their culture patterns and these were not African so much as Dutch and New England," he wrote. "The speech was an idiomatic New England tongue with no African dialect; the family customs were New England, and the sex mores."[11] Then, he wrote in *The Souls of Black Folk*, a schoolhouse snub by a White girl brought him to a sudden consciousness of his Blackness: "Then it dawned upon me with a certain suddenness that I was different from the others; or like, mayhap, in heart and life and longing, but shut out from their world by a vast veil. I had thereafter no desire to tear down that veil, to creep through; I held all beyond it in common contempt." He vowed to spend his life outdoing those who lived beyond that veil.[12] When Du Bois, still a proud son of New England, applied for admission to Harvard he was turned down. He went instead to Fisk University, a Black college in Nashville that was engaged mainly in turning out teachers for Black schools in the rural South. Du Bois was one such teacher during the summers. In other autobiographical writings, Du Bois located the critical era in the development of a Black consciousness in his college years at Fisk.[13]

According to his biographers, Du Bois remained in conflict about his racial identity even while he proclaimed his Blackness. Citing Rayford W. Logan and E. Franklin Frazier—two Du Bois disciples—David Levering Lewis wrote:

> Du Bois insisted . . . that he had embraced his racial identity only at Fisk. "Henceforward I was a Negro," Du Bois would proclaim, and then soar into a grand vision of his place in the race, knowing full well that Anglo-Saxon America was objectively blind by custom and law to intermediate racial categories. Logan always said that Du Bois's claim of belated racial self-discovery was a polemical contrivance to give greater punch to his writings about race relations. To claim that his identity as a Negro was in some sense the exercise of an option, an existential commitment, was to define Willie's celebration of and struggle for his people as an act of the greatest nobility and philanthropy. He was a Negro not because he had

to be—was born immutably among them—but because he had embraced the qualities of that splendid race and the moral superiority of its cause. . . . Willie's feelings about race in these early years were more labile or tangled, not to say conflictive, than his public professions revealed. . . . [He wrote] diary entries flashing over Franco-Caribbean roots like far-off lightning, enhancing a lordly sense of self. Willie's racial shape in his last year at Fisk was still congealing, and it would always be an alloy, never entirely pure. . . . Willie's ambivalence endowed him with a resilient superiority complex, and . . . his lifelong espousal of the "Darker World" was an optional commitment based above all upon principles and reason, rather than a dazzling advocacy he was born into.[14]

The most famous passage from Du Bois's writings expresses ambivalence about mixedness.

The Negro is a sort of seventh son, born with a veil, and gifted with second-sight in this American world—a world which yields him no true self-consciousness, but only lets him see himself through the revelation of the other world. It is a peculiar sensation, this double-consciousness, this sense of always looking at one's self through the eyes of others, of measuring one's soul by the tape of a world that looks on in amused contempt and pity. One ever feels his twoness—an American, a Negro; two souls, two thoughts, two unreconciled strivings; two warring ideals in one dark body, whose dogged strength alone keeps it from being torn asunder. The history of the American Negro is the history of this strife—this longing to attain self-conscious manhood, to merge his double self into a better and truer self.[15]

Formally, this passage is about the tension between a unitary African American racial identity and an ambiguous civic identity as an American whose citizenship is not fully credited. Here Du Bois does not speak directly to the racial ambiguity his other writings reveal. Yet might it be that, behind the veil of that formal duality, Du Bois was also questioning

Fig. 8.1.
W. E. B. Du Bois in Sisters Chapel, Spelman College, February 1938. Courtesy of Special Collections and Archives, W. E. B. Du Bois Library, University of Massachusetts, Amherst.

Fig. 8.2.
A darkened, stylized
view of W. E. B. Du Bois.
Portrait by Laura Wheeler
Waring. Courtesy of Special
Collections and Archives, W. E. B.
Du Bois Library, University of
Massachusetts, Amherst.

monoracial Blackness? Could his sensitivity to "this longing . . . to merge his double self into a better and truer self" have been shaped by a racial double consciousness? I have not yet located the private documents that would settle this question definitively, yet certain published writings are suggestive.

Throughout *Dusk of Dawn*, which Du Bois revealingly subtitled *An Essay toward an Autobiography of a Race Concept*, he was careful to note both African and White ancestries and mark the color of each character. Othello Berghardt was his "very dark grandfather," his grandmother Sally Burghardt "a thin, tall, yellow, and hawk-faced woman." His mother, Mary Sylvina, "was brown and rather small with smooth skin and lovely eyes, and hair that curled and crinkled." His father, Alfred, was "a light mu-

Fig. 8.3.
A view of W. E. B. Du Bois darkened for the cover of an important biography of the great man. Portrait by Addison N. Scurlock. Courtesy of the National Portrait Gallery, Smithsonian Institution.

latto." Stories and an elaborate genealogical chart laid out all the ancestors Du Bois knew and highlighted the race of the White ones.[16]

Du Bois elaborated his thinking about racial construction and mixedness in a chapter titled "The Concept of Race."[17] As he did in much of his writing, here Du Bois presented his personal struggles as emblematic of the struggles of the African American people. He proclaimed the racial binary: "I was born in the century when the walls of race were clear and straight; when the world consisted of mutually exclusive races; and even though the edges might be blurred, there was no question of exact definition and understanding of the meaning of the word." Yet most of his discussion surrounding that proclamation was not binary; it was, rather, an embrace of multiplicity. He went on at length about his White ancestry. He noted his cousins who lived as White. And in the same sentence in which he stated his strongest affirmation of solidarity with Africa, he also asserted that "this heritage binds together not simply the children of Africa, but extends through yellow Asia and into the South Seas."[18]

Surely, no African American intellectual was more unambiguously Black than W. E. B. Du Bois. And none was more expressive of multiplicity. Yet recent generations of readers and writers, in contemplating

Du Bois, have seen only the monoracial Black and not the embrace of multiplicity. This monoracial assumption has gone so far that often paintings and photographs of Du Bois are darkened and stylized to emphasize African-derived features and minimize the European-derived aspects of Du Bois's countenance. The first picture below shows Du Bois untinted: a beige man who could easily pass for Italian or Spanish. The second, a portrait of Du Bois by Laura Wheeler Waring, shows the same angular features but kinkier hair and sepia skin tones, highlighting a stylized Africanity. The third, very dark indeed, is from the cover of Lewis's Pulitzer Prize–winning biography. It is as if Du Bois, in order to stand in the role of honored Black intellectual and political forebear, must be presented as darker than he was in real life.[19]

JEAN TOOMER

Jean Toomer was an icon of Blackness who embodied racial multiplicity— indeed, who changed his race, more than once. No more powerful or controversial figure exists in Black letters. Born Nathan Pinchback Toomer in 1894, he grew to adolescence in the Washington home and psychic shadow of his grandfather P. B. S. Pinchback. Pinchback served as governor and was elected US senator in Louisiana during Reconstruction. He won on the strength of Black votes and his constituents' understanding that, though born the free son of a White planter, he possessed slave ancestry.[20]

Toomer's identity was flexible. Born Nathan, he changed his name to Eugene in childhood and Jean later. He attended high school among Washington's light, bright, and almost White African American upper class. The young Jean Toomer identified as Black but traveled socially on the White side of the line nearly as much as on the Black. He then flitted through several colleges without telling anyone about his African ancestry. His life from beginning to end was personalist, a spiritual search for the center of himself, and through that center for the universally human. Because of his grandfather's prominence and the racial angle of his own first coming to public notice, race was always part of that search, and he resented it.

For a brief time in the early 1920s Jean Toomer was a writer and a Black American. His spiritual search and the need for employment led him to live briefly in rural Georgia and to write about the experience. *Cane*, a jumble of prose, poetry, drawings, and a novella disguised in play form, ignited the imaginations of the makers of the Harlem Renaissance of the 1920s and two generations later the makers of the Black Revolution of the 1960s. Toomer thought he was drawing from a dying well of Black peasant culture with which he had only the most tenuous personal connection. Readers, by contrast, from Langston Hughes to Alice Walker, found the well Toomer tapped to be deep, rich, and ever self-renewing.[21]

Within a year of the publication of *Cane*, Toomer was off on his spiritual quest, leaving behind both the New York intellectual world to which he had briefly aspired and the Black identity he had tried on. He became successively a disciple of the mystic Georges Gurdjieff, an itinerant teacher, a seldom-published philosopher, a Quaker leader, and a recluse. He died in 1967, just before his masterwork was republished and spoke to a new generation of monoracial African Americans. Black critics saw and valued the powerful talent at work in the making of *Cane*, as well as the celebration of Black peasant life and the horrifying account of White racial oppression. But they tended to see Toomer the man as racially confused. Alice Walker confessed to "feelings of disappointment and loss."

> Disappointment because the man who wrote so piercingly of "Negro" life in *Cane* chose to live his own life as a white man, while [Langston] Hughes, [Zora Neale] Hurston, Du Bois, and other black writers were celebrating the blackness in themselves as well as in their work. Loss because it appears this choice undermined Toomer's moral judgment: there were things [White racism] in American life and in his own that he simply refused to see.[22]

This account suggests that, whatever Toomer's talent and contribution, he did not know who he really was, a Black man in a racist nation. Indeed, Walker's assessment might imply self-hatred on Toomer's part, the internalization of White America's contempt for Black people. It is clear that Walker thinks Du Bois and the others made a nobler choice when they embraced an unambiguous Black identity.

Fig. 8.4.
Jean Toomer, herald of the Harlem Renaissance, ca. 1934. From the Marjorie
Toomer Collection. Copyright Estate of Marjorie Content. Courtesy of the National
Portrait Gallery, Smithsonian Institution.

Yet, in addition to the remarkable sensitivity toward the Black folk to
be found in *Cane*, Toomer's writings show that he saw things differently
from the way Walker understood him. He thought he knew who he was—
not simply a monoracial Black man, but a man of multiple ancestries and
identities in a nation that did not yet recognize multiplicity. Many decades
before others took up the theme, Toomer asserted the constructedness of

race and proclaimed a vision of a society that went beyond race. He believed he was a universal man—not, as Walker would have it, a Black man who eschewed Blackness for Whiteness, but a man who did not fit in racial boxes, whose very existence challenged monoracial categories and, behind them, the viciousness of racism. Thus, he could write in later years:

> I would liberate myself and ourselves from the entire machinery of verbal hypnotism. . . . I am simply of the human race. . . . I am of the human nation. . . . I am of Earth. . . . I am of sex, with male differentiations. . . . I eliminate the religions. I am religious. . . .
> What then am I?
> I am at once no one of the races and I am all of them.
> I belong to no one of them and I belong to all.
> I am, in a strict racial sense, a member of a new race. . . .
> I say to the colored group that, as a human being, I am one of them. . . . I say to the white group that, as a human being, I am one of them. As a white man, I am not one of them. . . . I am an American. As such, I invite them [both], not as [colored or] white people, but *as Americans*, to participate in whatever creative work I may be able to do.[23]

Toomer's was a personal vision, born out of mystical seeking, written into a vague program for humankind. It spoke in no concrete way to the needs of people in America who were marked off by color for domination and abuse. Rather, it was a psychological vision of a person who knew his mixedness and his wholeness, and who believed them to be more important than group strivings. Ultimately, neither White nor Black America in the first half of the twentieth century had room for a racially multiple man like Jean Toomer, at least not for public recognition of his multiplicity. Perhaps now, in a new century, there is room.

WALTER WHITE

Walter White was the Whitest, and the Blackest, of the multiracial people I discuss in this essay. Physically, he was short, blond, and blue-eyed. By history and by choice, he was Black. Like Toomer, White grew up in a nearly White family on the margin between African American and European American social circles, in his case in Atlanta. Unlike Toomer, his family was not wealthy or well connected. His father carried the mail. Both the elder White and his wife were light-skinned enough to pass for White, but either they chose, or circumstances forced them, to remain on the Black side of the racial margin.

In middle age White declared his racial allegiance, with none of the ambivalence of Du Bois or Toomer. Perhaps it was because he did not come from the interstitial class and color position of the mulatto elite, or perhaps it was that by midcentury the one-drop rule imposed by Whites had so taken hold among African-derived people that they could imagine no other. Or maybe it was his own personal history that led Walter White to make such an unequivocal statement of his identity.

> I am a Negro. My skin is white, my eyes are blue, my hair is blond. The traits of my race are nowhere visible upon me. Not long ago I stood one morning on a subway platform in Harlem. As the train came in I stepped back for safety. My heel came down upon the toe of the man behind me. I turned to apologize to him. He was a Negro, and his face as he stared at me was hard and full of the piled-up bitterness of a thousand lynchings and a million nights in shacks and tenements and "nigger towns." "Why don't you look where you're going?" he said sullenly. "You white folks are always trampling on colored people." Just then one of my friends came up and asked how the fight had gone in Washington—there was a filibuster against legislation for a permanent Fair Employment Practices Committee. The Negro on whose toes I stepped listened, then spoke to me penitently:
>
> "Are you Walter White of the NAACP? I'm sorry I spoke to you that way. I thought you were white."
>
> I am not white. There is nothing within my mind and heart which tempts me to think I am. Yet I realize acutely that the only characteristic which matters to either the white or the colored race— the appearance of whiteness—is mine. There is magic in a white

skin; there is tragedy, loneliness, exile, in a black skin. Why then do I insist that I am a Negro, when nothing compels me to do so but myself? . . .

There is no mistake. I am a Negro. There can be no doubt.[24]

The dawning of this monoracial, one-drop consciousness came suddenly to young White. In August 1906, when White was thirteen, a race riot struck Atlanta. When the rioters came to the White family's house, the racial line was forever drawn:

A voice which we recognized as that of the son of the grocer with whom we had traded for many years yelled, "That's where that nigger mail carrier lives! Let's burn it down! It's too nice for a nigger to live in!" In the eerie light Father turned his drawn face toward me. In a voice as quiet as though he were asking me to pass him the sugar at the breakfast table, he said, "Son, don't shoot until the first man puts his foot on the lawn and then—don't you miss!"

In the flickering light the mob swayed, paused, and began to flow toward us. In that instant there opened up within me a great awareness; I knew then who I was. I was a Negro, a human being with an invisible pigmentation which marked me a person to be hunted, hanged, abused, discriminated against, kept in poverty and ignorance, in order that those whose skin was white would have readily at hand a proof of their superiority. . . .

Yet as a boy there in the darkness amid the tightening fright, I knew the inexplicable thing—that my skin was as white as the skin of those who were coming at me. . . . I was gripped by the knowledge of my identity, and in the depths of my soul I was vaguely aware that I was glad of it. I was sick with loathing for the hatred which had flared before me that night and come so close to making me a killer; but I was glad I was not one of those who hated; I was glad I was not one of those made sick and murderous by pride. . . .

It was all just a feeling then, inarticulate and melancholy, yet reassuring in the way that death and sleep are reassuring, and I have clung to it now for nearly half a century.[25]

The monoracial identification was reinforced when Walter White's father died in 1931 after being hit by a car. He was taken by the car's White driver to the city hospital, where he was placed in the White ward. Neighbors who had witnessed the accident told Walter White's darker-skinned brother-in-law that the elder White was in the hospital. He went looking in the Black ward and did not find him. When he looked in the White ward, the hospital workers realized they were tending a Black-identified man in the wrong ward. Horrified at having sullied their pristine Whiteness, they delivered White senior to the Black ward across the street. There, as Walter White recounted the story, in a dirty, vermin-infested, densely packed facility, his father died.[26]

Walter White's vision, then, was purely monoracial. He worked for the NAACP, the premier Black organization, for thirty years, twenty of them as executive director. Yet he had his multiracial moments, too. His masterwork as a novelist, *Flight*, is a tale of color and passing. This is as close as White came to contemplating the constructedness of racial categories in print. In 1949 White divorced his African American wife of more than twenty years and married a White woman, Poppy Cannon, who was several shades darker than he. There was a great hue and cry in both Black and White circles. In the former, White was accused of having sold out his race for a piece of White flesh, and Cannon, of having seduced one of Black America's most beloved leaders. Some White segregationists leered that this proved that all Black men wanted was to bed White women.[27]

Only in the final chapter of his autobiography did Walter White confess to some feelings of racial multiplicity, and then only in the context of a starry-eyed paean to interracial harmony.

> Yet I know, I know, I know that there is no reason for this killing, this hatred, this demarcation. There is no difference between the killer and the killed. Black is white and white is black. . . .
>
> I am one of the two in the color of my skin; I am the other in my spirit and my heart. It is only a love of both which binds the two together in me, and it is only love for each other which will join them in the common aims of civilization that lie before us. . . .
>
> I am white and I am black, and know that there is no difference. Each casts a shadow, and all shadows are dark.[28]

Granted that Walter White adopted a formal monoracial identity, the degree to which observers have credited monoracial Blackness to him is still remarkable. The cover of the reprint of his autobiography, *A Man Called White*, bills it as "the life story of a man who crossed the color line to fight for civil rights." By that the publishers mean, it turns out, not that a phenotypically White man crossed the color line to identify himself as Black and fight racism for decades but rather that on one brief occasion in 1918 the Black man Walter White posed as a White man in order to investigate a racist group. Surely, vital though that was as a political moment, it was the less significant color line crossing in White's personal life.

In choosing a monoracial Black identity, Walter White was making a personal response to a political situation, making his personal racial decision conform to his politics. He did not sustain this monoracialism throughout all aspects of his life. Nonetheless, a monoracial, essentialist Blackness is the main theme that more recent commenters have attributed to the life and work of Walter White, as of Du Bois.

FREDERICK DOUGLASS

W. E. B. Du Bois was the archetypal African American whose actual embrace of racial multiplicity and ambiguity has not generally been recognized. Walter White chose to eschew phenotype and embrace monoracial Blackness. Jean Toomer was the sole individual among those examined here who allowed himself a sustained encounter with the fact of his mixedness. White and Du Bois worked politically, publicly, in a monoracial space. But all three lived in a racial space that had great fluidity, ambiguity, and mixedness. In a later age, when other people, operating from an uninterrogated monoracial framework, came to write the histories of Du Bois, White, and the others, they saw only the public positioning and not the personal lives.

Gregory Stephens points to Frederick Douglass as an emblem of the ambiguity these people's life choices present. Although Douglass, unlike White, Toomer, and perhaps Du Bois, probably could not have passed for White, he possessed multiracial ancestry and inhabited a multiracial social space. Indeed, even as he was the nineteenth century's most ardent and honored agitator for the rights of Black Americans in slavery and freedom, he worked and socialized with White people, married a White woman, and pointed toward a hoped-for future of the sort that Nelson Mandela would one day call a nonracial democracy. Stephens characterizes Douglass's racial stance thus:

> In 1886, he told an audience: "[A man painting me insisted I show] my full face, for that is Ethiopian. Take my side face, said I, for that is Caucasian. But should you try my quarter face you would find it Indian. I don't know that any race can claim me, but being identified with slaves as I am, I think I know the meaning of the inquiry." Douglass' public persona was that of a defender of the rights of Afro-Americans. But his private identity was multiethnic. . . . He believed that his multiethnic identity and community were not abnormal, but rather represented the future of America.[29]

Stephens presents Douglass as a meta-mulatto, a larger-than-life advocate of nonracial democracy and an end to racial thinking. In that characterization Stephens goes too far.[30] Whatever measure of multiplicity Douglass—or Du Bois, White, or even Toomer—may have experienced in his private life, his embrace of a complex identity did little to undermine the social power of what G. Reginald Daniel calls the Law of the Excluded Middle.[31] Du Bois, White, and others like them embraced political Blackness and confraternity with monoracial African Americans and were tireless advocates of the cause of Black America, monoracially defined.[32] From sometime in the late nineteenth century until very late in the twentieth, multiracial people, part of whose ancestry was Black, almost always passed as unmixed African Americans. They constituted an anomaly in the binary racial system, not a challenge to it, and their multiraciality was covered over. Those few people like Jean Toomer who attempted to challenge the binary racial system were rendered irrelevant and invisible. In this period, the monoracial fact overwhelmed the multiracial fact. Such was the power of Blackness.

Fig. 8.5.
Abolitionist Frederick Douglass. Photo by Mathew Brady Studio. Courtesy of Ronald L. Harris.

NOTES

This essay originally appeared in *Racial Thinking in the United States: Uncompleted Independence*, which I edited with G. Reginald Daniel (Notre Dame, IN: University of Notre Dame Press, 2004). An earlier version was presented to the Collegium for African American Research, Münster, Germany, March 20, 1999. Several people there made comments that improved the work. In addition, I am grateful for the patient suggestions of Patrick Miller, Reginald Daniel, Puk Degnegaard, and Lori Pierce. Ingrid Dineen-Wimberly has explored this territory more thoroughly in "By the Least Bit of Blood: The Allure of Blackness among Mixed-Race Americans of African Descent, 1862–1935" (unpublished MS) and "Mixed-Race Leadership in African America: The Regalia of Race and National Identity in the US, 1862–1903" (PhD diss., University of California, Santa Barbara, 2009), and she has taught me a lot.

1. Other prominent members of the beigeoisie in those decades included P. B. S. Pinchback, Reconstruction-era acting governor and senator-elect from Louisiana; Adella Hunt Logan, fighter for women's suffrage and professor at Tuskegee Institute; Homer Plessy, challenger of Louisiana's Jim Crow railroad car law; Charles W. Chesnutt, the first major novelist in the African American literary pantheon; John Hope, president of Atlanta University; Archibald Grimké, political rival of Du Bois and Booker T. Washington; Mary Church Terrell, first president of the National Association of Colored Women; Mordecai Johnson, first African American president of Howard University; Charles Drew, surgeon and pioneer in blood plasma research and blood banking; and Adam Clayton Powell Jr., member of Congress from Harlem.

2. See G. Reginald Daniel, "Passers and Pluralists: Subverting the Racial Divide," in *Racially Mixed People in America*, ed. Maria P. P. Root (Newbury Park, CA: Sage, 1992), 91–107. On multiracial people passing for White, see Adrian Piper, "Passing for White, Passing for Black," *Transition*, no. 58 (1992): 4–32; Paul R. Spickard, *Mixed Blood: Intermarriage and Ethnc Identity in Twentieth-Century America* (Madison: University of Wisconsin Press, 1989), 329–39; F. James Davis, *Who Is Black? One Nation's Definition* (University Park: Pennsylvania State University Press, 1991); Robert McG. Thomas Jr., "Thyra Johnston, 91, Symbol of Racial Distinctions, Dies," *New York Times*, November 29, 1995; Countee Cullen, "Two Who Crossed the Line," in *Color* (New York: Harper, 1925), 16–17; almost any issue of *Ebony* from the 1950s; Daniel J. Sharfstein, *The Invisible Line: Three American Families and the Secret Journey from Black to White* (New York: Penguin, 2011); Heidi Ardizzone, *An Illuminated Life: Bella De Costa Greene's Journey from Prejudice to Privilege* (New York: Norton, 2007); Heidi Ardizzone and Earl Lewis, *Love on Trial: An American Scandal in Black and White* (New York: Norton, 2002); Allyson Hobbs, *A Chosen Exile: A History of Racial Passing in American Life* (Cambridge, MA: Harvard University Press, 2014).

Passing for Black is a phenomenon that has not been critically examined, although it is implied in works such as Martha Sandweiss, *Passing Strange: A Gilded Age Tale of Love and Deception across the Color Line* (New York: Penguin, 2009); Martha Hodes, *The Sea Captain's Wife: A Tale of Love, Race, and War in the Nineteenth Century* (New York: Norton, 2007); Kathy Russell, Midge Wilson, and Ronald Hall, *The Color Complex: The Politics of Skin Color among African Americans* (New York: Harcourt Brace Jovanovich, 1992); E. Franklin Frazier, *Black Bourgeoisie: The Rise of a New Middle Class* (New York: Free Press, 1957); Charles S. Johnson, "The Social Significance of Color in Negro Society" (Charles Spurgeon Johnson Papers, Fisk University Archives, Nashville, Box 173, folder 35); Verna M. Keith and Cedric Herring, "Skin Tone and Stratification in the Black Community," *American Journal of Sociology* 97.3 (1991): 760–78. Even unmixed White people sometimes chose to pass for Black; see John Howard Griffin, *Black Like Me* (Boston: Houghton Mifflin, 1961); Grace Halsell, *Soul Sister* (New York: Fawcett, 1969).

3. Throughout this essay I shall be speaking of the construction of race in terms of Black and White races. It is essential to note that there have always been more than just African- and European-derived peoples on this continent and that the others are part of the equation of any racial construction, as other chapters in this volume make clear.

4. Winthrop D. Jordan, *White over Black* (Chapel Hill: University of North Carolina Press, 1968), 3–43, 136–78; Joel Williamson, *New People: Miscegenation and Mulattoes in the United States* (New York: Free Press, 1980), 5–59; Spickard, *Mixed Blood*, 235–52; Martha Hodes, *White Women, Black Men: Illicit Sex in the 19th-Century South* (New Haven, CT: Yale University Press, 1997); Winthrop D. Jordan, "American Chiaroscuro: The Status and Definition of Mulattoes in the British Colonies," *William and Mary Quarterly*, 3rd ser., 19 (1962): 183–200; Carter G. Woodson, "The Beginnings of Miscegenation of Whites and Blacks," *Journal of Negro History* 3 (1918): 335–53; Winthrop D. Jordan, "Historical Origins of the One-Drop Racial Rule in the United States," ed. Paul Spickard, *Journal of Critical Mixed-Race Studies* 1 (2013): 98–132; Joshua D. Rothman, *Notorious in the Neighborhood: Sex and Families across the Color Line in Virginia, 1787–1861* (Chapel Hill: University of North Carolina Press, 2003).

5. James Thomas Flexner, *The Young Hamilton* (Boston, Little Brown, 1978), 8–26. So much of race making and the constraints placed on race choosing depends on context. The possibility of African ancestry in Hamilton's case was a certainty for Alexander Pushkin and Alexandre Dumas, larger-than-life figures in Russian and French letters a generation later. Yet though their ancestry was known, they were not marked by the dominant cultures of Russia and France as Black, and their artistic work did not take shape in ways that reflected a Black consciousness or identity. See T. J. Binyon, *Pushkin* (New York: Vintage, 2004); Tom Reiss, *The Black Count: Glory, Revolution, Betrayal, and the Real Count of Monte Cristo* (New York: Crown, 2012).

6. Daniel, "Passers and Pluralists"; Davis, *Who Is Black?*, 31–42; William-son, *New People*, 5–59; Sybil Kein, ed., *Creole: The History and Legacy of Louisi-ana's Free People of Color* (Baton Rouge: Louisiana State University Press, 2000); Virginia R. Domínquez, *White by Definition: Social Classification in Creole Loui-siana* (New Brunswick, NJ: Rutgers University Press, 1986); Sister Frances Jerome Woods, *Marginality and Identity: A Colored Creole Family through Ten Genera-tions* (Baton Rouge: Louisiana State University Press, 1972); Arnold R. Hirsch and Joseph Logsdon, eds., *Creole New Orleans: Race and Americanization* (Baton Rouge: Louisiana State University Press, 2000).

7. Williamson, *New People*, 61, 3, 109.

8. David Forcacs, ed., *An Antonio Gramsci Reader* (New York: Schocken Books, 1988), 189–21, 422–24; Bill Ashcroft, Gareth Griffiths, and Helen Tiffin, *Key Concepts in Post-Colonial Studies* (London: Routledge, 1998), 116–17.

9. W. E. B. Du Bois, "The Advance Guard of the Race," *Booklovers Maga-zine* 2 (July 1903): 3; Willard B. Gatewood, *Aristocrats of Color: The Black Elite, 1880–1920* (Bloomington: Indiana University Press, 1990).

10. Contrast the interpretations of Du Bois, "Advance Guard"; Reuter, *The Mulatto in the United States* (New York: Negro Universities Press, 1969; orig. 1918), 183–215 passim. I write here about leaders simply because they left writings that give us some clues to their thoughts on these issues. Lives of everyday people of multiracial ancestry and various identifications can be examined in Domín-guez, *White by Definition*; Shirlee Taylor Haizlip, *The Sweeter the Juice: A Family Memoir in Black and White* (New York: Simon and Schuster, 1994); Kent Ander-son Leslie, *Woman of Color, Daughter of Privilege* (Athens: University of Georgia Press, 1995); Victoria E. Bynum, "'White Negroes' in Segregated Mississippi: Mis-cegenation, Racial Identity, and the Law," *Journal of Southern History* 64.2 (1998): 247–76; Edward Ball, *Slaves in the Family* (New York: Ballantine, 1999).

11. W. E. Burghardt Du Bois, *Dusk of Dawn: An Essay toward an Autobiog-raphy of a Race Concept* (New Brunswick, NJ: Transaction, 1984; orig. 1940), 18–19, 115.

12. W. E. B. Du Bois, *The Souls of Black Folk* (New York: Fawcett, 1961; orig. 1903), 16.

13. Du Bois, *Dusk of Dawn*, 25–49, 115.

14. David Levering Lewis, *W. E. B. Du Bois: Biography of a Race* (New York: Holt, 1993), 72–73.

15. Du Bois, *Souls of Black Folk*, 16–17.

16. Du Bois, *Dusk of Dawn*, 11–12, 104–13.

17. Ibid., 97–133.

18. Ibid., 116–17.

19. David Levering Lewis, *W. E. B. Du Bois: The Fight for Equality and the American Century, 1919–1963* (New York: Henry Holt, 2000), photo following

206; Lewis, *Biography of a Race*, cover and photo following 304. The book's darkness may well be the work of someone in marketing at Holt and not reflect Lewis's reading of Du Bois's racial identity. When the first version of this essay was being considered for publication, one of the reviewers asked Professor Lewis if in fact the cover picture had been darkened. According to the reviewer's report, Lewis denied that it had been tinted darker. I have seen the original portrait by Addison N. Scurlock in the National Portrait Gallery in Washington, DC, and it is much lighter than the cover of Lewis's book. The second volume of Lewis's biography has a much lighter—and truer to life—image of Du Bois on its cover; see Lewis, *W. E. B. Du Bois: The Fight for Equality and the American Century*. Lewis is one of the most distinguished historians of African America. I do not wish to impute any particular motives to him, nor to impugn his scholarship. I am just pointing out a trend in images.

20. Toomer biographies include Cynthia Earl Kerman and Richard Eldridge, *Lives of Jean Toomer: A Hunger for Wholeness* (Baton Rouge: Louisiana State University Press, 1989); Charles R. Larson, *Invisible Darkness: Jean Toomer and Nella Larsen* (Iowa City: University of Iowa Press, 1993); Charles Scruggs and Lee Vandemarr, *Jean Toomer and the Terrors of American History* (Philadelphia: University of Pennsylvania Press, 1998); Jon Woodson, *To Make a New Race: Gurdjieff, Toomer, and the Harlem Renaissance* (Jackson: University Press of Mississippi, 1999); H. William Rice, "Searching for Jean Toomer," *American Legacy* 3.3 (Fall 1997): 16–22. On Pinchback, see Dineen-Wimberly, "By the Least Bit of Blood."

After this essay was first published, I received a nice letter from Toomer's stepdaughters, his literary heirs, who gave permission for the photo that appears in this essay. They thanked me for the copy of the book I had sent and said that they were grateful I had interpreted Toomer's identity and personality correctly.

21. Jean Toomer, *Cane*, introd. Darwin T. Turner (New York: Liveright, 1975; orig. 1923).

22. Alice Walker, "The Divided Life of Jean Toomer," *New York Times*, July 13, 1980, reprinted in Alice Walker, *In Search of Our Mothers' Gardens* (New York: Harcourt Brace Jovanovich, 1983). It is worth noting that Langston Hughes owned his multiplicity even as he chose a mainly Black identity; see Hughes, *The Big Sea* (New York: Hill and Wang, 1940), esp. 50–51. It is important to understand that Toomer was emphatically not attacking African Americans after the fashion of the racially mixed Negrophobe William Hannibal Thomas. John David Smith, *Black Judas: William Hannibal Thomas and the American Negro* (Athens: University of Georgia Press, 2000).

23. Kerman and Eldridge, *Lives of Jean Toomer*, 341–42.

24. Walter White, *A Man Called White* (Athens: University of Georgia Press, 1995; orig. 1948), 3–4; Walter White, "Why I Remain a Negro," *Negro Digest* (February 1948), 12–19.

25. White, *A Man Called White*, 11–12.

26. Ibid., 134–38.

27. Poppy Cannon, *A Gentle Knight: My Husband, Walter White* (New York: Rinehart, 1952); Poppy Cannon, "How We Made Our Mixed Marriage Work," *Ebony* (June 1952): 24–40; Poppy Cannon, "How We Erased Two Color Lines," *Ebony* (July 1952): 47–59; Poppy Cannon, "Love That Never Died," *Ebony* (January 1957): 17–20.

28. White, *A Man Called White*, 366.

29. Gregory Stephens, "Douglass, Not Lincoln, Bolsters GOP," *Los Angeles Times*, December 31, 2000, M2–M3; original brackets. See also Maria I. Diedrich, *Love across Color Lines: Ottilie Assing and Fredrick Douglass* (New York: Hill and Wang, 1999).

30. Gregory Stephens, *On Racial Frontiers: The New Culture of Frederick Douglass, Ralph Ellison, and Bob Marley* (Cambridge: Cambridge University Press, 1999). G. Reginald Daniel explores the concept of the meta-mulatto in *Machado de Assis: Multiracial Identity and the Brazilian Novelist* (University Park: Pennsylvania State University Press, 2012).

31. G. Reginald Daniel, "Either Black or White: Race, Modernity, and the Law of the Excluded Middle," in Spickard and Daniel, *Racial Thinking in the United States*, 21–59.

32. For other leaders who blended multiracial social lives with monoracial political lives, see Adam Clayton Powell Jr., *Adam by Adam* (New York: Dial, 1971); Wil Haygood, *King of the Cats: The Life and Times of Adam Clayton Powell, Jr.* (Boston: Houghton Mifflin, 1993), 10–12, 18, 78ff., 87, 104, 252, 265, 323–25; Mary Church Terrell, *A Colored Woman in a White World* (Salem, NH: Ayer, 1966; orig. Washington, DC: Ransdell, 1940).

9

Pacific Islander Americans and Multiethnicity

A Vision of America's Future?

At a basketball game in a schoolyard in Kaneʻohe, Hawaiʻi, two players began to argue. As basketball players will, they started talking about each other's families. One, who prided himself on his pure Samoan ancestry, said, "You got a Hawaiian grandmother, a Pake [Chinese] grandfather. Your other grandfather's Portegee [Portuguese], and you mom's Filipino. You got Haole [White] brother-in-law and Korean cousins. Who da heck are you?" The person with the bouquet of ethnic possibilities smiled (his team was winning) and said, simply, "I all da kine [I'm all of those things]. Le's play." This chapter attempts to explain that interaction. Specifically, it seeks to understand how ethnicity works for Pacific Islander Americans and what that might mean for other people.

ETHNICITY IN AMERICA

Throughout most of American history, the rhetoric of race and ethnicity presumed a hegemonic role for American identity. Until the last quarter century, nearly all analytical public discourse, scholarly and popular, pictured ethnicity as something primordial that people brought with them from some other place, which they then lost progressively as they lived in America for decades and generations. In this new country they became, as the ideas were enunciated in the generation of the American Revolution by Hector St. John de Crèvecouer, "the American, this new man[,] . . . that strange mixture of blood, which you will find in no other country. . . . *He* is an American who, leaving behind him all his ancient prejudices and manners, receives new ones. . . . Here individuals are melted into a new race of men."[1] These words, and the melting pot ideology to which they gave voice, have echoed throughout the history of Americans' thinking about racial and ethnic matters. In recent generations, America has indeed finally become a place where people from all over the world mix and mate, but Crèvecouer may not be quite right about the outcome of that mixing for ethnic identity.

Scholars have conceived ethnicity in various ways—as biology, as culture, as economic or political interests, as networks of social connectedness.[2] But, however American observers have conceived it and measured it, most of them have regarded ethnicity as a doomed commodity. In short order or long, they have believed, a more general American identity would obliterate it. Italian immigrants would become Italian Americans and then just Americans. It may be unnecessary to add that this vision of an inevitable shift to an American identity was advanced mainly by those people of northwest European descent who ran the country and defined the terms of the rhetoric of race and ethnicity. This, the dominant discourse, was the assimilationist view.[3]

In the past several decades, another vision of a multicultural America has come to the front. People of color and others who were denied determinative roles in the former rhetoric of race and ethnicity have begun to describe a different pattern of understanding. They have prescribed an America of many more or less permanent cultural islands, to be honored and preserved in their diversity. African Americans, Chinese, Puerto Ricans, Anglos, and many others would all maintain separate identities—whether in harmony or in conflict—far into the future. This, the subdominant discourse, is the pluralist view.[4]

Both these descriptions assume that an individual or group possesses only one ethnic identity. It is a very Cartesian enterprise, this assigning people to ethnic boxes and measuring the shapes and contents of the boxes. In the assimilationist view, nearly every person who comes to America (as well as those native peoples who preceded northwest European Americans on the continent) at first possesses an identity different from what the assimilationists regard as the American norm. Over time and perhaps generations of contact with northwest European American people and culture, that separate identity gradually fades into insignificance as the person takes on an amorphously American identity. In the pluralist view, each person retains more or less the identity with which she began, or some descendant of that identity, separately evolved.

MULTIETHNICITY

Both the assimilationists and the pluralists recognize that most people in fact are descended from multiple, not single, ethnic sources. They know that most African Americans are in fact part European American and Native American, most Jews have some Gentile ancestry, most Swedish Americans have some German or Norwegian relatives, and so forth. But both the dominant and subdominant paradigms treat ethnicity as if each person had only one ethnic identity. They say (along with census takers and school forms until quite recently), "Choose one box." Thus a person of African, Native American, and European ancestry has long been regarded—and has regarded himself—as an African American. Even as he may have acknowledged privately that he was descended from multiple roots, nonetheless he identified with only one. Reginald Daniel refers to this as the "rule of hypodescent"—the one-drop rule, whereby Whites and Blacks agree that one drop of Black blood makes one Black.[5] The system was not so clear-cut for other groups; some measure of mixture was acknowledged in the cases of people whose ancestors came from different European sources, for instance. But even then, people tended to see themselves as predominantly one sort of person, ethnically speaking.

In the last third of the twentieth century and into the twenty-first, two things have happened that have caused this to begin to change. In the first place, for nearly half a century, intermarriage across racial as well as religious and national lines has increased steadily. Almost no White American extended family exists today without at least one member who has married across what a few generations ago would have been thought an unbridgeable gap. Anglo-American has married Irish, Lutheran has married Baptist; such marriages would have scandalized many families in the early twentieth century, but they scarcely are noticed anymore. Formerly endogamous groups like Japanese Americans and Jews now experience an out-marriage rate of over 50 percent. Intermarriage is on the rise, although the rate of increase seems to be declining: according to US Census figures, the number of interracial marriages rose 65 percent between 1990 and 2000, plus another 20 percent between 2000 and 2010.[6] Because of the increase in intermarriage, there are a larger number of mixed people than ever before. In the 1980 census and again in 1990, the fastest-growing ethnic category was "Other," and most of these people were probably mixed.[7] The cover of a famous 1993 special issue of *Time* magazine proclaimed mixed people "The New Face of America."[8] Now, in the second decade of the twenty-first century, mixture is so common that if does not attract all that much attention.

The second thing that has happened to change the discourse of American ethnicity is that, over the past three decades, people of mixed ancestry have begun to claim both or all parts of their ancestry. They claim multiethnicity; they refuse to choose just one box. Scores of organizations of multiethnic persons dot the landscape. In the 1990s, some of those organizations lobbied for changes in the census (hence school forms, etc.) to allow people to check more than one box.[9] In 1997, the Office of Management and Budget, which establishes the categories for the US Census, held hearings and decided to allow people to check more than one racial box. The subsequent censuses in 2000 and 2010 showed increasing numbers of people exercising this option.[10] The situation of Pacific Islander Americans can provide some clues to what may lie in store for other American ethnic groups in this ever more mixed situation.

PACIFIC ISLANDER AMERICAN MULTIETHNICITY

The term *Pacific Islander Americans* is a bit problematic, for, like Asian Americans and Latinos, Pacific Islander Americans are not a single ethnic group but rather an artificial collection of groups. They appear as a sub-category of the human species in the US Census, on affirmative action forms, and the like, often mixed with Asian Americans and paralleled by Native, African, Hispanic, and White Americans. Yet almost no one rises in the morning thinking of herself as a Pacific Islander American. Most think of themselves as Tongans (or Tongan Americans), Samoans, Fijians, and so on. A few would recognize "Polynesian," "Melanesian," and "Micronesian" as somewhat larger categories that they have been told apply to them. But those are not indigenous categories either. They are constructs of the northwest European imagination.[11]

As it happens, nearly all the Pacific Islanders surveyed, interviewed, and read for this project were Polynesians of various sorts: Hawaiians, Tongans, Samoans, and Maori in about that order of frequency, with a few Fijians (who are more or less Melanesians) thrown in for good measure. The observations made in this chapter, therefore, may not represent the experiences of other sorts of Pacific Islander Americans as well as they do these groups.[12] Here I treat Pacific Islander Americans more or less as if they were a single group despite their obvious multiplicity. That is, I do not try to differentiate systematically between, for instance, Samoan American ethnicity and Maori American ethnicity. That is due both to the eclectic nature of the research and to the problem at hand: multiethnicity by its nature cuts across neat ethnic boundaries. It is important to note as well that I do not attempt to prescribe what ought to be; rather, I describe what seems to be and then muse about what may be becoming.

Pacific Islanders historically have constructed their ethnic identities rather more complexly than have many other peoples. Pacific Islanders have long had a greater consciousness than other American groups of being mixed peoples, of having multiple ethnic identities—Samoan and Tongan, Marquesan and Tahitian, Maori and European, and so forth. They seem more comfortable than other Americans with holding in tension two or more ethnic identities, with being deeply involved in more than one at the same time.[13] This consciousness of multiplicity is borne out by 2010 US Census data: 55.9 percent of people who listed Hawaiian or other Pacific Islander as their race, also listed a second or third racial identity, compared to 7.4 percent for Blacks and 3.2 percent for Whites.[14]

Take the case of the late William Kauaiwiulaokalani Wallace.[15] Bill was a Hawaiian rights activist, lawyer, and director of Hawaiian studies at Brigham Young University (BYU)–Hawai'i. When he spoke in public he would begin by chanting his genealogy for five minutes and playing his nose flute and drum. As a child on the island of Moloka'i, his parents were Hawaiian and his first language was Hawaiian. He dug taro and talked story and knew himself to be completely Hawaiian.

Then at the age of ten or eleven Bill went to live with his grandmother in La'ie on the island of O'ahu. There he found out—much to his dismay at first—that he was Samoan. He hung out with his Samoan cousins and their friends. He learned some Samoan words, ate Samoan food, and began to feel *fa'a samoa*—the Samoan way. So he was half Hawaiian and half Samoan. But then, on questioning his elders, he found that his Samoan side had relatives in Tonga. And he found that his Hawaiian family went back to Tahiti. So he was Hawaiian and Samoan and Tongan and Tahitian.

Then, as he emerged into adulthood, Bill married a Maori woman from New Zealand. In time, he visited her family and was accorded a position of honor. And he began to discover other pieces of himself. He worked for a couple of years in Samoa and discovered that his Samoan side included a fair amount of British and some German ancestry, that some of his relatives were members of what some call the *afakasi* class, part Samoan and part European. Back in Hawai'i, Bill learned that the name Wallace stemmed from a Scottish ancestor. And he found that among his plantation ancestors on Moloka'i was a Chinese man, back some three or four generations. Bill had a pretty clear hierarchy among these identities. The Hawaiian side organized his life's activities, shaped his values, and determined his identity more than the others. Next came the Samoan, although the Maori connection was not far behind. The other ethnic connections were quite dim. He confessed to feeling an occasional twinge of fellow feeling for each of the peoples that contributed smaller portions to his genealogy, but only three—Hawaiian, Samoan, and Maori—organized much of his life.

Bill Wallace was not at all unusual. In the mid-1990s, the Pacific Islander American Research Project surveyed people in three rural villages on the windward coast of the island of O'ahu, Hawai'i.[16] We surveyed 406 people, of whom 289 said they had at least some Pacific Islander ancestry. Of those, 91 said they were purely one or another sort of Pacific Islander, and 198—more than two-thirds—said they were biologically mixed (table 9.1). Many of the mixed people interviewed chose to identify with all parts of their ancestry: 42 out of 115 people who had part Hawaiian ancestry; 32 out of 86 part Samoans; 13 out of 38 part Tongans (table 9.2).

One suspects that even some people who said they were unmixed actually possessed some mixed ancestry. Ao Pauga wrote after a class discussion on ethnic mixing, "I went home and tried to [find] my genealogy.... [I]t really hit me because ... there is a possibility that I am not a full blood Samoan. I always thought that I am a pure Samoan and I am proud for that.... In Samoa, we (full-blood Samoan) always make fun of the 'Afakasi' half-caste.... I started to wonder.... So far I have found that there [is] some Tongan blood in me. My research also revealed one White (Palagi) name. As I continue my research, I am ... coming to realize that I am not a pure Samoan."

Many Polynesians tell stories like Bill Wallace's. Kookie Soliai has five names to represent the four ethnicities she feels. Her full name is Shazzelma Reiko Reremai Ku'uipo Soliai. The first name is a family concoction, but the others bespeak, in turn, Japanese, Maori, Hawaiian, and Samoan ethnicity. Her biological inheritance is equal parts Japanese (maternal grandfather), Hawaiian (maternal grandmother), English (paternal grandfather), and Maori (paternal grandmother), but the English person

Table 9.1. Ancestry

Report Single Ancestry		Report Multiple Ancestries	
Total	91	Total	198
Hawaiian	19	Including Hawaiian	115
Samoan	41	Including Samoan	86
Tongan	28	Including Tongan	38
Maori	1	Including Maori	11
Cook Islander	1	Including Other Pacific Islander	10
Fijian	1		

Table 9.2. Identity Choices of People Who Report Multiple Ancestries

Ancestry	Identify with All Parts of Ancestry	Simplify to Multiple Identity	Simplify to Identify with This Single Ancestry	Simplify to Identify with Another Single Ancestry
Mixed people with some Hawaiian ancestry	42	15	49	10
Mixed people with some Samoan ancestry	32	16	28	8
Mixed people with some Tongan ancestry	13	11	4	9
Mixed people with some Maori ancestry	2	1	5	2
Mixed people with some other Polynesian ancestry	2	3	1	4

was adopted and raised in Aotearoa/New Zealand, so she does not feel the English connection. Kookie says that her names make her "feel the relationship" to each of her inherited identities, as well as to the Samoan group into which she married. She says she feels completely at home in a room filled entirely with Japanese Americans, and also in a room made up entirely of Maori or Hawaiians, but perhaps not in a room full of Haoles.

Features of Pacific Islander American Multiethnicity

Pacific Islander ethnicity is perhaps not unique in the way it is constructed and operates, but it has several features that mark it as unusual. In the first place, Pacific Islander American ethnicity seems to be *situational*.[17] Dorri Nautu has Hawaiian, Filipino, Portuguese, and several other ancestries. She lives in a mixed community of part Hawaiians, Hawaiians, and several other ethnic groups, and she qualified to attend university on an ethnic Hawaiian scholarship. She identifies herself more than anything else as Hawaiian. But she says, "If I'm with my grandmother I'm Portuguese. If I'm with some of my aunts on my dad's side I'm Filipino. If I'm hanging around I'm just local. If I'm on the mainland I'm Hawaiian."

Dorri reports that her Filipino relatives accept her as a Filipina. But they see her (and she sees herself) as a little less completely Filipina than other family members. This is primarily, she says, because she has less Filipino cultural knowledge (about food, language, etc.) than do other family members. Secondarily, it is because she has a smaller historical quantum of Filipino ancestry. Dorri says that her relatives excuse her lack of cultural knowledge because she is not purely Filipina in ancestry or upbringing, whereas they would be critical if a pure Filipina exhibited a similar deficiency. Her Hawaiian relatives, on the other hand, do not seem to make any distinction regarding purity of ancestry. So how Dorri identifies herself depends on which of her groups she is with; she feels significantly connected with each of her major ethnic derivations, and she is accepted in each of the groups as an insider.

Lori Atoa reports the opposite situation. She is treated as a Samoan by her mother's Idaho Haole family and as *palagi* by her relatives and schoolmates at home in Samoa. Alexis Siteine reports a more complex dynamic.

My high school friend . . . asked me, "What do you tell people that you are?" My answer was, "It depends on who's doing the asking." I do not choose to sometimes be one thing and at other times another, but I have learned to identify what I think people are really asking. Sometimes they are actually asking, "What makes you the same as me?" Yet, more often it is, "What makes you different?" If asked this question in New Zealand by a non-Samoan, I identify myself as Samoan. If the asker is Samoan, I acknowledge my heritage: My mother is palagi and my father is Samoan. When I am out of New Zealand and am asked by a non-Samoan, I identify myself as a New Zealander; if a Samoan asks, my answer is the same, but I qualify it with "but my father is Samoan." These replies are generally satisfactory.

These various testimonies also point to some geographic differences. How one thinks about one's ethnicity seems to vary depending on where one is. Dorri Nautu feels "local"—mixed, polyglot, native to Hawai'i, but not specifically ethnically Hawaiian—most of the time when she is in Hawai'i. On the mainland she feels Hawaiian, not just placed in that box by others but actively, primarily, ethnically Hawaiian in her own imagination. This may be due in part to the difference between active and latent ethnicity. When one is with one's ethnic fellows, one seldom thinks about one's ethnicity except on ritual occasions. One just *is* ethnic—behaves in ways that embody the ethnic culture, associates with other ethnic people, and so forth. The time when one feels one's ethnicity more vividly is when one is confronted by a large group of outsiders. Thus many White people in America imagine they have no ethnicity; yet if they spend an afternoon in Harlem or Tokyo they are bound to feel their ethnicity quite strongly. So, too, the half Samoan woman noted above may not feel that identity very strongly while in the company of other Samoans (although an outsider is bound to see them all as being Samoan together), yet her Samoan identity comes to the fore when she is among non-Samoans in Idaho.

The greater recognition of one's Pacific Islander identity when in a contrast situation also may be related to a phenomenon one may observe among Tongans and Samoans in California, Washington, or Utah. Pacific Islanders are more willing to express their multiplicity in an overtly multiple place like Hawai'i than they are in the continental United States. The same person who in Hau'ula or on the multicultural campus of BYU–Hawai'i is primarily a Samoan but also admits to some palagi and Asian Indian ancestors in Los Angeles sees herself and is treated only as a Samoan, without the multiethnic consciousness.

Even farther afield from centers of Pacific Islander American population, one's Pacific Islander identity may become fuzzier, not necessarily in one's own mind but in the minds of the people around. In several western metropolitan areas, most non-Pacific people know that there are Samoans and Hawaiians, and they may know that there are Tongans, although other groups such as Fijians, Marshall Islanders, and I-Kiribati are beyond their ken.[18] But elsewhere in the United States, Pacific Islanders are frequently mistaken for someone of a different ethnicity. On a plane from the West Coast to Illinois, a curious passenger leaned across the aisle and asked Debbie Hippolite Wright, "What tribe are you from?," assuming she was a Native American. When she told him she was not a Native American, he replied, "Oh, you must be Mexican." When she told him she was flattered, but she was not that either, he said, "Well, what *are* you?" He had never heard of Maori, but ultimately he was comfortable with the label "Polynesian." Hawaiians are Polynesians, and he knew about Hawaiians.[19]

Another feature of Pacific Islander American multiethnicity is the common practice of choosing one from among the available identities for emphasis, at the same time holding onto other identities. Thus, Bill Wallace and Dorri Nautu were many things, but they chose to be mainly Hawaiian most of the time. Debbie Hippolite Wright is English and French in part but chooses Maori as her primary identity. Jon Jonassen is Rarotongan and Norwegian and several other things but is vociferously a Cook Islander.[20] Lori Atoa is Samoan and palagi but chooses Samoan because she grew up in Western Samoa and because she feels she looks more Samoan. Tupou Hopoate has ancestors from Germany, Portugal, England, Fiji, and Samoa, but she is militantly Tongan even as she acknowledges the others.[21]

The survey showed people choosing to simplify their ancestry (see table 9.2). Fifteen out of 115 part Hawaiians, 16 out of 86 part Samoans, and 11 out of 38 part Tongans simplified their ancestry but still expressed more than one identity; they simplified from as many as eight or nine biological branches down to just two or three. Others chose a single identity: 49 part Hawaiians identified simply as Hawaiians; 28 part Samoans, simply as Samoans. There were discernible patterns. Since the survey was taken in Hawai'i and since in recent decades there has been a resurgence of the prestige of Hawaiian identity, it should surprise no one that many people who knew of mixed ancestry chose to identify with the Hawaiian branch of their family tree more than with any other. Generally, the ancestry most likely to be left out in the simplifyings was European. The second most likely to be left out were Asian ancestries. Only very seldom did any of the people interviewed choose to ignore a Pacific Islander ancestry; in most cases when this occurred, it was when a person chose to embrace a single Hawaiian identity.

The choice of which identity to emphasize may shift in the course of one's life. Kookie Soliai says that in her heart she feels more strongly Maori than anything else. But when she lived in the continental United States she identified herself as Hawaiian because that was easier for a lot of people to figure out and because it gave her a bond of sisterhood with other islanders far from home. Back in Hawai'i, she identifies publicly as part Hawaiian despite her greater psychic affiliation with her Maori heritage, for reasons both political and financial (in Hawai'i there are tangible benefits to being Hawaiian).

The pattern of simplifying one's ethnicity, and of choosing one heritage to emphasize while still acknowledging some others, is a bit like the pattern among White Catholics that Mary Waters found in her study *Ethnic Options*. In both situations, the people in question acknowledge more than one possible identity; many simplify their ethnicity in practice; and many emphasize just one ethnic identity. The difference between Waters's White Catholics and the Pacific Islander Americans interviewed for this study has to do with the *importance* of ethnicity. For the people Waters studied, "ethnicity is increasingly a personal choice of whether to be ethnic at all, and, for an increasing majority of people, of which ethnicity to be. An ethnic identity is something that does not affect much in everyday life."[22] For Waters's Catholics, ethnicity does not have much content; it is merely "symbolic ethnicity."[23] For Pacific Islander Americans, on the other hand, ethnicity is much more important. As for White Catholics, Pacific Islander Americans' ethnicity is multiple, but theirs is no mere symbolic ethnicity. It is not something to be put on and taken off, not something to be trotted out only for ceremonial occasions. In the case of all the Pacific Islander Americans interviewed, the ethnicity is powerful, it is deeply felt, and it organizes quite a lot of the person's life. The fact of multiplicity and the act of choosing do not imply lack of content in ethnicity, and they in no way diminish ethnicity's importance.

A final feature of Pacific Islander American multiethnicity is that the group tends to admit individuals who have mixed ancestry on more or less the same basis as people who have pure ancestry. That is not always the case in the Pacific, as indicated by the ridicule heaped on *afakasis* in Samoa.[24] But it seems to be true of Pacific Islanders in America. There is little residue of the Samoan pure-blood/half-blood split in the United States, either in Hawai'i or on the continent. The same is true for other Pacific Islander groups in the United States. Dorri Nautu is accepted by both Filipinos and Hawaiians, although she is treated a bit more specially by the Filipinos on account of her mixture than by the Hawaiians. The difference in her reception is probably partly because Hawaiians and other Pacific peoples see themselves as fundamentally mixed peoples, whereas Filipinos and other Asians see themselves as more purely one thing. It may also be because Pacific Islander American ethnicity focuses not on the boundaries between groups but on the centers of group ethnicity and the glue that holds the group together—not on who is out but on who is in, and on what they do together.

Defining features, then, of Pacific Islander American multiethnicity include the following. It is situational, depending on whom one is with and where one is located geographically. People are conscious of and affiliate with multiple identities, but they commonly choose one for primary emphasis. And Pacific Islander Americans, perhaps more than other groups, seem to receive mixed people on more or less the same basis as they do unmixed people.

Bases of Pacific Islander American Multiethnicity

The identity choices of Pacific Islanders who possess multiple inheritances are based on several factors. A person's ethnicity may proceed from any of several bases, and the group seems willing to admit people to membership on the basis of any of several items. One such basis is consciousness of *ancestry*—bloodline, as many would call it. Samoans especially talk a lot about the importance of "blood," but all the Pacific Islanders interviewed stressed ancestry as an essential basis of ethnic identity.

In order to identify yourself as a Hawaiian, you must possess at least one Hawaiian ancestor. Being able to trace that ancestor gives you location. As Haunani-Kay Trask writes:

In Polynesian cultures, genealogy is paramount. Who we are is determined by our connection to our lands and to our families. Therefore, our bloodlines and birthplace tell our identity. When I meet another Hawaiian, I say I am descended of two genealogical lines: the Pi'ilani line through my mother who is from Hana, Maui, and the Kahakumakaliua line through my father's family from Kaua'i. I came of age on the Ko'olau side of the island of O'ahu. This is who I am and who my people are and where we come from.[25]

Most Hawaiians do not begin their conversations in Pizza Hut by reciting their entire genealogies. But if one is meeting someone in a slightly more formal way—if one, say, is being introduced to the aunt of one's friend—then the conversation is likely to begin with each person telling the other about who their relatives are and where they are from, until the two people arrive at a point of recognition whereby each can place where the other is located among the Hawaiian people. And reciting genealogy is something that the *ali'i*, the Hawaiian nobility, are said to have done of old; the memory of that act anciently performed resonates for many modern Hawaiians. Like Hawaiians, Maori in Aotearoa/New Zealand are likely to introduce themselves on formal occasions by means of a genealogical chant.

It is probably true that the idea of blood as the carrier of identity is not native to the Pacific; in fact, it seems to have come quite late—as late as the 1870s in Hawai'i.[26] And the idea of blood quantum, of calculating percentages, is found only in Hawai'i and can be traced to American government impositions from the 1920s on.[27] But genealogy is nonetheless a very old Pacific imperative. The *Kumulipo* and other ancient chants recite long genealogies that give location and substance to the Hawaiian people.[28] Lilikala Kame'eleihiwa expounds on the importance of genealogies to Hawaiian identity.

The genealogies *are* the Hawaiian concept of time, and they order the space around us. Hawaiian genealogies are the histories of our people. Through them we learn of the exploits and identities of our ancestors—their great deeds and their follies, their loves and their accomplishments, and their errors and defeats. Even though the great genealogies are of the *Ali'i Nui* and not of the commoners, these *Ali'i Nui* are the collective ancestors, and their *mo'olelo* (histories) are histories of all Hawaiians, too. . . . Genealogies anchor Hawaiians to our place in the universe. . . . Genealogies also brought Hawaiians psychological comfort in times of acute distress. . . . [T]heir genealogy . . . is comprised of the character of their ancestors. This is the sum total of their identity. From the Hawaiian view, it is pointless to discuss the actions of any character in Hawaiian history without a careful examination of his or her genealogy. . . . [W]ithout their identities the account would be unintelligible. . . . Ancestral identity is revealed in the names that Hawaiians carry, for the names of our ancestors continue as our names also. . . . Names of the *Ali'i Nui* are repeated for successive generations to enhance and share the honor of the original ancestor. In this process, the name collects it own *mana* [power, spirit, authority, identity] and endows the successor who carries it. It is said that the name molds the character of the child. . . . It is as if the Hawaiian stands firmly in the present, with his back to the future, and his eyes fixed upon the past, seeking historical answers for present-day dilemmas.[29]

This celebration of the mystic chords of memory is perhaps as important as the actual content of the genealogical account in gluing together Hawaiians as a people.

There is something incantatory about certain ethnic political speech. It is as invigorating to ethnicity when a Pacific Islander American politician recites the history of abuse that her people have suffered as when an island spiritual leader chants a genealogy. The ground of ethnicity in this case is almost rhetorical. It is a public remembering. Like Thomas Jefferson's recitation in the US Declaration of Independence of the dastardly deeds done by King George, such a catalogue of wrongs galvanizes the slumbering feeling of a people. Thus, for example, it is essential to the reawakening of Hawaiian political identity that Haunani-Kay Trask begins her book on Hawaiian nationalism by recounting the wrongs done to Hawaiians by Americans and others.[30] It is true history, but it is more than that: it is the act of rhetorically, publicly remembering, and thus it serves to strengthen the ethnic bond.

On a more prosaic level, who one's relatives are constitutes an essential ingredient in one's identifying with and being accepted by a Pacific Islander American group. If you have relatives in a particular Pacific Islander American people, then you are a legitimate member of that group. As a mixed New Zealander, Alexis Siteine, puts it, "Maoris seem to have adopted the 'one drop' rule about themselves: If you can claim any Maori ancestor, then you are part of the *tangata whenua* (people of the land). The members of the Maori club [in school] then, ranged in appearance from the blonde, blue-eyed, freckled variety to dark-haired, dark-eyed brownness."[31]

Much of what happens that is ethnic happens within the extended family. Almost all community ceremonies and obligations are organized on a family basis. The place, above all others, where Tongan or Fijian or Samoan culture is passed on is in the *family*. As Lori Atoa explained, "In the Samoan way of life, the extended family is first priority. Anytime there is a crisis in the family, we are always ready to give whatever is needed. . . . [T]he aunts and cousins on the Samoan side were always around to follow through on straightening us out. There again, we were totally exposed to the Samoan way of doing things." Among Maori, both in New Zealand and in the United States, it is not just ancestry or phenotype, but ties to the *marae* (tribal meeting grounds) that give one ethnic location. Nikki Mozo ended a student paper with the following declaration of her identity, based on genealogy and family tie.

> I am of the proud Ngati Kahununu tribe, who sailed the mighty Takitimu canoe and arrived on the islands of Aotearoa which is commonly known today as New Zealand. My marae was built at Nuhaka during the second world war in memory of our proud warriors of Ngati Kahununu. The river my people lived from is called Nuhaka. The mountain that my people lived on is called Momokai, which stands to the west of my dad's my grandfather's, and his father's village tucked in the quiet peaceful valleys of the hills. My name is Nicolette Roimatta Mozo and I am a Maori.

The family tie does not necessarily have to be genetic in order to be powerful. Ricky Soliai (Kookie's husband) is biologically Hawaiian-Tongan-Irish, but his father was adopted and raised by a Samoan family. Ricky regards himself as full Samoan, his family and other people (Samoans and non-Samoans) treat him as a Samoan without qualification, and he insists on raising the couple's children as Samoans only, despite their strongly Maori-Hawaiian-Japanese mother. Contrast that to the situation of many other interethnic adoptees: African Americans raised by White families or Korean babies in Swedish American families. Growing up, everyone thinks of them as interracial adoptees, not as natural members of the racial group of their adopted parents. On reaching their teen years, many such people go searching for their ancestral roots (there is in fact a thriving industry that puts Korean youths from the American Midwest in touch with the land and culture of their biological ancestors).[32] There seems to be less of this in the Pacific Islander case. One's adoption into a particular Pacific Islander ethnic group seems to entitle one to a more complete membership in that group than is the case with other American groups.

Bill Wallace's experience suggests that you may be able to marry into another ethnic group, although Dorri Nautu's and Kookie Soliai's experiences suggest that perhaps identity acquired through marriage is less strong than identity that comes from the home of your childhood. There is also a possibility that Hawaiians may be more accepting of outside infusions than other peoples for identifiable historical reasons. Wallace pointed out that, in the middle of the nineteenth century, "with the Hawaiian people dying out, the kings brought in people from the Pacific Rim—Chinese, Japanese, Koreans—to try to restock the Hawaiian blood." Whatever the case in specific historical situations, and whether or not people may marry into or be adopted into specific ethnic groups, it remains clear that the family is one of the primary bases of Pacific Islander American ethnicity.

Equally important in determining Pacific Islander American ethnicity is *cultural practice*.[33] One is Tongan because one behaves like a Tongan, speaks the Tongan language, has a Tongan heart. Inoke Funaki, in a moving personal exploration titled "Culture and Identity in the Pacific," finds

Tongan identity in "*fe'ofo'ofani* (brotherly love)," in "family spirit," in "willingness to help each other," in "kindness and neighborly generosity," in the "art of living together in harmony and peace."[34] One is Samoan because one speaks Samoan and one understands and lives *fa'a samoa*. Many Pacific Islander Americans would argue, indeed, that language is the sine qua non of ethnicity, the essential variety of cultural practice, because so much that is powerful is shared through language. Cy Bridges, keeper of things Hawaiian at the Polynesian Cultural Center, can talk long and movingly about the cultural bases of the Hawaiian way—about the daily practices, the heart qualities, which if one exemplifies them declare that one is a Hawaiian.

Another basis of Pacific Islander American ethnic connectedness is one's relationship to *place*. In Hawaiian, it is the *aina*, the land, and one must *malama aina*—care for the land. The caring is reciprocal, for the land also cares for the people, and the relationship is a deep, family bond.[35] Leaders of the Hawaiian cultural and political renaissance of the past three decades have stressed the importance of reclaiming the *aina* above almost everything else.[36] But it is not only ethnic nationalist politicians who revere the land. Elderly Hawaiians of no particular political convictions speak of feeling roots reaching down through their feet, deep into the earth of their islands. The stories of Auntie Harriet Ne, which resonate for Hawaiians of many political persuasions, speak intimately of the land and its inhabitants, animals and *menehune* (an ancient Hawaiian race, small of stature and possibly mythical), as well as humans.[37]

Pacific Islanders of other derivations also celebrate their ethnicity by reference to place. Tupou Hopoate, a Tongan raised in Australia who now lives in California, fled her Tongan ethnicity until her mother forced her to return to Tonga. She now speaks in hushed tones of her first encounter with the village and the hut where she was born and the intense love for her people and her culture that grew from that encounter to become one of the central forces of her life.[38] She later wrote a poem to express the depth of her commitment. It reads in part:

> When I speak of Tonga,
> I speak of Me.
> A person made up of multiple identities

> Through my veins flow the blood of various cultures
> But I only identify myself as one from Tonga.
> There, my heart will always stay true,
> For Tonga is my home; My island and My taboo.

Hopoate's subsequent life choices—to work as a missionary in Tonga, to attend a university made up mainly of Pacific Islander students, to marry a Tongan American, to live in a Tongan community in Southern California—have all stemmed from her experience of that intensely Tongan place.

Not all Pacific Islander Americans have had personal contact with places that symbolize their ethnicity. But nearly all have heard about such places from their relatives, and the collective memory of those ethnic places is a powerful reinforcer of their ethnic identity.

At least these bases, then—ancestry, family, practice, and place—are important determinants of Pacific Islander American ethnicity. Jocelyn Linnekin, Lin Poyer, and several colleagues have asserted that cultural identites in the Pacific are mainly "Lamarckian"; that is, they proceed from the notions that "acquired characteristics are heritable" and "shared identity comes from sharing." They would differentiate between such Pacific identities, based, they say, in practice and what they call "Mendelian" models of ethnicity based in kinship or bloodline. Linnekin and Poyer may be right about ethnic identities in some parts of the Pacific. But as far as ethnicity constructed among Pacific Islander Americans in Hawai'i and in the continental United States, Linnekin, Poyer, and their colleagues go too far. Yes, group identities among Pacific Islander Americans are based on place and practice. But they are also based profoundly on ancestry and family connection. Linnekin, Poyer, and their colleagues argue that blood is not the issue; in the crassest meaning of that term they may be right.[39] But while it may be argued that the blood quantum approach of some Hawaiians, for example, to participation in Hawaiian sovereignty was picked up from White American cultural definitions, nonetheless, every Pacific Islander American people of whom we have much knowledge has a strong sense of blood, of lineage, of clan connectedness, and of history as a basis for identity and group membership.

CONCLUSION: MULTIPLE ETHNIC CENTERS

Nearly all American and European ethnic thinking is about boundaries. Perhaps no writer on ethnic theory has been so frequently and reverently quoted as Fredrik Barth; his very influential book on the subject, *Ethnic Groups and Boundaries*, says in part, "The critical focus of investigation from this point of view becomes the ethnic *boundary* that defines the group, not the cultural stuff that it encloses."[40] Since Barth wrote those words in 1969, few people seem to have doubted that boundaries are the important things about ethnic groups. Barth may be right about ethnicity in some other contexts, but his ideas will not work for Pacific Islander American ethnicity. The boundaries surrounding Pacific Islander American ethnic groups are not very important at all. Pacific Islander Americans have inclusive, not exclusive, ethnic identities. What is important for Pacific Islander American ethnicity is not boundaries but centers: ancestry, family, practice, place. If one qualifies for acceptance at the centers of ethnicity, then one is of that ethnic group, no matter to what other ethnic groups one may also belong.

In a multicultural age, maybe this is a better model of ethnicity than any other. Pacific Islander Americans are in some ways a model of what is happening to America at large. Some may argue that Pacific Islander Americans are not a model for much of anything; a critic of an earlier version of this chapter did just that. That person observed that most of the data for this chapter came from Hawai'i and asserted that Hawai'i is so different from other places that it is a lousy example of anything except exceptions. The critic contended that ethnic relations in other places are much more conflictual, more categorical, more hostile than those in Hawai'i. I must disagree. Hawai'i is far from an interracial paradise. Every interpersonal encounter in Hawai'i is carefully calibrated in ethnic terms. A conversation between two Haoles is different from a conversation between a Haole and a Korean on the same subject, and very different again from a conversation between two Samoans. There is quite a bit of interethnic stereotyping and hostility in Hawai'i, between Haole and Hawaiian, between Japanese and Samoan, between Filipino and Korean, and so on.

What is different about Hawai'i—and what makes it not a bad model but a particularly *good* model for America's apparent future—are two things: (1) it is multicultural in the extreme, as America is becoming; and (2) in Hawai'i, as among Pacific Islander Americans generally, the consciousness of individuals and groups that they are multiethnic is very strong.[41]

The American people are becoming a people of multiple identities. We are, at last, biologically fulfilling Crèvecouer's vision of a mixed America, but we are not melting. Instead, we are becoming vividly multiethnic within each person. Some other American ethnic groups are beginning to face up to this multiethnic reality. It used to be (and still is for the Orthodox) that to be a Jew one had to be either a convert or the child of a Jewish mother. In recent decades, mindful of dwindling numbers in an era of 40 percent out-marriage or more, not a small number of Reform Jewish synagogues have been holding Get to Know Your Jewish Roots classes and encouraging anyone who can identify a Jewish ancestor to consider joining the faith. In similar fashion, where before World War II the small number of mixed offspring of Japanese American intermarriages were shunned by Japanese American community institutions, now they are among the leaders of Japanese American communities, and their numbers are quite large.[42] In an age of emerging multiplicity, Pacific Islander American formulations of multiethnicity are especially fruitful for understanding ethnicity as it is coming to be in the United States.[43]

Nearly a century ago, W. E. B. Du Bois expressed a tension of duality. He was not referring to racial duality, to feeling his White ancestry at the same time that he felt his Black ancestry. The tension Du Bois expressed was between race and nation. But his words provide a picture of an earlier era's torment when struggling to come to terms with multiple identities: "One ever feels his two-ness—an American, a Negro; two souls, two thoughts, two unreconciled strivings; two warring ideals in one dark body, whose dogged strength alone keeps it from being torn asunder."[44] Now, for Pacific Islander Americans at least, it seems possible to reconcile two or more ethnic identities in one person, without torment, and without one being subordinated to the other. Perhaps what is needed in our era is an understanding of ethnicity that does not presume that a person must check just one box. Perhaps, by focusing as Pacific Islander Americans do on the centers of ethnicity, and not on boundaries between groups, we can better prepare ourselves for an age when most if not all of us will be biologically and functionally multiethnic.

NOTES

A version of this chapter originally appeared in *Social Forces* 73.4 (June 1995): 1365–83. I have updated some language and provided a few more references, but I have not made a systematic attempt to bring the references completely up to date.

1. Hector St. John [Michel-Guilliame Jean] de Crèvecouer, *Letter from an American Farmer*, quoted in William Petersen et al., *Concepts of Ethnicity* (Cambridge, MA: Harvard University Press, 1982; orig. 1782); original emphasis.

2. Stephen Cornell, "The Variable Ties That Bind: Content and Circumstance in Ethnic Processes," *Ethnic and Racial Studies* 19.2 (1996): 265–89; Stephen Cornell and Douglas Hartmann, *Ethnicity and Race*, 2nd ed. (Thousand Oaks, CA: Pine Forge Press, 2007).

3. Richard D. Alba, *Italian Americans: Into the Twilight of Ethnicity* (Englewood Cliffs, NJ: Prentice-Hall, 1984); Oscar Handlin, *Race and Nationality in American Life* (Boston: Little, Brown, 1954); Robert Ezra Park, *Race and Culture* (New York: Free Press, 1950); Philip Perlmutter, *Divided We Fall: A History of Ethnic, Religious, and Racial Prejudice in America* (Ames: Iowa State University Press, 1992); Richard Alba and Victor Nee, *Remaking the American Mainstream: Assimilation and Contemporary Immigration* (Cambridge, MA: Harvard University Press, 2003). For my quite different take on their proposition, see *Almost All Aliens: Immigration, Race, and Colonialism in American History and Identity* (New York: Routledge, 2007), esp. 4–25.

4. Robert Blauner, *Racial Oppression in America* (New York: Harper and Row, 1972); Joe R. Feagin and Clairece Booher Feagin, *Racial and Ethnic Relations*, 4th ed. (Englewood Cliffs, NJ: Prentice-Hall, 1993); Nathan Glazer and Daniel Patrick Moynihan, *Beyond the Melting Pot* (Cambridge, MA: MIT Press, 1963).

5. G. Reginald Daniel, "Passers and Pluralists: Subverting the Racial Divide," in *Racially Mixed People in America* (Newbury Park, CA: Sage, 1992), 91–107. See also F. James Davis, *Who Is Black? One Nation's Definition* (University Park: Pennsylvania State University Press, 1991); Winthrop D. Jordan, "Historical Origins of the One-Drop Racial Rule in the United States," ed. Paul Spickard, *Journal of Critical Mixed-Race Studies* 1 (2013): 98–132.

6. Paul Spickard, *Mixed Blood: Intermarriage and Ethnic Identity in Twentieth-Century America* (Madison: University of Wisconsin Press, 1989); "Interracial

Marriage Rising but Not as Fast," Associated Press story, *CBS News Online* (June 4, 2010).

7. US Bureau of the Census, *1980 Census of Population. 1B. General Population Characteristics. United States Summary* (PC80-1-B1) (Washington, DC: Government Printing Office, 1983); US Bureau of the Census, *1990 Census of Population. General Population Characteristics. United States* (CP-1-1) (Washington, DC: Government Printing Office, 1992).

8. *Time*, "Special Issue: The New Face of America" (November 18, 1993).

9. Multiracial Americans of Southern California, [no title], *Spectrum* 7.4 (Oct.–Dec. 1993); Teresa Williams-León and Cynthia L. Nakashima, eds., *The Sum of Our Parts: Mixed Heritage Asian Americans* (Philadelphia: Temple University Press, 2001); Kim M. Williams, *Mark One or More: Civil Rights in Multiracial America* (Ann Arbor: University of Michigan Press, 2006).

10. Joel Perlmann and Mary C. Waters, eds., *The New Race Question: How the Census Counts Multiracial Individuals* (New York: Russell Sage Foundation, 2005).

11. Although many anthropologists at least would assert that these labels do assort languages into meaningful divisions: Ron G. Crocombe, "The Pan-Pacific Person: Staffing the Regional Organizations," *Pacific Perspective* 12 (1984): 51–60; Ron G. Crocombe, "Ethnicity, Identity and Power in Oceania," in *Islands and Enclaves: Nationalisms and Separatist Pressures in Island and Littoral Contexts*, ed. Gary Trompf (New Delhi: Sterling, 1993), 195–223.

12. It may be worth noting, however, that three of the four largest Pacific Islander American groups are represented here: Hawaiians, Samoans, and Tongans. Only Chamorros (Guamanians) are missing.

13. This multiple ethnic consciousness has something in common with *mestizaje*, mestiza consciousness, which Gloria Anzaldúa talks about in *Borderlands/ La Frontera: The New Mestiza*, and more generally with the Mexican consciousness of being a mixed people, even *la raza cósmica*. See Anzaldúa, *Borderlands/La Frontera: The New Mestiza* (San Francisco: Aunt Lute Press, 1987); Stan Steiner, *La Raza* (New York: Harper and Row, 1970); José Vasconcelos, *La Raza Cósmica*, trans. D. T. Jaen (Los Angeles: California State University, Centro de Publicaciones, 1979; orig. 1925).

14. United States Census Bureau, *The Two or More Races Population: 2010*, 2010 Census Briefs, C2010BR-13 (September 2012), 21.

15. When Bill died in 2009, many in Hawaiʻi wept. I miss him so. More of his story appears in an oral history interview at http://onlyinlaie.com/view_featured _story.php?story=43 (retrieved December 19, 2011).

16. The survey was conducted by the Pacific Islander Americans Research Project, of which I was then director. Sponsoring institutions were the Institute for Polynesian Studies and Brigham Young University–Hawaiʻi. The interviewers

were Blossom Fonoimoana, Inoke Funaki, David Hall, Debbie Hippolite Wright, Tupou Hopoate, Karina Kahananui, Dorri Nautu, and Ina Nautu.

17. Judith Nagata, "What Is a Malay? Situational Selection of Ethnic Identity in a Plural Society," *American Ethnologist* 1 (1974): 331–50; Orlando Patterson, "Context and Choice in Ethnic Allegiance: A Theoretical Framework and Caribbean Case Study," in *Ethnicity: Theory and Experience*, ed. Nathan Glazer and Daniel P. Moynihan (Cambridge, MA: Harvard University Press, 1975), 305–49.

18. For reasons probably deriving from Gaugin's legacy, most non–Pacific Islanders have a category for Tahitians—indeed, a sexualized stereotype of Tahitians—although almost none has ever met a Tahitian. Paul Spickard and Dorri Nautu, "Ethnic Images and Social Distance among Pacific Islander Americans," *Social Process in Hawai'i* 36 (1994): 69–85.

19. Sometimes the mistake is mystifyingly, perhaps willfully obtuse. Jamaica Kincaid's novel *Lucy* is about a young woman from the Caribbean who comes to New York and works as a nanny for an American couple. Yet the publisher put on the cover a reproduction of Paul Gauguin's *Young Girl with Fan* (1902, in the Museum Folkwang, Essen, Germany). The young woman in the painting has brown skin but is not a West Indian at all, as anyone who has even a rudimentary knowledge of Impressionism knows. She is Tohotaua, Gauguin's Tahitian mistress. But for the publisher, and perhaps for the reading public, it was enough that she be brown and an islander—a Pacific Islander made to stand for a West Indian. See Jamaica Kincaid, *Lucy* (New York: Farrar, Straus and Giroux, 1990).

20. In Jon's case, he has ancestry in several of the Cook Islands, and he emphasizes the national Cook Island identity over any specific island tie. His secondary allegiance is to a pan-Pacific Islander identity rather than to any of his ancestral European stocks.

21. An extreme—in fact an unusual—case is that of a student in a course on Asian and Pacific Islander ethnic issues. When the class went around the room sharing the multiplicities of their backgrounds, her answer was an emphatic, "I'm half Hawaiian!," and she would say no more. Throughout the semester she would not budge, would not admit any significance attaching to anything that might be in the other half, although she admitted the other half existed. For reasons social, ideological, and perhaps political, she would speak only of her Hawaiian side. But this student was an extreme case; most Pacific Islander Americans will admit their multiethnicity even as they choose to emphasize one aspect of their ancestry.

22. Mary C. Waters, *Ethnic Options: Choosing Identities in America* (Berkeley: University of California Press, 1990), 147.

23. Herbert Gans, "Symbolic Ethnicity: The Future of Ethnic Groups and Cultures in America," *Ethnic and Racial Studies* 2 (1979): 1–20; Waters, *Ethnic Options*, 7.

24. Paul Shankman, "Race, Class, and Ethnicity in Western Samoa," in *Ethnicity and Nation-Building in the Pacific*, ed. Michael C. Howard (Tokyo: United Nations University, 1990).

25. Haunani-Kay Trask, *From a Native Daughter* (Monroe, ME: Common Courage Press, 1993), 1.

26. Lilikala Kameʻeleihiwa, *Native Land and Foreign Desires* (Honolulu: Bishop Museum, 1992); Jon Jonassen, former executive secretary of the South Pacific Commission, interviewed by the author, Laʻie, Hawaiʻi, 1993; William Kauaiwiulaokalani Wallace III, director of Pacific Islands Studies, BYU–Hawaiʻi, interviewed by the author, Laʻie, Hawaiʻi, 1993.

27. The blood quantum idea entered Hawaiʻi formally in the 1920s as part of the US government's plan to return certain lands to people of substantial Hawaiian ancestry through the Office of Hawaiian Home Lands. See J. Kehaulani Kauanui, *Hawaiian Blood: Colonialism and the Politics of Sovereignty and Indigeneity* (Durham, NC: Duke University Press, 2008).

28. Martha Warren Beckwith, *The Kumulipo* (Honolulu: University of Hawaiʻi Press, 1972; orig. 1951).

29. Kameʻeleihiwa, *Native Land*, 19–22.

30. Trask, *From a Native Daughter*, 4–25.

31. John Harré makes much the same point in *Maori and Pakeha* (London: Institute of Race Relations, 1966). I am indebted to Nikki Mozo for the insight.

32. Joyce A. Ladner, *Mixed Families: Adopting across Racial Boundaries* (Garden City, NY: Doubleday, 1977); Jane Jeong Trenka et al., eds., *Outsiders Within: Writing on Transracial Adoption* (Boston: South End Press, 2006); Eleana J. Kim, *Adopted Territory: Transnational Korean Adoptees and the Politics of Belonging* (Durham, NC: Duke University Press, 2010).

33. G. Carter Bentley, "Ethnicity and Practice," *Comparative Studies in Society and History* 29 (1987): 24–55.

34. Inoke Funaki, "Culture and Identity in the Pacific: A Personal Expression," convocation address, BYU–Hawaiʻi, October 1993.

35. Kameʻeleihiwa, *Native Land*, 25–33.

36. Trask, *From a Native Daughter*, 87–110.

37. Harriet Ne, with Gloria L. Cronin, *Tales of Molokai* (Laʻie, Hawaiʻi: Institute for Polynesian Studies, 1992).

38. Tupou Hopoate, "My Life in Four Cultures," *Social Process in Hawaiʻi* 36 (1994): 5–15.

39. Jocelyn Linnekin and Lin Poyer, eds., *Cultural Identity and Ethnicity in the Pacific* (Honolulu: University of Hawaiʻi Press, 1990), 9–10.

40. Fredrik Barth, *Ethnic Groups and Boundaries* (Boston: Little, Brown, 1969), 15; original emphasis.

41. There is no room here to summarize, much less sort through, the right- and left-wing critiques of multiculturalism. Readers with an interest in that debate might start by consulting Tariq Modood, *Multiculturalism* (Cambridge: Polity Press, 2007); Charles Taylor et al., *Multiculturalism: Examining the Politics of Recognition* (Princeton, NJ: Princeton University Press, 1994); Susan Moler Okin et al., *Is Multiculturalism Bad for Women?* (Princeton, NJ: Princeton University Press, 1999); Will Kymlicka, *Multiculturalism: A Liberal Theory of Minority Rights* (New York: Oxford University Press, 1996); Alvin J. Schmidt, *The Menace of Multiculturalism: Trojan Horse in America* (New York: Praeger, 1997); David Theo Goldberg, ed., *Multiculturalism: A Critical Reader* (Malden, MA: Blackwell, 1994); Dennis McCallum, ed., *The Death of Truth: What's Wrong with Multiculturalism, the Rejection of Reason, and the New Postmodern Diversity* (Minneapolis: Bethany House, 1996); Avery Gordon and Christopher Newfield, eds., *Mapping Multiculturalism*, 2nd ed. (Minneapolis: University of Minnesota Press, 2008); James Kyung-jin Lee, *Urban Triage: Race and the Fictions of Multiculturalism* (Minneapolis: University of Minnesota Press, 2004).

42. Spickard, *Mixed Blood*; Paul Spickard, *Japanese Americans: The Formation and Transformations of an Ethnic Group*, rev. ed. (New Brunswick, NJ: Rutgers University Press, 2009).

43. There is, of course, the possibility that politics may intrude and current trends toward multiethnicity will be reversed. Sarajevo was long thought by some to be a happily multicultural place, and then in the 1990s it became an interethnic war zone. But despite the power of continuing racial oppression in America and despite the strength of regional political trends such as the sovereignty movement among Native Hawaiians, the United States is in my judgment quite far from the sort of ethnic division and warfare that occurred in the former Yugoslavia or the former Soviet Union. See, e.g., Victor Roudometof, *Nationalism, Globalization, and Orthodoxy: The Social Origins of Ethnic Conflict in the Balkans* (New York: Praeger, 2001); Christopher Zürcher, *The Post-Soviet Wars: Rebellion, Ethnic Conflict, and Nationhood in the Caucasus* (New York: New York University Press, 2009); Jonathan Y. Okamura, *Ethnicity and Inequality in Hawai'i* (Philadelphia: Temple University Press, 2008).

44. W. E. B. Du Bois, "Strivings of the Negro People," *Atlantic Monthly* 80 (August 1897).

10

Carving Out a Middle Ground

Making Race in Hawai'i

WITH JEFFREY MONIZ

Race, class, and gender constitute the holy trinity of late-twentieth- and early-twenty-first-century ethnic and cultural studies.[1] Though frequently invoked together, they seldom make their way together into the substance of scholarly studies. Almost invariably a scholar will emphasize one of these and treat the others only cursorily. I am as guilty of this neglect as anyone. In this chapter, Jeffrey Moniz rescues me at least briefly. He is at pains to delineate the class-based affinities that spurred the creation of a panethnic cultural and social unit called Local. Local is a panethnicity unique to Hawai'i that brings together peoples who in other places would not be grouped together and who would not be seen as part of the same race in the biologistic schemes of Gobineau and Blumenbach. In making this class move, Jeff is the leader and I am the follower. In this chapter we propose the idea of the midaltern as a way out of the Native-Hawaiians-versus-everybody-else dichotomy that has paralyzed Hawai'i's racial politics since the 1990s. The idea is more Jeff's than mine, but I am happy to tag along.

Hawai'i has long been linked to ideas and images about race and particularly about multiraciality. Those ideas and images have in turn been linked to a racial hierarchy that has sustained racial injustice in the islands. For several generations the hierarchy has meant racial injustice, primarily for Kanaka Maoli (Native Hawaiians)[2] but also for other peoples of color, masked by a tourist discourse celebrating happy, docile Polynesians and a genial multicultural society. Late in the twentieth century and early in the twenty-first, a new racial discourse championing Native Hawaiian sovereignty arose to challenge Haole (White) supremacy. This has the potential to affect racial justice in ways both positive and negative for Hawai'i's people. The new racial discourse incited our critique and inspired our development of a conceptual cultural space, a middle space that we call the midaltern. We introduce the concept of the midaltern as a more precise and inclusive way to describe the identities of those ignored or erased by the current discourse.

COLONIAL THINKING IN HAWAI'I

Captain Cook and nineteenth-century Euro-American missionaries saw Hawaiians as a race apart from themselves, physically different and characterologically inferior.[3] European-descended outsiders emphasized the strangeness, and the strange attractiveness, of Hawai'i and Hawaiians. They wrote about the natural wonders of the Hawaiian landscape—volcanoes, gleaming sands, teeming reefs, deep jungles, and tall waterfalls—and set those images alongside descriptions of Native Hawaiian people, portraying them as part of the landscape, too, as childlike, primitive, violent, irresponsible, gloriously sexual, and in need of benevolent colonial rule by such people as themselves.[4]

By the final third of the nineteenth century, European diseases had reduced the Kanaka Maoli population by 95 percent. Entrepreneurs, mainly Euro-Americans, brought in tens of thousands of Chinese, then Japanese, Filipinos, Koreans, and others to work the islands' growing sugar plantations.[5] Thus the population of the islands quickly came to include substantial numbers of people from many parts of the Pacific, from Asia, and from North America. In short order, the Haole minority seized control of most of Hawai'i's agricultural land, overthrew the Native Hawaiian monarchy, made Hawai'i a formal US colony, and set about marketing the islands abroad.[6]

A central theme in the Haole attempt to market Hawai'i was to characterize it as "the melting pot of the Pacific" and "the meeting place of East and West." The theme of multiracial harmony was a crucial support for the Haole attempt to take over and make over the islands. Lori Pierce, a historian of territorial-era Hawai'i, characterizes it this way:

> Racial tensions lay just beneath the surface of daily life in Hawai'i, but race as a source of conflict or distress was rarely if ever discussed publicly. Instead, the Haole ruling class constantly depicted Hawai'i as a racial paradise, a place where the Hawaiians, Haole, Japanese, and Chinese lived cooperatively. Civic celebrations such as Balboa Day that featured all of the ethnic groups of Hawai'i were typical. These parades, pageants, and public celebrations were a way of depicting life in Hawai'i to tourists, residents, and mainland audiences, who read about them in *Paradise of the Pacific* and *Mid-Pacific Magazine*. The message being communicated was that ethnic diversity was not a threat to the Haole ruling class. In fact, Euro-Americans were firmly in control and turning Hawai'i into a thoroughly American territory.[7]

Pierce links this celebration of harmony to Americanization campaigns in the continental United States and to uses of social science to subjugate Asian and Pacific peoples.[8]

The Haole elite that created the story of intercultural harmony as a mask for its own racial privilege then sold that image abroad, in the United States and elsewhere, as a way to bring tourists and money into the islands. Hawai'i was marketed, in the 1910s as in the 2000s, as a place of warm, conflict-free interaction among peoples where tourists would be welcome to come and spend their dollars and yen. Outrigger Hotels sold Hawai'i this way:

Modern Hawaii has often been referred to as the "Melting Pot of the Pacific" as the children of immigrants and subsequent generations of immigrants have harmoniously made their home in the islands. Through the years, each group has taken their distinct talents from the plantation fields to the forefront of Hawaii's evolution to a modern society. Descendants of these foreign immigrant groups today make their contributions among the ranks of entrepreneurs in businesses and banking, in government and health care, in the travel and hospitality industries, and many other areas of island enterprise. In addition, each ethnic group also has gifted the islands with the color and pageantry of their cultural observances, traditional attire, music and dance.[9]

Note the erasure of Kanaka Maoli from the hotel chain's description, the naturalization of Euro-Americans as if they were native to Hawai'i, and the assumption of the inevitability and superiority of "modern" Euro-American culture.

MULTIRACIALITY IN HAWAI'I

Some of the most influential books about Hawai'i stress multiraciality. Sidney Gulick, an American missionary to Japan born in the Marshall Islands to missionary parents, lived his later years in Hawai'i and wrote *Mixing the Races in Hawaii: The Coming Neo-Hawaiian American Race* in 1937. The book's first several pages, even before the title page or a paragraph of text, consist of pictures of twenty-eight high school and college students, most of them racially mixed. Each of the students is labeled racially, and many are fractionated—"6/8 Hawaiian, 1/16 French, 1/16 Hindu, 1/16 Negro, 1/16 Arabian"—but none is given a name. What was important, apparently, was not their persons, but the pseudoscientific racial categorization that could be imposed on them. Gulick began the written portion of his rhapsody to multiraciality and American triumphalism thus:

Hawaii is a land of many wonders. But the most striking of them all is its people. Here are some 400,000 men, women and children, of many races, languages, social traditions and varieties of moral and religious ideals, living together in remarkable harmony. Here a poly-racial, poly-chrome, poly-linguistic, poly-religious and thoroughly heterogeneous population is being transformed into a homogeneous people, speaking a common language—English—holding common political, ethical, social and religious ideas and ideals, putting into practice with remarkable success the principles of racial equality, and maintaining a highly effective, democratic form of government. The races are actually growing together—fusing biologically. . . . A new race is in the making. The physiological characteristics of the new race will be a mixture of Hawaiian, Caucasian and Asiatic, while its psychological, social, political and moral characteristics will be distinctly American.[10]

The most widely read book about Hawai'i in the territorial period was the University of Hawai'i sociologist Romanzo Adams's magnum opus, *Interracial Marriage in Hawaii*.[11] While it was more scholarly than Gulick's, it also had racially labeled pictures, and it celebrated racial mixing and told a story of interracial harmony. So, it appears, what was important about Hawai'i was race—specifically, racial harmony—and intermarriage and multiracial people were the emblems of that harmony.

As the territory slipped toward statehood, James Michener wrote the novel *Hawaii*, a thousand-page tribute to "those Golden Men who see both the West and the East, who cherish the glowing past and who apprehend the obscure future"—and that future would necessarily be framed by Euro-American cultural imperatives.[12] This was a variation on the melting pot theme that stressed not racial blending so much as Hawai'i's location as the place where the peoples of Asia met the peoples of Europe and America in harmony and mutual understanding. The meeting place theme is the very raison d'être for the East-West Center, Hawai'i's most prominent intellectual factory. It is located behind a major Baha'i temple and near the headquarters of innumerable East-West internationalist societies. The Center's mission statement begins:

The East-West Center is an internationally recognized education and research organization established by the US Congress in 1960 to strengthen understanding and relations between the United States and the countries of the Asia Pacific region. The Center helps promote the establishment of a stable, peaceful and prosperous Asia Pacific community in which the United States is a natural, valued and leading partner.[13]

Note that Hawai'i and Hawaiians are not mentioned, that they are subsumed under "the Pacific," which is in turn subsumed under "Asia," and that the United States is assumed to be the leader and the agenda-setter of this dialogue with Asia.

Some parts of this picture are accurate. There are in fact a lot of people in Hawai'i whose ancestors came, or who themselves came from different countries. Hawai'i's identity as a land of many different kinds of immigrants reflects demography as well as Haole propaganda. Hawai'i is in fact the only state in the United States where Whites have never constituted a numerical majority of the population, despite their disproportionate power, and the only one with an Asian and Pacific Islander majority.[14] A higher percentage of people in Hawai'i acknowledge multiple racial ancestries than in any other US state, perhaps more than anywhere else in the world. Hawai'i is the only US state or territory that has long kept statistics that record racial multiplicity. For many years people of mixed Kanaka Maoli and Haole parentage constituted something of a distinct social group, and their numbers were recorded separately in state records.[15]

In 2010, 23.6 percent of Hawai'i's residents voluntarily checked more than one racial box on US Census forms, compared to a national rate of 2.9 percent. Far more could have qualified: many mixed people checked only one box, and others had mixed ancestry that fell within one of the census's "racial" categories (for instance, a person with both Chinese and Japanese parentage would still be an "Asian" and not counted as mixed).[16] Hawaiians and other islanders are especially mixed. A survey in the mid-1990s found that 69 percent of Pacific Islanders who lived in Hawai'i and 86 percent of Native Hawaiians recognized they possessed multiple ancestries. Despite substantial social pressure to identify only with their island ancestries, 53 percent of Pacific Islanders and 49 percent of Native Hawaiians identified with another ancestry as well.[17] One accompaniment of all this actual mixing has been the rise and celebration of a mixed culture and identity called Local, including Local food, Local styles of dress, Local modes of human relationship, and a Local language, Pidgin.[18] More about Local identity in a moment.

So the motif of racial mixture in Hawai'i is not just a tourist marketer's myth; it is also a social fact. Yet the multiracial characterization does run the risk of glamorizing multiplicity and ignoring the harder racial realities of colonial domination in the islands, not just in the past but currently. What Lori Pierce calls "the discourse of aloha" makes the islands seem an attractive tourist paradise. At the same time, it obscures the racial domination by Haoles over other island residents and hierarchies among those peoples of color.[19]

Insofar as it treats non-Native peoples of color in Hawai'i, the discourse of aloha speaks of them in heroic terms of Asian immigrant uplift from plantation near-slavery to middle-class achievement by way of virtuous behavior, hard work, and not openly challenging Haole domination. Eiko Kosasa describes "the immigrant ideological perspectives Nisei [second-generation Japanese] settlers wanted to pass on to the Sansei and Yonsei [their children and grandchildren]." They represented "the Japanese experience as *willingly traveling* on the American 'immigrant' journey—beginning in poverty and ending in riches, moving from a simple, rural culture on the plantation to the sophistication of Western urban culture."[20] Dorothy Hazama and Jane Komeiji cast their community's history as the "story about the struggles and successes of the Japanese in Hawai'i," which was achieved by "belief in strong family ties, hard work, and perseverance, . . . education, and sensitivity and humility."[21]

The discourse of aloha ignores Native Hawaiians almost completely, treating them as museum curiosities, tourist entertainers, and a dying breed. This is true even in as fine a book as Ronald Takaki's *Pau Hana: Plantation Life and Labor in Hawaii*. After the first chapter, Kanaka Maoli are all but invisible; the plantation laborers are almost all Asians of one sort or another, and no questions are asked about the status of Hawaiians. The standard histories of Hawai'i attend to the radical decline of the

Hawaiian population and then, after the 1898 annexation by the United States, act as if Native Hawaiians all but ceased to exist and turn their attention almost exclusively to Haoles and Asians.[22] Ralph S. Kuykendall and A. Grove Day lament what they regard as the inevitable "native population . . . extinction."[23] In the "modern Hawaii" celebrated by Outrigger Hotels, Native Hawaiians have ceded the islands to entrepreneurial Asians and Euro-Americans. They contribute culture that others then get to perform and from which others take the profit, but they are no longer actors in their own land. The action has been taken over by other racial groups.

KANAKA MAOLI SOVEREIGNTY

In the past several decades, Native Hawaiians have created a political movement to reestablish their political and cultural sovereignty. A cultural renaissance of Hawaiian music, dance, and language use in the 1970s and 1980s led to increasingly insistent demands for restoration to the Hawaiian people of the independence that was taken away in the nineteenth century.[24] There are as many strategies for sovereignty as there are groups of Hawaiians active in the strident public debate. Some organizations, like Ka Lāhui Hawai'i, advocate creation of a self-governing Hawaiian nation within the nation that is the United States, in a relationship roughly analogous to that of federally recognized Native American tribes in the continental United States. Such an arrangement would involve creation of a Hawaiian government from within the Kanaka Maoli population and the transfer to that government of substantial public lands. Others advocate a greater degree of autonomy, in a compact of free association with the United States like that employed by the Federated States of Micronesia. Some call for full independence.[25]

The push for Native Hawaiian sovereignty is a movement with which both authors of this chapter are in sympathy. At its heart, the sovereignty movement is a quest for racial justice. Haunani-Kay Trask describes the situation in Hawai'i and the Pacific this way:

> We in the Pacific have been pawns in the power games of the "master" races since colonialism first brought Euro-Americans into

our vast ocean home. After Western contact destroyed millions of us through introduced diseases, conversion to Christianity occurred in the chaos of physical and spiritual dismemberment. Economic and political incorporation into foreign countries (Britain, France, the Netherlands, the United States) followed upon mass death. Since the Second World War, we Pacific Islander survivors have been witnesses to nuclear nightmare.

Now, our ancestral homelands—Hawai'i and the Pacific—are planned convergence points of the realigned New World Order. In our geographic area, a coalition of wealthy political entities has resulted in extreme American militarization of our islands and increasing nuclearization of the Pacific Basin; exploitation of ocean resources (including toxic dumping) by Japan, Taiwan, Korea, the United States, and others; commodification of island cultures by mass-based corporate tourism; economic penetration and land takeovers by Japan and other Asian countries; and forced outmigration of indigenous islanders from their nuclearized homelands. . . .

Because of this colonized condition, and in the face of increasing loss of control over our lives, Hawaiians have been agitating for federal recognition of the following:

1. Our unique status as Native people;
2. the injury done by the United States at the overthrow, including the loss of lands and sovereignty;
3. the necessity of reparation of that injury through acknowledgment of our claim to sovereignty, recognition of some form of autonomous Native government, the return of traditional lands and waters, and a package of compensatory resources, including monies.[26]

PROBLEMS WITH THE NEW RACIALIZED DISCOURSE

One unfortunate feature of the sovereignty movement, at least among certain of its advocates, has been a racial essentialism that fails to account for the dominant fact of multiplicity in the population of Hawai'i and, by that failure, threatens at least rhetorically to create another kind of racial injustice.[27] That is, the rhetoric of certain prominent sovereignty advocates ignores the multiraciality of nearly all Native Hawaiians and at the same time lumps together all non–ethnic Hawaiians as "settler colonialists."[28] The argument is advanced by Candace Fujikane, who ranks herself among the Asian settler colonialists.

> Our presence as local Asians in Hawai'i was established through a colonial process, and Hawai'i's history, like that of Native Americans, is a violent one of genocide and land theft. . . . In 1954, the Democratic Party "Revolution" ushered in a new era of local Asian political ascendancy. Although Asians in Hawai'i and on the continent are settlers, Hawai'i has become a white and Asian settler colony in which Asian settlers, particularly Japanese settlers, now dominate state institutions and apparatuses.

Fujikane repudiates the "master narrative of hard work and triumph that has been adopted by a new 'democratically' elected Asian ruling class." She charges that "local Asians' efforts to differentiate themselves from Haole or Whites in Hawai'i mask Native struggles against Asian settler colonialism. In a colonial situation, Haole and Asian settlers actively participate in the continued dispossession of Native Hawaiians."[29]

What, in such a schema, is the place of people who are native to the Hawaiian Islands but who are not Native Hawaiians? Granted that Asians who came on labor contracts to work in sugar and pineapple fields were taking part in a colonial process, it is not the case that they came on the same terms as Haoles who seized the lands and government. One may criticize the self-glorification of their descendants and those descendants' habit of erasing Native Hawaiians from their historical narrative (as we have criticized them in this chapter) without dismissing all non–Kanaka Maoli as foreign to the islands and illegitimate usurpers of places there. In particular, this extreme, essentialist version of sovereignty racializes all non–Kanaka Maoli together and blurs pertinent distinctions among some of the settler peoples who live in the islands. Any survey, scholarly or popular, of Hawai'i's current social structure would put three ethnic groups at the top in terms of wealth, education, status, and access to power: Haoles, Chinese, and Japanese (in that order). But such a survey would put these three groups at the bottom: Hawaiians, Samoans, and Filipinos (in that order). Samoans, by the definition of Fujikane and others, are settler colonialists, and Filipinos are Asian settler colonialists. But if they are settler colonialists, then their colonialism is of rather a different sort than that of Chinese, Haoles, or Japanese.

Further, the advocates of this particular, racialized version of Kanaka Maoli sovereignty ignore the multiracial lineage of many people in Hawai'i. Nearly all the advocates of Native Hawaiian sovereignty are themselves ancestrally mixed. That does not make them less Hawaiian or less able to represent the aspirations of the Hawaiian people (see chapter 9). But the discourse of Hawaiian sovereignty, at least in the extreme racialist form advocated by Fujikane and others, does tend to mask that multiraciality, and to set up extreme oppositions between Native people and others.

THE MIDALTERN

As a way out of the current impasse of essentialism and opposition in Hawaiian racial politics, we propose the concept of the *midaltern*. We have coined "the midaltern" and its associated state of *midalternity* in reference to subaltern studies as postcolonial criticism. They are useful notions for moving beyond a dominant/dominated dichotomy toward a deeper understanding of the complex and dynamic interplay of social identities in Hawai'i. While efforts to essentialize and dichotomize may seem useful for simplifying arguments aimed at critiquing colonial domination, thinking only in terms of a settler colonialist/Kanaka Maoli binary fails to acknowledge those who do not fit neatly into those categories. Three examples germane to the Hawai'i context challenge the binary and necessitate the further conceptual understanding made available in the concepts of the midaltern and midalternity.

First, the settler colonialist/Kanaka Maoli binary fails to acknowledge the multiraciality that is so ubiquitous in Hawai'i. According to the 2010 census, nearly a quarter of Hawai'i's population chose to report being more than one race. Most of them include Kanaka Maoli in their ancestry.[30] If the rule of hypodescent applies in cases of determining Kanaka Maoli ancestry, what becomes of the other, often unacknowledged, aspects of their identities? Midalternity readily permits one the possibility to claim membership in more than one social group.

Second, binary thinking obscures the status of those in Hawai'i who are from groups who were also directly colonized by the United States. For example, Filipinos, Puerto Ricans, Chamorros, and Samoans were all colonized during the same American expansion that overtook Hawai'i, at the time of the Spanish-American War.[31] Focusing on the plight of Kanaka Maoli as a colonized people, but ignoring or discounting others whose homelands were also colonized only serves further to oppress members of these other groups who also live in Hawai'i. The midaltern provides a more pertinent conceptual space for the colonized in Hawai'i who are not Kanaka Maoli. While they are not indigenous to the islands, they, too, are subjugated peoples who should not simply be branded as oppressors.

Third, binary thinking does not allow us to understand and conceptualize beyond the dominant/dominated, colonizer/colonized relationship, especially in the cases of those whose personal cultural values are not consistent with those typically ascribed to their particular racial identities. What about Native Hawaiians who espouse Euro-American cultural values more than Kanaka Maoli values? Or, consider a Native Hawaiian who acts Haole in public but lives as a Kanaka Maoli at home. These are examples of those who do not fit neatly into the binary but who, instead, would be suited to a midaltern understanding of their identities.

The midaltern is a middle space that allows for the inclusion and a richer understanding of these kinds of phenomena. While the midaltern was named in relation to the subaltern and the superaltern (figure 10.1), the concept is actually based on a kind of worldview common to Hawai'i and much of the Pacific. In Hawai'i, this kind of worldview clearly manifests itself in the culture, language, and identity known simply as Local. Local identity,[32] frequently characterized by the use of Pidgin[33] and the celebration of mixedness, is a viable and often salient identity choice available to multiracial people in Hawai'i. While this midaltern identity pro-

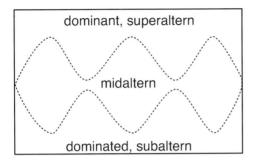

dominant, superaltern

midaltern

dominated, subaltern

Fig. 10.1.
Conceptualizing Midaltern
Space

vides for hybridity, it is also a conceptual space for fluidity, ambiguity, and contradiction. Local midaltern identities include those formed between and among particular, indigenous ways of being and dominant Western, colonial, even so-called global ways. Other terms that reflect this midalternity are *duality, multiplicity, multiple identities,* and *strange compromises*—language that commonly describes the social identities of many navigating race in Hawai'i.

LOCAL AS MIDALTERN

The Emergence of Local from the Old Racial Discourse

While the older racialized discourse of aloha is merely being replaced by a newer racialized settler/Kanaka Maoli discourse, it is important to take stock of the most significant contribution of the old discourse. The unexpected consequence of promoting aloha and celebrating diversity is the multiethnic identity commonly referred to in Hawai'i as Local. A clear dichotomy existed that divided the population during the plantation period in Hawai'i history. Haoles held most of the positions of power as plantation owners, managers, supervisors, financiers, and merchants. Non-Haoles did the backbreaking work at meager wages as plantation laborers, service workers, and domestics. The roots of Local identity developed out of this shared class experience, but the egalitarian attitudes toward other ethnic groups also grew out of familiarity facilitated by the passage of time and expedited by living and working in close proximity. Most important, non-Native and non-Haole residents took up the prevailing attitude of aloha, from both the authentic Native source and the Haole discourse. Non-Haoles embraced the melting pot ideal promoted by the Haole oligarchy and readily bought into the myth. The discourse of aloha that Pierce described was easy to buy into, simply because it was based on truth and the social conditions of the islands were ripe for panethnic alliances among its working class. Indeed, aloha was the glue that facilitated the formation of alliances that crossed ethnic boundaries.

Non-Haoles forged alliances that reflected their common subordinate status to the dominant Haole group. An alliance evidently appeared in the sugar strike of 1920. Although this was not the first strike against plantation ownership and management, the 1920 strike was significant because it was the first interethnic strike in Hawai'i. Workers, mainly Filipinos and Japanese, cooperated with each other, but as soon as Filipinos struck, large numbers of Spanish, Portuguese, and Chinese joined in. Their solidarity prevented the planters from effectively pitting ethnic groups against each other as strikebreakers, which had previously been the planters' prevailing strategy. Although the planters claimed victory after weathering the six-month strike, in hindsight strikers considered the strike of 1920 a success, because three months later the planters quietly met the strikers' demands. The time was marked by a sense of cooperation and unity that transcended ethnic boundaries.[34]

More evidence of this interethnic unity exploded onto the public landscape through sentiment surrounding the Massie Case of 1931–32. The sensationalized case, which made national headlines, concerned a Haole woman, the wife of a naval officer, who was allegedly raped by a group of five young men. Two of the men were Native Hawaiian, two were Japanese, and one was Native Hawaiian–Chinese. The rape case ended in a mistrial. The husband and mother of Thalia Massie, the alleged victim, with the help of two naval midshipmen, took matters into their own hands and lynched Joseph Kahahawai, one of the accused five. The Haole vigilantes were found guilty of manslaughter. They were sentenced to ten years of hard labor, only to have their sentences commuted to one day served in the territorial governor's office. Hawai'i residents were outraged by the inequitable handling of the case by Haole leadership. It was an insult to non-Haoles, who overwhelmingly identified with the "local boys." Discussions of the Massie Case, whether in the print media or on the lips of gossips, are often cited as the first time that the term *Local* was used with any salience.[35]

This unity further solidified during World War II, when the distinction between non-Haoles and the hordes of Haole servicemen stationed in the islands became even more apparent. Solidarity manifested itself once again, in the form of the large-scale sugar strikes of 1946. Workers of all the various ethnic groups drew on their shared experiences of mistreatment by American Haoles and combined in one labor organization—the CIO-ILWU.[36] This alliance, nurtured by harmonious race relations reinforced by the discourse of aloha, developed into a common identity.

This common identity coalesced over time as a result of social interactions among different ethnic groups at work, school, church, in the community, in leisure activities, and in the home, most notably through intermarriage. Various character traits are associated with a Local identity. They include being "easygoing, friendly, open, trusting, humble, generous, loyal to family and friends, and indifferent to achieved status distinctions." These are attributes that characterize the positive perceptions of Hawaiians and are in opposition to conventional Haole values: "directness, competition, individualism, achievement of status, and the necessity for impersonal, contractual relationships." Okamura provided this description of Local: "Local has come to represent the common identity of the people of Hawai'i and their appreciation of the inherent value of the land, peoples, and cultures of the islands."[37]

This common identity transcends ethnicity but does not assume that being Local guarantees equal status between ethnic groups. Okamura pointed out that differences between groups tend to be ignored in certain situations, especially when non-Locals are involved. Locals often emphasize their links of class and racial solidarity. Differences become highlighted in situations where disparate access to positions of status is at issue. For example, Okamura described the contention by Kanaka Maoli and Filipino groups that the public school system, at the hands of mostly Japanese administrators and teachers, does not provide equal educational opportunities or attend to the special educational needs of Kanaka Maoli and Filipino students.[38]

Jeff Chang addressed these differences within Local identity when he wrote, "From the social, political and economic margins, Filipino and native Hawaiian activists often speak of how privileged Local elite (most often, Japanese and Chinese) have forgotten the memory of their oppression at the hands of haoles." Chang sees Local consciousness as split, "sometimes mimicking and other times resisting colonial narratives."[39] Chang's notion of Local consciousness accurately describes the fluid nature of Local identity that is so dependent on context. Sometimes Hawai'i Locals reflect more Euro-American values and sometimes they exhibit more Hawaiian values. Because of the range of fluidity between value systems that are often polar opposites, Localness can be difficult to pin down, that is, unless multiplicity and fluidity are considered to be the key descriptors of Local identity.

Local Types

There are many kinds of Locals in Hawai'i. The scope of Local diversity depends on one's definition of *Local*. While an important part of our argument is that midalternity allows for fluidity—namely, the shifting of identities depending on context—and we argue against essentializing identities, a typology can be a useful heuristic tool for beginning a closer examination of different kinds of Locals. The typology presented in table 10.1 represents a starting point for understanding the complexity involved in constructing racialized identities in Hawai'i.

The table illustrates the interactions of two variables, racialized identity and worldview. The identity categories used here are consistent with both the old and the new racialized discourse. For instance, the "Non-Haole" and "Hapa" categories from the old discourse are subdivided to reflect the further distinction from the new discourse categories "Kanaka Maoli" and "Settler." Four basic types of worldview categories represent the multitude of diverse ideologies held by those living in Hawai'i. Again, they correspond to categories drawn from the old and new racialized discourses. A Euro-American worldview is most associated with Haole identity, a Local worldview is associated with non-Haole identities in general, a Kanaka Maoli worldview specifically represents indigenous perspectives mostly

Table 10.1. Types of Midaltern Expressions in Hawai'i (shaded) and Racialized Identity by Worldview (including Indications of Local Identity)

	Haole	Hapa		Non-Haole	
		Part Hawaiian (Kanaka Maoli)	No Kanaka Maoli Ancestry (Settler)	Settler	Kanaka Maoli
Euro-American worldview	The most Haole kine Haole (one dimensional) *Not Local*	Part Hawaiian who internalized Haole values *Can be Local*	Hapa who lives as Haole *Can be Local*	e.g., "Coconut," "Banana," or even "Katonk" Does not feel Local but *can be Local*	Hawaiian who lives by Haole values *Can be Local*
Local worldview	e.g., Haole who performs Localness *May be Local*	Hawaiian *Local*	*Local*	*Local*	Hawaiian *Local*
Monocultural settler/ immigrant/non-Haole/ non-Hawaiian worldview	e.g., Haole guy who lives Japanese-style *May be Local*	*Local*	*May not feel Local but may be treated as Local*	Operates solely by culture of origin *May be Local*	*Local*
Indigenous Kanaka Maoli worldview	e.g., Haoles who are *hanaid* (adopted) into Hawaiian families and adopt Hawaiian worldview (e.g., park ranger, Volcanoes National Park) *Local*	e.g., Part Hawaiians who reject their Haole ancestry and wholly embrace a Kanaka Maoli worldview *Can choose to identify as Local*	e.g., Hapas who live with Hawaiian families and adopt Hawaiian worldview *Local*	e.g., Settlers or their descendants who live with Hawaiian families and adopt Hawaiian worldview *Local*	"Pureblood" who lives da Hawaiian way *Can choose to identify as Local*

Note: The unshaded areas of the table indicate those who are typically more unidimensional in character. They ordinarily identify, or are identified, with the cultural worldview usually attached to their identity. We also argue, of course, that these identities are not necessarily fixed. This table is supplied purely for heuristic purposes.

reserved for Native Hawaiians, and the monocultural Settler/Immigrant/
Non-Haole/Non-Hawaiian worldview category serves as a catchall for all
other monolithically defined settler worldviews (Japanese, Chinese, Filipino, etc.). The intersections of these identity and worldview categories
begin to depict the kinds of diverse possibilities for identity that actually
exist in Hawai'i.

Each cell provides a description or example of a type of potential identity, based on the interaction of one's racialized identity and one's personal
worldview. For example, the identity of a person racialized as Haole and
possessing a Euro-American worldview is not considered Local. The identity represented in that particular cell is prototypically Haole. In this example, the visual physical cues linked with the Haole racialized identity
are directly paired with the views and behaviors most associated with a
Euro-American, or Haole, worldview. In contrast, consider someone racialized as Haole who actually possesses an indigenous Kanaka Maoli
worldview. An example of this is someone adopted or married into a
Kanaka Maoli family, who may have internalized a Kanaka Maoli worldview while being embraced by his or her Kanaka Maoli family. In this case,
someone whose racialized appearance is Haole may actually be considered Local, possibly even Kanaka Maoli. So this typology makes it possible
to distinguish differences in identity that go beyond superficial classification based on physiognomy or ancestry. This typology also considers the
ideological perspectives of an individual in the construction of her or
his identity.

In addition, the typology presented here includes an indication of
the degree to which each particular interaction of racialized identity and
worldview can be considered Local. All but one of the cells in this table
represent identities that can potentially be regarded as Local. Some have
more claim to Local identity than others. For instance, a Kanaka Maoli
who possesses an indigenous worldview may choose to identify as Local.
This would not be contested because Kanaka Maoli are usually considered
the most authentically Local identity associated with Hawai'i. By contrast,
a Haole possessing a Kanaka Maoli or Local worldview is not automatically granted Local status, due to his appearance. In order to prove one's
Localness, he would have to perform Localness or Hawaiianness by prac-

ticing language or cultural expressions associated with being Local or Kanaka Maoli. This can often be accomplished by speaking Pidgin or Hawaiian or adopting Hawaiian cultural practices like surfing, performing hula, or any of a number of traditions associated with Local culture in Hawaiʻi.

Multiraciality, though not expressly mentioned in the Local/Haole and Kanaka Maoli/Settler dichotomies, is an undeniable aspect of Localness in the old discourse but is totally obscured in the new. This virtual erasure of Hapa in the new discourse further masks the undeniable diversity among people of mixed backgrounds. What is apparent in the new discourse is the inclusion of part Hawaiians in the Kanaka Maoli category, regardless of their personal worldviews. In terms of Localness, a Hapa person, whether or not that person has Kanaka Maoli ancestry, is prototypically Local. In fact, next to being Kanaka Maoli, being multiracial in Hawaiʻi is considered the next most quintessentially Local marker. Hapa represents the value of sharing and mixing linked with Local culture built on aloha. This valuing of multiplicity, essential to being Local, is nowhere to be found in the new discourse. While the indigenous Kanaka Maoli, who are the original people of this Locality, are, logically, the most Local, two characteristics help to define the concept of being Local. Multiplicity, whether in terms of racial background, a syncretic worldview, or a worldview different from that usually associated with one's racialized identity, is an essential characteristic of being Local.

Fluidity, the other essential characteristic, is not easily represented in the typology table. The lack of hard lines separating the cells is meant to suggest the permeability of these boundaries. This permeability allows for the fluidity of identity—the fluidity that accounts for the perception of Locals possessing split consciousnesses that vary depending on context. A visual model created to represent Local identity was conceived as a more helpful heuristic device for showing this fluidity.

Local Identity Models

Imagine a globular blob with the consistency of the lava in a lava lamp. The blob represents everyone living in Hawaiʻi. The blob morphs into a form shaped like an hourglass and eventually pulls apart and separates at its middle (fig. 10.2). This description serves as a metaphor for the current direction that identity politics in Hawai'i are heading. It describes the effect of the change in racialized discourse and the corresponding decrease in the salience of Local identity. The dwindling salience of Local is the result of a number of factors, including the diminution of Pidgin, the language of Local culture, and the increasing influence of American popular culture, especially MTV and hip-hop. It is also an effect of the ever-increasing number of people of Kanaka Maoli ancestry who identify more strongly with the Hawaiian sovereignty movement, focusing primarily on their identity as indigenous people instead of their Local identity. This is, of course, consistent with the new shift in discourse.

The Local part of each model pictured, bounded by dashed lines, represents the middle space that includes both Haole and Hawaiian portions. Local Identity, which includes elements of Haole and Hawaiian cultures, in addition to major contributions from other settler cultures, is the space

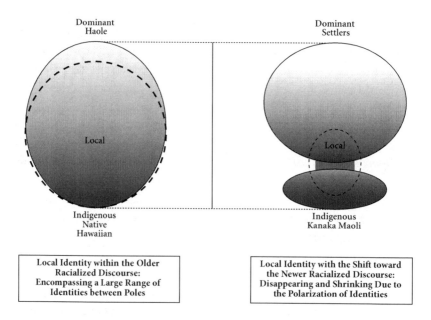

Fig. 10.2. Local Identity Models

that allows for fluid movement between the poles, depending on context. While Local identity emerged as a direct resistance to colonial domination, it also encompasses resistant and compliant responses that have incorporated and internalized the values of the colonizer. In other words, Local includes both those who resist and those who mimic dominant colonial narratives, consciously or unconsciously. In midaltern terms, the Local midaltern identity represents an inclusive middle position between superaltern and subaltern identities.

In the first model, pictured on the left, Local identity is shown as encompassing most people in Hawai'i, excluding dominant Haoles. In the second model, there is clumping at the poles, resulting in a shrinking middle space. Most people are grouped in the Dominant Settler category, with indigenous Kanaka Maoli clearly separate. Local identity is portrayed as shrinking and fading, reflecting its dwindling significance.

The process of supplanting the colonial resistance narrative with a postcolonial indigenous rights narrative will certainly contribute to the diminution of Local as a salient identity. This change is already being reflected in observable trends indicating a continuing cultural shift. Of the three major languages spoken in Hawai'i —English, Hawaiian, and Pidgin— Pidgin is the only language not taught in Hawai'i's schools. Rampant consumerism and materialism, the pervasiveness of mainstream American media, and the indigenous movements of Native Hawaiian sovereignty and nationalism combine simultaneously to give Hawaiian and English currency and prestige at the expense of Hawai'i Pidgin. This analogue is significant because it considers the forces that are diminishing Hawai'i Pidgin and the Local identity it represents. While the once-dying Hawaiian language is experiencing a resurgence, Pidgin is gradually losing its status as the primary language of most non-Haoles. Codified into law as official languages of the state of Hawai'i, English and Hawaiian continue to increase in prominence, while the use of Pidgin is frowned upon in schools and is mostly utilized in public discourse for comic relief and the telling of ethnic jokes. At the same time that the decline of Pidgin and Local identity is becoming increasingly noticeable so are efforts to maintain and preserve them. The publication of a Pidgin translation of the Bible's New Testament and a growing body of Local literature written in Pidgin have contributed to its legitimization as a language and have helped perpetuate the cultures to which Pidgin is tied. Books and plays written and performed in Pidgin continue to gain in popularity, resulting in a strong enough following to support performing arts dedicated to Local culture.[40]

While these Local identity models are useful for understanding phenomena at the societal level, they can also illuminate the fluidity that occurs at the individual level. The model can represent the identity of a single individual and the details depicted by the figure would represent aspects of that individual. Consider the example of a Native Hawaiian who acts Haole in public but lives as a Kanaka Maoli in the privacy of his own home. Imagine that both models pictured in figure 10.3 represent this same person in two different contexts. The first one represents our subject's apparent identity at work, and the second one represents him at home.

In the first model, on the left, note the large Haole portion and the smaller Hawaiian portion. Imagine that our subject works in a business office in Honolulu, a context primarily governed by Haole values. To act

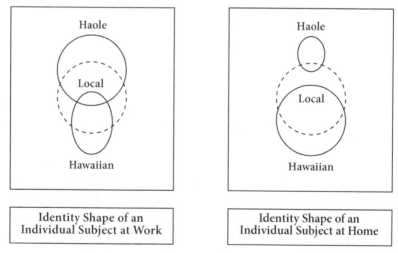

Fig. 10.3. Local Identity Model Illustrating the Fluidity of an Individual's Identity

more Haole would likely be advantageous in this situation. Once our subject leaves the workplace and retreats to the sanctuary of his home, the model transforms into a different shape. In the version of the model pictured on the right, note the small Haole portion and the larger Hawaiian portion. Away from his Haole-dominated workplace, our subject is able more fully to assert the Kanaka Maoli portion of his identity. The presence of the Local part of the model, the middle space that includes both Haole and Hawaiian portions, represents a salient identity in which all this operates.

Multiplicity and fluidity are the hallmarks of Local identity. Various kinds of identities in Hawai'i are included under the Local umbrella, making it a diverse and dynamic identity that defies strict categorization. Local identity is Hawai'i's organic manifestation of midalternity. It is akin to mestizaje and borderlands theoretical projects in terms of how it constructs a sanctioned space devoted to conceptualizing identities for those left out or pushed out by dominant paradigms, especially dichotomies.[41] The Local cases described here were presented to help define midalternity and the midaltern. It is impossible to describe the potentially limitless ways that Local identities play out, nevertheless it is apparent that Local identity challenges dichotomous thinking, creates more possibilities, and allows for more precise identification.

MIDALTERN THEORY

In midaltern terms, the Local midaltern identity represents the center between superaltern and subaltern identities. Although theories of middle or third spaces may not be new, the introduction of the midaltern to postcolonial discourse about the subaltern provides an additional dimension to the discussion. Asserting Local identity as midaltern proposes a way out of the current impasse of essentialism and opposition in Hawai'i racial politics—hence, a move in favor of racial justice—but the concept of the midaltern can also be useful for understanding colonial and postcolonial situations in places other than Hawai'i. This would involve rethinking the notion of the subaltern.

The Subaltern

The concept of the subaltern comes from Antonio Gramsci's writings about fascism in post–World War I Italy. *Subaltern* refers to subordination in the context of dominant/dominated relationships in history. This subordination can be in terms of class, caste, gender, race, language, or culture. Although subaltern studies have witnessed differences and shifts in the use of the concept of subalternity, the idea of subordination has remained central. The effort to rethink history from the perspective of the subordinated, the subaltern, has also remained a consistent goal of subaltern studies. This "history from below," focusing on critiques of colonialism and Western domination, prompted the question, What about a history-from-the-middle approach? Again, thinking only in terms of a dominant/dominated dichotomy fails to recognize those who reside, figuratively, somewhere in the middle. Subaltern scholars seem to relegate persons in the middle simply to the subaltern. Those who are meandering somewhere between and throughout dominant and dominated spaces are simply thought of as a kind of subaltern expression. In other words, the subaltern would subsume all those who, somewhere, in some way, reside in the middle. In our opinion, distinguishing the midaltern from the subaltern is an important distinction that bears valuable implications.[42]

Da "So What?"

We propose the midaltern because it allows the conceptualization of a wider range of possibilities. Rather than assigning people to static, essentialized, either/or categories, midalternity recognizes the existence and importance of multiplicity, thus creating the possibility for more precise accounting of peoples' identities. The fluidity of the midaltern also allows us to take context and worldview into consideration. The performance of one's identity can shift dramatically between contexts. Midalternity provides the conceptual space to consider such shifts. Its recognition of the contextual nature of identity allows the potential for one's identity to broaden beyond just one dimension.

In addition, midalternity provides the potential for more inclusive co-alition building in the quest for racial justice. In Hawai'i, this quest would not be only for justice for Native Hawaiians, but also for all Local multi-racial people and settler people who have not shared fully in the blessings of settler colonialism. For example, non–Kanaka Maoli Locals who feel threatened by the rhetoric of some sovereignty activists would not be as defensive if they did not also feel under attack. In fact, many of these Locals might turn out to be the best allies for Kanaka Maoli and their quest for sovereignty. When faced with the extermination of cultures, whether indigenous or midaltern, employing all the assistance that is available instead of alienating potential allies would seem to have a better chance of success in preserving those threatened cultures.

A shift toward a more inclusive and thoughtful discourse may result in an important realization for Locals who feel threatened by the sovereignty movement. They may finally realize that it is actually in the best interest of all Locals to support wholeheartedly all efforts to achieve Kanaka Maoli sovereignty in Hawai'i. As the original inhabitants of Hawai'i, with a history of experience in the islands stretching back for many hundreds of years, Kanaka Maoli possess indigenous cultural values that are almost certainly those best suited for living in Hawai'i. Local culture is heavily interconnected with Kanaka Maoli culture. If protection and active support are not given to Kanaka Maoli efforts to attain sovereignty, there will be a greater chance of both Kanaka Maoli and non-Hawaiian Locals being engulfed and extinguished by those whose worldviews emphasize economic exploitation over the preservation of Hawai'i's limited and valuable resources—which include, most notably, its people.

NOTES

An earlier version of this chapter appeared in *Mixed Messages: Multiracial Identities in the "Color-Blind" Era*, ed. David L. Brunsma (Boulder, CO: Lynne Rienner, 2006), 63–82.

1. The landmark work often cited on this subject is Paula Rothenberg's *Race, Class, and Gender: An Integrated Study*, currently in its ninth edition (New York: Worth, 2013). While this is an admirable, thought-provoking collection, it is not

an integrated study. Rather, Rothenberg and her contributors simply lay up next to each other an array of studies, each of which emphasizes one of the three themes. There is a small but growing number of studies that genuinely explore how gender, class, and race are related to, even co-create each other. One such study is Karen Brodkin, *How Jews Became White Folks and What That Says about Race in America* (New Brunswick, NJ: Rutgers University Press, 1998).

2. We use "Kanaka Maoli" and "Native Hawaiians" interchangeably to refer to those people who are descended from inhabitants of the islands who lived there before Europeans first arrived.

3. Karina Kahananui Green, "Colonialism's Daughters: Eighteenth- and Nineteenth-Century Westerners' Perceptions of Hawaiian Women," in *Pacific Diaspora: Island Peoples in the United States and across the Pacific*, ed. Paul Spickard, Joanne L. Rondilla, and Debbie Hippolite Wright (Honolulu: University of Hawai'i Press, 2002), 221–52.

4. Stanley D. Porteus, *Calabashes and Kings: An Introduction to Hawaii* (Palo Alto, CA: Pacific Books, 1945). For a critique, see Isaiah Helekunihi Walker, *Waves of Resistance: Surfing and History in Twentieth-Century Hawai'i* (Honolulu: University of Hawai'i Press, 2011).

5. Edward D. Beechert, *Working in Hawai'i: A Labor History* (Honolulu: University of Hawai'i Press, 1985); Jonathan Kamakawiwoʻole Osorio, *Dismembering Lāhui: A History of the Hawaiian Nation to 1887* (Honolulu: University of Hawai'i Press, 2002); David E. Stannard, *Before the Horror: The Population of Hawai'i on the Eve of Western Contact* (Honolulu: University of Hawai'i Social Science Research Institute, 1989); Ronald Takaki, *Pau Hana: Plantation Life and Labor in Hawai'i* (Honolulu: University of Hawai'i Press, 1983).

6. Helena G. Allen, *The Betrayal of Liliuokalani, Last Queen of Hawaii* (Honolulu: Mutual Publishing, 1982); Michael Dougherty, *To Steal a Kingdom* (Waimanalo, Hawai'i: Island Style Press, 1992); Lilikalā Kameʻeleihiwa, *Native Land and Foreign Desires* (Honolulu: Bishop Museum Press, 1992); Noel J. Kent, *Hawaii: Islands under the Influence* (New York: Monthly Review Press, 1983); Jonathan Kamakawiwoʻole Osorio, "'What Kine Hawaiian Are You?' A Moʻolelo about Nationhood, Race, History, and the Contemporary Sovereignty Movement in Hawai'i," *Contemporary Pacific* 13.2 (2002): 359–79. For comic relief, see Thurston Twigg-Smith, *Hawaiian Sovereignty: Do the Facts Matter?* (Honolulu: Goodale, 1998).

7. Lori Pierce, "'The Whites Have Created Modern Honolulu': Ethnicity, Racial Stratification, and the Discourse of Aloha," in *Racial Thinking in the United States*, ed. Paul Spickard and G. Reginald Daniel (Notre Dame, IN: University of Notre Dame Press, 2004), 124–54.

8. Lori Pierce, "Creating a Racial Paradise: Citizenship and Sociology in Hawai'i," in *Race and Nation: Ethnic Systems in the Modern World*, ed. Paul Spickard (New York: Routledge, 2005).

9. Outrigger Hotels, "Island Culture," http://ohanahotels.com/travelguide_region.aspx?regiondetail=1&destination=5 (retrieved May 20, 2004).

10. Sidney L. Gulick, *Mixing the Races in Hawaii: The Coming Neo-Hawaiian American Race* (Honolulu: Hawaiian Board Book Rooms, 1937), v.

11. Romanzo Adams, *Interracial Marriage in Hawaii: A Study of the Mutually Conditioned Processes of Acculturation and Amalgamation* (New York: Macmillan, 1937).

12. James A. Michener, *Hawaii* (New York: Random House, 1959), 937.

13. East-West Center, "WEC Mission and Overview" (1999), www.eastwestcenter.org/about-ov.asp (retrieved May 20, 2004).

14. Campbell Gibson and Kay Jung, *Historical Census Statistics on Population Totals by Race, 1790 to 1990, and by Hispanic Origin, 1970 to 1990, for the United States, Regions, Divisions, and States*, Working Paper No. 56 (Washington, DC: US Census Bureau Population Division, September 2002), 44, 86–120.

15. Robert C. Schmitt, *Demographic Statistics of Hawaii: 1778–1965* (Honolulu: University of Hawai'i Press, 1968); Robert C. Schmitt, *Historical Statistics of Hawaii* (Honolulu: University Press of Hawai'i, 1977).

16. United States Bureau of the Census, *The Two or More Races Population: 2010*, 2010 Census Briefs, C2010BR-13 (September 2012), 11.

17. Paul Spickard, "Pacific Islander American Multiethnicity: A Vision of America's Future?," *Social Forces* 73.4 (June 1995): 1365–83.

18. Glen Grant and Dennis M. Ogawa, "Living Proof: Is Hawaii the Answer?," *Annals of the American Academy of Political and Social Science* 530 (November 1993): 137–54; Jonathan Y. Okamura, "Why There Are No Asian Americans in Hawai'i: The Continuing Significance of Local Identity," *Social Process in Hawai'i* 35 (1994): 161–78; Gary Pak, *Watcher of Waipuna and Other Stories* (Honolulu: Bamboo Ridge Press, 1992); Kent Sakoda and Jeff Siegel, *Pidgin Grammar: An Introduction to the Creole Language of Hawai'i* (Honolulu: Bess Press, 2003); Lee A. Tonouchi, *Da Word* (Honolulu: Bamboo Ridge Press, 2001); Lee A. Tonouchi, *Living Pidgin: Contemplations on Pidgin Culture* (Kāne'ohe, Hawai'i: Tinfish Press, 2002); Kathleen Tyau, *A Little Too Much Is Enough* (New York: Farrar, Straus and Giroux, 1995); Eric Yamamoto, "The Significance of Local," *Social Process in Hawai'i* 27 (1979): 101–15.

19. Pierce, "Whites Have Created Modern Honolulu."

20. Eiko Kosasa, "Ideological Images: U.S. Nationalism in Japanese Settler Photographs," in *Whose Vision? Asian Settler Colonialism in Hawai'i*, ed. Peggy Myo-Young Choy, Candace Fujikane, Momiala Kanahele, and Jonathan Okamura, special issue, *Amerasia Journal* 26.2 (2000): 66–91; original emphasis.

21. Dorothy Ochiai Hazama and Jane Okamoto Komeiji, *Okage sama de: The Japanese in Hawai'i, 1885–1985* (Honolulu: Bess Press, 1986), 255. See also Clarence E. Glick, *Sojourners and Settlers: Chinese Migrants in Hawaii* (Honolulu: Hawaii Chinese History Center and University Press of Hawaii, 1980); Yukiko

Kimura, *Issei: Japanese Immigrants in Hawai'i* (Honolulu: University of Hawai'i Press, 1988); Andrew Lind, *Hawaii's Japanese: An Experiment in Democracy* (Princeton, NJ: Princeton University Press, 1946); Dennis M. Ogawa, *Jan Ken Po: The World of Hawaii's Japanese Americans* (Honolulu: University of Hawai'i Press, 1978).

22. Takaki, *Pau Hana*; Gavan Daws, *Shoal of Time: A History of the Hawaiian Islands* (New York: Macmillan, 1968); Lawrence H. Fuchs, *Hawaii Pono: A Social History* (New York: Harcourt, Brace and World, 1961).

23. Ralph S. Kuykendall and A. Grove Day, *Hawaii: A History. From Polynesian Kingdom to American State*, rev. ed. (Englewood Cliffs, NJ: Prentice-Hall, 1961), 127. The saga of Hawaiian extinction is celebrated from a somewhat different angle in Martha H. Noyes, *And Then There Were None* (Honolulu: Bess Press, 2003).

24. George H. S. Kanahele, *Kū Kanaka: Stand Tall. A Search for Hawaiian Values* (Honolulu: University of Hawai'i Press, 1986).

25. Mililani B. Trask, "Ka Lāhui Hawai'i: A Native Initiative for Sovereignty," *Turning the Tide: Journal of Anti-Racist Activism, Research, and Education* 6.5–6 (December 1993); Haunani-Kay Trask, *From a Native Daughter: Colonialism and Sovereignty in Hawai'i*, rev. ed. (Honolulu: University of Hawai'i Press, 1999); Haunani-Kay Trask, "Native Social Capital: The Case of Hawaiian Sovereignty and Ka Lāhui Hawai'i, *Policy Sciences* 33 (2000): 149–59; Osorio, "What Kine Hawaiian Are You?"; Davianna Pomaika'i McGregor, "Recognizing Native Hawaiians: A Quest for Sovereignty," in Spickard, Rondilla, and Wright, *Pacific Diaspora*, 331–54; Poka Laenui, *Another View on Hawaiian Sovereignty and Self-Determination* (Waianae, Hawai'i: Self-published, 1994); Michael Kioni Dudley and Keoni Kealoha Agard, *A Call for Hawaiian Sovereignty* (Honolulu: Nā Kāne O Ka Malu Press, 1993).

A sampling of Hawaiian sovereignty websites (all active as of August 10, 2013) will give the reader an idea of the range of opinions and proposals: www .hawaiiankingdom.org/; www.hawaii-nation.org/; http://www.oha.org/prog/sov .html; www.mauiculture.net/kuhikuhi/ea.html; www.alohaquest.com/; www.pixi .com/~kingdom/; www.freehawaii.org/; http://nahuihawaii.tripod.com/.

26. Trask, *From a Native Daughter*, 58, 27.

27. That is not the case for other sovereignty proponents, e.g., Laenui, *Another View on Hawaiian Sovereignty*; and McGregor, "Recognizing Native Hawaiians."

28. See, e.g., J. Kehaulani Kauanui, "Off-Island Hawaiians 'Making' Ourselves 'at Home': A [Gendered] Contradiction in Terms?," *Women's Studies International Forum* 21.6 (1998): 681–93; J. Kehaulani Kauanui, "Rehabilitating the Native: Hawaiian Blood Quantum and the Politics of Race, Citizenship, and Entitlement" (PhD diss., University of California, Santa Cruz, 2000); J. Kehaulani Kauanui, "The Politics of Blood in *Rice v. Cayetano*," *Polar* 25.1 (2002): 110–28; J. Kehaulani

Kauanui, *Hawaiian Blood: Colonialism and the Politics of Sovereignty and Indigeneity* (Durham, NC: Duke University Press, 2008).

29. Candace Fujikane, "Asian Settler Colonialism in Hawai'i," in Choy et al., *Whose Vision?*, xv–xxii.

30. Bureau of the Census, *Two or More Races*, 11.

31. See the foreword by Russell C. Leong, ed., in the special issue of *Amerasia Journal*, 26.2 (2000) and the work cited in note 22 above. And see Deborah Wei and Rachael Kamel's *Resistance in Paradise: Rethinking 100 Years of U.S. Involvement in the Caribbean and the Pacific* (Philadelphia: American Friends Service Committee and Office of Curriculum Support, School District of Philadelphia, 1998), v–vii.

32. Throughout this essay we use *Local identity* as an umbrella term for what are actually several Local identities (emphasizing plurality). In the same respect, Local culture can arguably be viewed as a unitary panethnic culture within which are nested various Local subcultures (e.g., Local Japanese, Local Filipino, Hawaiian).

33. "Pidgin" here refers to the vernacular associated with Local identity and culture in Hawai'i. Hawai'i Pidgin is a Creole language based primarily on Hawaiian and English, with significant contributions from the languages of other ethnic groups that settled in Hawai'i. See note 18 above.

34. Jonathan Y. Okamura, "Aloha Kanaka Me Ke Aloha 'Aina: Local Culture and Society in Hawaii," *Amerasia Journal* 7.2 (1980): 119–37; Takaki, *Pau Hana*.

35. John P. Rosa, "The Massie Case Narrative and the Cultural Production of Local Identity in Hawai'i," *Amerasia Journal* 26.2 (2000): 93–115; David E. Stannard, *Honor Killing: How the Infamous "Massie Affair" Transformed Hawai'i* (New York: Viking, 2005).

36. J. A. Rademaker, "Race Relations in Hawaii, 1946," *Social Process in Hawaii* 11 (1947).

37. Okamura, "Aloha Kanaka Me Ke Aloha 'Aina"; Jonathan Y. Okamura, "The Illusion of Paradise: Privileging Multiculturalism in Hawai'i," in *Making Majorities: Constituting the Nation in Japan, Korea, China, Malaysia, Fiji, Turkey, and the United States*, ed. Dru C. Gladney (Stanford, CA: Stanford University Press, 1998), 264–84; Jonathan Y. Okamura, *Ethnicity and Inequality in Hawai'i* (Philadelphia: Temple University Press, 2008).

38. Okamura, "Aloha Kanaka Me Ke Aloha 'Aina"; Jeff Chang, "Local Knowledge(s): Notes on Race Relations, Panethnicity and History in Hawai'i," *Amerasia Journal* 22.2 (1996): 1–29.

39. Chang, "Local Knowledge(s)."

40. Pidgin Bible Translation Group, *Da Jesus Book: Hawai'i Pidgin New Testament* (Orlando, FL: Wycliffe Bible Translators, 2000); Pak, *Watcher of Waipuna*.

41. Rafael Pérez-Torres, *Mestizaje: Critical Uses of Race in Chicano Culture* (Minneapolis: University of Minnesota Press, 2006); Gloria Anzaldúa, *Borderlands/La Frontera: The New Mestiza* (San Francisco: Aunt Lute Books, 1987); Edwina Barvosa, *Wealth of Selves: Multiple Identities, Mestiza Consciousness, and the Subject of Politics* (College Station: Texas A&M University Press, 2008); Alexander Diener and Joshua Hagen, eds., *Borderlines and Borderlands: Political Oddities at the Edge of the Nation-State* (Lanham, MD: Rowman and Littlefield, 2010); *"Borderlands" History Comes of Age*, special issue, *Journal of American History* 98.2 (September 2011).

42. Antonio Gramsci, *Selections from the Prison Notebooks of Antonio Gramsci* (New York: International Publishers, 1971); Catherine Hall, "Introduction: Thinking the Postcolonial, Thinking the Empire," in *Cultures of Empire: A Reader. Colonisers in Britain and the Empire in the Nineteenth and Twentieth Centuries* (Manchester: Manchester University Press, 2000), 1–33; G. Prakash, "Subaltern Studies as Postcolonial Criticism," in Hall, *Cultures of Empire*, 120–36. History from the middle is not to be confused with the construction of Asians and Latinos as middle peoples on a two-ended racial spectrum, with Blacks at one end and Whites at the other—the sort of thing proposed in a silly book by Eileen O'Brien, *The Racial Middle: Latinos and Asian Americans Living beyond the Racial Divide* (New York: New York University Press, 2008).

11

Does Multiraciality Lighten?

Me-Too Ethnicity and the Whiteness Trap

MULTIRACIALITY STUDIES AND WHITENESS STUDIES

The two most striking themes—some would say movements—in ethnic studies literature of the past quarter century are expressions of multiraciality and studies of Whiteness. There are similarities and perhaps connections between the two themes. Both depend on an understanding that race is a constructed entity rather than a biological essence. Both Whiteness studies and multiracialism have been put forth by their advocates as expressions of antiracism. In addition, both have been accused by their detractors of selling out the interests of people of color. It is true that there are potential dangers for monoracial communities of color in both the Whiteness studies movement and the multiracial movement. It is also true that the multiracial movement has been more concerned with the psychological needs of individuals than with the needs of monoracial communities. However, as we will see, the dangers are greater in Whiteness studies than in the multiracial idea. Critics' fears to the contrary, the acknowledgment of multiraciality, even the assertion of a multiracial identity, is not necessarily an indicator that one is abandoning one's community of color and seeking Whiteness.

Whether for good or for ill, the last decade and a half of the twentieth century and the first decade of the twenty-first saw the rise of a new consciousness of racial multiplicity, both on the part of people who were claiming multiracial identities and in the minds of monoracial observers. The shelf of books on multiraciality has been growing rapidly.[1] Ethnic studies departments have begun to recognize this trend. Courses on multiraciality are taught at a steadily growing number of universities across the country.[2] Courses and textbooks on race and ethnicity routinely now include units on multiraciality.[3] At least one university has hired and tenured a professor whose job is specifically to teach multiracial issues.[4] There is even a high school course on multiracial identity, at the Los Angeles School for Global Studies, taught for credit in the spring semester of 2012.[5] Multiracial student organizations have sprouted on scores of college campuses.

Alongside the heightened attention to multiraciality, the 1990s and 2000s witnessed a boom in Whiteness studies. Scholars began to examine the experiences of European Americans as a racial group. The impetus came from left-wing White scholars who wanted to examine the bases and processes of White privilege so that they might undermine it. The list of books in this field is just as long as that in multiraciality studies.[6] The American Historical Association and the American Studies Association have held sessions on the history and culture of Whiteness. Can the establishment of faculty positions in Whiteness studies be far behind?[7]

RACIAL CONSTRUCTIONS

The notion of multiraciality and the advocacy of Whiteness studies both depend on a constructivist concept of ethnicity, of the sort I described in chapter 1. In *The Sweeter the Juice*, Shirlee Taylor Haizlip shows half of her racially mixed family creating themselves as Black people and the other half creating themselves as White.[8] In "A Bill of Rights for Racially Mixed People," Maria Root argues passionately that people of mixed ancestry ought not be bound by someone else's notions of racial categories or appropriate racial behavior. She argues that, as a multiracial person,

I have the right . . .

not to keep the races separate within me

not to be responsible for people's discomfort with my physical
    ambiguity

not to justify my ethnic legitimacy

I have the right

to identify myself differently than strangers expect me to identify

to identify myself differently than how my parents identify me

to identify myself differently than my brothers and sisters

to identify myself differently in different situations.[9]

This is a powerful statement about race as individual choice, as something plastic that may—and perhaps must—be molded by individuals on a daily basis.

In an equally constructivist vein, Matthew Jacobson writes of Whiteness as "alchemy." He portrays the White group in American history as a coalition with ever-changing boundaries around it and constantly morphing glue holding it together. Karen Brodkin writes (although I believe her argument is overstated) about "how Jews became White folks." David Roediger, in a much more careful exposition with less sweeping claims, shows how White working people in the nineteenth century gathered in class solidarity, in part on the basis of an increasing sense of racial solidarity. The most boldly constructivist of all the Whiteness studies writers is Noel Ignatiev. He argues that Whiteness itself is not a matter of skin color, ancestry, or anything else that might be attributed to historical or biological background. Rather, he says, Whiteness is defined by the very act of oppressing Black people.[10]

UNDERMINING RACISM

The main expressions in each literature, Whiteness and multiraciality studies, assert that they are antiracist in intent and impact. Multiracialists contend their work undermines the very categories of racism. Aubyn

Fulton says, "I think the existence of [interracial individuals] is corrosive to and undermining of the current racial status quo (in this context I think that 'corrosive' and 'undermining' are *good* things, since I think that the current racial status quo is a bad thing and should be corroded and undermined)."[11] Ronald Glass and Kendra Wallace insist:

> Race cannot be ignored as a conceptual framework because of its theoretical inadequacy for capturing the phenomenon of race, nor because of its simplistic use of reified notions for historically dynamic meanings and practices. Nor can the politics of race be transcended by a mental act of some sort (like a change in belief, or an act of will) nor wished away in a fantasy of color-blindness. . . . But an even stronger challenge to race can come from people at the margins to all racial centers; that is, from people expressive of multiracial existence and evident human variation, who resist efforts to be subdued and brought within racial orders.[12]

Reginald Daniel submits that people who maintain multiracial identities are "subverting the racial divide." I have written that multiracial people, by their very choice to assert a multiracial identity, are "undermining the very basis of racism, its categories."[13]

In similar fashion, students of Whiteness say they are interrogating and thereby undermining the processes of White privilege. Some of them call their collective project "critical White studies." Noel Ignatiev and John Garvey call themselves "race traitors."[14] In addition, some scholars of Whiteness do, in fact, examine their subject in such a way as to critique White privilege. David Roediger, echoing W. E. B. Du Bois, writes of "the wages of Whiteness": "The pleasures of Whiteness could function as a 'wage' for White workers. That is, status and privileges conferred by race could be used to make up for alienating and exploitative class relationships, North and South. White workers could, and did, divine and accept their class positions by fashioning identities as 'not slaves' and as 'not Blacks.'"[15] George Lipsitz writes of "the possessive investment in Whiteness" and calls into question "the content of [White people's] character.[16]

CRITIQUES OF MULTIRACIALITY AND
WHITENESS STUDIES

Despite aspirations to undermine racial privilege on the part of scholars and advocates of multiraciality and Whiteness studies, some critics have nonetheless derided each of these modes of study as tending to reinforce racial hierarchy and White privilege. Monoracialist critics say that advocacy of a multiracial interpretation encourages individuals to flee identification with communities of color and seek a middle social position, lightened by recognition of their ancestral multiplicity. Jon Michael Spencer accuses advocates of a multiracial identity of trying to create in America a three-tiered racial hierarchy like the one he perceives to exist in South Africa: White on top, multiracial in the middle, and Black on the bottom.[17] In a more sophisticated analysis, Rainier Spencer agrees and argues that asserting multiraciality constitutes a racist embrace of the one-drop rule. Because nearly every person in America who has some African ancestry also has other ancestries, the only logical thing to do would be to call all African Americans multiracial people. To do so, he argues, would be to ignore the real social disabilities suffered by African Americans. He argues that good census data are needed to measure racial progress or the lack thereof, and that monoracial categories are the necessary categories of analysis. "The challenge for America," he says, "lies in determining how to move away from the fallacy of race while remaining aggressive in the battle against racism."[18]

Both of these critics—indeed, most of the criticism of the multiracial movement—have focused on the successful 1990s movement to change the racial categories employed by the US Census. That is curious, for I read the census debate as a significant but ultimately minor issue in a much broader multiracial social movement.[19] Nonetheless, their opposition to both commonly espoused options, a multiracial category and multiple box checking, is echoed by some members of the public who identify themselves monoracially despite possessing multiple ancestries. Declaring his intention to eschew the chance to check more than one box on the 2000 census and determined to check the "Black" box only, Michael

Gelobter asked, "Should Frederick Douglass have checked white and black? Should W. E. B. Du Bois have checked white and black?" For African American leaders such as Du Bois and Douglass to have acknowledged their patent multiracial ancestry, argues Gelobter, would have been for them to have abandoned common cause with other African Americans.[20] This is the core of the monoracial argument against the expression of a multiracial identity: claiming a multiracial identity means abandoning Black America.[21]

Critics of Whiteness studies are equally caustic. The critics complain that, whatever their antiracist intentions may be, the authors of Whiteness studies place White people at the center of attention, thus distracting from the real needs of peoples of color. Noel Ignatiev wrote a book with the title *How the Irish Became White* and Karen Brodkin followed with *How Jews Became White Folks and What That Says about Race in America*.[22] Soon scholars and laypeople alike could be heard to remark, "You know, once [X White group] were not White, but then they became White." This amounted to a kind of me-too ethnicity. White people were saying, "Look at us. We have race, too. We are the ones who merit attention." Significant energy in ethnic studies began to shift away from examining the lives and experiences of people of color. Instead, that attention began to go to White people, who, I contend, already were the subject of nearly the entire curriculum. Many studies of Whiteness, in this interpretation, amount to little more than me-too ethnic self-absorption on the part of White people.

It is that quality of self-absorption in each movement and a related individualism that are troubling. The central claim of the multiracial movement is that America must recognize the multiplicity in their identities as multiracial individuals. They tend to be opposed by the group claims of monoracially defined communities of color. Marie Hara and Nora Okja Keller have edited a stunning collection of poetry and prose by multiracial women. However, in sixty-three sensitive evocations of the various authors' life experiences, almost no attention is paid to group needs. It is all about their own individual identity and relationship issues.[23] Many multiracial activists are in practical fact committed to the needs of the communities of color to which they have connections, but their multiracial claim is essentially an individualistic concern. Similarly, Whiteness studies have resulted in a significant turning away from the issues of communities of color and redirecting of that scholarly energy toward White people as a group. In addition to individualism and self-concern, both intellectual movements have a trendy quality. As Danzy Senna writes, "Hybridity is in"; the same can be said of Whiteness.[24]

CONNECTING MULTIRACIALITY AND WHITENESS STUDIES

Whatever the merits of multiraciality and of Whiteness studies, the critics have pointed to at least potentially problematic tendencies in these two intellectual movements. It now remains to be ascertained whether there is a connection between these two fields of concern. From a certain skeptical angle, one may view the assertion of a multiracial identity as a kind of Whiteness experience: centering Whiteness, decentering monoracial oppression, and deemphasizing the needs of communities of color. This we may call the Whiteness trap.

A University of California, Berkeley, student, himself multiracial, complains about his classmates in Hapa Issues Forum, one of the multiracial groups on campus: "They're all Japanese-White kids from the suburbs who think that because they are part White their shit don't stink." Lisa Jones writes:

By marketing themselves as anything but black, do light-complexioned entertainers such as [Mariah] Carey become, in the eyes of most Americans, de facto whites? And do Carey and other people of color who feel more at ease representing themselves by their combination ethnic heritages, and not by race[,] . . . teach the world how to be "raceless"? Or are they positioning themselves as a separate class along the lines of South African "coloreds"?[25]

There may be some evidence that the assertion of a multiracial identity is related to middle-class status and experience in White contexts. Kerry Ann Rockquemore surveyed 250 college students, each of whom had one

White parent and one Black parent. She found that those raised in middle-class White neighborhoods tended to identify themselves as biracial, whereas those raised in Black communities tended to identity themselves as monoracially Black.[26]

Jon Michael Spencer suggests that White parents with Black partners who have advocated a multiracial census category have done so partly out of a wish for their children to avoid the disabilities of being Black in American society: "[It] is not all about the self-esteem of their mixed-race children. Some of this behavior has to do with the self-esteem of these interracially married White parents who have difficulty accepting their mixed-race children choosing black as an identity." The most insistent advocate of a multiracial census option, Susan Graham of Project RACE, lends some support to such a suggestion when she says, "Nobody can tell me my children are more black than white."[27]

The conservative activist Charles Byrd, who is also a multiracialist, says, "What we need to do as a country is get rid of these stupid [racial] boxes altogether." Royce Van Tassell echoes this opinion, setting forth multiraciality as a station on the way to getting rid of talking about race entirely. Van Tassel, affiliated with a right-wing action group that sponsors the Race Has No Place Project, wants to drum any consideration of race—of the causes, patterns, and consequences of racial discrimination—out of American public life. As evidence to support his claim that Americans do not want to think about race, talk about race, or collect data about the status of America's various racial communities, he cites a survey his group sponsored that claims that a large majority of Americans would describe a person of a Black parent and a White parent as multiracial. He skips several logical steps to the conclusion that "Americans want to reclaim their racial privacy, and they are tired of the government's intrusive race questions."[28]

There are considerable grounds, then, to make the argument that multiraciality lightens. At the very least, the multiracial idea can give support to the position that the most important thing is an individual's self-identity. As in the cases of Van Tassel and Byrd, the concept of multiraciality may be used by people with malign motives to attack communities of color.

DOES MULTIRACIALITY LIGHTEN? EVIDENCE FROM HISTORY

One may grant that there may be some measure of evidence for Rainier Spencer's fears. Some people who are not persons of goodwilll—who do not support the interests of communities of color in the United States and who do not want White Americans to have to take race seriously—may welcome the multiracial movement. They may try to turn it to their ends, as a way station on the path to ignoring race (and, therefore, their own guilt) entirely. Yet does that mean that the critics' contention is true? Does multiraciality necessarily lighten? Contrary to the contentions of Spencer, Gelobter, and others, there is not much historical evidence that it does.

Consider the cases of several prominent Americans who acknowledged multiracial ancestry. Frederick Douglass was the most widely known African American of the nineteenth century. He was the son of a slave woman and a White man, although his features were such that he could not easily have passed for White. There was no fiercer advocate of the rights of African Americans, yet throughout his life Douglass acknowledged his White ancestry along with the Black. He insisted on traveling in an interracial social world and in his later years married a White woman. Douglass acknowledged his multiraciality, even as he embraced Black America fully.[29]

Alice Dunbar-Nelson was a turn-of-the-century African American writer and the wife of the poet Paul Laurence Dunbar. She was Black in her writing and in her political commitments. However, her social world was racially mixed, and she passed for White frequently in her private life, for instance, to shop in segregated White stores or to attend the theater. Reading out from Dunbar-Nelson's life to those of several of her contemporaries and successors in African American letters, Hanna Wallinger concludes that "although racial thinking determined the public utterances and creative writing of many prominent African Americans— . . . Charles Chesnutt, Wallace Thurman, Langston Hughes, Hallie E. Queen, and Josephine and Senator Blanche Bruce—it did not determine their personal lives to an exclusive degree."[30]

Edith Maude Eaton was another of that same generation that spanned the turn of the twentieth century. She has widely been honored as the foremother of Asian American fiction. The child of English and Chinese parents, she lived in North America, took the pen name Sui Sin Far, and wrote in humane and sympathetic tones about the plight of Chinese Americans. Nonetheless, although she has been honored for her public persona as a Chinese American, she lived her personal life as a White woman.[31]

Perhaps there is no more revered figure in African American history than W. E. B. Du Bois—historian, sociologist, journalist, cofounder of the NAACP, pan-Africanist. Indeed, a Pulitzer Prize–winning author subtitled Du Bois's story *Biography of a Race*. Du Bois was fervently committed to his identity as an African American, to the African American people, and later to the entire African diaspora. Yet in *Dusk of Dawn*, one of several autobiographies, Du Bois discusses at great length the various strands of his European ancestry, some of it quite recent, and the degrees of his affinity with those strands. Du Bois was light of skin and European of feature, and he could easily have passed for White had he chosen to do so. He consistently recognized his multiraciality. However, that did not mitigate his embrace of Blackness or his effectiveness in serving the cause of African Americans.[32]

Similar stories could be told of other important figures of African American history: Mary Church Terrell, first president of the National Association of Colored Women; Mordecai Johnson, first African American president of Howard University; Walter White, novelist and longtime executive secretary of the NAACP; Jean Toomer, herald of the Harlem Renaissance; Adam Clayton Powell Jr., flamboyant congressmember from Harlem in the 1950s and 1960s. All these were multiracial people who acknowledged, even embraced, their multiraciality and who nonetheless were leaders in one way or another of communities of color. Even Wallace D. Fard, the mysterious figure behind the founding of the Nation of Islam, and Malcolm X, the Black Muslims' fiery leader, were multiracial men who acknowledged their multiraciality, although they were less sanguine about it than Douglass or Du Bois.

Earlier in this chapter, I reported that Michael Gelobter asked, "Should Frederick Douglass have checked white and black? Should W. E. B. Du

Bois have checked white and black?" I think it is possible, given the shape of those men's careers and the contents of their public utterances, that they might well have chosen to check both "Black" and "White" boxes if they had lived to the time of the 2000 and 2010 census. Both they, and all the other individuals to whom I have just referred, identified themselves emphatically with communities of color (Black and Chinese in these cases). Yet they all also acknowledged their multiplicity and did not try to mask it. Some, like Dunbar-Nelson and Sui Sin Far, lived part of the time on the White side of the line. Some, like Du Bois, gloried in their multiraciality even as they chose monoracial lives. Some, like Malcolm X, hated their White ancestry. However, all recognized their multiplicity even as they chose to serve communities of color. There is just not adequate historical evidence to conclude that acknowledgment or embrace of a multiracial identity necessarily lightens. The important issue for monoracial communities of color is not whether multiracial people claim their multiraciality but whether, having done so, they continue to serve the needs of those communities of color.

The criticism of the multiracial movement—that it is a form of seeking after Whiteness—has theoretical validity. It points to a real danger. There are those who advocate a multiracial identity who also would like to do away with consideration of race in American society, who in effect would abandon the needs of communities of color. However, examining the actual lives of several multiracial people in historical context suggests that recognition, even embrace, of a multiracial identity does not mean that multiracial people fall into the Whiteness trap.

NOTES

A quite different version of this essay appeared in *New Faces in a Changing America: Multiracial Identity in the 21st Century*, ed. Loretta I. Winters and Herman L. DeBose (Thousand Oaks, CA: Sage, 2003), 289–300. I have updated many references and clarified some language but preserved the original argument.

1. Places to begin on the multiracial phenomenon include G. Reginald Daniel, *More than Black? Multiracial Identity and the New Racial Order* (Philadelphia: Temple University Press, 2002); Maria P. P. Root, ed., *Racially Mixed People in*

America (Newbury Park, CA: Sage, 1992); Maria P. P. Root, ed., *The Multiracial Experience* (Thousand Oaks, CA: Sage, 1995); Jayne O. Ifekwunigwe, ed., *"Mixed Race" Studies* (New York: Routledge, 2004); Teresa Williams León and Cynthia L. Nakashima, eds., *The Sum of Our Parts: Mixed Heritage Asian Americans* (Philadelphia: Temple University Press, 2001); and Naomi Zack, *Race and Mixed Race* (Philadelphia: Temple University Press, 1993). Other prominent writings on multiracial people and the movement include Suki Ali, *Mixed-Race, Post-Race: Gender, New Ethnicities, and Cultural Practices* (New York: Berg, 2003); Gloria Anzaldúa, *Borderlands/La Frontera: The New Mestiza* (San Francisco: Aunt Lute Press, 1987); Katya Gibel Azoulay, *Black, Jewish, and Interracial* (Durham, NC: Duke University Press, 1997); James F. Brooks, ed., *Confounding the Color Line: The Indian-Black Experience in North America* (Lincoln: University of Nebraska Press, 2002); David L. Brunsma, ed., *Mixed Messages: Multiracial Identities in the "Color-Blind" Era* (Boulder, CO: Lynne Rienner, 2006); David Brunsma and Kerry Ann Rockquemore, *Beyond Black: Biracial Identity in America*, 2nd ed. (Lanham, MD: Rowman and Littlefield, 2008); Carol Camper, ed., *Miscegenation Blues: Voices of Mixed Race Women* (Toronto: Sister Vision, 1994), Greg Carter, *The United States of the United Races: A Utopian History of Racial Mixing* (New York: New York University Press, 2013); Kimberly McClain DaCosta, *Making Multiracials: State, Family, and Market in the Redrawing of the Color Line* (Stanford, CA: Stanford University Press, 2007); Sui Sin Far, *Mrs. Spring Fragrance and Other Writings* (Urbana: University of Illinois Press, 1995); Jack D. Forbes, *Black Africans and Native Americans: Color, Race and Caste in the Evolution of Red-Black Peoples* (New York: Basil Blackwell, 1988); Kip Fulbeck, *Paper Bullets* (Seattle: University of Washington Press, 2001); Kip Fulbeck, *Part Asian–100% Hapa* (San Francisco: Chronicle Books, 2006); Lise Funderburg, *Black, White, Other: Biracial Americans Talk about Race and Identity* (New York: Morrow, 1994); Rudy P. Guevarra Jr., *Becoming Mexipino: Multiethnic Identities and Communities in San Diego* (New Brunswick, NJ: Rutgers University Press, 2012); Patricia Penn Hilden, *When Nickels Were Indians: An Urban, Mixed-Blood Story* (Washington, DC: Smithsonian Institution Press, 1995); Gerald Horne, *The Color of Fascism: Lawrence Dennis, Racial Passing, and the Rise of Right-Wing Extremism in the United States* (New York: New York University Press, 2006); Margaret L. Hunter, *Race, Gender, and the Politics of Skin Tone* (New York: Routledge, 2005); Kevin R. Johnson, *How Did You Get to Be Mexican? A White/Brown Man's Search for Identity* (Philadelphia: Temple University Press, 1999); Kevin R. Johnson, ed., *Mixed Race America and the Law* (New York: New York University Press, 2003); Ralina L. Joseph, *Transcending Blackness: From the New Millennium Mulatta to the Exceptional Multiracial* (Durham, NC: Duke University Press, 2012); Randall Kennedy, *Interracial Intimacies: Sex, Marriage, Identity, and Adoption* (New York: Pantheon, 2003); Yelena Khanga, *Soul to Soul: The Story of a Black Russian American Family, 1865–*

1992 (New York: Norton, 1992); Rebecca Chiyoko King-O'Riain, *Pure Beauty: Judging Race in Japanese American Beauty Pageants* (Minneapolis: University of Minnesota Press, 2006); Rebecca Chiyoko King-O'Riain, Stephen Small, Minelle Mahtani, Miri Song, and Paul Spickard, eds., *Global Mixed Race* (New York: New York University Press, 2014); Kathleen Odell Korgen, ed., *Multiracial Americans and Social Class: The Influence of Social Class on Racial Identity* (New York: Routledge, 2010); Karen Isaaksen Leonard, *Making Ethnic Choices: Punjabi-Mexican Americans* (Philadelphia: Temple University Press, 1994); James McBride, *The Color of Water: A Black Man's Tribute to His White Mother* (New York: Riverhead, 1996); Robert S. McKelvey, *Dust of Life: America's Children Abandoned in Vietnam* (Seattle: University of Washington Press, 1999); Tiya Miles, *Ties That Bind: The Story of an Afro-Cherokee Family in Slavery and Freedom* (Berkeley: University of California Press, 2005); Tiya Miles and Sharon P. Holland, eds., *Crossing Waters, Crossing Worlds: The African Diaspora in Indian Country* (Durham, NC: Duke University Press, 2006); Stephen Murphy-Shigematsu, *When Half Is Whole: Multiethnic Asian American Identities* (Stanford, CA: Stanford University Press, 2012); Kien Nguyen, *The Unwanted: A Memoir* (Boston: Back Bay Books, 2002); Barack Obama, *Dreams from My Father: A Story of Race and Inheritance* (Tokyo: Kodansha, 1995); Jill Olumide, *Raiding the Gene Pool: The Social Construction of Mixed Race* (London: Polity Press, 2002); David Parker and Miri Song, eds., *Rethinking "Mixed Race"* (London: Pluto Press, 2001); Theda Perdue, *"Mixed Blood" Indians: Racial Construction in the Early South* (Athens: University of Georgia Press, 2003); Clara E. Rodríguez, *Changing Race: Latinos, the Census, and the History of Ethnicity in the United States* (New York: New York University Press, 2000); Joanne L. Rondilla and Paul Spickard, *Is Lighter Better? Skin-Tone Discrimination among Asian Americans* (Lanham, MD: Rowman and Littlefield, 2007); Maria P. P. Root and Matt Kelley, eds., *Multiracial Child Resource Book* (Seattle: Mavin Foundation, 2003); Claudio Saunt, *Black, White, and Indian: Race and the Unmaking of an American Family* (New York: Oxford University Press, 2005); Daniel J. Sharfstein, *The Invisible Line: Three American Families and the Secret Journey from Black to White* (New York: Penguin, 2011); Miri Song, *Choosing Ethnic Identity* (London: Polity, 2003); Paul Spickard, *Mixed Blood: Intermarriage and Ethnic Identity in Twentieth-Century America* (Madison: University of Wisconsin Press, 1989); Spickard and Daniel, *Racial Thinking*; Cathy J. Tashiro, *Standing on Both Feet: Voices of Older Mixed Race Americans* (Boulder, CO: Paradigm, 2012); Circe Sturm, *Blood Politics: Race, Culture, and Identity in the Cherokee Nation of Oklahoma* (Berkeley: University of California Press, 2002); Barbara Tizard and Ann Phoenix, *Black, White, or Mixed Race?* (New York: Routledge, 1993); Dorothy West, *The Wedding* (New York: Doubleday, 1995); Gregory Howard Williams, *Life on the Color Line* (New York: Penguin, 1995); Joel Williamson, *New People: Miscegenation and Mulattoes in the United States* (New York: Free Press, 1980);

Winters and DeBose, *New Faces in a Changing America*; Marguerite Wright, *I'm Chocolate, You're Vanilla: Raising Healthy Black and Biracial Children in a Race-Conscious World* (San Francisco: Jossey-Bass, 1998).

2. In recent years, they have included the University of California campuses at Berkeley, Davis, Los Angeles, and Santa Barbara; California State University campuses at Northridge, Pomona, Sacramento, San Francisco, and San Jose; Brigham Young University–Hawai'i; University of Hawai'i; Brown University; Portland State University; University of Illinois; University of Texas at Austin; Golden Gate University Law School; Mills College; Oregon State University; Dartmouth College; Scripps College; University of Vermont; University of Oregon; University of Southern California; New York University; Stanford University; Saint Louis University; Simmons College; University of Washington; Pomona College; University of Wisconsin–Milwaukee; and Berklee College of Music. This list came from the author's personal knowledge and from a Google survey of courses in credible online listings conducted on August 11, 2013. It is likely that there are others I have missed.

3. E.g., Becky Thompson and Sangeeta Tyagi, eds., *Names We Call Home: Autobiography on Racial Identity* (New York: Routledge, 1996); Stephen Cornell and Douglas Hartmann, *Ethnicity and Race*, 2nd ed. (Thousand Oaks, CA: Pine Forge Press, 2007).

4. San Francisco State University, in the College of Ethnic Studies.

5. www.mascsite.org/programs/multiracialstudies/ (retrieved August 11, 2013).

6. A sampling: Theodore Allen, *The Invention of the White Race*, 2 vols. (London: Verso, 1994, 1997); Tomás Almaguer, *Racial Fault Lines: The Historical Origins of White Supremacy in California* (Berkeley: University of California Press, 1994); Valerie Babb, *Whiteness Visible: The Meaning of Whiteness in American Literature and Culture* (New York: New York University Press, 1998); Maurice Berger, *White Lies: Race and the Myths of Whiteness* (New York: Farrar, Straus and Giroux, 1999); Karen Brodkin, *How Jews Became White Folks and What That Says about Race in America* (New Brunswick, NJ: Rutgers University Press, 1998); Walter Bronwen, *Outsiders Inside: Whiteness, Place, and Irish Women* (New York: Routledge, 2001); Christine Clark and James O'Donnell, eds., *Becoming and Unbecoming White: Owning and Disowning a Racial Identity* (Westport, CT: Bergin and Garvey, 1999); Dalton Conley, *Honky* (Berkeley: University of California Press, 2000); Kalpana Seshari Crooks, *Desiring Whiteness: A Lacanian Analysis of Race* (New York: Routledge, 2000); Chris J. Cuomo and Kim Q. Hall, eds., *Whiteness: Feminist Philosophical Reflections* (Lanham, MD: Rowman and Littlefield, 1999); Renee R. Curry, *White Women Writing White* (New York: Greenwood, 2000); Richard Delgado and Jean Stefancic, eds., *Critical White Studies* (Philadelphia: Temple University Press, 1997); Philip Deloria, *Playing Indian* (New Haven, CT: Yale University Press, 1998); Richard Dyer, *White* (London:

Routledge, 1997); Abby L. Ferber, *White Man Falling: Race, Gender, and White Supremacy* (Lanham, MD: Rowman and Littlefield, 1998); Michelle Fine, Lois Weis, Linda C. Powell, and L. Mun Wong, eds., *Off White: Readings on Race, Power, and Society* (New York: Routledge, 1997); Neil Foley, *The White Scourge: Mexicans, Blacks, and Poor Whites in Texas Cotton Culture* (Berkeley: University of California Press, 1997); Ruth Frankenberg, *White Women, Race Matters: The Social Construction of Whiteness* (Minneapolis: University of Minnesota Press, 1993); Ruth Frankenberg, ed., *Displacing Whiteness* (Durham, NC: Duke University Press, 1997); John Gabriel, *Whitewash: Racialized Politics and the Media* (New York: Routledge, 1998); Jim Goad, *The Redneck Manifesto: How Hillbillies, Hicks, and White Trash Became America's Scapegoats* (New York: Touchstone, 1998); Grace Elizabeth Hale, *Making Whiteness: The Culture of Segregation in the South, 1890–1940* (New York: Vintage, 1998); Ian F. Haney López, *White by Law: The Legal Construction of Race* (New York: New York University Press, 1996); John Hartigan, *Racial Situations: Class Predicaments of Whiteness in Detroit* (Princeton, NJ: Princeton University Press, 1999); Mike Hill, ed., *Whiteness: A Critical Reader* (New York: New York University Press, 1997); Noel Ignatiev, *How the Irish Became White* (New York: Routledge, 1995); Noel Ignatiev and John Garvey, eds., *Race Traitor* (New York: Routledge, 1996); Matthew Frye Jacobson, *Whiteness of a Different Color: European Immigrants and the Alchemy of Race* (Cambridge, MA: Harvard University Press, 1998); Joe Kincheloe, Shirley R. Steinberg, Nelson M. Rodriguez, and Ronald E. Chennault, eds., *White Reign: Deploying Whiteness in America* (New York: St. Martin's, 1998); Jane Lazarre, *Beyond the Whiteness of Whiteness: Memoir of a White Mother of Black Sons* (Durham, NC: Duke University Press, 1996); Robert G. Lee, *Orientals: Asian Americans in Popular Culture* (Philadelphia: Temple University Press, 1999); George Lipsitz, *The Possessive Investment in Whiteness: How White People Profit from Identity Politics* (Philadelphia: Temple University Press, 1998); Dana D. Nelson, *National Manhood: Capitalist Citizenship and the Imagined Fraternity of White Men* (Durham, NC: Duke University Press, 1998); Maureen Reddy, *Crossing the Color Line: Race, Parenting, and Culture* (New Brunswick, NJ: Rutgers University Press, 1994); Nelson M. Rodriguez and Leila E. Villaverde, eds., *Dismantling White Privilege: Pedagogy, Politics, and Whiteness* (New York: Peter Lang, 2000); David Roediger, *The Wages of Whiteness: Race and the Making of the American Working Class* (London: Verso, 1991); David Roediger, *Towards the Abolition of Whiteness* (London: Verso, 1994); David Roediger, *Black on White: Black Writers on What It Means to Be White* (New York: Schocken, 1998); Alexander Saxton, *The Rise and Fall of the White Republic: Class Politics and Mass Culture in Nineteenth-Century America* (London: Verso, 1990); Thandeka, *Learning to Be White: Money, Race, and God in America* (New York: Continuum, 1999); *Transition: The White Issue*, no. 73 (1996); Matt Wray and Annalee Newitz, eds., *White Trash: Race and Class in America* (New York: Routledge, 1997). For further examples, see the notes to chapter 3.

7. Some would argue that the majority of faculty positions in the humanities and social sciences are, in fact, already dedicated to Whiteness studies: European philosophy, English literature, Western Civilization, European art, etc.

8. Shirlee Taylor Haizlip, *The Sweeter the Juice: A Family Memoir in Black and White* (New York: Simon and Schuster, 1994).

9. Maria P. P. Root, "A Bill of Rights for Racially Mixed People," in Root, *Multiracial Experience*, 3–14.

10. Jacobson, *Whiteness of a Different Color*; Brodkin, *How Jews Became White Folks*; Roediger, *Wages of Whiteness*; Ignatiev, *How the Irish Became White*. For a more careful exposition of racial construction on the part of African Americans in the same period, see Michael A. Gomez, *Exchanging Our Country Marks: The Transformation of African Identities in the Colonial and Antebellum South* (Chapel Hill: University of North Carolina Press, 1998). For theoretical formulations of racial construction, see Cornell and Hartmann, *Ethnicity and Race*; Michael Omi and Howard Winant, *Racial Formation in the United States*, rev. ed. (New York: Routledge, 1994); Paul Spickard and W. Jeffrey Burroughs, eds., *We Are a People: Narrative and Multiplicity in Constructing Ethnic Identity* (Philadelphia: Temple University Press, 2000).

11. Aubyn Fulton, message posted to interracial individuals discussion list, ii-list@hcs.Harvard.edu (May 30, 1997); quoted in Rainier Spencer, *Spurious Issues: Race and Multiracial Identity Politics in the United States* (Boulder, CO: Westview, 1999), 197.

12. Ronald David Glass and Kendra R. Wallace, "Challenging Race and Racism: A Framework for Educators," in Root, *Multiracial Experience*, 341–58.

13. G. Reginald Daniel, "Passers and Pluralists: Subverting the Racial Divide," in Root, *Racially Mixed People*, 91–107; Paul Spickard, Rowena Fong, and Patricia Ewalt, "Undermining the Very Basis of Racism, Its Categories," *Social Work* 40.6 (1995): 725–28.

14. Delgado and Stefancic, *Critical White Studies*; Ignatiev and Garvey, *Race Traitor*.

15. Roediger, *Wages of Whiteness*.

16. Lipsitz, *Possessive Investment*.

17. In this early work, Spencer sees only two races in America: Black and White. He offers essentially no evidence for his South African analogy; Spencer, *New Colored People*.

18. Spencer, *Spurious Issues*, 167. Rainier Spencer's critique has become somewhat more subtle and discerning in subsequent volumes; see *Challenging Multiracial Identity* (Boulder, CO: Lynne Rienner, 2006) and *Reproducing Race: The Paradox of Generation Mix* (Boulder, CO: Lynne Rienner, 2011).

19. See my review of Werner Sollors, *Neither Black nor White Yet Both*, and Jon Michael Spencer, *The New Colored People: The Mixed-Race Movement in America*, in the *Journal of American Ethnic History* 18.2 (1999): 153–56.

20. Diana Jean Schemo, "Despite Options on Census, Many to Check 'Black' Only," *New York Times*, February 12, 2000, A1, A9.

21. Two other outstanding examples of critiques of the multiracial idea and movement are Jared Sexton, *Amalgamation Schemes: Antiblackness and the Critique of Multiracialism* (Minneapolis: University of Minnesota Press, 2008); and Michele Elam, *The Souls of Mixed Folk: Race, Politics, and Aesthetics in the New Millennium* (Stanford, CA: Stanford University Press, 2011). For analysis of Sexton's unfortunate book, see my review in *American Studies* 50.1–2 (Summer 2009): 125–27. Elam's is much more nuanced in its analysis, though it is marred by sloppy research.

22. Ignatiev, *How the Irish Became White*; Brodkin, *How Jews Became White Folks*.

23. Marie Hara and Nora Okja Keller, eds., *Intersecting Circles: The Voices of Hapa Women in Poetry and Prose* (Honolulu: Bamboo Ridge, 1999).

24. Danzy Senna, "The Mulatto Millennium," in *Half + Half*, ed. C. C. O'Hearn (New York: Pantheon, 1998), 12–27.

25. Lisa Jones, *Bulletproof Diva: Tales of Race, Sex, and Hair* (New York: Doubleday, 1994).

26. Kerry Ann Rockquemore, "Between Black and White: Exploring the Biracial Experience," *Race and Society* 1.2 (1998), 197–212; Brunsma and Rockquemore, *Beyond Black*.

27. Spencer, *Colored People*, 87; Schemo, "Despite Option."

28. Schemo, "Despite Option"; M. Royce Van Tassell, "Americans Are Tired of Racial Boxes: Vast Majority Want Government to 'Leave My Race Alone!,'" *The Egalitarian* 3.2 (2000): 1, 5.

29. Gregory Stephens, *On Racial Frontiers: The New Culture of Frederick Douglass, Ralph Ellison, and Bob Marley* (Cambridge: Cambridge University Press, 1999).

30. Hanna Wallinger, "Not Color but Character: Alice Dunbar-Nelson's Uncompleted Argument," in *Racial Thinking in the United States*, ed. Paul Spickard and G. Reginald Daniel (Notre Dame, IN: University of Notre Dame Press, 2004).

31. Paul Spickard and Laurie Mengel, "Deconstructing Race: The Multiethnicity of Sui Sin Far," *Books and Culture* (November 1997): 4–5; Annette White-Parks, *Sui Sin Far/Edith Maude Eaton* (Urbana: University of Illinois Press, 1995).

32. David Levering Lewis, *W. E. B. Du Bois: Biography of a Race* (New York: Holt, 1993); W. E. B. Du Bois, *Dusk of Dawn: An Essay toward an Autobiography of a Race Concept* (New Brunswick, NJ: Transaction, 1984; orig. 1940).

12

It's Not That Simple

Multiraciality, Models, and Social Hierarchy

WITH INGRID DINEEN-WIMBERLY

I am pointing to the moon with my finger in order to show it to you.

Why do you look at my finger and not at the moon?

—Shinran (thirteenth-century founder of Pure
Land Buddhism), *Collected Works of Shinran*

*When Ingrid Dineen-Wimberly and I were asked to contribute
an essay to a book on multiraciality and social class, it seemed
a good idea. It offered the chance to try to deal with class and
race together, something that we had been hoping to do in a
theoretical way. We are historians; the other seventeen contributors were sociologists or nearby sorts of social scientists. The
social scientific project yearns to discover what are presumed to
be the constant, underlying, universal laws of human behavior—
something like Plato's ideal types. In pursuit of that discovery,
social scientists make models and test them, trying to get ever
closer to the master model they believe lies beneath the surface
of human experience. That is what we perceived the other*

*authors in the volume to be doing, and it struck Ingrid and me
as slightly wide of the mark. Both this essay and chapter 13 describe my unease with the model-making aspect of social scientific inquiry. As historians, Ingrid and I tend to ask descriptive
rather than hypothesis-driven questions first. We work outward
from the stories of particular humans' lives. We construct generalizations, to be sure, but we are wary of proclaiming universal laws of human behavior, and we find that models often
obscure as much as they enlighten. We are grateful to Kathleen
Korgen, the editor of the book, for her initial invitation, for
many insightful suggestions, and for her personal grace as our
essay took on a shape she may not initially have envisioned.*

This essay is a meditation on the usefulness of models or typologies for
understanding racial hierarchy and social class, and specifically the racial
and class positioning of multiracial people of various sorts and in various
contexts. We begin by examining five models that have been put forward
regarding racial hierarchy and the social positioning of multiracial people.
Each describes a particular social and historical context; each has an argument about that context that may seem plausible to some advocates;
and each has flaws that stand out to other onlookers. Each helps us see
some things, even as it obscures others. In the second half of this essay, we
will consider another model: the one-drop rule, and its corollary assumption that it has always been advantageous in social class terms for racially
mixed people who could "pass" as White to do so. We find that model—
and in particular, its corollary theory about class mobility— leaves something to be desired. That, in turn, may cast doubt on the class assumptions
of some of the other models we examine in the first part of the essay.

The first typology is the idea espoused by Susan R. Graham, Charles
Byrd, Newt Gingrich, Ward Connerly, and a few other activists that multiraciality necessarily is a good thing because it constitutes a move toward
a postracial social order.[1] A leader in this vector of assertion is Graham,
who has pushed the notion that the creation of a multiracial category for

people of mixed ancestry is a step toward a happy future day when the United States will be "post racial[,] . . . [when] we have finally, gone beyond race, transcended it, and have become . . . color-blind."[2]

Newt Gingrich, spasmodically the darling of the Republican Party, in June 2007 spoke in favor of multiracialism as a step toward stopping all talk about race:

> [We need to take] action of the sort which will dramatically change people's lives. Let me now suggest 10 practical steps which, started today can build a better America and, in the process, close the racial divide: . . .
>
> RACIAL CLASSIFICATION —We must break down rigid racial classifications. A first step could be to add a "multiracial" category to the census and other government forms to begin to phase out the outdated, divisive, and rigid classification of Americans as "blacks" or "whites" or other single races. Ultimately, our goal is to have one classification—"American."[3]

Susan Graham regarded Gingrich as one of the great friends of the multiracial movement as she understood it.[4] Neither Graham nor Gingrich nor others like Ward Connerly, who made similar arguments, ever mentioned class in their campaigns for a particular version of multiraciality; they more or less pretended that class was not an issue. But it is worth pointing out that their individualistic ethic appealed mainly to middle- and upper-class Americans of whatever racial identity.

Racial conservatives, like Gingrich and Graham, who advocate multiraciality as a step toward a nonracial future have been the targets of a few writers like Rainier Spencer and Jared Sexton who oppose the very idea of a multiracial identity because they see the whole idea as tending in the direction that Graham and Gingrich advocate—toward a conservative-dream future where no one would ever talk about race again, and Black Americans would be left to rot.[5] The problem, of course, is that Gingrich and Graham do not stand for the multiracial movement, neither its activists nor its scholars. The notion espoused by Spencer and Sexton, that the goal of a multiracial identity is to end all talk about race, is nonsense. Most serious students of the multiracial movement, like most activists (and unlike Graham and Gingrich), do not see the advocacy of a multiracial identity as a step toward not talking about race any more. Rather, they see it as a practical, sensible, and humane way of understanding the complex racial identities of a large and growing number of people in a world that is racially very complex. Nonetheless, it is true that for most multiracialists, as for Graham and Gingrich (and also for their critics Sexton and Spencer), the question of class position never really comes up.[6]

A second, sometimes popular typology in the realm of multiraciality is the Brazilian model of Mulatto upward mobility and racial harmony espoused by Gilberto Freyre and later modified by Thomas Skidmore and Carl Degler. Freyre contrasted the harsh US system of racial segregation in the first half of the twentieth century with what he described as a broad "racial democracy" in Brazil, with lots of social and marital mixing between two large racial groups, White and Black, and consequently lots of multiracial people. Degler saw this, not as simple racial harmony across Brazil's entire population, but instead as a many-layered hierarchy of class, color, and racial mixture strung out between poor Blackness and rich Whiteness. He saw an attempt at upward mobility in the highlighting of one's multiraciality, and he called this the "Mulatto escape hatch"—out of Blackness and toward semi-Whiteness. Skidmore took this line of thinking further, contending that the ultimate goal of all this was to support White hegemony by Whitening most of the population as much as possible, and observed that this giving in to the White ideal stunted any real move for Black racial uplift.[7] More recently, G. Reginald Daniel and other critics have highlighted long-standing and pervasive Black-White racial conflict that Freyre, Degler, and even Skidmore's models tended to obscure. They have discerned, in the late twentieth and early twenty-first centuries, a move in Brazil and elsewhere in Latin America toward a North American–style Black-White divide.[8]

A third typology is the Mexican and Central American model of *mestizaje* first articulated by José Vasconcelos. Vasconcelos glorified Mexico's population as *la raza cósmica* (the cosmic race), which he represented as a spiritual and biological blending of Castilian and Indian peoples whose very mixture made Mexico a more spiritual and vigorous nation than any other. Vasconcelos and those who followed his lead in other parts of Central America were trying to provide ideological foundations for nationhood in an ideology of racial mixedness. Yet, even as this formulation recognized and built upon the racial blending of Native and European, it denied the existence of African, Asian, or other roots in the national experiment. It obscured the existence (and low class position) of Black- and Asian-descended people, and it tended to erase the troubles of Native peoples themselves by pretending they all were mestizos.[9]

Fourth, we turn to the idea pursued by George Yancey, that the US racial order is currently moving to a two-category, Black/non-Black division. Yancey believes that, in the not too distant future, Asian and Latino Americans will assimilate more or less completely and become White people, in their own eyes and in the eyes of other Americans, leaving only African-descended people as racial outsiders in American society (he doesn't tell us what will happen to other racialized groups like Native or Arab Americans). Yancey's vision has no room for multiracial people, except to imply that they should accept an uncomplicatedly monoracial Black identity. He writes:

> The changing nature of race relations will result in the merging of nonblack racial minorities into the dominant culture. . . . [T]he processes of assimilation that characterize European ethnic groups are the same social forces that influence nonblack racial minorities today. . . . [W]e may eventually see the development of a society in which blacks are separated from all, or at least most, other racial groups—or a black/nonblack society. . . . The development of a black/nonblack society challenges the notion . . . that our future racial reality will include a multiracial community that fights for racial justice. . . . African Americans will soon find themselves relatively alone in their struggle for racial justice.[10]

Almost all serious students of Latinos, Native Americans, Asian Americans, Arab Americans—or for that matter, of multiracial people—would simply disagree. Yancey offers very little evidence to support his argument, which seems to be based on little more than naked assertion. However, we should note that it is at least possible to infer a class critique from Yancey's typology. That is, his permanently Black group does seem like a working-class or lumpen proletarian bunch of people, and the other people he calls non-Blacks seem to occupy middle-class or upper-class positions. One might presume that he is making a class argument using racial terminology and saying that there is no place in this class argument for the multiracial possibility.

Fifth and finally, we turn to the admittedly speculative typology put forward by Eduardo Bonilla-Silva and David Embrick, which posits a subtler reconfiguration of American society than does Yancey: a three-part hierarchical division into White, Honorary White, and Collective Black. They write that "racial stratification in general and the rules of racial (re)cognition in the United States in particular are slowly coming to resemble those in Latin America." Here is their "Preliminary Map of the Triracial System in the United States":

Whites
Whites
New Whites (Russians, Albanians, etc.)
Assimilated white Latinos[11]
Some multiracials (white-looking ones)
Assimilated (urban) Native Americans
A few Asian-origin people

Honorary Whites
Light-skinned Latinos
Japanese Americans
Korean Americans
Asian Indians
Chinese Americans
Middle Eastern Americans
Most multiracials

Collective Black
Filipinos
Vietnamese

Hmong
Laotians
Dark-skinned Latinos
Blacks
New West Indian and African Immigrants
Reservation-bound Native Americans[12]

Again, as with Yancey, in Bonilla-Silva and Embrick's model the bottom group—the Collective Black—looks like a social class grouping more or less, though one marked using racial terminology. Indeed, the authors find some of the evidence for their model in income data (along with survey data on racial self-classification, degrees of intergroup warmth, and stereotypes). A strength of this model is that it helps us to see some gross class dynamics among different racialized groups. Yet, leaving aside whether their characterization of Latin America is apt, their model has several other flaws, chiefly that its generalizations about the United States are far too sweeping. It suggests that all Chinese and Middle Eastern Americans, for example, are pretty well off and that no African Americans, African immigrants, or Filipinos are; this is far from the case. The model posits a high race/class position for "white-looking" multiracial people but no place at all for darker people who have multiple ancestries; this omission goes unexplained. It misses the very important class and political dynamics between so-called mixed bloods and full-bloods on many American Indian reservations. And the model positively misplaces the majority of urban Indians in class terms (many are among the poorest dwellers of cities like Minneapolis, Seattle, and Los Angeles). No one who has spent much time in the western United States could put a lot of faith in a model as superficial and stereotypical as this.

Each of these typologies helps us understand some important things about the ways that race and class have worked in the United States and elsewhere in the Americas. So far we have described some of the distinctive contributions of each of these typologies and the things they help us see, even as we have offered a few gentle criticisms of their conclusions.

There are also important social dynamics that each model tends to obscure. For example, the Graham-Gingrich, Freyre-Degler-Skidmore, and Vasconcelos models suggest a far greater degree of racial harmony than actually has been the case in the three societies—the United States, Brazil, and Mexico—that they purport to describe. Vasconcelos, for example, describes the Mexican people as a triumphant blend of Castilian and Indian peoples while ignoring the very large quantum of African ancestry in the Mexican population and enduring racial and class discrimination against people with African ancestry, as well as the small but significant numbers of Filipinos, Chinese, and others.[13]

The Brazilian, Yancey, and Bonilla-Silva and Embrick typologies lay race out on a single Black-to-White racial continuum (although Bonilla-Silva and Embrick do so with somewhat more sophistication). The simple Black-to-White linearity of these models suggests that one's social position is a function of one's degree of Whiteness, for one is always being measured in terms of one's conformity to a White standard and proximity to White people. To the contrary, in both Brazil and the United States race has always been, from the sixteenth century to the present, not a bipolar continuum but a multipolar juxtaposition of several different racialized groups—always at least White, Black, and Red, and usually Brown and Yellow as well.[14]

With any model, it is easy for researchers, students, or policy makers to lose sight of the fact that it is a model, not the actual stuff of human experience. When a typology becomes reified—when people treat the model as if it were the real thing—danger of serious error creeps in. It is not the case that any of these is a complete representation of social experience. It is not the case that any of these—the Brazilian model, the White/Honorary White/Collective Black model, or any of the others (or for that matter, the one-drop rule)—in fact describes the central social experience of its time and place, compared to which individual examples may be seen as exceptions. Rather, such models are lenses that help us see certain things, even as they obscure other things.

FROM MODELS TO LIVES: THE ONE-DROP RULE AND ACTUAL SOCIAL EXPERIENCES

The one-drop rule, which is said by many commentators to have defined American race relations from sometime in the eighteenth or nineteenth century until past the middle of the twentieth, was a formal articulation of dominant ideas about how social relationships between White and Black (but not between White and Indian, White and Asian, White and Brown, Black and Brown, Asian and Black, Asian and Latino, or Black and Indian) people ought to be understood. The one-drop rule said that if one had "one drop of Black blood" (i.e., if one had a single known African-descended ancestor), then one was defined socially and legally as Black. Yet, even though the one-drop rule existed for a long time and had legal sanction in some places, it was only a social ideal. The actual social experience of racially mixed people in that era was much more complex.[15]

We want to explore some of that complexity, and we want to relate racial hierarchy to social class. To do this, we will look historically to the era of the one-drop rule, try to ascertain what shapes people's lives actually took, and compare those lives with the One Drop typology. The remainder of our essay describes the lives of several people of racially mixed ancestry who made different racial and class moves at various times over the course of the late nineteenth and early twentieth century.

There is a tendency in the study of mixed-race ethnicity to assume that individuals who could physically pass for White, and who chose to do so, did this in order to avoid racial discrimination or violence and to improve their life chances in social and economic terms. Many states, at various times in the nineteenth and twentieth centuries, had laws that allowed those who had one quarter or less Black ancestry to sue to become legally White. Even irrespective of the law, many thousands of light-skinned people who had some Black ancestry passed into the White population.

The advantages that might accrue from taking on a White identity would seem obvious. Jean Toomer, author of Cane, a novella that helped launch the Harlem Renaissance of the 1920s, came from a family that had lots of White ancestors and a few Black ones. Of his grandfather's several siblings, Toomer wrote, "Two . . . had left home . . . and were thereafter known as white. They had discarded a reputation less true to the racial facts for a reputation more true to the racial facts. They became in social fact what they so largely were in racial fact. Such an act, curiously enough, is called 'passing.' Speaking correctly, it would be much more accurate to say that my grandfather passed for a Negro, than to say that these brothers of his passed for white."[16]

From a shifted vantage point, however, our research has uncovered pivotal times in US history when mixed-race individuals and communities aligned more with their African or Native heritage than with their European, and accrued tangible benefits on account of that choice. After the Civil War, because new positions in Black leadership became available in US politics, business, and government, many racially ambiguous people passed for Black (if we may echo Toomer's phrase) and enjoyed a newfound upward mobility on account of their chosen Black identity. Among those in the next few generations whose physiognomies allowed them to choose, and who made the choice to be Black, were the pioneering Black journalist T. Thomas Fortune, the Reconstruction-era politician Blanche K. Bruce, the Progressive reformer Mary Church Terrell, the writer Alain Locke, the poet Langston Hughes, and the anti-lynching crusader Walter White, who led the NAACP for many years.[17]

We can see some of the complications of such matters in the lives and racial identity choices of the members of one family. For Belle da Costa Greene, passing from a Black identity to a White one indeed meant moving to a higher social class standing. Because her father was a well-known Black leader, she had to take on a new name in order to assume a White identity. This enabled her to apply for and win the position of director of the private library of J. P. Morgan, a White banker and at the time America's richest man. This move to Whiteness and name change were necessary for her, even though Morgan and her Black father were acquaintances.[18]

Greene's father, Richard T. Greener, had quite a different racial and career trajectory. Born a free man of color in Philadelphia in the 1840s, he associated with prominent abolitionists while still a teenager, and he attended Oberlin College, Phillips Academy, and Harvard, where he was remembered as the university's first African American graduate. In the 1880s he was prominent enough as a Black man to be appointed secretary to the board of the Ulysses S. Grant Monument. For the next few decades he worked closely in Black politics with Booker T. Washington and other luminaries. He served as dean of Howard Law School and later as a US foreign diplomat. Then, for reasons that are obscure, Richard Greener removed himself from the ranks of Black leadership. In so doing, he also reduced his legacy and, consequently, his status. He disappeared from the historical record; critics said he took on a White racial identity.[19]

Fig. 12.1.
US Senator Blanche K. Bruce of Mississippi. Courtesy of the Library of Congress.

P. B. S. Pinchback moved the other direction in much the same era. At the start of the Civil War, Pinchback met only modest success as a White sergeant in the Union Army. Then, changing his racial identity, as a Black captain he commanded a company of troops. After the war, as a Black politician, he became the Reconstruction-era lieutenant governor and then governor of Louisiana; he was elected to both the US House of

Fig. 12.2.
Mary Church Terrell, founder of the National Association of Colored Women.
Courtesy of the Library of Congress.

Fig. 12.3.
Belle da Costa
Greene. Courtesy of
the Morgan Library.

Representatives and the Senate; and he remained a powerful figure in African American politics throughout his life. Pinchback, in later conversations with his grandson Jean Toomer, did not fault his brothers for having chosen to pass for White, nor did he apologize for his own choice to pass for Black: "They had every right to be white. I have every right to be colored. They saw it to their advantage to do what they did. I saw it to my advantage to do what I did. . . . I realized I could make more head way if I were known as black. . . . Besides . . . I was more attached to our mother."[20]

Fig. 12.4.
Governor P. B. S. Pinchback of Louisiana. Courtesy of the Library of Congress.

Just as racial politics after the Civil War opened up Black leadership opportunities for part Black multiracial people, so racial politics at various times in the nineteenth century made the choice of an Indian identity advantageous for multiracial people of mixed White and Native descent. John Ross was the dominant figure in Cherokee national politics throughout the middle third of the nineteenth century, elected principal chief of the tribe in every election from 1828 to 1860. He was the son of a Scotch father and a Cherokee mother. He achieved and maintained his leadership position, not because of his proximity to Whiteness on account of his paternity, but on account of his mother's clan position within the Cherokee Nation. Among the Cherokee and other southeastern Indians, an individual's identity and tribal membership were reckoned according to the social location of one's maternal uncles. In another twist of racial hierarchy, even as Ross led a fierce defense of his people against the White invasion of Cherokee territory and the forcible removal of the Cherokee on the Trail of Tears, he also owned twenty slaves who produced the bulk of his personal wealth. When the Civil War came he tried to keep his tribe out of the conflict, though eventually they entered on the Confederate side.[21]

It is not that the lives of people such as Ross, Pinchback, Greener, and the other multiracial people who took on Black and Native identities and prospered were exceptions to a socially determinative one-drop rule. It is that the One Drop typology captures only certain features of the racial and class dynamics of the United States in the nineteenth and early twentieth century. Social reality was far more complicated than the model. In similar fashion, for all that the other models—Graham's romance of multiraciality as a path to a raceless future, Degler's Mulatto escape hatch, Vasconcelos's cosmic race, Yancey's Black/non-Black divide, and Bonilla-Silva and Embrick's triracial hierarchy—help us see certain possibilities and limits for multiracial people, we must remember that no model represents social reality fully. People's lives are not defined by any of these six models, nor are their personal struggles and choices simply a function of a model—in accordance with it or exceptions to it. Rather, their lives are their lives; their struggles are their struggles; their choices are their choices. Sometimes the models can help us see some things about those

Fig. 12.5.
Paramount chief John Ross of the Cherokee Nation. Courtesy of the J. B. Milan
Collection, Oklahoma Historical Society Research Division.

lives and struggles and choices, but inevitably they tend to prevent us from perceiving other things that may be just as important.

We do not mean to say that typologies are not helpful. Each of them is a lens that can help us see some things. Sociological models are aimed at helping us see social structural issues, and they may help us define and pursue positive social ends. If we can make better lenses, then perhaps we can see things more clearly and comprehensively and in turn begin to make a more just society. So it is important to consider models of reality that other scholars make as guides to our thinking when that seems helpful, and perhaps as encouragements to make better models of our own. Yet we ought not imagine that this is a simple, linear process of building better and better models to get closer and closer to some imagined underlying reality, like ancient Greek sculptors trying to make images ever more like, not the human bodies they saw around them, but the ideal types that Platonic philosophy told them were superior to actual human frames.

Models are useful, but they are not all equal. Models that work in one place do not always work equally well in another place. The model that Soviet imperial scholars constructed to understand the peoples of Central Asia looks very different from the model constructed by British imperial scholars for understanding the peoples of southern Africa.[22] What is more, in any single place, human life patterns shift over time, for, as the novelist L. P. Hartley put it, "The past is a foreign country: they do things differently there."[23] Things were different a hundred years ago than they are today; they will be different again in the future. And as we have seen, even in a single place and time—the United States at the recent turn of the century—different models may be constructed by people who wish to understand different aspects of a problem, or to pursue different sorts of outcomes, in this case the meaning and class implications of multiraciality.

Models are not magic; they must be used with care. The lens or typology or model is not the goal; it is a finger pointing in a direction that may help us see that goal. In the end, the loyalty of the authors of this chapter is not to models—sociological, philosophical, political, or any other sort—but to human lives as they have been lived and as they continue to be lived, in all their shifting complexity. We hope that the reader of this essay, of the other chapters in this book, and of other works of sociology will consider the models that are offered, learn from them, and then look beyond them for subtler shadings of insight than any model can give into the complex relationships that have existed between multiracial ancestry, racial identity choices, and social class.

NOTES

This essay appeared in *Multiracial Americans and Social Class*, ed. Kathleen Korgen (New York: Routledge, 2010), 205–21. I have made some corrections to errors that the copy editor of that book introduced and changed the reference format, but otherwise the essay is little changed from the original.

1. Charles Michael Byrd, *Interracial Voice* (magazine 1995–2003); Charles Michael Byrd, *The Bhagavad-Gita in Black and White: From Mulatto Pride to Krishna Consciousness* (Palm Coast, FL: Backintyme Books, 2007). On Connerly, see G. Reginald Daniel and Josef Manuel Castañeda-Liles, "Race, Multiraciality, and the Neoconservative Agenda," in *Mixed Messages: Multiracial Identities in the "Color-Blind" Era*, ed. David L. Brunsma (Boulder, CO: Lynne Rienner, 2006), 125–45.

2. Susan Graham, "Is This President Obama's Post-Racial America?," January 20, 2009, Project RACE website, www.projectrace.com/fromthedirector/archive/012009_obama_post_racial_america.php (retrieved April 25, 2009). See also Susan R. Graham, "The Real World," in *The Multiracial Experience*, ed. Maria P. P. Root (Thousand Oaks, CA: Sage, 1995), 15–36; Susan R. Graham, "Grassroots Advocacy," in *American Mixed Race*, ed. Naomi Zack (Lanham, MD: Rowman and Littlefield, 1995), 185–90; www.projectrace.com.

3. Newt Gingrich, speech to the Orphan Foundation of America, June 27, 2007; on Gingrich's website, newt.org/EditNewt/NewtNewsandOpinionDB/tabid/102/ArticleType/ArticleView/ArticleID/748/Default.aspx (retrieved April 25, 2009).

4. She wrote in 2001, after Gingrich had resigned from public office in the midst of personal scandal and rebellion in his own party, "He was on our side. The Speaker of the House, Newt Gingrich, was in our corner. Now he has resigned. . . . At our first one-on-one meeting I quickly outlined the problem of multiracial children and adults without a racial classification. I handed Newt a bound report with the history of the movement and statistics. He quickly flipped through the report, put it aside and said, 'This is the right thing to do for the children.' He outlined what he would do to help—it was an impressive list. Newt Gingrich sent a personal letter to the Director of the U.S. Bureau of the Census on our behalf. Newt Gingrich repeatedly included us in speeches. Newt Gingrich spoke to educators about the multiracial classification. . . . Newt's downfall was that he

surrounded himself with the wrong people," not that he had been forced to resign from his post as Speaker of the US House of Representatives in 1999 because of 84 charges of ethics violations, the loss of his leadership position in the house, a rebellion by House Republicans, and allegations of other improprieties. "Multiracial Life after Newt," November 9, 2001, Project RACE website, www.project race.com/fromthedirector/archive/fromthedirector-110998.php (retrieved April 25, 2009).

5. Rainier Spencer, "Census 2000: Assessments in Significance," in *New Faces in a Changing America: Multiracial Identity in the 21st Century*, ed. Loretta I. Winters and Herman L. DeBose (Thousand Oaks, CA: Sage, 2002), 99–110; Rainier Spencer, *Spurious Issues: Race and Multiracial Identity Politics in the United States* (Boulder, CO: Westview, 1999); Jared Sexton, *Amalgamation Schemes: Antiblackness and the Critique of Multiracialism* (Minneapolis: University of Minnesota Press, 2008).

6. For expositions of this view, see Maria P. P. Root, ed., *The Multiracial Experience* (Thousand Oaks, CA: Sage, 1996); G. Reginald Daniel, *More than Black? Multiracial Identity and the New Racial Order* (Philadelphia: Temple University Press, 2002); Teresa Williams-León and Cynthia Nakashima, eds., *The Sum of Our Parts: Mixed-Heritage Asian Americans* (Philadelphia: Temple University Press, 2001); Greg Carter, *The United States of the United Races: A Utopian History of Racial Mixing* (New York: New York University Press, 2013).

7. Gilberto Freyre, *The Masters and the Slaves: A Study in the Development of Brazilian Civilization*, trans. Samuel Putnam (New York: Knopf, 1956; orig. 1933); Carl N. Degler, *Neither Black nor White: Slavery and Race Relations in Brazil and the United States* (New York: Macmillan, 1971); Thomas E. Skidmore, *Black into White: Race and Nationality in Brazilian Thought*, rev. ed. (Durham, NC: Duke University Press, 1993, orig. 1974).

8. G. Reginald Daniel, *Race and Multiraciality in Brazil and the United States* (University Park: Pennsylvania State University Press, 2006).

9. José Vasconcelos, *The Cosmic Race/La raza cósmica*, trans. Didier T. Jaén (Baltimore: Johns Hopkins University Press, 1997; orig. 1979); Colin M. MacLachlan and Jaime E. Rodriguez O., *The Forging of the Cosmic Race: A Reinterpretation of Colonial Mexico* (Berkeley: University of California Press, 1980). For critiques, see Virginia Q. Tilley, "*Mestizaje* and the 'Ethnicization' of Race in Latin America," in *Race and Nation: Ethnic Systems in the Modern World*, ed. Paul Spickard (New York: Routledge, 2004), 53–68; and Marilyn Grace Miller, *The Rise and Fall of the Cosmic Race: The Cult of Mestizaje in Latin America* (Austin: University of Texas Press, 2004). For reassertions of the concept, see Raphael Pérez-Torres, *Mestizaje: Critical Uses of Race in Chicano Culture* (Minneapolis: University of Minnesota Press, 2006); and Peter Wade, "Rethinking *Mestizaje*: Ideology and Lived Experience," *Journal of Latin American Studies* 37 (2005): 239–57.

10. George Yancey, "Racial Justice in a Black/Nonblack Society," in Brunsma, *Mixed Messages*, 49–62. See also George Yancey, *Who Is Black? Latinos, Asians, and the New Black/Nonblack Divide* (Boulder, CO: Lynne Rienner, 2003). Yancey is also the editor, along with his wife, Sherelyn Whittum Yancey, of *Just Don't Marry One: Interracial Dating, Marriage, and Parenthood* (Valley Forge, PA: Judson Press, 2003).

11. We assume they mean "White-looking Latinos." We have no idea what "White Latinos" might be. Presumably these are lighter people than the "Light-skinned Latinos" in the second section, but one cannot know for sure.

12. Eduardo Bonilla-Silva and David G. Embrick, "Black, Honorary White, White: The Future of Race in America?," in Brunsma, *Mixed Messages*, 33–48; see also Eileen O'Brien, *The Racial Middle: Latinos and Asians Living beyond the Racial Divide* (New York: New York University Press, 2008).

13. Daniel, *Race and Multiraciality in Brazil and the United States*; Jeffrey Lesser, *Negotiating National Identity: Immigrants, Minorities, and the Struggle for Ethnicity in Brazil* (Durham, NC: Duke University Press, 1999); Lillian Guerra, *The Myth of José Martí: Conflicting Nationalisms in Early Twentieth-Century Cuba* (Chapel Hill: University of North Carolina Press, 2005); Stephen Small, "Muste-finos are White by Law: Whites and People of Mixed Racial Origins in Historical and Comparative Perspective," in *Racial Thinking in the United States*, ed. Paul Spickard and G. Reginald Daniel (Notre Dame, IN: University of Notre Dame Press, 2004), 60–79; Ada Ferrer, *Insurgent Cuba: Race, Nation, and Revolution, 1868–1898* (Chapel Hill: University of North Carolina Press, 1999).

14. See the references in note 13 above, and also Tomás Almaguer, *Racial Fault Lines: The Historical Origins of White Supremacy in California* (Berkeley: University of California Press, 1994); Gary B. Nash, *Red, White, and Black: The Peoples of Early America*, 5th ed. (Upper Saddle River, NJ: Prentice Hall, 2006); Paul Spickard, *Almost All Aliens: Immigration, Race, and Colonialism in American History and Identity* (New York: Routledge, 2007); Martha Menchaca, *Recovering History, Constructing Race: The Indian, Black, and White Roots of Mexican Americans* (Austin: University of Texas Press, 2001); David Luis-Brown, *Waves of Decolonization: Discourses of Race and Hemispheric Citizenship in Cuba, Mexico, and the United States* (Durham, NC: Duke University Press, 2008).

15. Spickard and Daniel, eds., *Racial Thinking in the United States*; F. James Davis, *Who Is Black? One Nation's Definition* (University Park: Pennsylvania State University Press, 1991); Daniel, *More than Black?*; Matthew Guterl, *The Color of Race in America, 1900–1940* (Cambridge, MA: Harvard University Press, 2004); Winthrop D. Jordan, "Historical Origins of the One-Drop Racial Rule in the United States," ed. Paul Spickard, *Journal of Critical Mixed-Race Studies* 1 (2013): 98–132.

16. Jean Toomer Papers, James Weldon Johnson Collection, JWJ MSS. Series 1, b. 18: f. 493, handwritten draft of autobiography (Yale College of American Life, Beinecke Rare Book and Manuscript Library, Yale University, New Haven, CT), 41.

17. Ingrid Dineen-Wimberly, "Mixed-Race Leadership in African America: The Regalia of Race and National Identity in the US, 1862–1903" (PhD diss., University of California, Santa Barbara, 2009); Ingrid Dineen-Wimberly, "By the Least Bit of Blood: The Allure of Blackness among Mixed-Race Americans of African Descent, 1862–1935" (unpublished MS).

18. The reader should note that Belle changed her surname by dropping the letter *r* in order to make her transition from Black to White. In the hope of affecting a Portuguese heritage, which might then explain her olive complexion, she added "da Costa." The first official reference to Belle da Costa Greene (from her birth name, Marion Greener) was recorded in the US Census in 1900. See Heidi Ardizzone, *An Illuminated Life: Belle da Costa Greene's Journey from Prejudice to Privilege* (New York: Norton, 2007). Compare the mobility experienced due to White connections or a White identity move in the lives of Amanda America Dickson and Anatole Broyard: Kent Anderson Leslie, *Woman of Color, Daughter of Privilege: Amanda America Dickson, 1849–1893* (Athens: University of Georgia Press, 1996); Anatole Broyard, *Kafka Was the Rage: A Greenwich Village Memoir* (New York: Vintage, 1997); Bliss Broyard, *One Drop: My Father's Hidden Life—A Story of Race and Family Secrets* (Boston: Back Bay Books, 2008).

19. Allison Blakely, "Richard Theodore Greener and the 'Talented Tenth's' Dilemma," *Journal of Negro History* 59.4 (1974): 305–21; "Richard T. Greener: The First Black Harvard College Graduate," in *Blacks at Harvard*, ed. Werner Sollors, Caldwell Titcomb, and Thomas A. Underwood (New York: New York University Press, 1993), 37–41; Michael Robert Mounter, "Richard Theodore Greener: The Idealist, Statesman, Scholar and South Carolinian" (PhD diss., University of South Carolina, 2002). Compare the life trajectories of the novelists Nella Larsen and the young Jean Toomer: Thadious M. Davis, *Nella Larsen, Novelist of the Harlem Renaissance: A Woman's Life Unveiled* (Baton Rouge: Louisiana State University Press, 1996); George Hutchinson, *In Search of Nella Larsen: A Biography of the Color Line* (Cambridge, MA: Harvard University Press, 2006); Cynthia Earl Kerman and Richard Eldridge, *The Lives of Jean Toomer: A Hunger for Wholeness* (Baton Rouge: Louisiana State University Press, 1989).

20. Toomer draft autobiography, JWJ MSS. Series 1, b. 18: f. 493 (Beinecke Library), 30; James Haskins, *Pinckney Benton Stewart Pinchback* (New York: Macmillan, 1973). For a move in the direction of postracialism, compare the life of Philippa Schuyler and the later career of Jean Toomer: Kathryn Talalay, *Composition in Black and White: The Life of Philippa Schuyler* (New York: Oxford University Press, 1997); Kerman and Eldridge, *Lives of Jean Toomer*; Rudolph P. Byrd, *Jean Toomer's Years with Gurdieff* (Athens: University of Georgia Press, 1991).

21. Gary E. Moulton, *John Ross, Cherokee Chief* (Athens: University of Georgia Press, 1978); Theda Perdue, *"Mixed Blood" Indians: Racial Construction in the Early South* (Athens: University of Georgia Press, 2003); Circe Sturm, *Blood Politics: Race, Culture, and Identity in the Cherokee Nation of Oklahoma* (Berkeley: University of California Press, 2002). See also Claudio Saunt, *A New Order of Things: Property, Power, and the Transformation of the Creek Indians, 1733–1816* (Cambridge: Cambridge University Press, 1999); John Walton Caughey, *McGillivray of the Creeks* (Columbia: University of South Carolina Press, 2007; orig. 1939).

22. This is one of the major theoretical points in Paul Spickard, ed., *Race and Nation: Ethnic Systems in the Modern World* (New York: Routledge, 2005). See especially Adrienne Edgar, "The Fragmented Nation: Genealogy, Identity, and Social Hierarchy in Turkmenistan," 257–72; and T. Dunbar Moodie, "Race and Ethnicity in South Africa: Ideology and Experience," 319–36.

23. L. P. Hartley, *The Go-Between* (New York: Stein and Day, 1967; orig. 1953), 1; cf. David Lowenthal, *The Past Is a Foreign Country* (Cambridge: Cambridge University Press, 1985).

13

Obama Nation?

Race, Multiraciality, and American Identity

I am the son of a black man from Kenya and a white woman from Kansas. I was raised with the help of a white grandfather who survived a Depression to serve in Patton's Army during World War II and a white grandmother who worked on a bomber assembly line at Fort Leavenworth while he was overseas. I've gone to some of the best schools in America and lived in one of the world's poorest nations. I am married to a black American who carries within her the blood of slaves and slaveowners—an inheritance we pass on to our two precious daughters. I have brothers, sisters, nieces, nephews, uncles, and cousins, of every race and every hue, scattered across three continents, and for as long as I live, I will never forget that in no other country on Earth is my story even possible.[1]

Thus spoke Barack Obama on March 18, 2008, at the National Constitution Center in Philadelphia. Responding to widespread public criticism of his pastor, Rev. Jeremiah Wright, candidate Obama issued what many took to be a call for Americans to look beyond race in thinking about the future of their country. I believe he was hoping to point us in rather a different direction: toward an honest conversation about race, something the United States has not had in a very long time.

Obama is an iconic figure in America's racial history. On one hand, he represents racially what the United States has always been—a complicated mixing of peoples and identities that defies simple categorization. He also represents something distinctive about this particular moment in our racial history. In both these senses, historical and contemporary, we may be something like an Obama nation.[2]

Barack Obama is, to be sure, a man of multiracial parentage. Yet, at least since his university days, he has chosen to identify himself, not as a multiracial person, but simply as a Black American. He described his student years as a struggle

> to escape from . . . my own inner doubt. . . . I was more like the students who had grown up in the suburbs, kids whose parents had already paid the price of escape. You could spot them right away by the way they talked, the people they sat with in the cafeteria. When pressed, they would sputter and explain that they refused to be categorized. They weren't defined by the color of their skin, they would tell you. They were individuals.
>
> That's how Joyce liked to talk. . . . "I'm not black," Joyce said. "I'm *multiracial*." Then she started telling me about her father, who *happened* to be Italian and was the sweetest man in the world; and her mother, who *happened* to be part African and part French and part Native American and part something else. "Why should I have to choose between them?" she asked me. Her voice cracked, and I thought she was going to cry. "It's not white people who are making me choose. Maybe it used to be that way, but now they're willing to treat me like a person. No—it's *black people* who always have to make everything racial. *They're* the ones making me choose. *They're* the ones who are telling me that I can't be who I am. . . . "
>
> They, they, they. That was the problem with people like Joyce. They talked about the richness of their multicultural heritage and it sounded real good, until you noticed that they avoided black people.[3]

Obama took another path—into the heart of monoracial, political Blackness. As much as he loves body surfing with his friends back in Honolulu, as much as he cherishes the memory of his young years in Indonesia and his Kenyan relatives, it was in Black Chicago as a community organizer that he found his racial home. Obama, in his own mind, is *from* Hawai'i, but he is *of* Chicago. He is a Black man.[4]

Yet Obama is a special kind of Black man—maybe the only kind who could be elected president, even in an era that imagines itself enlightened about race. I trust I will not incite the feigned horror of the conservative press if I observe that one of the things that made Barack Obama acceptable to White voters was that we knew his story, and we knew it to be different from the story of, say, Jesse Jackson or Al Sharpton or Charlie Rangel. We knew that he was raised not in Philadelphia or Shreveport but in exotic Hawai'i, not by his Black father (who in any case was descended not from American slaves but from seemingly elite Kenyans); rather he was nurtured and taught life's ways by his hippie mother and his cracker grandparents. Those features of Obama's biography moved him enough off the center of Blackness that White voters could hear his voice in a way they could not hear Jackson's or Sharpton's or Rangel's: not through a filter of Blackness, but as a comforting presence they knew to be as skilled in the ways of Whiteness as he was in the ways of Blackness.

Let me be clear. Barack Obama is not a savior of America's racial soul. His presidency, even if it comes to be regarded universally as a splendid success, will not put an end to the relevance of race in American public life. Obama knows this, as do most thoughtful Americans.[5] Race dwells too deeply in the warp and woof of everything we are and do for it to suddenly become irrelevant. Nonetheless, this is an unprecedented, hopeful moment in our history, and we ought not despise that.

In this chapter, I would like first to offer some reflections on America's racial history, and in particular the history of racial mixing. Then I will attempt to assess the ways that scholars and popular writers have portrayed the meaning of racial mixing. In the past two decades a new field—multiracial studies—was born and has grown like Topsy. I had a hand in that founding and growth.[6] I will suggest a few ways that I believe that movement has fallen short, and also some directions that it might take from here. Finally, I will attempt to assess the meaning of Barack Obama as a racial figure in America's history.

RACE IN AMERICA

Race in America is not, and has never been, just about White and Black. The racial systems that Americans have devised and periodically revised have always been about Black, Red, and White, and in many places and times about Brown and Yellow as well.[7] African American slavery is America's national sin, but it is not the only set of racialized relationships in play in any time or any place in United States history.

I say "racialized relationships" because I do not take race to be a tangible thing but rather a set of relationships between groups of people who perceive themselves to be different, and usually unequal. I have argued elsewhere that race is a language, used to describe the power relationships that exist and are carried out between peoples; that race is a story about power that is written on the body. It is a story that tells who I think you are, who your parents were, and what your life chances ought to be, a story written on your features as I perceive them.[8] That is, race makes use of physical markers (and, increasingly these days, of genetic markers) in order to pursue political ends between peoples. Although, like most racial theorists, I argue that race is a set of ideas fashioned by people whose identities we know, for purposes we can at least guess, that is not to say that race is not consequential. People kill people over race, and even in less extreme cases, many people's life chances are sharply curtailed and others' superabundantly blessed on account of their racial placements.

The US racial system has evolved in such a way that five very large panethnicities, or races—Black, White, Native American, Asian American, and Latino—have taken on the role of major categories.[9] Each of these panethnicities brings together in one conceptual whole a congeries of different peoples. Recent African immigrants, Haitians, Jamaicans, and other West Indians, and African Americans whose ancestors were slaves in North America (themselves with roots from many African groups) all are treated more or less as Black people in the American system.[10] American Indians include people of many different tribes, people whose ancestry is a mixture of different tribal origins, and people whose ancestry also contains European- or African-descended people.[11] Similar lumping together of disparate people has attended the forming and sustaining of the White, Asian, and Latino panethnic groups.[12]

There is nothing natural or inevitable about this configuration. The racialized map of Germany, Japan, Brazil, or Malaysia looks quite different from the US variety. In the census of the United Kingdom, when last I checked, the eight racial categories were "White, Black Caribbean, Black African or Black Other (please specify), Indian, Pakistani, Bangladeshi, Chinese, and Any Other Ethnic Group (please describe)."[13] In Malaysia, the relevant racialized groups are Malay, Chinese, and Indian.[14] In Germany, the major divide that is ordinarily recognized lies between ethnic Germans (who are simply German, whether or not they were born in Germany or hold German citizenship) and non-ethnic-German peoples, who are all presumed to be immigrants, are racialized as other and experience little to no social inclusion.[15]

RACIAL MIXTURE IN AMERICAN HISTORY

Racial mixing is not a new thing in the United States. We are commonly told that since the 1970s and with increasing velocity there has been a "multiracial baby boom." That is, it is asserted that in the last third of the twentieth century and into the twenty-first, more people have been marrying, having sex, and bearing babies across racial boundaries than ever before in history.[16]

Well, maybe not so much. In fact, there has always been a whole lot of racial mixing in the United States. Gary Nash, in his 1995 presidential address to the Organization of American Historians, called this the "hidden history of mestizo America."[17] As Winthrop Jordan taught us four decades ago and Martha Menchaca reminded us more recently, interracial sex—among Europeans, Africans, and Native North Americans—was probably more common in the eighteenth century than at any later time in US history.[18] In what was to become the northern provinces of Mexico, and still later the US Southwest from Texas to California, Spaniards, Africans, and many different sorts of Native peoples mixed under conditions that sometimes involved compulsion, sometimes contract, sometimes romance, and oftentimes more than one of those dimensions. The mixing, and fluctuating racial positionings for the complicatedly mixed offspring, continued in that region through the nineteenth century and on through the twentieth.[19]

In the eastern provinces of central North America (what became the eastern and southeastern United States), interracial mixing took three predominant forms in the eighteenth century. In one instance, sex, cohabitation, and marriage were common between White indentured servants (usually women) and African-derived men (sometimes slaves, sometimes servants). The children of such unions sometimes became free Blacks, but probably just as often, they slid into the White working-class population; a third portion were enslaved.[20] In another colonial-era instance of meeting and mating, White men who lived and worked in Indian Country were taken as husbands by Native women; their children most often followed the lineage customs of Native peoples and became members (sometimes leaders) of tribes like the Cherokee and Creek. The third common pattern in this period consisted of unions that were formed between runaway slaves and members of various Native American tribes in the Southeast; their children, too, most often became Indians.[21]

As the slave regime hardened over the course of the first half of the nineteenth century, so too did the line between Black and White. It is to this era that we owe the invention of the one-drop rule: the custom, sometimes codified in law, that one drop of Black blood—one known African-descended ancestor—made one Black. In the Antebellum era, it is likely that interracial mixing between White and Black declined in frequency, and it took on a new characteristic shape. Now most interracial sex occurred between men of the master class and women and girls of the slave class. Usually it was brutally compelled; that is the dominant fact we must not forget. Yet in some instances there seem to have been long-standing arrangements between White masters and slave women that approximated marriage. And there are hints of a small number of relationships that broke what at that time had fairly recently become the strongest taboo: sex between Black men and White women.[22]

The fact that interracial sex was forbidden by law and custom meant that any such unions, whether fully compelled or possessing an element of volition, could not be publicly acknowledged. The emerging one-drop rule and the financial imperatives of slavery meant that most children born of interracial sex in the Antebellum period became Black slaves, but some small number were set free or ran away to freedom in the North. In time they came to form the beigeoisie—the light-skinned leadership class of African America—that emerged more fully after the Civil War.[23]

Just as racial mixing is not a new thing, so, too, complex, shifting relationships to racial identity on the part of racially mixed people are not new things, despite the seeming solidity of the one-drop rule. P. B. S. Pinchback was born in Georgia in the era of slavery, a free person who was known to have a little African parentage. He entered the Civil War on the Union side as a White sergeant and emerged a Black captain; his brothers remained on the White side of the color line. Pinchback went on to become a Reconstruction-era politician in Louisiana, served as lieutenant governor and governor, and was elected to but not seated in both the US House of Representatives and the Senate. He lived out his days on the Gold Coast in Washington, DC, home to the beigeoisie of the nation's capital, one of the most prominent African American leaders in the Republican Party, even though he always maintained a consciousness of his mixed identity and only gingerly embraced unmixed African Americans.

Similarly complicated racial positionings were carried out by many other figures who are often thought of as monoracial African Americans, including the abolitionist Robert Purvis; the great Black novelist Charles W. Chesnutt; Jean Toomer, herald of the Harlem Renaissance; the archetypal African American intellectual, W. E. B. Du Bois; the NAACP executive secretary and anti-lynching crusader Walter White; and the reform leaders Adella Hunt Logan and Mary Church Terrell.[24]

People of part Native ancestry also led racially complex lives. Alexander McGillivray led his people, the Creek Indians, in defiance of White encroachment in the late 1700s. John Ross served the Cherokee Nation as paramount chief for half a century, from before the Trail of Tears until after the Civil War. Both had Native mothers and Scotch fathers. By contrast, Charles Curtis, as Indian of ancestry as either Ross or McGillivray, was elected vice president of the United States in the 1920s as a more-or-less White man, although one known to have some Native ancestry.[25] And

Fig. 13.1.
Abolitionist Robert Purvis. Courtesy of the Simon Gratz Collection, Image no. 2137,
Historical Society of Pennsylvania.

Fig. 13.2.
Novelist Charles W.
Chesnutt. Courtesy
of the Cleveland
Public Library.

people from other racial groups also mixed, mated, and took on complicated racial identities. At the dawn of the twentieth century, Edith Maude
Eaton and her sister Winnifred, the children of a White British man and
a Chinese woman, pursued literary careers in the United States under the
pen names Sui Sin Far and Onoto Watanna. About the same time, Robert
Wilcox was just one of many part-Hawaiian, part-White people who attempted to defend Hawai'i against American imperialism.[26]

All this manifest racial mixing, however, was obscured in the public
imagination with the rise in the second half of the nineteenth century of
a mania for racialist science. This movement, which also led to immigration restriction and eugenics, held that there were four or five distinct
races of humankind and that mixing between them was unnatural and led
inevitably to physical, mental, and moral decline.[27] Even though a very
large part of the American population had mixed ancestry, some of it
quite recent, and even though a lot of people were mating and marrying

Fig. 13.3.
Vice President Charles Curtis. Courtesy of the Kansas State Historical Society.

Fig. 13.4.
Novelist and screenwriter Winnifred Eaton before she became Onoto Watanna.
Courtesy of the Glenbow Museum, Calgary, image no. NA-4320-2.

Fig. 13.5. Hawaiian nationalist Robert Wilcox. Courtesy of the Hawaiian Historical Society.

across racial lines, the intellectual pressure to see only pure, discrete races was overwhelming. The monoracial myth prevailed.

So, if a whole lot of people mated and more than a few married, and in both instances a lot of them had children, across racial lines in earlier periods in American history, what then is new in the last decades of the twentieth century and the first decades of the twenty-first? It is not that we have a dramatically larger number of mixed people but that we are beginning to see those people as mixed. We are also beginning to see racial mixing, mating, and marriage as normal, not aberrant—as part of the core experience of being Americans, not as something epiphenomenal. That is a huge change, but it is as much a change of consciousness as it is a change of demography or social behavior. This change of consciousness is built on the positive social value attached to interracial socializing that arose out of the Civil Rights movement. In that sense, it is a change of social etiquette.

It is true that since the 1970s or so, and with increasing frequency and social penetration each decade since, more people who have seen themselves as members of one racialized group—say, Latinos—have met, worked, studied, and socialized with people who have perceived themselves as Blacks, Whites, Asians, Arabs, or members of other groups. In addition, as the stigma that once attached to interracial mating has abated, more and more people who know they possess multiple ancestries have come to embrace that multiplicity. Many of them, probably most, still think of themselves, and are perceived by those around them, as mono racial people, White or Black or whatever. But they no longer so freely ignore their multiplicity. And a rapidly increasing number of people have come to identify themselves as racially multiple.[28]

WRITING ABOUT MULTIRACIALITY—
SOME DEAD ENDS

We see all these things quite a bit more clearly today than we did twenty-five years ago, when I wrote a book called *Mixed Blood*.[29] This is largely because of an outpouring of literature—history, biography, sociology, literary and cultural criticism, even some psychological studies—the scope of which can only be suggested in the notes to this essay. Two and a half decades ago, I think I saw the outlines of what a couple of hundred scholars have come to find out in recent years. But I never cease to be amazed at how richly they have documented and analyzed the phenomenon of interracial mixing and mating, the constructed and performed qualities of race itself, the identity situations of multiracial people, and the political implications of all these things.

One of the ways that I misspent my time in writing *Mixed Blood* was in trying to seek out what many took to be the underlying sociological laws of intermarriage behavior and racial identification. In this move, I was a child of the sociological turn in historical studies that consumed so much effort during the 1960s, 1970s, and beyond.[30] Like social scientists dating back to early in the twentieth century, I tried to tease out and evaluate theories about

- what sociological circumstances tend to encourage or inhibit inter-marriage;
- which groups (and which sorts of individuals within such groups) tend to marry which other sorts of people from which other groups; and
- the ethnic identity placements of racially mixed people.

Very distinguished social scientists—people like Bruno Lasker, Romanzo Adams, Robert Merton, Kingsley Davis, Ruby Jo Reeves Kennedy, Milton Gordon, and Harry Kitano—had all spent enormous energy theorizing about such issues and then testing their hypotheses.[31]

It is not that I don't think there are discernible patterns to intergroup romance, mating, and marriage, nor to the identity situations of mixed people. But I have come over the years increasingly to be convinced that most of the so-called laws of intergroup mixing are just wrong. Seeking after them may be a fool's errand. For instance, Merton, Davis, and others posited the law of "hypergamy," where lower-caste men of unusual achievement or wealth marry up by partnering with higher-caste women. This law asserts that the men in question trade their tangible wealth or celebrity for the higher caste status of the women they marry.[32] This assumes some things that are by no means universally agreed upon: for example, that men are active and women passive, or that we all can agree on which direction is up, socially speaking. It also flies in the face of a whole lot of intergroup mating that has actually taken place, including slavery-era relationships between White men and slave concubines. If we are seeking after ironclad rules for who marries whom and why, or who takes on which identity, the only rule I can be sure of is this one: It depends.

Then there is the matter of "passing." Usually, this has been taken to refer to people of mixed ancestry (who according to the one-drop rule were really Black) choosing not to be Black but passing for White. Well, maybe. But if that be true, then were Walter White, W. E. B. Du Bois, and other multiracial, White-looking African American–identified leaders passing for Black? I asked that question gently in *Mixed Blood* and a subsequent essay, and I took a good deal of grief for having suggested it. I was told that passing went only one way, from truly Black to falsely White. I was told further that passing is a fraud, a deception, and an abandonment of one's people. Those who scolded me spoke in tones like those of Alice Walker, as she lamented the complex and fluctuating racial identity choices that the great Harlem Renaissance author, Jean Toomer, made over the course of his lifetime. Walker said she had

> feelings of disappointment and loss. Disappointment because the man who wrote so piercingly of "Negro" life in *Cane* chose to live his own life as a white man, while [Langston] Hughes, [Zora Neale] Hurston, Du Bois, and other black writers were celebrating the blackness in themselves as well as in their work. Loss because it appears this choice undermined Toomer's moral judgment: there were things [White racism] in American life and in his own that he simply refused to see.[33]

Regardless of whether Walker oversimplified the racial positionings of Hughes, Hurston, and Du Bois (I believe she did), I am quite certain that she mistook what Jean Toomer was up to. Toomer thought he knew who he was—not simply a monoracial Black man, but a man of multiple ancestries and identities in a nation that did not then recognize such multiplicity. Many decades before others took up the theme, Toomer asserted the constructedness of race and proclaimed a vision of a society that was not completely constrained by race. He lived his life accordingly, not as a White man as Walker contends, but not always as a monoracially Black man either.[34]

In the years since I wrote that if some mixed people were passing for unmixed White, then others surely were passing for Black, we have come to understand that not all mixed people who identify as White do so simply to escape Blackness. Some surely do, but some people of mixed origins like P. B. S. Pinchback have passed for unmixed Black, with the purpose to achieve tangible benefits in employment, power, and social status. Was Pinchback a fraud? And some like Toomer have moved back and forth between identities over the course of their lifetimes. Some other people with mixed ancestry like John Ross or Robert Wilcox have passed for Indian or for Hawaiian. Perhaps most important, we have begun to see that passing is not necessarily a fiction or a fraud. It may simply be an expression of who one actually is: like Jean Toomer (and, for that matter, White and Du Bois), a racially complex person. Perhaps it is time to recognize that we have been trapped in a trope for too long; perhaps it will serve us better to retire the term *passing* altogether.

WHAT RACE MIXING DOES NOT MEAN, AND WHAT IT DOES

There has been considerable dispute about what may be the meaning of interracial sex, intermarriage, and multiracial people. A lot of the people who wrote about intermarriage from the 1940s through the 1960s assumed that intermarriage was a sure sign that racialized divisions were on the decline and that in the case of the couples in question, at least, racial differences, and racism itself, had pretty much been erased. Milton Gordon suggested as much:

> If marital assimilation, an inevitable by-product of structural assimilation, takes place, fully, the minority group loses its ethnic identity in the larger host or core society, and identificational assimilation takes place. Prejudice and discrimination are no longer a problem, since eventually the descendants of the original minority group become indistinguishable, and since primary group relationships tend to build up an "in-group" feeling which encloses all the members of the group.[35]

In recent decades, a number of scholars have taken pains to point out that racialized relationships—indeed, pretty blatantly racist attitudes, words, and actions—often exist within interracial couples. Often, it is observed, White men, for example, choose Asian or Latina partners for reasons having to do with their own racist stereotypes about sexy, submissive women, and some scholars suggest that racism pervades a lot of mixed relationships. Similar racist imagery may affect a lot of Black or Asian men and women who choose White partners.[36] I think that some of the scholars who perceive and emphasize racist qualities in the partners to intermarriages probably overstate their case, but for sure, the fact of intermarriage does not mean that racism has disappeared.

Neither does multiracial identity mean the end of racism, much less the end of race. Susan Graham, the White mother of multiracial, part Black children, was in the 1990s the most prominent political activist working to add a multiracial category to the US Census. She continues well into the new century to push the notion that the creation of a multiracial category for people of mixed ancestry would be a step toward a happy future day when the United States would be "post racial[,] . . . [when] we have finally, gone beyond race, transcended it, and have become . . . color-blind."[37] Well, no. Graham is a social conservative who, it seems possible to me, may have been intent on saving her daughters from what she saw as the sad fate of having to grow up as Black people in America, and so she may have sought a middle racial status for them. But very few multiracial activists or scholars who study multiraciality would support Graham's extreme interpretation, and most would repudiate it. A great deal of the scholarship that has emerged in the past decade, in fact, has carefully examined the ways that racism continues to operate in the context of racial mixture, multiracial identity, and the multiracial movement.[38]

That has not kept a small cadre of monoracialists from attacking the multiracial movement and scholars who study racial mixture. Here I am thinking primarily of Lewis Gordon, Jon Michael Spencer, Rainier Spencer, and Jared Sexton. They point to a real tension that exists between some African American intellectuals and the multiracial idea over the lingering fear that, for some people, adopting a multiracial identity is a dodge to avoid being Black. If so, that might tend to sap the strength of a monoracially defined movement for Black community empowerment. So they open up the possibility of thinking critically about the political consequences of the multiracial idea. But sadly, all these authors argue from their conclusion to their evidence; that is, they start from the conviction that the multiracial idea is a bad one, and then they cherry-pick quotes and misrepresent the positions of key thinkers in order to pursue their point. They insist on monoraciality: one cannot be mixed or multiple; one must choose ever and only to be Black. I don't have a problem with that as a political choice for an individual, but to insist that it is the only possibility flies in the face of a great deal of human experience—as Henry Louis Gates Jr., says, "We are all mulattos"[39]—and it ignores the history of how modern racial ideas emerged. When nothing else seems likely to work, Sexton in particular simply resorts to ad hominem attacks on the motives and personal lives of the writers themselves.[40] Obama, in his critique of his college friend Joyce, made an argument similar to the one that these writers present, but he did it with more grace and intellectual integrity.

What the increasing acceptance of intermarriage over the past three or four decades, together with the rise of the multiracial movement, perhaps *does* mean is fairly simple. More than at any other time in US history, most Americans seem comfortable with the idea that people who are identified as members of different races should know each other, mix socially, and perhaps marry when they choose to do so. That is new in the current generations of adults. So, too, there is a new openness on the part of a lot of people to consider the constructed quality of racial identities and the contingent nature of racial affiliations.

STUDIES OF MIXED RACE: WHERE WE HAVE BEEN AND WHERE WE MIGHT GO

There is a long tradition of studies of Black-White mixing and multiracial people, dating back more than a century, to the novels of Charles Chesnutt and Nella Larsen, the sociology of W. E. B. Du Bois and Edward Reuter, and the philosophizing of Jean Toomer and George Schuyler.[41] Romanzo Adams and his Hawai'i colleagues added an Asian dimension beginning in the 1930s.[42] The current wave of mixed-race studies development began

much more recently, in the late 1970s and 1980s, with several disserta-
tions by people like Christine Hall, Nathan Strong, and Stephen Murphy-
Shigematsu.[43]

Every student of multiracial matters will be familiar with the First Book
of Root, the Second Book of Root, the Book of Davis, and the Book of
Daniel. Maria Root gathered the work of two dozen social scientists in two
edited volumes in 1992 and 1995, on topics as disparate as the psychology
of multiracial people passing for Black or White, the racialized politics of
Native American reservations, and the social dilemmas faced by Amerasians in Vietnam. One of her most celebrated achievements was the "Bill
of Rights for Racially Mixed People," a fierce statement of identity independence that has been much reprinted, and indeed has been known to
be chanted at retreats and to appear on T-shirts. F. James Davis in 1991
wrote a sociologically inflected history of the one-drop rule in the United
States, in a book called *Who Is Black? One Nation's Definition*. G. Reginald
Daniel gave us what may turn out to be the definitive account of the multiracial movement, together with its intellectual and cultural antecedents,
in *More than Black? Multiracial Identity and the New Racial Order*. These
are the foundational texts in this field.[44]

Other major markers in the growth of mixed-race studies include Mar-
tha Menchaca's *Recovering History, Reconstructing Race: The Indian, Black,
and White Roots of Mexican Americans*; Ramón Gutiérrez's *When Jesus
Came, the Corn Mothers Went Away*; Circe Sturm's *Blood Politics: Race,
Culture, and Identity in the Cherokee Nation of Oklahoma*; Karen Leon-
ard's *Making Ethnic Choices*; Theda Perdue's *"Mixed Blood" Indians: Racial
Construction in the Early South*; Jayne Ifekwunigwe's masterful synthesis,
"Mixed Race" Studies; Kip Fulbeck's *Part Asian—100% Hapa*; Martha
Hodes's *White Women, Black Men: Illicit Sex in the Nineteenth-Century
South*; and Kimberly McClain DaCosta's provocation, *Making Multi-
racials: State, Family, and Market in the Redrawing of the Color Line*.[45]

I admire these writers and many others who work in the field. Yet, when
I reflect on the development of mixed-race studies over the past couple of
decades, I think I see some ways in which the field has fallen short of what
it might have been. Some examples: For reasons that pretty much escape
me, a lot of writers in this field have failed to distinguish between the

study of interracial mating and marriage (the coming together of two monoracially defined people) and studies of multiraciality (the lives and identity choices of people who have mixed ancestry). It does not take a great deal of imagination to figure out that parents' issues are not necessarily their children's issues; anyone who has been either a parent or a child knows this. Yet somehow this distinction has escaped a whole lot of authors, including some very smart people like Werner Sollors. It is also an intergenerational issue that has plagued the multiracial movement and organizations like Multiracial Americans of Southern California and the Biracial Family Network.[46]

Writing, scholarly and otherwise, on the mixed-race question has run very heavily to personal and family stories about identity. The story these books tell is usually pretty much the same. A person finds out he or she has mixed ancestry—maybe a long-kept family secret, as in the case of Edward Ball, perhaps something more immediate about mommy and daddy, as in the story of Gregory Howard Williams. The person goes on a quest, finds out the family secret, writes that story, achieves self-understanding and racial closure, goes on *Oprah*, and becomes a blessing to countless other mixed people (and a titillation, perhaps, to monoracially identified people everywhere who wonder whether, just maybe, their family has a more interesting story than they have been led to believe). This genre is useful for helping readers identify with the issue of racial mixedness and the complicated ways that families work and, well, don't. Since the multiracial movement is largely a post-adolescent identity quest, books like these are helpful, even inspiring ones, and indeed I use them in my classes sometimes.[47]

I am less clear what I think about a new development, which has chosen to go by the name Critical Mixed Race Studies (always capitalized, sometimes abbreviated CMRS). An association has been founded—the CMRS Association has been meeting since 2010—a discipline proclaimed, and an excellent online journal inaugurated. I don't doubt the earnestness, insight, or skill of the scholars who are beginning this task. They say they want to look critically at racial issues, unpack received ideas about race, and bring a new, multiracialist perspective to scholarship and education, from universities down to secondary and even elementary schools. All well and good. But I do question whether critical mixed race studies is a *discipline*—we apply that term too loosely these days, when I think we really mean "field of study" or "point of view." In this case I respect the practitioners and support the task, but I am a bit wary about the triumphal tone with which some of the CMRS people seem to be proceeding.[48]

I do have a few ideas about where mixed-race studies might direct its energies with profit in the years to come. We have had a great deal of writing on the coming together of Black and White—both interracial couples and mixed-race people—and also on Asian and White mixing. The past decade has witnessed a spate of writing about the Black-Indian nexus.[49] We have had comparatively less writing on the complexities of Latino identities. What really is going on, racially and culturally speaking, in mixed Dominican–Puerto Rican families, for example? We don't know very much about the social and psychological dynamics that have attended the pairing of African Americans and Asian Americans, of Asian and Latino mixes, of Latinos and Native peoples, and so on. Rudy Guevarra's work on Mexipinos—interracial Filipino and Mexican working-class communities and families over several generations—is a start in this direction. I also am heartened by the writing of Julia Schiavone Camacho, Verónica Castillo-Muñoz, and others on the nexus of Mexicans, Native peoples, Chinese, and Japanese from the late nineteenth century up to the mid-twentieth, forming a multiracial working class, and in fact multiracial families, in northern Mexico and across the border into the US Southwest.[50]

We also can learn some things from thinking about mixed race in other places besides the United States and Britain, where most of the research to date has been situated. Schiavone Camacho and Castillo-Muñoz take us across the US-Mexico border and remind us that if we are to understand racial relationships we are going to have to get outside nationalist frames. It will be very helpful, I think, if other scholars follow their lead, not only in crossing borders, but also in looking at all the peoples who make up Mexicans, not just the mestizo myth of Castilians and Indians, but also Africans, Chinese, Filipinos, and others. The burgeoning literature on *mestizaje* may lead us in that direction.[51] We can learn a great deal about the role that empire has played in racial mixing if we follow Ann Laura

Stoler and Eric Alan Jones to Indonesia, Lily Welty to Japan and Okinawa, or other scholars to Malaysia and the Philippines and contemplate mixedness in such places. What is the meaning of mixedness for Chinese Thais or Vietnamese Cambodians, who have lived for generations as partly mixed, partly segregated minorities, who also have ties to the homelands of some of their great-grandparents? How do people of mixed *jati* parentage function in Indian society? Rebecca King-O'Riain, Stephen Small, and their colleagues have published *Global Mixed Race*, which offers a comparative look at multiraciality in a dozen different countries, none of them the United States. From a very different platform—not mixed-race studies but creole studies—Robin Cohen and Paola Toninato have begun to compare mixed identities in a lot of places. I would like to see more of that work in the years to come. I am not sure how creole studies and mixed-race studies ought to come together, but it would be a good idea if they started to talk with each other.[52]

I like very much the turn to beauty culture that Margaret Hunter, Joanne Rondilla, and others have been taking. It is a way of unpacking the issues attendant upon racial multiplicity, and of linking them with gender issues, for beauty is a far more important issue with regard to women's life chances than it is to men's. I would hope that someone would tackle the beauty issues related to race and mixedness for men as well.[53]

The biggest thing that long was missing from mixed-race studies was the intersection of racial mixing and sexuality. Were I to write *Mixed Blood* today instead of a quarter century ago, I would have to reframe the entire discussion, because except for a couple of paragraphs, the book has nothing at all to say about gay or lesbian couples. There are racialized dimensions in gay and lesbian sex, romantic relationships, and marriages, as there are for heterosexual couples. Where a quarter century ago there was not much scaffolding on which to build an interpretation of interracial issues in gay and lesbian couples, scholars have begun to explore the racial dimensions of LGBT relationships in the new century.[54] Martin Manalansan addresses these issues for Filipinos in *Global Divas*. Amy Sueyoshi examines the complex racial and sexual wanderings of turn-of-the-last-century writer Yone Noguchi. Judy Tzu-Chun Wu opens up the interracial lesbian life of Doctor Mom Chung. Pablo Mitchell explores race and sexuality among Mexican Americans in *Coyote Nation* and *West of Sex*, as does Horacio Rocque Ramírez in *Queer Latino San Francisco*. Nayan Shah and Amy Steinbugler have contributed solid monographs.[55] We need many more such efforts. We need a lot of studies of gay sexuality and relationship building, including racialized dynamics in cross-racial gay and lesbian couples. As we expand our exploration of the racialized dynamics of lesbian and gay relationships, we might want to ask questions like these: Who pairs with whom, how and why? What are the images that groups have of each other, and how do those images work in the sphere of gay sexual thinking, feeling, and doing? When lesbian and gay couples have children, what place does race play in the ways they raise those children, and how do the children shape their racial identities?

As this book goes to press, the US Supreme Court's decision invalidating the Defense of Marriage Act is still fresh. The arguments in that case, for and against gay and lesbian couples being allowed to marry, have been made for several years, but the judgment of history has not yet begun to coalesce.[56] At this early stage, it seems likely that the DOMA decision will take its place alongside 1967's *Loving v. Virginia* case, which ruled that laws forbidding interracial marriage were unconstitutional. Instead of the Court insisting that states must allow formerly prohibited marriages, as in the *Loving* decision, gay marriage seems to be coming about piecemeal, one state after another, with increasing velocity. The somewhat parallel legal history of the end to bans on interracial and homosexual marriages will surely be part of the story that will be told in multiracial studies in the future.

IS MIXED RACE AN ETHNIC GROUP?

In 1995, in a paper at a mixed-race conference in Hawai'i, I posed this grammatically awkward question: "Is there a groupness in mixedness?"[57] That is, given that people of mixed ancestry tend to have a complex of similar experiences, do they constitute a meaningful social group, or are these simply individual experiences that are similar? In particular, do mixed people constitute an ethnic or racial group of their own, independent from the groups with which they may share partial ancestry? That is, should we amend David Hollinger's racial pentagram (Black-White-Asian-Latino-Indian) to include a sixth group, multiracial people?[58] Two decades later, the question remains.

To be sure, there is an individual experience of mixedness, one that is increasingly acknowledged by the public in the United States and elsewhere. Susan Graham contends that this amounts to an ethnic group–like quality for mixed people as well. She argues for a separate multiracial category, alongside the five current racial categories, on census and other government forms. And she believes this sixth, multiracial group to be a good thing, possibly because, if it were acknowledged widely, it would get her kids out of the racial trap of being thought to be Black. Jared Sexton agrees with Graham that there is a group quality to multiraciality, and he says it's bad, because he sees it as a betrayal of monoracially defined Black people.

But Sexton and Graham are outliers in the conversation about multiraciality. Many people—from Maria Root and her "Bill of Rights for Racially Mixed People" to the MAVIN Foundation to a host of community groups and Internet communication sites—avoid both these extremes. They simply do their best to create group cohesion, a common set of principles, a network of connection, and ultimately a panethnicity as multiracial people.[59]

Still, there are a couple of problems with the idea that multiracial people can constitute a racial or ethnic group of their own. For one thing, it seems to me that the multiracial identity quest is something of a life-stage thing. I have spent more than a quarter century watching several thousand people of mixed ancestry struggle with their identity, encounter the multiracial idea, embrace it, become activists and students of the phenomenon, find stable places of identity, and then move on to other life tasks. Cathy Tashiro, a medical anthropologist and nursing scholar, interviewed elder multiracials—people in their sixties and seventies. What were their most pressing topics of concern? Their bodies did not work so well anymore. A spouse had died and they were lonely. Their children did not visit them enough. They were having a tough time getting by on a fixed income. Death loomed on the horizon. By that time in their lives, they had pretty much settled who they wanted to be, racially speaking, and other topics took center stage.[60] I have never heard of a similar study of aging issues for monoracially defined groups, so I don't know for sure that the racial issue recedes in similar fashion for monoracial people. I suspect that for some it does. But for many of those on whom American racial hierarchy falls most heavily, I am pretty sure race remains powerful throughout their lives. Still, I do wonder if it is possible for a stable racial grouping to exist if it is based on an issue that people address in their young adult years and then set to the side as they go on with their lives.

It also strikes me that, in twenty-first-century America, it will be hard to sustain a long-standing group of people called multiracials or mixed-race people. In certain other historical settings, particular groups such as the Métis in Canada, the Coloureds in southern Africa, or small groups of triracial isolates such as the Brass Ankles, Redbones, or Lumbee in the United States have maintained definable mixed-race communities over many generations.[61] But that was partly a matter of their being forced to form separate communities, because interracial mixing was officially forbidden. Racial boundaries between European and Native, European and African, and White and Black were officially kept solid, so people who in defiance of the rules in fact were mixed really had no choice but to stick together and mate within the pool of other (mostly related) mixed people.

In our time, by contrast, the very forces that gave rise to the multiracial movement and the acceptance of the multiracial idea—a society-wide openness to interracial interaction and to the idea of multiplicity—militate against the formation of an enduring, separate, mixed-race group. So while there surely are experiences—sociological, psychological, familial, perhaps political—that a lot of mixed folks have in common, and although there are a lot of support groups through which multiracial people cycle their activities for periods in their lives, it seems to me that there is not, in fact, an enduring groupness to multiracial mixedness.

What, then, does this multiracial moment—the Obama moment, if you will—suggest about the state and future of race in the United States? Well, it suggests that we do live at a moment when no one really blinks if a Black character kisses an Asian character on *Grey's Anatomy*, when public figures like the musician Lenny Kravitz and the speed skater Apolo Anton Ohno are known to have multiracial parentage, and when that mixedness is not seen as a problem. The social taboo against interracial intimacy seems to have declined to the point where antimiscegenist sentiments that were commonplace a generation ago now seem retrograde and impolite, the stuff of radical Tea Partying. In that sense, perhaps we are becoming an Obama nation. On the other hand, if Gary Nash was right when he wrote about the "hidden history of mestizo America," then maybe we have been an Obama nation all along.

BARACK OBAMA AS RACIAL EMBLEM

How are we to assess Barack Obama's impact as a racial figure?[62] He has not been a postracial president. Rather, for the most part, he has succeeded in performing a balancing act between Blackness and Whiteness in his self-presentation and in the public imagination. Obama has always performed Whiteness perfectly, and he has usually performed Blackness pretty convincingly—these are among the skills that have been crucial to his success. His breakthrough moment came at the 2004 Democratic National Convention in Boston, where the young Illinois state senator delivered the keynote speech. Showing promise of a future as Healer-in-Chief, he proclaimed:

> There is not a liberal America and a conservative America—there is the United States of America. There is not a Black America and a White America and Latino America and Asian America—there's the United States of America. . . .
> We worship an "awesome God" in the blue states, and we don't like federal agents poking around in our libraries in the red states. We coach Little League in the blue states, and yes, we've got some gay friends in the red states. There are patriots who opposed the war in Iraq and there are patriots who supported the war in Iraq. We are one people, all of us pledging allegiance to the Stars and Stripes, all of us defending the United States of America.[63]

Not everyone caught it, but in that speech Obama marked himself as an evangelical Christian. His God remark strummed the chords of "Awesome God," which was then the most popular praise song being sung in White evangelical churches across the nation.[64]

Obama performed racial legerdemain once again four years later when he won the Iowa Democratic Party caucuses—a first, surprising victory in his meandering path to the Democratic nomination and later the presidency. Iowans are a churchy lot, Democrats nearly as much as Republicans. They are good neighbors and family folk. Most of them are sincerely good, Christian, White people who want to do a good, generous thing when they can. They believe in hard work and, the Democrats among them at least, believe that it's important for people to work together and take care of one another. In Barack Obama, Iowa caucusers rightly perceived one of their own. He was that nice, clean-cut, well-spoken Negro young man who knew all the words to the hymns they sang on Sunday. It made them feel good to vote for someone Black who was like them in so many ways.

In that first campaign and as president, Obama performed his Blackness only sporadically, though with considerable fluency when he chose to do so. He was a Black man, but he was a particular kind of Black man, one whose multiracial, international growing-up story we knew: Kenya, Hawai'i, Indonesia, Occidental College, Columbia, Harvard Law. More conventional Black politicians were not the sort who could get elected to the presidency, for as smart and driven and well connected as they might be, they could not perform Whiteness the way that Obama could. And then, in office, Obama chose to perform simply as President, seldom as an explicitly racialized figure, despite some opponents' attempts to paint him as one.[65]

None of Obama's signature policy achievements—creating a national healthcare system, rescuing the auto industry, reforming the banking system, ending overt discrimination against gays in the military, exiting the Iraq war, avoiding a second Great Depression, killing Osama Bin Laden, surveillance of private citizens, drone attacks—had a racial or civil rights theme. It is as if, on the racial front, it was enough that a person of his race was elected. Obama chose to operate in a race-neutral manner throughout his first term and well into his second.

Does Barack Obama's double election to the presidency then mean that America has arrived at a postracial moment in our history? Hardly.[66] Despite the nonracialized way in which Obama has acted as president, both those who supported him and those who opposed him did so at least partly in racial terms. The enthusiasm for Obama among American voters (and those millions in other countries who celebrated with us in November 2008) was racialized. Liberals—and a lot of nonliberals who were people of goodwill—applauded Obama's ascendancy as a partial fulfillment of the promise of the Civil Rights movement. I confess that I did not think I would see a Black president in my lifetime, and I was pretty jazzed when it happened. The historic nature of this election was felt around the globe. On election night 2008 I was in a small city in Germany where five hundred university students took over an entire restaurant and stayed through the night, until five o'clock in the morning, awaiting the final news that Obama had been elected. Part of the enthusiasm, in the United States and abroad, was generated by Obama's political skills, his positions on issues, and the respite he promised from George Bush's mistakes. But much of it was that a Black man could be elected to America's highest office.

Likewise, opposition to President Obama was and remains racialized. Tea Party rally signs regularly depicted the president as a witch doctor with a bone through his nose or in other dehumanizing disguises that had African themes. On April 19, 2010, White gun rights activists brought loaded weapons and fiery rhetoric to two small national parks—Gravelly Point and Fort Hunt—in Virginia just across the Potomac from the White House. Can you imagine the outcry if Black loudmouths had brought guns and made threatening speeches across from the White House while a White president was in residence? Michael Steel, former Republican National chairman, commented on the Republican 2013 shutdown of the federal government in a vain attempt to stop the Affordable Care Act: "It's not about Obamacare. It's about Obama." He went on to label Obama's race as the reason they opposed vehemently any attempt to work with him or his party. Conservative commentators, from Fox News and elsewhere, piled on Michelle Obama. They objected to Barack and Michelle exchanging a congratulatory fist bump, calling their gesture gangland thuggery. They made demeaning comments about Mrs. Obama's arms, implying she lacked femininity, and the shape of her buttocks, suggesting she was no person to be lecturing the nation's youth on weight and diet. And they tried to make her out to be an Angry Black Woman rather than a warm, intelligent, articulate First Lady.[67]

Obama was repeatedly racialized as Other. It began during the Democratic primary campaign in 2008, with Hillary Clinton's reference to "real Americans, White Americans" not supporting Obama, implying that her opponent, because he was not fully White, was not a real American and not fit to lead Americans. When some ignorant critics contended that the Protestant Obama was a Muslim (and Muslims have come in for a lot of hate since 2001), Mrs. Clinton did not correct them. Instead, responding to a Steve Croft question on CBS's *60 Minutes*, she stared into the camera and said merely, "I take him on the basis of what he says"—that he is a Christian—"and, you know, there isn't any reason to doubt that." She knew better, but she wanted the top job and so was willing to say pretty much anything to get it.[68]

Then there were the contentions about the president's place of birth, which escalated as the 2012 election approached. Presidential faux-candidate and TV personality Donald Trump and other birthers contended that Barack Obama was not an American citizen because he was born, they said, in Kenya. Hence, he was not legitimately president. They had no evidence for their claim about his birthplace, but that did not stop them from declaring him illegitimate. Orly Taitz, while a 2012 birther candidate for the US Senate from California, promised that if elected she would "demand investigation and prosecution of governmental officials who are aiding and abetting Barack Obama in his occupation of the position of the US President without any valid identification papers."[69]

President Obama produced his 1961 Honolulu birth certificate and the Republican governor of Hawai'i pronounced it authentic. But Trump insisted that "a lot of people do not think it was an authentic certificate."[70] Yes, it was authentic. But it doesn't matter. Article 2 of the Constitution declares, "No person except a natural born citizen . . . shall be eligible to the office of President." It does not say the person has to be born in the United States.

Since the founding of the nation, US law has always recognized two ways to be a "natural born citizen." One can be born on US soil (the law of jus soli) or one can be born to a parent who is a US citizen (jus sanguinis). US law in this matter follows English Common Law, which has recognized both principles for many centuries. The first US Congress in 1790 passed a law declaring that "The children of citizens of the United States that may be born beyond the sea, or outside the limits of the United States, shall be considered as natural-born citizens of the United States."[71]

No one is arguing that President Obama's mother, Stanley Ann Dunham, was not a US citizen in 1961. Therefore, it doesn't matter if Barack Obama was born in Hawai'i, in Kenya, or in a rocket ship on the way to Mars. He still is a natural born US citizen.

In 2008 no one questioned John McCain's eligibility to hold the office of president. Yet McCain was born in—wait for it—Panama. He was born in a US naval hospital in the Canal Zone, territory that the United States controlled in much the same way that it controls Guantánamo Bay today. If the birthers want to argue that the Panama Canal Zone was US soil, then they will have to concede that Guantánamo Bay is US soil and subject to the rule of US law—hardly a position they are likely to advocate. Then there is the citizenship status of George Romney, the former Michigan governor and father of the 2012 presidential candidate. The elder Romney was born in Mexico and came to the United States with his US citizen parents when he was a small boy, apparently without papers. When George Romney ran for president in 1967, no one seriously questioned his citizenship status. Nor, to my knowledge, has anyone questioned the US citizenship of Mitt Romney.[72]

It is worth pointing out that some of the people who questioned President Obama's US citizenship, like US Senator Dean Heller (Republican of Nevada) and presidential candidate Ron Paul (then a Republican congressmember from Texas), also said they wanted to end jus soli—citizenship for immigrants' children by virtue of their birth on US soil. They really can't have it both ways. Without both jus sanguinis and jus soli, we would not have any natural born citizens at all, and no one would be eligible to run for president.[73]

This is all about race, not about citizenship or personal history. Questioning President Obama's US citizenship, like suggesting he is a secret Muslim, is thinly veiled code. What the conspiracy theorists really mean is that President Obama is not legitimately president because he is Black. It is long past time to end this birther nonsense. It doesn't matter where President Obama was born (it was in Hawai'i, but it doesn't matter). He is a US citizen, and he is president. He has been elected twice, and he has been exercising the powers of the office for years. The birthers need to get over it, but they show few signs of getting that message.

Barack Obama maintained his balancing act—performing Whiteness daily, making a nod toward Blackness now and then, but mainly trying to be president of all the people and not merely a racial figure—until 2013. The year before, Trayvon Martin, an unarmed, Black, seventeen-year-old Floridian, was stalked and killed by George Zimmerman, a volunteer neighborhood watchman and wannabe cop. The case became a cause célèbre, with liberals horrified at what they saw as a racial killing and conservatives complaining that Zimmerman was being lynched for having behaved reasonably.[74]

In the end, a jury acquitted Zimmerman. An uproar ensued. Barack Obama's response was instructive in his departure from his usual neutral racial stance. A few days after the verdict, while demonstrations and counterdemonstrations were going on across the country and the punditry was aflame, Obama walked into the White House briefing room without a script and said some very personal things about race. He did not criticize the verdict, but he did say:

> Trayvon Martin could have been me 35 years ago. . . . [T]he African American community is looking at this issue through a set of experiences and a history that doesn't go away.
>
> There are very few African American men in this country who haven't had the experience of being followed when they were shopping in a department store. That includes me. There are very few African American men who haven't had the experience of walking across the street and hearing the locks click on the doors of cars. That happens to me—at least before I was a senator. There are very few African Americans who haven't had the experience of getting on an elevator and a woman clutching her purse nervously and holding her breath until she had a chance to get off. That happens often. It happened to me. . . .
>
> The African American community is also knowledgeable that there is a history of racial disparities in the application of our

criminal laws—everything from the death penalty to enforcement of our drug laws.

Obama ended on a hopeful note:

> I don't want us to lose sight that things are getting better. Each successive generation seems to be making progress in changing attitudes when it comes to race. It doesn't mean we're in a post-racial society. It doesn't mean that racism is eliminated. But when I talk to Malia and Sasha, and I listen to their friends and I see them interact, they're better than we are—they're better than we were—on these issues. And that's true in every community that I've visited all across the country.[75]

Clearly, Barack Obama was experiencing the Zimmerman verdict and the killing of Trayvon Martin as a Black man, not just as the president of all the Americans. In making a personal statement, he was spending some of the goodwill he had earned in his years as president. Yet he kept his response personal rather than programmatic. It was a human response, not a policy intervention.

But, as he said, on race, American society is indeed getting better. The very fact of his presidency; our society's recognition of his racial mixedness; his ability to speak truth about the verdict instead of platitudes—all these point toward how far we have come since people like Emmett Till and Vincent Chin were targeted for murder on account of their race.[76] That he could not also speak his anger at the killing of Trayvon Martin and the acquittal of George Zimmerman, without losing the attention and assent of White Americans, shows how far we have yet to go.

NOTES

This chapter began life as the keynote address at a conference on Obama and multiraciality hosted by Ramón Gutiérrez and Matt Briones at the University of Chicago in 2010. I am grateful to them and to the other conference participants, particularly Martha Hodes, Ralina Joseph, and Juliette Maiorana, for their perceptive comments.

1. The text quoted here is from the *New York Times*, March 18, 2008. See also Clarence E. Walker and Gregory D. Smithers, *The Preacher and the Politician: Jeremiah Wright, Barack Obama, and Race in America* (Charlottesville: University of Virginia Press, 2009).

2. The title of this chapter represents an attempt to rescue a concept—a possible sense of historical identification between Barack Obama and the American people—from the clutches of a political hack named Jerome R. Corsi, whose screed, *Obama Nation: Leftist Politics and the Cult of Personality* (New York: Simon and Schuster, 2008), came out during Obama's first presidential campaign.

3. Barack Obama, *Dreams from My Father: A Story of Race and Inheritance* (New York: Kodansha, 1996), 91–92; original emphasis.

4. Oscar Avila, "Obama's Census Choice: 'Black,'" *Los Angeles Times*, April 4, 2010.

5. For a perceptive argument against the postracial fantasy, see Suki Ali, *Mixed-Race, Post-Race: Gender, New Ethnicities and Cultural Practices* (Oxford: Berg, 2003).

6. This essay is both theoretical and historiographical. The notes are extensive, but they can only suggest the rich scholarship that has come into being. I hope the reader will be forgiving if I have left out some of his or her favorite books. I have left out many of my favorites, too.

7. Gary B. Nash, *Red, White, and Black: The Peoples of Early America* (Englewood Cliffs, NJ: Prentice-Hall, 1974); Tomás Almaguer, *Racial Fault Lines: The Historical Origins of White Supremacy in California* (Berkeley: University of California Press, 1994); Paul Spickard, *Almost All Aliens: Immigration, Race, and Colonialism in American History and Identity* (New York: Routledge, 2007).

8. Paul Spickard, "Race and Nation, Identity and Power: Thinking Comparatively about Ethnic Systems," in *Race and Nation: Ethnic Systems in the Modern World*, ed. Paul Spickard (New York: Routledge, 2005), 1–29.

9. Michael Omi and Howard Winant, *Racial Formation in the United States: From the 1960s to the 1990s*, 2nd ed. (New York: Routledge, 1994); Yen Le Espiritu, *Asian American Panethnicity: Bridging Institutions and Identities* (Philadelphia: Temple University Press, 1992); C. Loring Brace, *"Race" Is a Four-Letter Word: The Genesis of the Concept* (New York: Oxford University Press, 2005). It may well be the case that a sixth racialized panethnicity—Arab or Middle Eastern or Muslim American—is currently being formed. See Anny Bakalian and Mehdi Bozorgmehr, *Backlash 9/11: Middle Eastern and Muslim Americans Respond* (Berkeley: University of California Press, 2009); Moustafa Bayoumi, *How Does It Feel to Be a Problem: Being Young and Arab in America* (New York: Penguin, 2008); Edward E. Curtis IV, *Muslims in America: A Short History* (New York: Oxford University Press, 2009); Yvonne Yazbeck Haddad, ed., *The Muslims of America* (New York: Oxford University Press, 1991); Amir Marvasti and Karyn D. McKinney,

Middle Eastern Lives in America (Lanham, MD: Rowman and Littlefield, 2004); Michael W. Suleiman, ed., *Arabs in America* (Philadelphia: Temple University Press, 1999).

10. Michael A. Gomez, *Exchanging Their Country Marks: The Transformation of African Identities in the Colonial and Antebellum South* (Chapel Hill: University of North Carolina Press, 1998); Gwendolyn Midlo Hall, *Slavery and African Ethnicities in the Americas: Restoring the Links* (Chapel Hill: University of North Carolina Press, 2005); John A. Arthur, *Invisible Immigrants: African Immigrant Diaspora in the United States* (Westport, CT: Praeger, 2000); Reuel R. Rogers, *Afro-Caribbean Immigrants and the Politics of Incorporation: Ethnicity, Exception, or Exit* (New York: Cambridge University Press, 2006); Nancy Foner, ed., *Islands in the City: West Indian Migration to New York* (Berkeley: University of California Press, 2001); Mary C. Waters, *Black Identities: West Indian Immigrant Dreams and American Realities* (Cambridge, MA: Harvard University Press, 2001).

11. Stephen E. Cornell, *The Return of the Native: American Indian Political Resurgence* (New York: Oxford University Press, 1988); Hazel Hertzberg, *The Search for an American Indian Identity: Modern Pan-Indian Movements* (Syracuse, NY: Syracuse University Press, 1971); Joane Nagel, *American Indian Ethnic Renewal: The Resurgence of Identity and Culture* (New York: Oxford University Press, 1996).

12. On the formation of White race, see Theodore W. Allen, *The Invention of the White Race*, 2 vols. (London: Verso, 1994, 1997); Jennifer Guglielmo and Salvatore Salerno, eds., *Are Italians White?* (New York: Routledge, 2003); Thomas A. Guglielmo, *White on Arrival: Italians, Race, Color, and Power in Chicago, 1890–1945* (New York: Oxford University Press, 2003); Ian Haney López, *White by Law: The Legal Construction of Race* (New York: New York University Press, 1996); Noel Ignatiev, *How the Irish Became White* (New York: Routledge, 1995); Matthew Frye Jacobson, *Whiteness of a Different Color: European Immigrants and the Alchemy of Race* (Cambridge, MA: Harvard University Press, 1998); George Lipsitz, *The Possessive Investment in Whiteness* (Philadelphia: Temple University Press, 1998); David R. Roediger, *The Wages of Whiteness: Race and the Making of the American Working Class* (London: Verso, 1991); Alexander Saxton, *The Rise of the White Republic* (London: Verso, 1990).

On the formation of the Asian American race, see Espiritu, *Asian American Panethnicity*; Emma Gee, ed., *Counterpoint: Perspectives on Asian America* (Los Angeles: UCLA Asian American Study Center, 1976); Russell Jeung, *Faithful Generations: Race and New Asian American Churches* (New Brunswick, NJ: Rutgers University Press, 2005); Edward J. W. Park and John S. W. Park, *Probationary Americans: Contemporary Immigration Policies and the Shaping of Asian American Communities* (New York: Routledge, 2005); Lavina Dhingra Shankar and Rajini Srikanth, eds., *A Part, Yet Apart: South Asians in Asian America* (Philadelphia:

Temple University Press, 1998); Amy Tachiki et al., eds., *Roots: An Asian American Reader* (Los Angeles: UCLA Asian American Study Center, 1971); Linda Trinh Vo, *Mobilizing Asian American Community* (Philadelphia: Temple University Press, 2004); Linda Trinh Vo and Rick Bonus, eds., *Contemporary Asian American Communities* (Philadelphia: Temple University Press, 2002); William Wei, *The Asian American Movement* (Philadelphia: Temple University Press, 1992); Helen Zia, *Asian American Dreams* (New York: Farrar, Straus and Giroux, 2000).

On the formation of the Latino panethnicity, see William V. Flores and Rina Benmayor, eds., *Latino Cultural Citizenship* (Boston: Beacon, 1997); Juan Gonzalez, *Harvest of Empire: A History of Latinos in America* (New York: Penguin, 2000); David E. Hayes-Bautista, *La Nueva California: Latinos in the Golden State* (Berkeley: University of California Press, 2004); Roberto Suro, *Strangers among Us: Latino Lives in a Changing America* (New York: Knopf, 1998); Hector Tobar, *Translation Nation: Defining a New American Identity in the Spanish-Speaking United States* (New York: Riverhead, 2005).

13. Floya Anthias and Nira Yuval-Davis, *Racialized Boundaries: Race, Nation, Gender, Colour and Class and the Anti-Racist Struggle* (New York: Routledge, 1992), 148–55.

14. Judith A. Nagata, "What Is a Malay? Situational Selection of Ethnic Identity in a Plural Society," *American Ethnologist* 1.2 (1974): 331–50; Daniel P. S. Goh, Matilda Gabrielpillai, Philip Holden, and Gaik Cheng Khoo, eds., *Race and Multiculturalism in Malaysia and Singapore* (New York: Routledge, 2009).

15. I hasten to point out that very few ethnic Germans would be comfortable with the concept of an "ethnic German"—in their perception, they are simply Germans, and others are simply not Germans. Most Germans, even people versed in racial analysis of other places, take offense if it is suggested that the divisions in German society are racial. Surely, this is understandable, given Germany's troubled racial history, and the degree to which the German government and public have unflinchingly faced up to the racial atrocities of the 1930s and 1940s. But that does not make the patently racialized quality of intergroup relations in Germany today any less real, and obvious to the outside observer. See Richard Alba, Peter Schmidt, and Martine Wasmer, eds., *Germans or Foreigners? Attitudes toward Ethnic Minorities in Post-Reunification Germany* (New York: Palgrave, 2003); Betigül Ercan Argun, *Turkey in Germany: The Transnational Sphere of Deutschkei* (New York: Routledge, 2003); William A. Barbieri Jr., *Ethics of Citizenship: Immigration Rights and Group Rights in Germany* (Durham, NC: Duke University Press, 1998); Rita Chin, *The Guest Worker Question in Postwar Germany* (Cambridge: Cambridge University Press, 2007); Rita Chin, Heide Fehrenbach, Geoff Eley, and Atina Grossmann, eds., *After the Nazi Racial State: Difference and Democracy in Germany and Europe* (Ann Arbor: University of Michigan Press, 2009); Deniz Göktürk, David Gramling, and Anton Kaes, eds., *Germany in Transit: Nation and Migration, 1955–2005* (Berkeley: University of California Press, 2007).

16. www.mavinfoundation.org/generationmix/about_faqs.html (February 6, 2010); Maria P. P. Root, "A Bill of Rights for Racially Mixed People," in *The Multiracial Experience: Racial Borders as the New Frontier* (Thousand Oaks, CA: Sage, 1995), 6.

17. Gary B. Nash, "The Hidden History of Mestizo America," presidential address, Organization of American Historians, Washington, DC, March 31, 1995, printed in *Journal of American History* 82.3 (1995): 941–62; Gary B. Nash, *Forbidden Love: The Secret History of Mixed-Race America* (New York: Holt, 1999).

18. Winthrop D. Jordan, *White over Black: American Attitudes toward the Negro, 1550–1812* (Chapel Hill: University of North Carolina Press, 1969), 136–78; Martha Menchaca, *Recovering History, Constructing Race: The Indian, Black, and White Roots of Mexican Americans* (Austin: University of Texas Press, 2001).

19. Ramón A. Gutiérrez, *When Jesus Came, the Corn Mothers Went Away: Marriage, Sexuality, and Power in New Mexico, 1500–1846* (Stanford, CA: Stanford University Press, 1991); Laura E. Gómez, *Manifest Destinies: The Making of the Mexican American Race* (New York: New York University Press, 2007); Neil Foley, *The White Scourge: Mexicans, Blacks, and Poor Whites in Texas Cotton Culture* (Berkeley: University of California Press, 1997); Ilona Katzew and Susan Deans-Smith, eds., *Race and Classification: The Case of Mexican America* (Stanford, CA: Stanford University Press, 2009); James F. Brooks, *Captives and Cousins: Slavery, Kinship, and Community in the Southwest Borderlands* (Chapel Hill: University of North Carolina Press, 2002).

20. Jordan, *White over Black*; Winthrop D. Jordan, "Historical Origins of the One-Drop Racial Rule in the United States," ed. Paul Spickard, *Journal of Critical Mixed Race Studies* 1 (2013): 98–132; Martha Hodes, ed., *Sex, Love, Race: Crossing Boundaries in North American History* (New York: New York University Press, 1999), 35–138.

21. Theda Perdue, *"Mixed Blood" Indians: Racial Construction in the Early South* (Athens: University of Georgia Press, 2003); Circe Sturm, *Blood Politics: Race, Culture, and Identity in the Cherokee Nation of Oklahoma* (Berkeley: University of California Press, 2002), 27–51; James F. Brooks, ed., *Confounding the Color Line: The Indian-Black Experience in North America* (Lincoln: University of Nebraska Press, 2002), 21–134.

On the continuing mixing of Native-identified people with people of European and African ancestry, see the other sections of Sturm and Brooks, as well as Tiya Miles, *Ties That Bind: The Story of an Afro-Cherokee Family in Slavery and Freedom* (Berkeley: University of California Press, 2005); Claudio Saunt, *Black, White, and Indian: Race and the Unmaking of an American Family* (New York: Oxford University Press, 2005); Tiya Miles and Sharon P. Holland, eds., *Crossing Waters, Crossing Worlds: The African Diaspora in Indian Country* (Durham, NC: Duke University Press, 2006).

22. Martha Hodes, *White Women, Black Men: Illicit Sex in the Nineteenth-Century South* (New Haven, CT: Yale University Press, 1997); Hodes, *Sex, Love, Race*, 141–327; Joel Williamson, *New People: Miscegenation and Mulattoes in the United States* (New York: Free Press, 1980); Bernie D. Jones, *Fathers of Conscience: Mixed-Race Inheritance in the Antebellum South* (Athens: University of Georgia Press, 2009); Joshua D. Rothman, *Notorious in the Neighborhood: Sex and Families across the Color Line in Virginia, 1787–1861* (Chapel Hill: University of North Carolina Press, 2003).

23. Willard B. Gatewood, *Aristocrats of Color: The Black Elite, 1880–1920* (Fayetteville: University of Arkansas Press, 2000); Ingrid Dineen-Wimberly, "By the Least Bit of Blood: The Allure of Blackness among Mixed-Race Americans of African Descent, 1862–1935" (unpublished MS); Audrey Elisa Kerr, *The Paper Bag Principle: Class, Colorism, and Rumor and the Case of Black Washington, D.C.* (Knoxville: University of Tennessee Press, 2006); Kent Anderson Leslie, *Woman of Color, Daughter of Privilege: Amanda America Dickson, 1849–1893* (Athens: University of Georgia Press, 1995); Ira Berlin, *Slaves without Masters: The Free Negro in the Antebellum South* (New York: Random House, 1974).

24. Dineen-Wimberly, "Least Bit of Blood"; Ingrid Dineen-Wimberly and Paul Spickard, "It's Not That Simple: Multiraciality, Models, and Social Hierarchy," in *Multiracial Americans and Social Class*, ed. Kathleen Korgen (New York: Routledge, 2010), 205–21; Margaret Hope Bacon, *But One Race: The Life of Robert Purvis* (Albany: State University of New York Press, 2007); Jean Toomer, draft autobiography, JWJ MSS. Series 1, b. 18: f. 493 (Beinecke Library, Yale University); Cynthia Earl Kerman and Richard Eldridge, *The Lives of Jean Toomer: A Hunger for Wholeness* (Baton Rouge: Louisiana State University Press, 1989); Thomas Dyja, *Walter White: The Dilemma of Black Identity in America* (New York: Ivan Dee, 2008); W. E. B. Du Bois, *Dusk of Dawn: An Essay toward an Autobiography of a Race Concept* (New York: Harcourt, Brace, 1940); Mary Church Terrell, *A Colored Woman in a White World* (Amherst, NY: Humanity Books, 2005; orig. 1940).

25. John Walton Caughey, *McGillivray of the Creeks* (Columbia: University of South Carolina Press, 2007; orig. 1938); Gary E. Moulton, *John Ross, Cherokee Chief* (Athens: University of Georgia Press, 1978); William E. Unrau, *Mixed Bloods and Tribal Dissolution: Charles Curtis and the Quest for Indian Identity* (Norman: University of Oklahoma Press, 1971).

26. Sui Sin Far, *Mrs. Spring Fragrance and Other Writings* (Urbana: University of Illinois Press, 1995); Annette White-Parks, *Sui Sin Far/Edith Maude Eaton* (Urbana: University of Illinois Press, 1995); Diane Birchall, *Onoto Watanna: The Story of Winnifred Eaton* (Urbana: University of Illinois Press, 2006); Onoto Watanna, *The Half Caste and Other Writings* (Urbana: University of Illinois Press, 2002). On Wilcox, see Lauren L. Basson, *White Enough to Be American? Race*

Mixing, Indigenous Peoples, and the Boundaries of State and Nation (Chapel Hill, NC: University of North Carolina Press, 2008), 95–140.

27. Spickard, *Almost All Aliens*, 262–73; Bruce Baum, *The Rise and Fall of the Caucasian Race* (New York: New York University Press, 2006); Emmanuel Chukwudi Eze, ed., *Race and the Enlightenment* (Oxford: Blackwell, 1997); Stephen Jay Gould, *The Mismeasure of Man*, rev. ed. (New York: Norton, 1996); Jonathan Marks, *Human Biodiversity: Genes, Race, and History* (New York: Aldyne de Gruyter, 1995); William H. Tucker, *The Science and Politics of Racial Research* (Urbana: University of Illinois Press, 1994).

28. Loretta I. Winters and Herman L. DeBose, eds., *New Faces in a Changing America: Multiracial Identity in the 21st Century* (Thousand Oaks, CA: Sage, 2003).

29. Paul R. Spickard, *Mixed Blood: Intermarriage and Ethnic Identity in Twentieth-Century America* (Madison: University of Wisconsin Press, 1989).

30. Journals like *Social History, Comparative Studies in Society and History*, and especially *Social Science History* are fruit of that intellectual movement.

31. Bruno Lasker, *Filipino Immigration* (New York: Arno, 1969; orig. 1931); Romanzo Adams, *Interracial Marriage in Hawaii* (New York: Macmillan, 1937); Robert K. Merton, "Intermarriage and the Social Structure," *Psychiatry* 4 (1941): 361–74; Kingsley Davis, "Intermarriage in Caste Societies," *American Anthropologist* 43 (1941): 376–95; Ruby Jo Reeves Kennedy, "Single or Triple Melting Pot? Intermarriage Trends in New Haven, 1870–1940," *American Journal of Sociology* 49 (1944): 331–39; Milton M. Gordon, *Assimilation in American Life* (New York: Oxford University Press, 1964), 224–32; Harry H. L. Kitano, *Japanese Americans*, 2nd ed. (Englewood Cliffs, NJ: Prentice-Hall, 1976), 210–11.

32. Merton, "Intermarriage and the Social Structure"; Davis, "Intermarriage in Caste Societies"; David M. Buss, "Human Mate Selection," *American Scientist* 73 (January–February 1985): 47–51.

33. Alice Walker, "The Divided Life of Jean Toomer," *New York Times*, July 13, 1980, reprinted in Alice Walker, *In Search of Our Mothers' Gardens* (New York: Harcourt Brace Jovanovich, 1983).

34. This paragraph follows closely my argument in "The Power of Blackness: Mixed-Race Leaders and the Monoracial Ideal," in *Racial Thinking in the United States*, ed. Paul Spickard and G. Reginald Daniel (Notre Dame, IN: University of Notre Dame Press, 2004), 103–23, which is reproduced elsewhere in this volume. Toomer's surviving relatives confirmed my analysis in subsequent correspondence.

35. Gordon, *Assimilation in American Life*, 80. Unfortunately, too many people still make this assumption, despite abundant evidence to the contrary. Jessica Vasquez echoes Gordon's argument in an otherwise very smart book, *Mexican*

Americans across Generations: Immigrant Families, Racial Realities (New York: New York University Press, 2011).

36. Gin Pang and Larry Shinagawa, "Interracial Relationships and the Language of Denial" (unpublished manuscript, ca. 1998).

37. Susan Graham, "Is This President Obama's Post-Racial America?," January 20, 2009, Project RACE website, www.projectrace.com/fromthedirector /archive/012009_obama_post_racial_america.php (retrieved April 25, 2009). See also Susan R. Graham, "The Real World," in Root, *The Multiracial Experience,* 15–36; Susan R. Graham, "Grassroots Advocacy," in *American Mixed Race,* ed. Naomi Zack (Lanham, MD: Rowman and Littlefield, 1995), 185–90; www.project race.com.

38. E.g., Margaret L. Hunter, *Race, Gender, and the Politics of Skin Tone* (New York: Routledge, 2005); Joanne L. Rondilla and Paul Spickard, *Is Lighter Better? Skin-Tone Discrimination among Asian Americans* (Lanham, MD: Rowman and Littlefield, 2007); Cedric Herring, Verna M. Keith, and Hayward Derrick Horton, eds., *Skin/Deep: How Race and Complexion Matter in the "Color-Blind" Era* (Urbana: University of Illinois Press, 2004); Kimberly McClain DaCosta, *Making Multiracials: State, Family, and Market in the Redrawing of the Color Line* (Stanford, CA: Stanford University Press, 2007); G. Reginald Daniel, *More than Black? Multiracial Identity and the New Racial Order* (Philadelphia: Temple University Press, 2002); David L Brunsma, ed., *Mixed Messages: Multiracial Identities in the "Color-Blind" Era* (Boulder, CO: Lynne Rienner, 2006).

39. Gates is quoted in Mateo Gold, "'Faces of America' Reveals Family Ties," *Los Angeles Times,* February 10, 2010.

40. Lewis R. Gordon, *Her Majesty's Other Children: Sketches of Racism from a Neocolonial Age* (Lanham, MD: Rowman and Littlefield, 1997); Jon Michael Spencer, *The New Colored People: The Mixed-Race Movement in America* (New York: New York University Press, 1997); Rainier Spencer, *Spurious Issues: Race and Multiracial Identity Politics in the United States* (Boulder, CO: Westview, 1999); Rainier Spencer, *Challenging Multiracial Identity* (Boulder, CO: Lynne Rienner, 2006); Jared Sexton, *Amalgamation Schemes: Antiblackness and the Critique of Multiracialism* (Minneapolis: University of Minnesota Press, 2008). For more detail, see my reviews of Sexton's book in *American Studies* 50.1–2 (2009): 125–27, and of Jon Michael Spencer's in *Journal of American Ethnic History* 18.2 (1999): 153–56.

41. Charles W. Chesnutt, *The Wife of His Youth and Other Stories* (Boston: Houghton Mifflin, 1899); Charles W. Chesnutt, *The House Behind the Cedars* (Boston: Houghton Mifflin, 1900); Charles W. Chesnutt, *The Marrow of Tradition* (Boston: Houghton Mifflin, 1901); Charles W. Chesnutt, *Charles W. Chesnutt: Essays and Speeches,* ed. Joseph R. McElrath Jr., Robert C. Leitz III, and Jesse S. Crisler (Stanford, CA: Stanford University Press, 1999); Nella Larsen, *Quicksand* (New York: Knopf, 1928); Larsen, *Passing* (New York: Knopf, 1929); Du Bois,

Dusk of Dawn; Edward Byron Reuter, *The Mulatto in the United States, Including a Study of the Role of Mixed-Blood Races Throughout the World* . . . (Boston: Badger, 1918); Reuter, *Race Mixture: Studies in Intermarriage and Miscegenation* (New York: Whittlesey House, 1931); Jean Toomer, *A Jean Toomer Reader: Selected Unpublished Writings*, ed. Frederik L. Rusch (New York: Oxford University Press, 1993); George S. Schuyler, *Racial Intermarriage in the United States: One of the Most Interesting Phenomena in Our National Life* (Girard, KS: Haldeman-Julius Publications, 1929).

42. Adams, *Interracial Marriage in Hawaii*; Sidney L. Gulick, *Mixing the Races in Hawaii: A Study of the Coming Neo-Hawaiian American Race* (Honolulu: Hawaiian Board Book Rooms, 1937).

43. Christine C. I. Hall, "The Ethnic Identity of Racially Mixed People: A Study of Black-Japanese" (PhD diss., UCLA, 1980); Nathan Oba Strong, "Patterns of Social Interaction and Psychological Adjustment among Japan's Konketsuji Population" (PhD diss., University of California, Berkeley, 1978); Stephen Murphy-Shigematsu, "Voices of Amerasians: Ethnicity, Identity and Empowerment in Interracial Japanese Americans" (EdD diss., Harvard University, 1987).

44. Maria P. P. Root, ed., *Racially Mixed People in America* (Newbury Park, CA: Sage, 1992); Root, *The Multiracial Experience*; F. James Davis, *Who Is Black? One Nation's Definition* (University Park: Pennsylvania State University Press, 1991); Daniel, *More than Black?*

45. Martha Menchaca, *Recovering History, Reconstructing Race: The Indian, Black, and White Roots of Mexican Americans* (Austin: University of Texas Press, 2001); Gutiérrez, *When Jesus Came*; Sturm, *Blood Politics*; Karen Isaksen Leonard, *Making Ethnic Choices: California's Punjabi Mexican Amereicans* (Philadelphia: Temple University Press, 1992); Perdue, *"Mixed Blood" Indians*; Jayne Ifekwunigwe, *"Mixed Race" Studies: A Reader* (New York: Routledge, 2004); Kip Fulbeck, *Part Asian—100% Hapa* (San Francisco: Chronicle Books, 2006); Hodes, *White Women, Black Men*; DaCosta, *Making Multiracials*.

46. Werner Sollors, *Neither Black nor White Yet Both: Thematic Explorations of Interracial Literature* (New York: Oxford University Press, 1997); Werner Sollors, ed., *Interracialism: Black-White Intermarriage in American History, Literature, and Law* (New York: Oxford University Press, 2000); Werner Sollors, ed., *An Anthology of Interracial Literature: Black-White Contacts in the Old World and the New* (New York: New York University Press, 2004).

47. Some examples (though their name is legion): Edward Ball, *Slaves in the Family* (New York: Farrar, Straus and Giroux, 1998); Gregory Howard Williams, *Life on the Color Line: The True Story of a White Boy Who Discovered He Was Black* (New York: Dutton, 1995); Shirlee Taylor Haizlip, *The Sweeter the Juice: A Family Memoir in Black and White* (New York: Simon and Schuster, 1994); Lawrence Hill, *Black Berry, Sweet Juice: On Being Black and White in Canada* (Toronto: HarperCollins, 2001); Neil Henry, *Pearl's Secret: A Black Man's Search for*

His White Family (Berkeley: University of California Press, 2001); Kevin R. Johnson, *How Did You Get to Be Mexican? A White/Brown Man's Search for Identity* (Philadelphia: Temple University Press, 1999); James McBride, *The Color of Water: A Black Man's Tribute to His White Mother* (New York: Riverhead, 1996); Kym Ragusa, *The Skin between Us: A Memoir of Race, Beauty, and Belonging* (New York: Norton, 2006).

There is, however, a more sinister subgenre: self-indulgent diva writings by multiracial children who have a more or less famous Black parent. At least Danzy Senna and Zadie Smith can write, even if they don't have much to say that makes much sense. Not even that much can be said for the autobiographical writings of Bliss Broyard, Lisa Jones, or Rebecca Walker. See Danzy Senna, *Caucasia* (New York: Riverhead, 1998); Zadie Smith, *White Teeth* (New York: Random House, 2000); Bliss Broyard, *One Drop: My Father's Hidden Life—A Story of Race and Family Secrets* (New York: Little, Brown, 2007); Lisa Jones, *Bulletproof Diva: Tales of Race, Sex, and Hair* (New York: Doubleday, 1994); Rebecca Walker, *Black, White, and Jewish: Autobiography of a Shifting Self* (New York: Riverhead, 2001).

48. http://las.depaul.edu/aas/About/CMRSConference/index.asp (retrieved July 21, 2010). The journal's website is http://escholarship.org/uc/ucsb_soc_jcmrs.

49. Sturm, *Blood Politics*; Brooks, *Confounding the Color Line*; Miles, *Ties That Bind*; Miles and Holland, *Crossing Waters, Crossing Worlds*; Claudio Saunt, *Black, White, and Indian: Race and the Unmaking of an American Family* (New York: Oxford University Press, 2006); Gabrielle Tayac, ed., *indiVisible: African-Native American Lives in the Americas* (Washington, DC: Smithsonian Books, 2009); Celia E. Naylor, *African Cherokees in Indian Territory: From Chattel to Citizens* (Chapel Hill: University of North Carolina Press, 2008); Melinda Maynor Lowery, *Lumbee Indians in the Jim Crow South: Race, Identity, and the Making of a Nation* (Chapel Hill: University of North Carolina Press, 2010).

50. Rudy P. Guevarra Jr., *Becoming Mexipino: Multiethnic Identities and Communities in San Diego* (New Brunswick, NJ: Rutgers University Press, 2012); Julia María Schiavone Camacho, *Chinese Mexicans: Transpacific Migration and the Search for a Homeland* (Chapel Hill: University of North Carolina Press, 2012); Schiavone Camacho, "Crossing Boundaries, Claiming a Homeland: The Mexican Chinese Transpacific Journey to Becoming Mexican, 1930s–1960s," *Pacific Historical Review* 78.4 (2009): 545–77; Verónica Castillo-Muñoz, "Divided Communities: Agrarian Struggles, Transnational Migration and Families in Northern Mexico, 1910–1952" (PhD diss., University of California, Irvine, 2009); Grace Peña Delgado, *Making the Chinese Mexican: Global Migration, Localism, and Exclusion in the U.S.-Mexico Borderlands* (Stanford, CA: Stanford University Press, 2012); Jason Oliver Chang, "Racial Alterity in the Mestizo Nation," *Journal of Asian American Studies* 14.3 (2011): 331–59. See also the fascinating international transformations of Native American–Hawaiian–Chinese families and individuals

portrayed by David A. Chang in "Borderlands in a World at Sea: Concow Indians, Native Hawaiians, and South Chinese in Indigenous, Global, and National Space, 1860s–1880s," *Journal of American History* 98 (2011): 384–403.

51. Gloria Anzaldúa, *Borderlands/La Frontera: The New Mestiza* (San Francisco: Aunt Lute Press, 1986); José Vasconcelos, *The Cosmic Race/La raza cósmica*, trans. Didier T. Jaén (Baltimore: Johns Hopkins University Press, 1997; orig. 1979); Colin M. MacLachlan and Jaime E. Rodriguez O., *The Forging of the Cosmic Race: A Reinterpretation of Colonial Mexico* (Berkeley: University of California Press, 1980). For critiques, see Virginia Q. Tilley, "*Mestizaje* and the 'Ethnicization' of Race in Latin America," in Spickard, *Race and Nation*, 53–68; and Marilyn Grace Miller, *The Rise and Fall of the Cosmic Race: The Cult of Mestizaje in Latin America* (Austin: University of Texas Press, 2004). For reassertions of the concept, see Raphael Pérez-Torres, *Mestizaje: Critical Uses of Race in Chicano Culture* (Minneapolis: University of Minnesota Press, 2006); and Peter Wade, "Rethinking *Mestizaje:* Ideology and Lived Experience," *Journal of Latin American Studies* 37 (2005): 239–57.

52. Schiavone Camacho, "Crossing Boundaries, Claiming a Homeland"; Castillo-Muñoz, "Divided Communities"; Ann Laura Stoler, *Carnal Knowledge and Imperial Power: Race and the Intimate in Colonial Rule* (Berkeley: University of California Press, 2002); Eric Jones, *Wives, Slaves, and Concubines: A History of the Female Underclass in Dutch Asia* (DeKalb: Northern Illinois University Press, 2010); Lily Anne Yumi Welty, "Advantage Not Crisis: Multiracial American Japanese in Post–World War II Japan and U.S., 1945–1972" (PhD diss., University of California, Santa Barbara, 2012); Rebecca Chiyoko King-O'Riain, Stephen Small, Minelle Mahtani, Miri Song, and Paul Spickard, eds., *Global Mixed Race* (New York: New York University Press, 2014); Robin Cohen and Paola Toninato, eds., *The Creolization Reader: Studies in Mixed Identities and Cultures* (New York: Routledge, 2010).

53. Hunter, *Race, Gender, and the Politics of Skin Tone*; Margaret L. Hunter, "Buying Racial Capital: Skin-Bleaching and Cosmetic Surgery in a Globalized World," *Journal of Pan African Studies* 4.4 (2011): 142–64; Rondilla and Spickard, *Is Lighter Better?*; Ingrid Banks, *Hair Matters: Beauty, Power, and Black Women's Consciousness* (New York: New York University Press, 2000); Evelyn Nakano Glenn, ed., *Shades of Difference: Why Skin Color Matters* (Stanford, CA: Stanford University Press, 2009); Herring, Keith, and Horton, *Skin/Deep*; Rebecca Chiyoko King-O'Riain, *Pure Beauty: Judging Race in Japanese American Beauty Pageants* (Minneapolis: University of Minnesota Press, 2006); Noliwe M. Rooks, *Hair Raising: Beauty, Culture, and African American Women* (New Brunswick, NJ: Rutgers University Press, 1996); Solomon Leong, "Who's the Fairest of Them All? Television Ads for Skin-Whitening Cosmetics in Hong Kong," *Asian Ethnicity* 7.2 (2006): 167–81.

54. The first steps in this direction were taken by two pioneering essays: George Kitahara Kich, "In the Margins of Sex and Race: Difference, Marginality, and Flexibility," in Root, *Multiracial Experience*, 263–76; and Karen Maeda Allman, "(Un)Natural Boundaries: Mixed Race, Gender, and Sexuality," in Root, *Multiracial Experience*, 277–90.

55. Martin Manalansan, *Global Divas: Filipino Gay Men in the Diaspora* (Durham, NC: Duke University Press, 2003); Amy Sueyoshi, *Queer Compulsions: Race, Nation, and Sexuality in the Affairs of Yone Noguchi* (Honolulu: University of Hawai'i Press, 2012); Judy Tzu-Chun Wu, "Was Mom Chung a 'Sister Lesbian'? Asian American Gender Experimentation and Interracial Homoeroticism," *Journal of Women's History* 13.1 (2001): 58–82; Judy Tzu-Chun Wu, *Doctor Mom Chung of the Fair-Haired Bastards: The Life of a Wartime Celebrity* (Berkeley: University of California Press, 2005); Pablo Mitchell, *Coyote Nation: Sexuality, Race, and Conquest in Modernizing New Mexico, 1880–1920* (Chicago: University of Chicago Press, 2005); Pablo Mitchell, *West of Sex: Making Mexican America, 1900–1930* (Chicago: University of Chicago Press, 2012); Nayan Shah, *Stranger Intimacy: Contesting Race, Sexuality and the Law in the North American West* (Berkeley: University of California Press, 2011); Amy C. Steinbugler, *Beyond Loving: Intimate Racework in Lesbian, Gay, and Straight Interracial Relationships* (New York: Oxford University Press, 2012). See also Jason Lee Crockett, "Narratives of Racial Sexual Preference in Gay Male Subculture" (PhD diss., University of Arizona, 2010); Christopher Cutrone, "The Child with a Lion: The Utopia of Interracial Intimacy," *GLQ* 6.2 (2000): 249–85; Kenneth Chan, "Rice Sticking Together: Cultural Nationalist Logic and the Cinematic Representations of Gay Asian-Caucasian Relationships and Desire," *Discourse* 28.2–3 (2006): 178–96; Arnaldo Cruz-Malave and Martin F. Manalansan, eds., *Queer Globalizations: Citizenship and the Afterlife of Colonialism* (New York: New York University Press, 2002); Daniel Hurewitz, *Bohemian Los Angeles and the Making of Modern Politics* (Berkeley: University of California Press, 2007); Michael Harms-García and Ernesto Javier Martínez, eds., *Gay Latino Studies: A Reader* (Durham, NC: Duke University Press, 2011); and Kevin J. Mumford, *Interzones: Black/White Sex Districts in Chicago and New York in the Early Twentieth Century* (New York: Columbia University Press, 1997). I am grateful to Maribel Mira Martinez and Ashkon Moleai for helping me begin research in this area.

56. Robert Barnes, "At Supreme Court, Victories for Gay Marriage," *Washington Post*, June 26, 2013.

57. Some of the papers from that conference, though not my final presentation, were published in *We Are a People: Narrative and Multiplicity in Constructing Ethnic Identity*, ed. Paul Spickard and W. Jeffrey Burroughs (Philadelphia: Temple University Press, 2000).

58. David A. Hollinger, *Postethnic America: Beyond Multiculturalism* (New York: Basic Books, 1995). I have argued elsewhere that the pentagram is already a hexagram—that is, that Arab Americans, Muslims, and other people of Middle Eastern and North African origin have come to be racialized gradually since the 1970s; *Almost All Aliens*, 425–27, 453–56. See also Nabeel Abraham, Sally Howell, and Andrew Shryock, eds., *Arab Detroit 9/11: Life in the Terror Decade* (Detroit, MI: Wayne State University Press, 2011); Moustafa Bayoumi, *How Does It Feel to Be a Problem? Being Young and Arab in America* (New York: Penguin, 2008); Warren J. Blumenfeld, Khyati Y. Joshi, and Ellen E. Fairchild, eds., *Investigating Christian Privilege and Religious Oppression in the United States* (Rotterdam: Sense Publishers, 2009); Amaney Jamal and Nadine Naber, eds., *Race and Arab Americans before and after 9/11: From Invisible Citizens to Visible Subjects* (Syracuse, NY: Syracuse University Press, 2008); Junaid Rana, *Terrifying Muslims: Race and Labor in the South Asian Diaspora* (Durham, NC: Duke University Press, 2011).

59. The MAVIN Foundation can be found at www.mavinfoundation.org/; Swirl is at http://swirlinc.wordpress.com/; the Mixed Network is at http://the mixednetwork.com/; Multiracial Americans of Southern California is at www .ameasite.org/masc.asp; etc.

60. Cathy J. Tashiro, "Identity and Health in the Narratives of Older Mixed Race Asian Americans," *Journal of Cultural Diversity* 13.1 (2006): 41–49; Cathy J. Tashiro, *Standing on Both Feet: Voices of Older Mixed Race Americans* (Boulder, CO: Paradigm, 2012).

61. Jennifer S. H. Brown and Jacqueline Peterson, eds., *New Peoples: Being and Becoming Métis in North America* (Winnipeg: University of Manitoba Press, 1985); George M. Fredrickson, *White Supremacy: A Comparative Study of American and South African History* (New York: Oxford University Press, 1982), 94–135; Juliette Bridgette Milner-Thornton, *The Long Shadow of the British Empire: The Ongoing Legacies of Race and Class in Zambia* (New York: Palgrave Macmillan, 2012); Brewton Berry, *Almost White* (New York: Macmillan, 1963); Karen I. Blu, *The Lumbee Problem: The Making of an American Indian People* (Cambridge: Cambridge University Press, 1980).

62. Thoughtful takes on Obama's racial persona appear in *Obama and the Biracial Factor: The Battle for a New American Majority*, ed. Andrew J. Jolivette (Bristol: Policy Press, 2012); and Thomas J. Sugrue, *Not Even Past: Barack Obama and the Politics of Race* (Princeton, NJ: Princeton University Press, 2010). An excellent account of Obama's presidency and the 2012 elections is Jonathan Alter, *The Center Holds: Obama and His Enemies* (New York: Simon and Schuster, 2013). See also H. Samy Alim and Geneva Smitherman, *Articulate While Black: Barack Obama, Language, and Race in the U.S.* (New York: Oxford University Press, 2012). The next half-dozen pages of this essay owe much to a chapter, "Obama, Race, and the 2012 Election," in *Race and the Obama Phenomenon: The Vision of*

a More Perfect Multiracial Union, ed. G. Reginald Daniel and Hettie V. Williams (Jackson: University Press of Mississippi, 2014), 329–38; and to an op-ed piece I wrote for the *San Jose Mercury News* under the title "Birthers' Attack on Obama Is Not Only Bogus, It's Irrelevant" (June 16, 2012); I am grateful to Salim Yaqub for hounding me until I wrote it.

63. Barack Obama, Keynote Speech, Democratic National Convention, Fleet Center, Boston, July 27, 2004, www.americanrhetoric.com/speeches/convention2004/barackobama2004dnc.htm (retrieved November 21, 2012).

64. Michael W. Smith, "Awesome God," www.sing365.com (retrieved November 21, 2012). The refrain goes, "Our God is an awesome God, He reigns from Heaven above. With wisdom, power and love, Our God is an awesome God."

65. Patrice Peck, "Biracial versus Black: Thought Leaders Weigh in on the Meaning of President Obama's Biracial Heritage," http://thegrio.com/2012/11/19 (retrieved November 19, 2012).

66. Sugrue, *Not Even Past*; Donald R. Kinder and Allison Dale-Riddle, *The End of Race? Obama, 2008, and Racial Politics in America* (Chicago: University of Chicago Press, 2010); Michael Tesler and David O. Sears, *Obama's Race: The 2008 Election and the Dream of a Post-Racial America* (Chicago: University of Chicago Press, 2010); Desmond S. King, *Still a House Divided: Race and Politics in Obama's America* (Princeton, NJ: Princeton University Press, 2011).

67. Ashley Fantz, "Obama as Witch Doctor: Racist or Satirical?," CNN .com, September 18, 2009 (retrieved November 24, 2012); Fredrick Kunkle and Ann Gerhart, "Gun-Rights Advocates Gather in Va. and D.C. to Celebrate 'Historic Moment,'" *Washington Post*, April 20, 2010; Alexis Garrett Stodghill, "Tea Party Group Makes Racially-Tinged Obama Skunk Reference," http://thegrio .com/2011/12/12 (retrieved November 19, 2012); Michael Steele, on *Hardball with Chris Matthews*, MSNBC (October 1, 2013).

68. "Clinton Says Obama Muslim Rumor Not True 'As Far as I know,'" ABC News blog *Political Punch* (retrieved November 25, 2012).

69. http://orlytaitzforussenate2012.com/platform.html (retrieved May 29, 2012).

70. Steve Peoples, "Trump Overshadows Romney with 'Birther' Talk," Associated Press, May 29, 2012.

71. Michael LeMay and Elliott Robert Barkan, eds., *US Immigration and Naturalization Laws and Issues* (Westport, CT: Greenwood, 1999), 17.

72. Apparently there was some question raised by the American Independent Party about the elder Romney's citizenship, but the matter went nowhere. In his 2012 stump speech, Mitt Romney frequently alluded to his birth in Michigan and that of his wife as proof of their US citizenship, and contrasted that to the birthers' questioning of Obama's citizenship.

73. http://deanheller.com (retrieved May 29, 2012); www.ronpaul.com/on -the-issues/border-security (retrieved November 24, 2012).

74. George Yancy and Janine Jones, eds., *Pursuing Trayvon Martin: Historical Contexts and Contemporary Manifestations of Racial Dynaics* (Lanham, MD: Lexington Books, 2012); Earl Ofari Hutchinson, *America on Trial: The Slaying of Trayvon Martin* (Los Angeles: Hutchinson Report E-books, 2013); Hunter Billings III, *The Lynching of George Zimmerman* (Amazon Digital Services, 2013).

75. www.businessinsider.com/obama-trayvon-martin-race-speech-video-text-2013-7 (retrieved July 19, 2013).

76. Stephen J. Whitfield, *A Death in the Delta: The Story of Emmett Till* (Baltimore: Johns Hopkins University Press, 1991); *Who Killed Vincent Chin?*, dir. Christine Choy and Renee Tajima-Peña, *POV* (PBS, 1989).

Suggested Reading

In addition to the works mentioned here, the notes to the essays constitute a rich trove of sources. This list is adapted, in abridged form, from Paul Spickard, "Ethnicity," in *Oxford Bibliographies in Sociology*, ed. Jeff Manza (New York: Oxford University Press, 2013). In each section I have arranged the entries in the order in which I think the general reader is likely to find them useful.

RACE IN US HISTORY

Takaki, Ronald T. *A Different Mirror: A History of Multicultural America.* Boston: Little, Brown, 1993. The best, most artful and comprehensive overview of the history and meaning of ethnicity, race, immigration, and membership in America.

Spickard, Paul. *Almost All Aliens: Immigration, Race, and Colonialism in American History and Identity.* New York: Routledge, 2007. A broad interpretation of race, ethnicity, migration, and colonialism across all major groups in American history.

JOURNALS

Ethnic and Racial Studies
Journal of American Ethnic History
Journal of Ethnic and Migration Studies

RACIAL AND ETHNIC THEORY

Cornell, Stephen, and Douglas Hartmann. *Ethnicity and Race: Making Identities in a Changing World*. 2nd ed. Thousand Oaks, CA: Pine Forge Press, 2007. The best introduction to contemporary constructivist ideas about ethnicity and race. In clear prose and with a multitude of concrete examples drawn from around the world, the authors lay out the various ways of thinking about the field and help the reader navigate among them.

Barth, Fredrik, ed. *Ethnic Groups and Boundaries: The Social Organization of Culture Difference*. Boston: Little, Brown, 1967. Eight essays by Scandinavian ethnographers that explore the contours of ethnicity in places as various as Laos, Afghanistan, Norway, Mexico, and Ethiopia. Barth's theories about the mutability of ethnic boundaries began the transformation of thinking about race and ethnicity.

Smedley, Audrey, and Brian Smedley. *Race in North America: Origin and Evolution of a Worldview*, 4th ed. Boulder, CO: Westview, 2011. The most widely used systematic study of the history of racial and ethnic ideas. It includes new chapters on a variety of current topics, from the contention that the presidency of Barack Obama heralds a "postracial" future to the emergence of a new generation of scientists who contend that race is a valid biological concept.

Sollors, Werner. *Theories of Ethnicity: A Classical Reader*. New York: New York University Press, 1996. Full texts of twenty-four influential essays by authors ranging across the twentieth century, including Max Weber, Charles Chesnutt, Randolph Bourne, Horace Kallen, Robert E. Park, Jean Toomer, Marcus Lee Hansen, Georg Simmel, Erik Erikson, Karl Mannheim, Fredrik Barth, Robert Merton, Abner Cohen, Ulf Hannerz, and Herbert Gans. The book mainly focuses on the United States and the United Kingdom and does not address the race-versus-ethnicity question.

Omi, Michael, and Howard Winant. *Racial Formation in the United States: From the 1960s to the 1990s*. 3rd ed. New York: Routledge, 2014. Possibly the most influential book put forth by the constructivists. The book's key contribution is chapter 4, "Racial Formation." Here Omi and Winant explain the dynamics by which many disparate peoples (Ibo, Hausa, Fon, Fulani, Mandinka, Bambara, etc.) came to be formed into one panethnicity or race (in this case, the Black or African American race). They describe this process of panethnic formation and suggest how the racial formation concept may also be applied historically to White or European Americans, as well as to Native Americans, Asian Americans, and Latinos or Hispanic Americans.

Espiritu, Yen Le. *Asian American Panethnicity: Bridging Institutions and Identities*. Philadelphia: Temple University Press, 1993. Shows the quite self-conscious process by which, beginning in the late 1960s, Chinese, Japanese, Koreans, and other Americans whom White Americans orientalized together, chose to form a panethnic coalition they called Asian Americans. Espiritu goes on to show how that panethnic or racial formation was reinforced by the building of panethnic institutions.

Hall, Stuart, and Paul du Guy, eds. *Questions of Cultural Identity*. Thousand Oaks, CA: Sage, 1996. Identified with the approaches broadly labeled cultural studies, Hall and du Guy bring together ten advocates of the notion that ethnic identities—indeed, all sorts of human identity—were constructed in particular times and places by particular sorts of people for purposes at which we can at least guess, and so those identities could be unpacked and perhaps reshaped. They question the very categories of race, nationality, class, and gender that had previously been such unquestioned features of modern social life.

Gilroy, Paul. *Against Race: Imagining Political Culture beyond the Color Line*. Cambridge, MA: Harvard University Press, 2002. A culmination of the evolution of one of the most influential contemporary thinkers about ethnic and racial matters. Here Gilroy, radically, advocates the position that racial thinking—not just racism—is a key obstacle to human freedom. He argues passionately that much of modern culture is tied up with the expression of ethnic, racial, and other identities and that the only way out is to eschew racial thinking entirely.

Crenshaw, Kimberlé, Neil Gotanda, Gary Peller, and Kendall Thomas, eds. *Critical Race Theory: The Key Writings That Formed the Movement*. New York: New Press, 1995. More than two dozen key essays, most substantially in their entirety.

RACE AND BIOLOGICAL THINKING

Eze, Emmanuel Chukwudi, ed. *Race and the Enlightenment: A Reader*. Malden, MA: Wiley-Blackwell, 1997. A nearly definitive reader on the history of the Enlightenment origins of scientific racialism. Selections from Linnaeus, Kant, Herder, Blumenbach, Cuvier, and others, nicely set in context.

Gould, Stephen Jay. *The Mismeasure of Man*. Rev. ed. New York: Norton, 1996. The history of modern scientific racialist ideas in exquisite detail and sparkling prose by the eminent paleobotanist and popular science writer.

Marks, Jonathan. *Human Biodiversity: Genes, Race, and History*. New York: Aldine de Gruyter, 1995. Sorts out the biological claims of the scientific racialists, tests them against the recent findings of geneticists, and finds them wanting. Marks, a biologist as well as an anthropologist, writes with knowledge, insight, and clarity. Highly recommended.

Graves, Joseph L., Jr. *The Emperor's New Clothes: Biological Theories of Race at the Millennium*. New Brunswick, NJ: Rutgers University Press, 2003. An evolutionary biologist traces the history of scientific racialism, from pre-Darwinian racial ideas, through Darwin, the eugenicists, Nazism, down to recent controversies over race and IQ and race and disease.

Briggs, Laura. *Reproducing Empire: Race, Sex, Science, and US Imperialism in Puerto Rico*. Berkeley: University of California Press, 2002. A brilliant exposé of the nexus between the science of eugenics, colonialism, racial domination, gender, the family, and sexuality. Briggs shows how eugenic ideas were used in Puerto Rico to pursue racially and colonially directed birth control and sterilization campaigns, how they were implicated in public-health and behavior-control campaigns against prostitution, and also to control entry to the United States.

Koenig, Barbara A., Sandra Soo-Jin Lee, and Sarah S. Richardson, eds. *Revisiting Race in a Genomic Age*. New Brunswick, NJ: Rutgers University Press, 2008. Scholars of biology, medicine, law, sociology, pharmacology, anthropology, linguistics, philosophy, political science, and environmental science expound on the implications of recent genetic research for ideas about race and ethnicity, as well as the future of medicine.

IDENTITY AND THE PRIMORDIALITY QUESTION

Epstein, A. L. *Ethos and Identity: Three Studies in Ethnicity*. London: Tavistock, 1978. Emphasizes the continuing significance of ethnic identities, despite predictions of ethnic group demise and absorption into larger social entities, in three situations: the Copper Belt of southern Africa, in Melanesia, and among American Jews.

Hobsbawm, Eric, and Terence Ranger, eds. *The Invention of Tradition*. Cambridge: Cambridge University Press, 1983. A key early collection of essays on places in Europe, Africa, and South Asia where what are widely regarded as primordial ethnic entities were created. On closer scrutiny, they all appear to be rather recent inventions.

Anderson, Benedict. *Imagined Communities: Reflections on the Origins and Spread of Nationalism*. Rev. ed. London: Verso, 2006. A much-admired but pretty confused book with no discernible outline or argument. Nonetheless, it contains a few scattered paragraphs that change everything. It articulates the revolutionary insight (at least in 1983 when the first edition was published) that nations, races, and ethnic groups—perhaps genders and classes, too—are "imagined communities," not biological facts or primordial social entities.

Nagata, Judith A. "What Is a Malay? Situational Selection of Ethnic Identity in a Plural Society." *Ethnology* 1 (1974): 331–50. Explores the ways that ethnically complicated people in Malaysia choose among possible ethnic identifications, and the continuous process of ethnic oscillation that results.

Keesing, Roger M. "Creating the Past: Custom and Identity in the Contemporary Pacific." *Contemporary Pacific* 1.1–2 (1989): 19–42. Examines the creation of myths of ancestral ways of life as a powerful tool for creating ethnic solidarity in the present.

COMPARING RACIAL AND ETHNIC SYSTEMS

Spickard, Paul, ed. *Race and Nation: Ethnic Systems in the Modern World*. New York: Routledge, 2005. An integrated conversation among eighteen scholars who analyze and compare the ethnic and racial dynamics in seventeen places around the world, from Japan to Turkmenistan to the

Punjab to the Maghreb to South Africa to Central America to the mid-Pacific to Cambodia. The introduction analyzes the relationship between ethnicity and race and other theoretical concerns.

Reilly, Kevin, Steven Kaufman, and Angela Bodino, eds. *Racism: A Global Reader*. Armonk, NY: M. E. Sharpe, 2003. A collection of more than fifty previously published pieces, scholarly and popular, from a variety of viewpoints, dealing with ethnic and racial issues and especially with the problem of racism here and there around the globe. Designed for classroom use.

Wade, Peter. *Race and Ethnicity in Latin America*. 2nd ed. London: Pluto Press, 2010. Eminent anthropologist sketches the shapes that ethnicity and race take in various parts of Latin America and contemplates the evolution and implications of plastic as well as enduring identities.

Telles, Edward E. *Race in Another America: The Significance of Skin Color in Brazil*. Princeton, NJ: Princeton University Press, 2006. Widely regarded as the definitive scholarly interpretation of race and ethnicity in Brazil, based on careful demographic, ethnographic, historical, and comparative analysis.

Daniel, G. Reginald. *Race and Multiraciality in Brazil and the United States: Converging Paths?* University Park: Pennsylvania State University Press, 2006. A convincing portrait of the evolving ethnic and racial shape of Brazilian society. Daniel sees Brazil moving from a society that understood itself as ethnically and racial multiple, mixed, and complicated toward a simpler, binary racial structure where one is either Black or White. At the same time, he sees the United States, which has long been dominated by binary, one-drop rule racial thinking (i.e., one drop of Black blood—one known African-identified ancestor—made one Black), moving toward the embrace of multiraciality and ethnic mixedness.

Harrell, Stevan, ed. *Cultural Encounters on China's Ethnic Frontiers*. Seattle: University of Washington Press, 2000. Ten Chinese and Western scholars explore the imperialist treatment within China of ethnic minorities by the Han Chinese majority. The book provides rich material for the comparative study of colonialism, imperialism, and nation building.

Honig, Emily. *Creating Chinese Ethnicity: Subei People in Shanghai, 1850–1980*. New Haven, CT: Yale University Press, 1992. Shows how an ethnic minority was created out of migrants from one rural area who were segregated, discriminated against, consigned to the worst jobs and housing, and despised by other residents of China's largest city.

Dirks, Nicholas. *Castes of Mind: Colonialism and the Making of Modern India*. Princeton, NJ: Princeton University Press, 2001. Argues that what has come to be called caste is not some primordial entity that has existed since time immemorial, nor is it a single system reflecting a core Indian value. Rather, Dirks, an anthropologist and a historian, portrays it as a modern phenomenon that arose out of concrete interactions between people of the Indian subcontinent and British colonizers.

Hawley, John C., ed. *India in Africa, Africa in India: Indian Ocean Cosmopolitanisms*. Bloomington: Indiana University Press, 2008. Explores the long-standing interactions between Africans and Indians across the Indian ocean, with several essays each on Indian populations and cultures in Africa and Africa populations and cultures in India.

Moodie, T. Dunbar. *The Rise of Afrikanerdom: Power, Apartheid, and the Afrikaner Civil Religion*. Berkeley: University of California Press, 2008. Examines the shaping of Afrikaner identity as both the colonizers (over Black Africans) and the colonized (at the hands of the British). A powerful challenge to easy assertions of racism at the same time that it emphatically undermines apartheid.

Milner-Thornton, Juliette Bridgette. *The Long Shadow of the British Empire: The Ongoing Legacies of Race and Class in Zambia*. New York: Palgrave Macmillan, 2011. A deeply researched and richly imagined account of racially complicated families and communities and also of the minds of their colonizers, who were sometimes their family members. Milner-Thornton explores evolving ideas about race and the shifting sands of race policy in the British Empire.

Fonseca, Isabel. *Bury Me Standing: The Gypsies and Their Journey*. New York: Vintage, 1996. A lyrical journalistic investigation of Gypsies, more properly known as Roma or Romani, who constitute a significant ethnic minority in nearly every part of Europe and are almost universally discriminated against.

Göktürk, Deniz, David Gramling, and Anton Kaes, eds. *Germany in Transit: Nation and Migration, 1955–2005*. Berkeley: University of California Press, 2007. More than three hundred documents and articles from the popular press and scholarly sources.

Hirsch, Francine. *Empire of Nations: Ethnographic Knowledge and the Making of the Soviet Union.* Ithaca, NY: Cornell University Press, 2005. An essential part of the Soviet nation-making project was recruiting ethnographers to describe (some would say create) a host of minority nationalities to make up the population of the further reaches of the Soviet empire. Hirsch tells the story of these ethnographers and the ethnic groups (the Soviets would say "nationalities") they created and analyzed.

Brubaker, Rogers. *Citizenship and Nationhood in France and Germany.* Cambridge, MA: Harvard University Press, 1998. In France, citizenship is reckoned according to the jus soli, the law of the soil. Anyone born in France and naturalized as French is a French citizen. This leads the French to ignore actual ethnic and racial differences and discriminations. Germany, by contrast, adheres to the rule of jus sanguinis, the law of blood. To be a true German citizen one must be descended from ethnic Germans.

Isaac, Benjamin. *The Invention of Race in Classical Antiquity.* Princeton, NJ: Princeton University Press, 2006. A refutation of the common belief that the ancient Greeks and Romans harbored ethnic and cultural, but not racial, prejudices, by comprehensively tracing the intellectual origins of racism back to classical antiquity. Isaac's systematic analysis of ancient social prejudices and stereotypes reveals that some of those represent prototypes of racism, which in turn inspired the early modern authors who developed the more familiar racist ideas.

RACE, WHITENESS, AND CLASS

Harris, Cheryl I. "Whiteness as Property." *Harvard Law Review* 106.8 (1993): 1707–91. All work in the Whiteness field stems from Harris's insight that American law and social practice have treated Whiteness, not simply as membership in an ethnic group, but as a form of property—an asset with tangible benefits.

Lipsitz, George. *The Possessive Investment in Whiteness: How White People Profit from Identity Politics.* Rev. ed. Philadelphia: Temple University Press, 2006. Racism is a matter of interests as well as attitudes. Lipsitz takes the reader systematically through American history, showing how White people used law, economics, and other forms of power systematically to enhance White people's life chances at the expense of

African Americans, Asians, Native Americans, and Latinos, in areas such as wealth accumulation, employment, education, housing, and health care.

Jacobson, Matthew Frye. *Whiteness of a Different Color: European Immigrants and the Alchemy of Race.* Cambridge, MA: Harvard University Press, 1998. Jacobson is sensitive to the racial positioning of White immigrant groups over the course of US history. There clearly was a hierarchy among Whites, with English-descended people at the top and people like Jews and Italians lower down. But contrary to the assumptions of some of the Whiteness studies scholars, no European-derived people ever was not White in America. Jacobson traces this history with sensitivity and nuance.

Roediger, David R. *The Wages of Whiteness: Race and the Making of the American Working Class.* Rev. ed. London: Verso, 2007. A massively influential book in the Whiteness studies canon, this is really about race, class, and the labor movement. Addresses the question why working-class Whites did not make common cause with working-class Blacks in the nineteenth century, since their class interests would seem to favor such a coalition. Finds the answer in the intensity of their identifying racially (and against their own class interests) with upper-class and middle-class Whites.

Kelley, Robin D. G. *Race Rebels: Culture, Politics, and the Black Working Class.* New York: Free Press, 1996. A loose collection of essays, some quite controversial, on the means and meanings of resistance by Black working-class Americans to racialized and class oppressions.

Wray, Matt. *Not Quite White: White Trash and the Boundaries of Whiteness.* Durham, NC: Duke University Press, 2006. Asserts that some poor southern White people suffer a semiracialized minority position on account of class. Indelible characteristics are written upon them by others, including filth, poverty, ignorance, violence, and a propensity toward incest.

RACE, GENDER, AND SEXUALITY

Moodie, T. Dunbar. *Going for Gold: Men, Mines, and Migration.* Berkeley: University of California Press, 1994. Detailed study of the proletarianized workforce of South African gold mines. Shows the formation of new ethnic groupings and social hierarchies, as well as complex framings of gender and sexuality. A model of sociological inquiry.

Nagel, Joane. *Race, Ethnicity, and Sexuality: Intimate Intersections, Forbidden Frontiers*. New York: Oxford University Press, 2003. Unpacks the interrelationships between ethnicity, race, sexuality, and nationality. Shows how sexual ideas, desires, and fears inform stereotypes about ethnic groups, races, and nations, and how this may result in conflict. Explores the creation of hybrid communities and cultures out of ethnic and sexual encounters, and shows how what Nagel calls "ethnosexual encounters" can both reinforce and undermine existing group categories and national boundaries.

Frankenberg, Ruth. 1994. *White Women, Race Matters: The Social Construction of Whiteness*. New York: Routledge, 1994. Interviews with thirty White women who explore their own racial positioning, how they got there, and what they do in the racial arena. Among the first books to explore Whiteness critically, and the first to do so with a feminist lens.

Carby, Hazel V. "White Woman Listen! Black Feminism and the Boundaries of Sisterhood." In *The Empire Strikes Back: Race and Racism in 70s Britain*. Edited by the Centre for Contemporary Cultural Studies. Pp. 212–35. London: Hutchinson, 1982. A Black British woman's clarion call for White women to understand their implicatedness in White racism, for Black feminists to stand together, and for women of both races to construct a nonracist feminism.

Brodkin, Karen. *How Jews Became White Folks and What That Says about Race in America*. New Brunswick, NJ: Rutgers University Press, 1998. Does not in fact establish that Jews were ever not White in America. But this is an excellent study of the interplay among ethnicity, class, and gender in the making of a people, their culture, and their position in society.

Hunter, Margaret L. *Race, Gender, and the Politics of Skin Tone*. New York: Routledge, 2005. A penetrating analysis of the impact of race, gender, and racial mixedness on beauty culture and women's self-images and relationships, primarily among Blacks and Latinas.

RACE AND THE COLONIAL CONNECTION

Fanon, Frantz. *The Wretched of the Earth*. Translated by Richard Philcox. New York: Grove Press, 2005. A Caribbean psychiatrist who took part in the Algerian Revolution, Fanon was one of the most important theorists of revolutionary struggle, colonialism, and the meanings of race. Since the 1960s *The Wretched of the Earth* has been a handbook for revolutionaries around the globe. *Time* magazine described it as "not so much a book as a rock thrown through the window of the West." Fanon saw race as the key issue in colonial encounters.

Memmi, Albert. *The Colonizer and the Colonized.* Rev. ed. Boston: Beacon Press, 1991. A fierce, lyrical contemplation of the minds both of those who colonize others and of those who are colonized, racialized persons. Viewed by many as a revolutionary document after its initial publication in 1965.

Césaire, Aimé. *Discourse on Colonialism.* New York: Monthly Review Press, 2001. Classic (1955) work that inspired generations of anticolonial revolutionaries in Africa, Latin America, and the Caribbean. Emphatically and eloquently refutes the racist ideas that lie at the heart of colonial encounters.

Said, Edward W. *Orientalism.* New York: Vintage, 1979. Eminent literary critic, Palestinian activist, and moral leader's classic statement of the ways Europeans racialized Arabs and other peoples to their east and south.

Stoler, Ann Laura. *Carnal Knowledge and Imperial Power: Race and the Intimate in Colonial Rule.* 2nd ed. Berkeley: University of California Press, 2010. Drawing mainly on the history of Dutch colonialism in what is now Indonesia, and using a Foucauldian interpretive lens, Stoler explores the interwoven dynamics of race, colonialism, sexuality, family, and power.

MULTIRACIALITY

Root, Maria P. P., ed. *Racially Mixed People in America.* Newbury Park, CA: Sage, 1992. An anthology of writings by psychologists, sociologists, historians, and others who explored the emerging idea that ethnic and racial complexity not only was possible, but in fact was quite common, even though it went unrecognized by mainstream scholars and social commentators. This book marked the public coming-out of the multiracial movement.

Daniel, G. Reginald. *More than Black? Multiracial Identity and the New Racial Order*. Philadelphia: Temple University Press, 2001. The most knowledgeable account of the multiracial movement, as well as a sensitive contemplation of the ambivalence that some monoracially identified African Americans have about that movement.

Williams-León, Teresa, and Cynthia L. Nakashima, eds. *The Sum of Our Parts: Mixed-Heritage Asian Americans*. Philadelphia: Temple University Press, 2001. Two dozen authors explore facets of racial mixedness for Asian-descended people in the United States and several other countries.

Ifekwunigwe, Jayne I., ed. *"Mixed Race" Studies: A Reader*. New York: Routledge, 2004. The definitive collection of forty sharply edited essays on multiraciality, from Gobineau and Darwin down to Maria Root and Gloria Anzaldúa.

Sturm, Circe. *Blood Politics: Race, Culture, and Identity in the Cherokee Nation of Oklahoma*. Berkeley: University of California Press, 2002. Sturm examines how Cherokee identity is socially and politically constructed, and how that process is embedded in ideas of blood, color, and race. Blood has long been a metaphor for belonging among Cherokee, an idea imposed by the US government on Native ways of membership. With nearly all Cherokee mixed, disputes over membership have become increasingly common. In particular, those Cherokees whose ancestry was mixed with Africans have experienced attempts to push them out of the nation.

Wade, Peter. *Blackness and Race Mixture: The Dynamics of Racial Identity in Colombia*. Baltimore: Johns Hopkins University Press, 1995. A complex, subtle ethnography exploring dynamics of race, class, Blackness, family, and mixture in a Colombian province, which has implications for other Latin American societies.

Index

PAUL SPICKARD is professor of history at the University of California, Santa Barbara. He is the author or editor/co-editor of a number of books, including *Global Mixed Race*.